Routledge Handbook of Organizational Change in Africa

Edited by Franca Ovadje and Samuel Aryee

Routledge
Taylor & Francis Group
LONDON AND NEW YORK

First published 2019
by Routledge

2 Park Square, Milton Park, Abingdon, Oxfordshire OX14 4RN
52 Vanderbilt Avenue, New York, NY 10017

Routledge is an imprint of the Taylor & Francis Group, an informa business

First issued in paperback 2020

British Library Cataloguing-in-Publication Data
A catalogue record for this book is available from the British Library

Library of Congress Cataloging-in-Publication Data
Names: Ovadje, Franca, editor. | Aryee, Samuel, editor.
Title: Routledge handbook of organizational change in Africa / edited by Franca Ovadje and Samuel Aryee.
Other titles: Handbook of organizational change in Africa
Description: Abingdon, Oxon ; New York, NY : Routledge, 2018. | Includes bibliographical references.
Identifiers: LCCN 2018009992 | ISBN 9781138642164 (hardback) | ISBN 9781315630113 (ebook)
Subjects: LCSH: Organizational change—Africa. | Organizational behavior—Africa.
Classification: LCC HD58.8 .R69364 2018 | DDC 658.4/06096—dc23
LC record available at https://lccn.loc.gov/2018009992

ISBN: 978-1-138-64216-4 (hbk)
ISBN: 978-0-367-65982-0 (pbk)

Typeset in Bembo
by Apex CoVantage, LLC

Routledge Handbook of Organizational Change in Africa

Although change management and therefore effective adaptation to environmental complexity is considered a uniquely human cultural activity, the extensive change management literature is largely based on the experiences of organizations in the advanced economies of the West. As the economies of African countries become increasingly open, African organizations will need to be agile in order to adapt and grow in a dynamic, global environment. Currently, there is a dearth of contextualized knowledge on change management within Africa, but this handbook aims to address this by bringing together a wide range of experts to explore organizational change and change management from an African perspective.

The handbook adopts a multidisciplinary (historical, philosophical, processual, and strategic) perspective as well as empirical accounts of change management. It addresses such issues as: What are the external and internal pressures for change? What is the content and process of change management? What are the essentials of effective change management? How can change management be theorized from an African perspective? What sort of leadership can best align with change management demands in an African context? How do organizations build internal change management capability? It is hoped that answers to these questions contained in the handbook will provide a contextualized understanding of change management which African organizations and scholars can leverage to respond to the threats and opportunities inherent in their increasingly dynamic environment.

The handbook should constitute an essential reference for academics, researchers, and advanced students of change management, development studies, and African studies, as well as practitioners.

Franca Ovadje is a Professor of Organizational Behaviour and the Founder of the Danne Institute for Research, Lagos, Nigeria. She is also a visiting Professor of the Strathmore Business School in Kenya.

Samuel Aryee is a Professor of Organisational Behaviour and Human Resource Management in Surrey Business School, University of Surrey, UK.

Contents

Figures

Tables

Appendices

Acknowledgments

Our sincere gratitude goes to each and every one of the contributors to this Handbook. This book would not exist without your invaluable contribution. Our contributors are not only experts on Africa, but are passionate about "bringing Africa in".

Every chapter went through a review process – editorial and peer review. Some contributors were also reviewers. We thank all our reviewers for helping us improve the quality of the chapters.

Special thanks to Routledge for believing in this project and for encouraging us all the way. We thank the editorial team: Helen Hurd, Helen Bell, Margaret Farrelly, and Matt Shobbrock for their patience, support and encouragement.

Finally, we would like to express our appreciation to SaroAfrica International Ltd for sponsoring the Contributors' Workshop which was held in March 2017 at the Four Points Sheraton, Lagos.

Notes on contributors

Christopher Akor studied Political Science at the University of Ibadan, graduating with a First Class Degree. He also holds a master's degree in African Studies from the University of Oxford. After a brief stint in academia and research, he has ventured into journalism, serving as the Op-Ed Editor and Head, Editorial Board of BusinessDay Newspaper.

Kenneth Amaeshi is Professor of Business & Sustainable Development at University of Edinburgh Business School, UK. His research focuses on entrepreneurship and business model innovation for sustainable development. His other interests include sustainability, corporate responsibility, ethics, and governance. His research has been published in *Journal of Business Ethics*, *Journal of World Business*, *Entrepreneurship Theory and Practice*, *Journal of Business Research*, and *International Business Review*, among others.

Samuel Aryee obtained his undergraduate degree from the University of Ghana, Legon and postgraduate degrees (MA, PhD) from McMaster University, Canada. He is currently a Professor of Organizational Behaviour and Human Resource Management in the Department of Management at the University of Surrey, where he also serves as Director of the Doctoral Programme. Prior to joining the University of Surrey, Samuel served for several years as Director of the PhD Programme at King's College London, Aston Business School, and Aston University, and also held academic positions in Singapore (National University of Singapore) and Hong Kong (Baptist University). He is currently an associate editor of *Human Relations* and serves on the editorial boards of the *Journal of Applied Psychology*, *Journal of Management Studies*, *Journal of Occupational and Organizational Psychology*, and *Management and Organization Review*, among others. Samuel's areas of research interest include strategic human resource management, organizational justice, work-family interface, abusive supervision, and services management. He pursues research in these areas in cross-cultural contexts. His research findings have been published in such journals as the *Academy of Management Journal*, *Journal of Applied Psychology*, *Journal of Management*, *Journal of Management Studies*, *Organizational Behavior and Human Decision Processes*, and *Journal of Organizational Behavior.*

Michael J.R. Butler is Reader in Transformational Change, and Founder/Director of The TRANSFORMATION Project (www.thetransformationproject.co.uk), Aston Business School, UK. His research interests understand change from a multi-disciplinary perspective. He is on the Editorial Board of the *International Journal of Complex Governance Networks* and *Asia Pacific Journal of Business Administration*. He has published in the *British Journal of Management*, *Human Relations*, *International Journal of Operations and Production Management*, *Journal of Management*, *Leadership Quarterly* and *Organization Science*. He has co-edited three books. His engaged scholarship (funded to c£1.5m) has been recognized (CMI and ESRC). The OECD used his research to evaluate international policy implementation.

Theresa A. Chika-James is an Assistant Professor of Organizational Behavior, Human Resources and Management at MacEwan University School of Business, Edmonton, Canada. She holds both a PhD from Cardiff Business School and an MBA from Glamorgan University (now known as University of South Wales), both in Wales, UK. She is an Associate Fellow of the UK Higher Education Academy and a member of the British Academy of Management. Dr. Chika-James conducts research in the areas of organizational transformation and change, international human resource management, and stakeholder management.

Glory Enyinnaya is the Founder and Lead Consultant of Kleos Advisory Services. She holds an MBA from Lagos Business School, Pan-Atlantic University, Nigeria. She is a Prosci-certified Change Management practitioner and a member of the Association of Change Management Practitioners. She also holds a First Class Honours degree in accountancy from the University of Nigeria. She is the President of Beta Gamma Sigma, an international honors society for high-performing MBAs. She has change management experience in Accenture and other blue-chip companies across the public service, energy, and FMCG sectors. She is a blogger, speaker, and author.

George Ferns is a Lecturer in Management, Employment and Organisation at Cardiff Business School, UK. His research broadly concerns how organizations engage with social and environmental issues, focusing on topics such as corporate sustainability, sustainable development, CSR, and environmental activism. George is also interested in the political economy of climate change. He has published in *Business & Society* and *Journal of Business Ethics*. He has also published in the *Guardian* and *Stanford Social Innovation Review* on corporations and social change.

Godson Ikiebey is a sustainability researcher. He holds an MSc in marketing communication from the School of Media and Communication, Pan-Atlantic University. He was a founding Research Fellow of the Knowledge Economy Group, a think tank that conducted research on the knowledge economy in Nigeria. Godson's research focuses on the interplay between developing and implementing sustainability strategies, strategy development, and socio-economic development. His research publications include: "The Meaning and Uses of Cause-Related Marketing," published in *The Marketing Review*, and "The Role of HR in Implementing CSR and Sustainability in Emerging Economies," published as a technical paper in the Case Centre (EECH).

Howard Jean-Denis is a PhD student in strategic management at the Isenberg School of Management, University of Massachusetts Amherst. His primary research interests are in strategic management, corporate governance, repatriation, and multinational corporations. His research has won multiple awards, including an international business research grant from General Electric, and Best Paper Award for social entrepreneurship research through the Southern Management Association. He holds an MBA from Bentley University, Massachusetts. His past work includes service as a US Army Non-Commissioned Officer, working as a social entrepreneur for clients globally, and representing MNCs in corporate strategy and analysis.

Bahar Ali Kazmi is a Lecturer at Aston Business School. His research interests are in the areas of business ethics, corporate social responsibility, human rights, and Business-NGO partnerships. His research work focuses on transnational business networks. He has worked with Save the Children UK, the International Labour Organization (ILO), the Resource

Centre – Prince of Wales Business Leader Forum (UK), the Department for International Development (UK), the European Commission, the Swiss Development Organisation, and the US Labor Department.

Bradford J. Knipes (PhD) is Professor and former Chair of the Department of Economics and Management, Westfield State University in Westfield, Massachusetts, USA. His research in strategic management, decision-making, crisis management, world business and economic issues, and corporate social responsibility has been presented at national and international conferences, and published in scholarly journals such as the *Journal of Business History* and the *Southern African Business Review*. His awards include the Halloran Best Paper Prize in the History of Corporate Responsibility, received at the 2010 Academy of Management Annual Meeting in Montreal, Canada.

Mzamo P. Mangaliso (PhD) is a Professor in the Management Department, and former Director of MBA Programs, University of Massachusetts, Amherst, MA. His research in strategic management has appeared in several scholarly journals, book chapters, and two books: *Strategic Choice Under Uncertainty* and *Protest and Prophesies: Ubuntu in Glocal Management.* Accolades include winning the Distinguished Teaching Award at UMass Amherst, and the 2010 Halloran Prize for Best Paper in the History of Corporate Responsibility. He is past President and Fellow of the Eastern Academy of Management (US), and former President of the National Research Foundation of South Africa. Prior to joining academia, he worked as a metallurgical research analyst at the Harmony Gold Mines, and as a production manager for Unilever (SA).

Nomazengele A. Mangaliso (PhD) is Professor and former Chair of the Sociology Department, Westfield State University in Westfield, MA. She is author of the book *The South African Mosaic: A Sociological Analysis of Post-Apartheid Conflict* and its sequel, *The South African Mosaic II: A Sociological Analysis of Post-Apartheid Conflict, Two Decades Later* (forthcoming in 2018). She has organized, presented papers, and chaired sessions at a number of conferences around the world. Her research on the processes and institutions that (re)produce stratification based on race and ethnicity, gender, and social class has been published as chapters in several books and scholarly journals. Prior to emigrating to the US, she spent several years in South Africa working as a field social worker and later for Unilever in Durban, KZN.

Santiago Martínez was born in Barcelona, and holds a master's degree in political science from the University of Helsinki and an MBA from the Helsinki School of Economics. Partner and CEO of Providentia Ltd, a company that offers leadership training, Santiago lectures on leadership, business ethics, and corporate social responsibility in several institutions in Finland and abroad. Santiago Martínez is a partner-member of IECO (Institute for Ethics in Communication and Organizations) in Valencia, Spain. He is also a founder and regular columnist of *hyvejohtajuus.fi*, the #1 blog in the Nordic Countries on leadership-related issues. Presently his topics of interest are excellence, happiness, and motivation, which he gets hiking in Finnish Lapland and running development cooperation programs in different countries.

Everlyne Misati is a PhD candidate in the Management and International Business Department at the Florida International University's College of Business. Her primary research interests lie at the intersection of strategy, international business, and entrepreneurship. She is also interested in examining the micro foundations of these macro areas, for example, the role of individuals, top management (leaders), and their interactions in driving firm-level outcomes.

Leah Z. B. Ndanga (Ph.D.) is an Assistant Professor of Management at West Chester University of Pennsylvania's College of Business and Public Management. She has a BSc (Agriculture) from the University of Fort Hare, South Africa, an MSc (Agricultural Economics) from the University of Pretoria, South Africa, and an MS (Agribusiness) from Purdue University, West Lafayette, IN and a PhD in Strategic Management from the University of Massachusetts Amherst. Earlier, she was an economist, focusing on emerging market segments and market actors. Her current research continues to have an international focus, especially the strategic management of emerging market multinationals, with a particular interest in international knowledge transfer, indigenous knowledge systems and culture.

Franklin N. Ngwu is a Senior Lecturer in Strategy, Finance and Risk Management, Lagos Business School, Pan-Atlantic University, Nigeria. He has a PhD in law and economics of banking regulation, MSc in economics, and Post-Graduate Diploma in development economics from University of Manchester, UK. In addition, he also has a MSc in comparative political economy from Cardiff University, UK and a BSc in sociology from University of Lagos, Nigeria. He has over 15 years of experience in teaching, private sector, policy research and consulting both in Nigeria and UK. He has consulted for both local and international organisations and worked in Barclays Bank UK for over five years. He has lectured at the Glasgow School of Business and Society, Glasgow Caledonian University; the School of Built Environment and Business, University of Salford; and the Department of Economics and School of Law, University of Manchester, UK. He has presented papers at international/local conferences, contributed many book chapters, and published papers in peer-reviewed journals. He is the author/editor of the corporate governance handbook titled *Corporate Governance in Developing and Emerging Markets* (Routledge, 2016). He is working on a second book titled *Enhancing Board Effectiveness: Institutional, Regulatory and Functional Perspectives for Developing and Emerging Markets.*

Ijeoma Nwagwu earned her doctorate and master's in law from Harvard Law School. After attending the Nigerian Law School, Ijeoma worked for the Civil Liberties Organisation, and produced documentaries on law, human rights, and development with Channels Television Lagos and the Institute for Democracy in South Africa. Ijeoma taught at St. Mary's University College, London and was on the team for the World Bank Assisted Science and Technology Education Post-Basic (STEP-B) project. She teaches Strategy, CSR, sustainability, and social entrepreneurship at Lagos Business School. Ijeoma also speaks and writes on business, law, and development in emerging markets.

Chris Ogbechie is a Professor of Strategic Management at the Lagos Business School, Pan-Atlantic University. His research interests include strategy in emerging markets, corporate governance, corporate social responsibility, and sustainability. He is also a visiting professor at the Strathmore Business School, Nairobi, Kenya. He is currently the Chairman of the Board of Diamond Bank Plc. His research publications include *Strategic Marketing of Financial Services in Nigeria* (2011), "Corporate Governance Practices of Publicly Quoted Companies in Nigeria" (*International Journal of Business Governance and Ethics*), and "Corporate Social Responsibility in SMEs: A Shift from Philanthropy to Institutional Works?" (*Journal of Business Ethics*).

Franca Ovadje has a PhD in business administration from the IESE Business School in Barcelona, Spain. She was a pioneer faculty member of the Lagos Business School (LBS) where she led sessions on Leadership, Change Management, and Human Resource Management. She also taught on the African AMP at the IESE Business School in Barcelona and on several programmes in South Africa and Ghana. She is a visiting Professor at the Strathmore Business School in Kenya. Her publications include articles in local and international journals as well as book chapters. Franca is the author of the book *Change Leadership in Developing Countries* (Routledge, 2014). She has presented research papers at several international conferences including the Academy of Management, European Academy of Management, British Academy of Management, Eastern Academy of Management, and the African Academy of Management. She has also written several case studies on African companies, including "What it Takes to Lead Change in Africa," published in the *Harvard Business Review* case collection. She was a recipient of the African Management Scholar Award in 2007. In 2017, Franca founded the Danne Institute for Research. The Institute is committed to carrying out and promoting research which will positively impact the African environment. Professor Ovadje strongly believes that Africa's growth and prosperity is hinged on rigorous, insightful research on the African environment. She is a passionate and engaged scholar.

Anastasia Pavlovic holds a bachelor's degree from Hanzehogeschool van Groningen, a master's degree in economics from Plekhanov University in Moscow, and an executive master's degree in finance from IE Business School in Madrid. She worked as Technical Assistant on tax legislation improvement in Russia under the TACIS umbrella, and later co-founded and managed the Russian franchise of Inlingua language schools. Since 2014, she has been working as the Academic and Research Director at the Institute for Small Business Initiatives (ISBI) at Strathmore Business School in Kenya.

Suncan Pavlovic's academic path includes an Executive MBA from IE Business School (Madrid), an AMP from IESE Business School (Barcelona), and a postgraduate diploma in financial strategy from Oxford University (SAID). Besides having held executive positions in multinational companies like Deutsche Bank (Head PWM Eastern Europe) and Raiffeisenbank Foreign Trade (CEO Russia) in his 30-year-long career, he successfully founded several private enterprises in different countries and industries. In 2014, he moved to Kenya to establish and manage the Institute for Small Business Initiatives (ISBI) at Strathmore Business School. He works at Strathmore University as a Visiting Professor of Finance.

Pat Utomi, Political Economist and Professor of Entrepreneurship, is Founder and CEO of the Centre for Values in Leadership (CVL). He is a fellow of the Institute of Management Consultants of Nigeria and founding Senior Faculty of the Lagos Business School, Pan-Atlantic University, and Chairman and Chief Executive of the Integrated Produce City (IPC), as well as Executive Vice Chairman of SmartCity Lagos, a joint holding with Dubai Holdings by SmartCity Dubai. He serves on the Africa Board of leading global professional service firm Deloitte, and was Director of The Centre for Applied Economics at the Lagos Business School. He has served in senior positions in government, as an Adviser to the President of Nigeria; he has also served in the private sector as Chief Operating Officer for Volkswagen of Nigeria, as well as in academia. He is the author of several management and public policy books, including the award-winning *Managing Uncertainty: Competition and Strategy in Emerging Economies* (1998), *Why Nations are Poor* (2006), and *The Art of Leading* (2016). He has passionately pursued the building of a viable opposition political party in Nigeria and transparent, accountable government. He was candidate for President of Nigeria in 2007 and 2011. He is a man of faith and family who is widely traveled through all the continents of the world. He has visited more than 80 countries.

Fred O. Walumbwa is a Professor and faculty member in the Department of Management and International Business at the Florida International University's College of Business. Fred has published over 80 academic research papers in a wide range of prestigious journals in business, management, and psychology, and as book chapters. His research focuses on leadership, positive organizational behavior and scholarship, organizational climate and justice, and cross-cultural issues in management.

David B. Zoogah (PhD, The Ohio State University), is Associate Professor of Management at the Williams College of Business, Xavier University, and Visiting Professor of Management at the Johannesburg Business School, College of Business and Economics, University of Johannesburg. His research is at the meso level, which combines micro and macro theories to examine issues related to management in Africa, corporate environmental sustainability, employee development, and strategic followership. He has several articles related to diverse areas – environmental sustainability, natural resources, followership and leadership, and strategy – of management in Africa. In addition, he is interested in strategic followership. He has authored book chapters on management in Africa. He is a co-winner of the Strategic Doing Award of the Academy of Management in 2012 that resulted in the establishment of the Africa Faculty Development Workshops, and received the Outstanding Author Contribution (2015) of Emerald's Literati Network Awards for Excellence on his chapter on Strategic Human Resources Management in Africa.

1
Introduction

Franca Ovadje and Samuel Aryee

History is littered with stories of once-successful organizations that went into terminal decline and eventual death (Cameron, Sutton, and Whetten, 1988; Whetten, 1980). Although organizational decline and death have not attracted much scholarly interest relative to organizational success, as adaptive systems, it is imperative that organizations respond to environmental changes or continuously adapt to their environment if they are to survive and grow (McKinley, Latham, and Braun, 2014; Probst and Raisch, 2005; Trahms, Ndofor, and Sirmon, 2013). The increasingly turbulent environment in which organizations operate has, therefore, made organizations more dependent than ever on their ability to understand the forces that precipitate change, how change is managed, and its impact on organizational performance. Despite the importance of effective change management to an organization's continued survival and growth, there are several stories of failed organizational change efforts (Beer and Nohria, 2000; Probst and Raisch, 2005). Indeed, some researchers estimate that between 70–80% of change initiatives fail or achieve only partial success (Coetsee and Flood, 2013: 4).

A defining feature of the extensive discourse on organizational change is its predominant focus on change efforts of organizations in the West (Armenakis and Bedeian, 1999; Rafferty, Jimmieson, and Armenakis, 2013). Over the past two decades or so, the previously underperforming economies of sub-Saharan African have been experiencing a form of economic renaissance, with some of these countries averaging annual growth rates in the region of 6% (Economic Commission for Africa, 2012). Indeed, so impressive has the performance of these economies been that this development is said to herald the emergence of the continent as a pole of global growth. Among the imperatives for the economic transformation is the ability of African organizations to ride the storm of change. While globalization has created opportunities for organizations in Africa, they face the challenge of effectively exploiting these opportunities in order to survive and grow. Unfortunately, how these organizations manage change has not been the subject of much systematic research. In fact, research within Africa is limited (George, Corbishley, Khayesi, Haas, and Tihanyi, 2016: 379). This is particularly unfortunate as sub-Saharan African countries have had their fair share of organizational failures exemplified by state-owned corporations (Amankwah-Amoah and Debrah, 2010). Although a multiplicity of factors may have precipitated these organizational failures, it is fair to argue that at the root of the failures of these once-successful organizations is the inability of their leaders to understand the changing environmental context in order to respond to the threats and opportunities inherent in these contexts.

The objective of this handbook is to address this lacuna in the change management literature in Africa and, ultimately, to provide an actionable knowledge base that organizations can draw on to effectively manage change. This handbook addresses, among others, such issues as change drivers, the process of change, winning commitment to change, and building change capacity in an organization.

Taken together, these issues are underpinned by the realization that organizational survival in an increasingly dynamic environment is contingent upon its agility and adaptability. Consequently, the handbook adopts a contextual, historical, processual, strategic (Pettigrew, Woodman, and Cameron, 2001), and philosophical orientation to change management in Africa. Scholars and managers will find the Handbook a useful source of insights and resources on change management in Africa. It is also hoped that the issues addressed in the handbook will provide theoretical inspiration for context-specific change management research, the findings of which will contribute to the scholarly conversation on change management.

The handbook is structured around five themes: the change context and the drivers of change; understanding the change process; leaders as change agents; enhancing change implementation; and embedding change and building change capability.

The context and drivers of organizational change in Africa

Part I introduces the African context and discusses the change drivers in this context. Leading change in Africa presents peculiar challenges because of the unstable macro-economic and political environment (Ovadje, 2014) and the presence of institutional voids (Khanna and Palepu, 2010).

Three chapters are dedicated to a discussion of this theme. The first chapter discusses the change drivers in the African macro-economic and socio-political environment. Pat Utomi and Christopher Akor discuss global- and national-level drivers of change. The global drivers include technology, new knowledge, labour costs, computing, telecommunications, and broadcasting (and social media).

The national-level drivers of change are perhaps particularly important to business in Africa. The Growth Drivers Framework is proposed as a tool for analyzing national-level drivers of change. According to Utomi and Akor, policy choices by government, institutions, human capital, entrepreneurship, culture, and leadership affect the business environment and thus impact organizational strategies.

Institutions are often a challenge to business even where policy choices are attractive. According to Utomi and Akor, business "runs into the headwind of weak institutions and the predatory actions of public officials and bureaucrats." While they provide tools for a systematic analysis of the social, political, and economic environment, they emphasize the role of institutions. According to them, "to deal with change in Africa is to understand institutions."

African firms are going international (Ovadje, 2014: 13) and internationalization is driving change not only in international firms, but also in the competitive environment. New entrants may increase the level of competition in an industry. For example, the entry of United Bank for Africa (UBA) into the banking industry in Ghana led to a shake up as incumbents struggled to improve their customer service models to compete with UBA's. In their chapter on "Firm internationalization as a driver of organizational change," Chris Ogbechie, Franklin N. Ngwu, and Godson Ikiebey argue that as firms expand across borders, they create new departments, employ international executives, and ultimately, manage an international business. Internationalization involves doing new things as the size and structure of the organization changes and the firm faces the challenge of managing in new cultures, geographies, legal environments, etc.

Internationalization may lead to a revision of the business model (to adapt to new markets), new processes, and governance structures. As the firm manages in several environments with specific environmental challenges, it must adapt to these local environments or implement change initiatives if it is to survive.

Ijeoma Nwagwu examines "Responsible Management Education" (RME) as a catalyst of change.

RME involves integrating ethics, corporate responsibility, and sustainability in the curricula, research, and other activities of business or management schools. It is hoped that undergraduate and graduate students, as well as senior executives, who attend these schools will learn the principles and implement what they have learnt in their organizations.

RME as a driver of change is predicated on the belief that business schools have an extensive reach and can influence the society significantly. RME is new in Africa; only about 26 schools on the continent are signatories of the Principles for Management Education (PRME). Of these, only six (five in South Africa and one in Nigeria) are champions of RME. These champions have reviewed their mission statements and are adapting their curricula, research, and core activities to reflect ethics, corporate responsibility, and sustainability. These institutions are undergoing change and are driving organizational change through the students and executives they impact through their teaching and research activities.

To summarize thus far: Because of the pervasiveness of government in African economies, the macro-economic and socio-political environment are major change drivers in this context. Frequent policy changes mean that companies have to be agile and adaptive if they are to survive. A growing driver of change is internationalization. A number of African firms have become international: they export goods to other African markets (usually neighbouring countries), and they have agents in foreign markets or have set up offices and manufacturing facilities in these markets. Many Africans think there is more similarity than difference across Africa (Ovadje, 2014). International companies are finding that this is not so. Internationalization brings more complexity to the organization: the need to comply with local regulations, manage different cultures, etc.

Another driver of change in the African context is Responsible Management Education. Though this is not yet a significant driver of change, Nwagwu argues that it could be significant in the near future. Business schools educate not only undergraduates but also senior executives. As more of these schools become signatories of PRME and embed the principles of RME into their teaching and research, they are likely to develop change agents who will drive change in their organizations.

Understanding the change process

Three chapters are presented in this section: two theoretical models and a model of the change process based on the African culture.

In the first chapter, David B. Zoogah proposes a circumstantiated model of organizational change and development in Africa. He argues that the internal and external context impacts the drivers, processes, and outcomes of organizational change and development. He asserts that unlike the environment of Western countries which are reliable, controllable, and appropriate for diagnostic and dialogic models, the African environment has different cultural, social, political, institutional, economic, and regulatory characteristics. Zoogah argues that the circumstantiated model is more appropriate for the African context which is unclear, unpredictable, and ambiguous.

The model is based on complexity theory, and proposes conversations in large groups as a way to implement change. These conversations should be about planned and unexpected events (common in an unpredictable environment). Change outcomes may be planned and unplanned as reversals occur and unexpected outcomes become the norm.

Mangaliso, Mangaliso, Knipes, Jean-Denis and Ndanga, in their chapter on "Ubuntu as essential inspiration for more humanistic organizational management," argue that the change process and outcomes in Africa cannot be divorced from the African context. They focus on the African cultural context as captured by Ubuntu, and tease out the characteristics of this context and its impact on the change process and outcomes.

According to them, language (social aspects of communication), decision making, the African concept of time, and leadership affect the change process and thus the outcomes.

In the African worldview, time is not a series of deadlines, but rather a series of opportunities to create or reinforce the social bonds among individuals. In the African context, decision making takes time, as the change process revolves around conversations. It requires wide consultation, typically in open forums such as town hall meetings, building a sense of community, consulting widely and reaching agreement results in greater commitment to the change.

Mangaliso and colleagues highlight the core values which underpin the Ubuntu philosophy: collectivism, harmonious relationships, kindness, etc. It is not surprising that African interpretation of change outcomes emphasize social wellbeing more than efficiency. The authors note that Africans are more concerned about the impact of the change on fellow team members than on the bottom line.

In the third chapter in this section, David B. Zoogah adopted a flow perspective of change and introduced a murmuration model of change in Africa. According to him, change in Africa is both complex and dynamic. A myriad of factors influence change in this context, change outcomes are varied and could include change reversals, and the change process is similar to a murmuration. Change drivers operate across different levels and move in tandem such that a change in one factor triggers change in the other factors. These change drivers (social, economic, political, cultural, and legal factors) drive change not only at organizational, but also at individual, levels.

Leaders as change agents

The focus in the third part of the book is on leaders as change agents. Part III contains four chapters. The role of authentic leadership and trust is the subject of the first chapter. Everlyne Misati and Fred O. Walumbwa, in their chapter on "Authentic leaders as change agents," point out that Africa still faces huge challenges in spite of its growth in recent years. A number of African companies, however, are re-inventing themselves and are clearly on a growth trajectory. To continue on this trajectory, they must manage change (innovation) more efficiently. The contributors posit that authentic leaders are needed to facilitate these changes.

Authentic leaders are sensitive to the needs of employees. They build credibility and trust and are willing to learn. These attributes are important for change implementation. While Misati and Walumbwa recognize that other types of leadership, such as transformational leadership, facilitate organizational change, they argue that authentic leaders are best suited to the African cultural context: they communicate with employees, empower them, and facilitate a favourable organizational culture and climate.

In his chapter on "Human resource function as change agent," Samuel Aryee adopts a strategic human resource management approach which is grounded in the resource-based view (RBV) and dynamic capabilities perspective. As a strategic partner, the HR function's primary responsibility is capability building as a competitive resource that facilitates strategy implementation. The chapter argues that product-market competition has meant that African organizations need to evidence marketplace agility through product and service innovation. As change agent, the HR function initiates change through the adoption of high-performance work systems for agility. The adoption of this change intervention triggers the development of a change management capability by institutionalizing a climate for agility which fosters skill and behavioural flexibility in the form of innovative behaviours leading to marketplace agility/organizational performance. However, the extent to which the HR function can effectively perform its change agent role is argued to be much dependent on top management's emphasis on employees as a strategic resource, the competencies and power of the HR function, and the quality of the employee-organization relationship. The quality of the employee-organization relationship is argued to be an important boundary condition because of the African cultural emphasis on the collective.

George Ferns and Kenneth Amaeshi, in their chapter on "Rethinking African business elites as change agents," highlight the importance of business elites in driving change in Africa. The contributors acknowledge that business elites are often accused of stimulating corruption and of rent-seeking behaviour, but argue that business elites sometimes play positive roles which have implications for change in Africa. They thus bring a novel perspective to the organizational change literature in Africa.

Business elites, because of the amount of power they wield in developing countries, have the power to influence governments and government policies which create the environment for business. They present a typology of business elites as change agents and argue that a small but growing number of them are leading change on the continent. The pervasive influence of government and government regulation in these countries makes business elites a formidable force for change in these countries.

We close Part III of the Handbook with an interview by Franca Ovadje and Glory Enyinnaya of a change agent in the public sector. Peter Obi, the former Governor of Anambra State of Nigeria, led a change initiative that transformed the State. In the interview, Obi argues that from his experience in Anambra State, to lead change in the public sector, the change agent must be "insanely" committed to the vision and have execution skills. The change leader must deliver on his campaign promises; he must execute. The choice of the change team is important. Team members must be open, accountable, and able to tell truth to power and ask questions, sometimes difficult questions.

According to Peter Obi, change agents need, above all, character; their conduct (their example), especially in public, is important as it sends signals regarding what is acceptable behaviour. They must be ethical and accountable as they manage funds that do not belong to them.

Enhancing change implementation

Many change initiatives fail. This part puts together two chapters which elucidate different ways to enhance change implementation and ensure some success. Theresa Chika-James presents an empirical study whose results suggest a number of the facilitators of culture change in Africa. Santiago Martinez develops a philosophical discourse on virtuous leadership and its role in change implementation.

Chika-James poses two questions in her chapter on "Fundamentals of organisational culture change," which was based on a case study of an African organization: Can organizations really change culture? Can frameworks be used to alter a people's underlying assumptions, beliefs, and values? The results of her empirical study show that some of the facilitators of organizational culture change include: a new CEO, the nature of the employment contract (temporary workers tend to be less committed to the change), and the influence of external stakeholders.

She notes the need to align both cognitive and symbolic structures with organizational culture change to ensure similarities of meaning across stakeholder groups. To this end, it is important to understand the context (organizational and societal) in which cultural change is proposed. The study concludes that frameworks for culture change may not guarantee changes in the values and beliefs of organizational members even if they espouse the values of the new culture. In effect, her results suggest that while it is possible to effect culture change, it is a complex process with unintended consequences.

Santiago Martinez, in his chapter on "Enhancing change implementation through virtuous leadership," argues that virtuous leadership, compared to other types of leadership, makes a unique contribution to our understanding of organizational change in Africa. Virtuous leadership facilitates organizational transformation in the design, implementation, and embedding of change. The chapter is a philosophical discourse on organizational change in Africa; it engages the African culture and posits that virtuous leaders help organizations win commitment to change, especially change that requires new attitudes and values (culture change). He argues that virtuous leadership has potential for contributing to organizational change effectiveness in Africa as it resonates with the African culture.

Embedding change and building change capacity

Perhaps one reason for the failure of change initiatives is that change leaders cry Uhuru ("Victory") too early, when the new ways have not been embedded. Change must be sustained over a reasonable length of time; otherwise, a reversal could occur (Ovadje, 2014). Given the uncertainties in the African environment, leaders must build change capacity into their organizations. It is to this issue that we turn our attention in this last part of the handbook.

Butler, Pavlovic, Pavlovic, and Kazmi, in their chapter on "Transformational change in Africa: A case study of sustainable economic growth in Kenya," focus on how to manage change in order to achieve sustainable economic growth in transition economies. The chapter provides evidence for a new framework for transformational change in Africa. The five dimensions of the framework are critically discussed and related to examples from the micro small medium enterprise (MSME) sector, which is seen as central to sustaining growth. The chapter also highlights the role of universities in building MSME capacity for change.

The last two chapters in this part present what two organizations (a Kenyan and a Nigerian organization) are doing to build change capacity in their organizations. In the first chapter, Franca Ovadje presents the case study of an organization which has renewed itself over the years. She argues that in dynamic environments such as African environments, organizations need to be ambidextrous if they are to survive. They must combine a focus on exploiting current opportunity and exploring future ones. This involves sensing the future and seizing current opportunities. Equity Bank is ambidextrous because it has a mechanism for sensing the environment, and for receiving and processing feedback. It also dedicates resources to seizing future opportunities and creates innovation spaces where these opportunities can be explored. Ovadje concludes that the most important reason for Equity Bank's renewal is its people, culture, and leadership.

The last chapter presents an interview with Mitchell Elegbe, the CEO of Interswitch, an electronic payment company, with operations in three African countries. In its 15 years of history, Interswitch has weathered many storms. The CEO talks about these changes, their drivers, and how regulators impose restrictions which reduce the level of innovation in spite of demanding customers. Over-regulation in Nigeria was one of the reasons for the internationalization of Interswitch. In the interview, Elegbe also talks about how he wins commitment to change and the role of trust in implementing change.

References

Amankwah-Amoah, J., and Debrah, Y. A. (2010) The protracted collapse of Ghana Airways: Lessons in organizational failure. *Group and Organization Management*, 35: 636–665.

Armenakis, A. A., and Bedeian, A. G. (1999) Organizational change: A review of theory and research in the 1990s. *Journal of Management*, 25: 293–315.

Beer, M., and Nohria, N. (2000) *Breaking the Code of Change*. Boston, MA: Harvard Business Press.

Cameron, K. S., Sutton, R. I., and Whetten, D. A. (Eds.). (1988) *Readings in Organizational Decline: Frameworks, Research, and Prescriptions*. Cambridge, MA: Ballinger.

Coetsee, J., and Flood, P. C. (2013) *Change Lessons From the CEO*. San Francisco, CA: Jossey-Bass.

Economic Commission for Africa. (2012) *Unleashing Africa's Potential as a Pole of Global Growth*. Addis Ababa: ECA.

George, G., Corbishley, C., Khayesi, J. N. O., Haas, M. R., and Tihanyi, L. (2016) Bringing Africa in: Promising directions for management research. *Academy of Management Journal*, 59(2): 377–393.

Khanna, T., and Palepu, K. G. (2010) *Winning in Emerging Markets*. Boston, MA: Harvard Business Press.

McKinley, W., Latham, S., and Braun, M. (2014) Organizational decline and innovation: Turnarounds and downward spirals. *Academy of Management Review*, 39: 88–110.

Ovadje, F. (2014) *Change Leadership in Developing Countries*. New York, NY: Routledge.

Pettigrew, A. M., Woodman, R. W., and Cameron, K. S. (2001) Studying organizational change and development: Challenges for future research. *Academy of Management Journal*, 44: 697–713.

Probst, G., and Raisch, S. (2005) Organizational crisis: The logic of failure. *Academy of Management Executive*, 19: 90–105.

Rafferty, A. E., Jimmieson, N. L., and Armenakis, A. A. (2013) Change readiness: A multilevel review. *Journal of Management*, 39: 110–135.

Trahms, C. A., Ndofor, H. A., and Sirmon, D. G. (2013) Organizational decline and turnaround: A review and agenda for future research. *Journal of Management*, 39: 1277–1307.

Whetten, D. A. (1980) Organizational decline: A neglected topic in organizational science. *Academy of Management Review*, 5(4): 577–588.

2

Change drivers in the macroeconomic and sociopolitical context

Pat Utomi and Christopher Akor

Introduction

It is a long-established cliché that the most certain thing in life is change. It seems not many can cope with it or manage it effectively. Understanding change, what drives it, and how to turn it into strategic advantage may indeed be the key to survival and superior performance in economic life. The enterprise of this chapter is therefore to provide the manager and leader in the public, private, and social enterprise sectors of African economies tools for systematic appraisal of factors that drive change, and for piloting transition organizations toward desired ends, using management insights.

Among the goals of the chapter is to draw from case studies in several African countries and contexts so as to arm managers with tools that can facilitate their response to unanticipated change or manage planned change thrown up by the evolution of the social, political, and economic environment of business. It should also provide a guide to how governance can be interrogated from within and outside the firm and government. Following that, frameworks for analysis will be offered. Flowing from these frameworks and case studies, evidence from praxis will be presented to illustrate how change has been managed. Underpinning this approach is acceptance of the axiom that unless the rate of learning in an organization is equal to or greater than the pace of change in the environment, that organization would be moving toward dinosaur status. Rewan's axiom, L ≥ C[1], and getting managers ready to respond to its imperative, is essential to the need for this volume.

25 years ago, Nigeria had less than 300,000 functional telephone lines servicing a population of about 150 million people, which was a teledensity ratio in the lower rungs of world averages. In September 2017, the teledensity stood at 99.93% with 139,905,123 active lines, compared to 0.59% and 588,374 active lines in December 2000, according to the Nigeria Communications Commission (NCC). The 2017 figure is actually a decline from the December 2016 peak of 110.38% with 154,592,780 active lines. At that time, the typical middle-class professional woman in Lagos, Nigeria spent most of her Saturday mornings, after a tiring week at work, in traffic to fruit, vegetable, meat, and fish bazaars in unsanitary conditions in the suburbs, shopping for foodstuffs that would feed the family for the coming week.

About the same time, South Africa's investment agency, the Industrial Development Corporation (IDC), was taking a stake to facilitate the building of an aluminium plant in Mozambique that would be good example to illustrate the severely challenged aluminium plant in Nigeria, ALSCON in Ikot Abasi, in the South East of Nigeria. Beyond the MOZAL-Mozambique and ALSCON-Nigeria comparison, the conditions in Nigeria and Mozambique were significantly affected by South African businesses crossing borders on the continent where perceptions of risk in Africa made it difficult for many global ventures from Europe and elsewhere to exploit yawning opportunities.

In Nigeria's telecommunications space, investments led by South African firms would yield one of the most rapid transitions in teledensity, with consequences for changing industry structure in many sectors of the economy. Years later, the plight of the professional woman shopping for food was transformed dramatically as the South African brand, Shoprite, surfaced in a mall in Lagos, offering those products in convenient air-conditioned outlets for prices competitive with what obtained in the mammy markets and bazaars, while offering location advantage in city centre shopping outlets, not only in Lagos and Abuja, but in far-flung provincial locations like Warri and Asaba in Delta State, Nnewi, and Onitsha in Anambra State, as well as elsewhere.

Just as South African enterprises' externalization of domestic competition led to the transformation of the context of the environment of business, and have affected the culture of management practice, the phenomenon of China rising has also affected how Ethiopia and Senegal are becoming light manufacturing African Antelopes.

What have been the consequences of these trends for how change is managed in an Africa facing the internet-propelled knowledge economy, in which change is taking place at the speed of thought and perhaps faster; at a time when robotics are reducing the number of people in the manufacturing line but Africa has a youth bulge, with some countries like Nigeria growing their population at 2.8% per annum; e-commerce is making the electronic mall an increasing source of access to fashion and consumer goods; and social media is attracting more advertising revenue than could be imagined a decade ago? This is a time during which conflict is raising the levels of uncertainty for decision makers. Mervyn King, the South African judge and academic who set global standards for corporate governance with his reports in South Africa, captures it well. Writing on a changed and changing world in the King IV Report Code of Corporate Governance in South African, King notes that financial instability is one of the drivers of these changes. Financial crises, arising from the capital crisis in the United States of America and the Sovereign Fund crisis in the European Union, have still not been resolved. Brexit created further uncertainty for financial systems. Adding to these are the ubiquitous issues of climate change, social media platforms, and disruptive technologies, leading to the belief that we are in the cusp of the fourth industrial revolution.

With change and its management as an imperative, it is important to better understand the context of that change which is rooted in the social, political, and economic environment of business.

The evolution of the social, political, and economic environment of business

When Vijay Mahajan, the Indian-born marketing professor at the University of Texas, published *Africa Rising: How 900 Million African Consumers Offer More Than You Think* in 2008, he was challenging a stereotype of underperforming countries that had resulted in a phenomenon that came to be known as Afro-pessimism. His lead was soon followed by many, including some who were reversing themselves. The UK's *Economist* magazine, which had once written of Africa as "the Hopeless Continent," would, on December 3rd, 2011 offer a leader story: "Africa Rising." Its rethink of Africa followed its observation that "over the past decade six of the world's ten fastest growing countries were African." The celebratory discussion of Africa rising was even more pronounced in *The Next Africa*, published in 2015 by Jake Bright and Aubrey Hruby.

This journey to reversal resurrected again as the commodities boom that fuelled some of the "Africa rising" narrative began to recede dramatically by 2014, unearthing one of the key points of the "Washington consensus" from the years of structural adjustment in the 1980s and 1990s, which focused on African countries building the capacity to respond to shocks. Africa, it seems, still remains quite vulnerable to shocks. Leaders therefore have to build capacity to cope with shocks and build shock absorbers.

Africa has had a chequered history of tumultuous change in its post-colonial journey. This has enormously challenged the strategy of companies and the choices of governments. As we shall see in the discussion that follows, the need to develop the capacity to anticipate and manage change, as well as to develop the discipline for executing planned change effectively, is critical if Africa is to gain speed towards the "great escape" which Deaton (2013) appropriately poses as the leadership challenge of our time in his interrogation of "health, wealth and the origins of inequality."

Most of the economies of Africa were subsistence agriculture communities until the Industrial Revolution and colonial incorporation made them raw material outposts. Many of the plantation economies experienced little or no industrialization in colonial times, and were quickly subject to terms of trade challenges after independence.

Several new nations had followed the lead offered by the work of yet another Nobel Prize laureate in economics, Arthur Lewis, who sought to domesticate into the African context Raul Prebisch's Import Substitution Industrialization (ISI) idea, which he advanced in his *Industrialization of the Gold Coast* (Ghana). Okigbo (1987), first economic adviser to the first Prime Minister of Nigeria, Tafawa Balewa, makes the point of how the Lewis book "influenced many new nations into promoting import substitution industries."

These approaches to development, influenced by bureaucrats returning from education at the University of London and London School of Economics, with the significant influence of Harold Laski, promoted a mixed economy: This mode, in which the public sector shared honours in the production of goods beyond the realm of non-appropriable goods (those public goods whose use could not exclude those who did not pay), would challenge public choice in Africa for a generation and become the reason for the Washington consensus (Adebayo, 1998). In some countries like Nigeria, the mixed economy idea would, as the confidence of the state grew with oil revenues, advance to a point where political leaders began to insist that the state had a duty, in the face of a weak indigenous private sector, to assume the "commanding heights" of the economy (Ayida, 1987; Asiodu, 1993). The push for more "collectivist" orientation in economic management in Nigeria was a significantly different thrust from countries such as Cote d'Ivoire, Botswana, and Mauritius.

Richard C. Crook and James Manor (1998), in their book *Democracy and Decentralization in South Asia and West Africa: Participation, Accountability and Performance*, suggest that "despite rapid urbanisation, Cote d'Ivoire's economy is still based on agricultural exports (of mainly coffee and cocoa)." Commercialized agriculture developed later and in more restricted way in Cote d'Ivoire than in Ghana, and when it did, it was associated with enormous waves of migration during the 1950s and 1960s. Remarkably, Cote d'Ivoire would overtake the earlier champions, Nigeria and Ghana, in cocoa production and become the world's dominant producer by far. Yet the failure to change, like several of Southeast Asia's so-called "tiger economies" did to manufacturing for export, has left Cote d'Ivoire one of the very poor countries of the world, earning far less from producing 70% of the world's cocoa than the leading chocolate producing companies like Nestle and Cadbury do from processing cocoa. Where Cote d'Ivoire earned a paltry $3.7 billion USD from cocoa exports, Nestle had a net profit of nearly $14.5 billion USD in 2015.

Africa's engagement with crisis and reform, and the need for change, has been the duty of politicians that emerged from liberation wars and constitutional challenges to colonial order. It also came from managers that hurriedly took on nationalized or indigenized firms, as well as beneficiaries of empowerment programs that saw them through to executive positions in African subsidiaries of multinational companies. Many were ill-prepared for the roles they were thrust into and the increasing problems created by factors such as changing technology, uncertainty created by fractious politics, and civil wars, as well as severe drought and global financial troubles. But whether it is the black empowerment executive in South Africa, leader of multilateral agencies like the African Development Bank and the Afrexim Bank, or even cabinet ministers and heads of government, these African leaders have been products of perceptions that complicate their tasks far beyond what their counterparts in the industrialized market economies have to deal with.

As John Reader (1997), who set sail for Africa on his 18th birthday in 1955 and lived there for decades, meeting the who's who in emerging Africa, from the anti-Apartheid leaders to belligerents in the Nigerian civil war and residents in East Africa, observes in his book: Africa has been woefully misunderstood and misused by the rest of the world. This perception problem has affected investment flows and the culture of management in both multinational corporations and entrepreneurial ventures, such that the skills required by the manager in Africa to manage the change he confronts may be more peculiar than his colleague in Europe would need. Where, for example, compliance with instructions from an expatriate manager is taken for granted, variables such as ethnicity, age – a major factor in a gerontocratic culture – and level of education would determine compliance by an African executive.

Like Reader, many Africanists have ringside seats as activists, politicians, professionals, and academics observing political, economic, and corporate efforts to manage change in Africa since independence. They have interrogated the change question as participant observers, seeking novel ways of understanding the challenge of change in Africa, combining insights to global academic thinking and trends on the subject, and proposing a new pedagogy for developing managers. They believe that an African approach to managing change is possible.

Even though contact between Europe and Africa predates colonial ambitions in Europe, with Kings of the Benin kingdom dispatching viceroys to the court of Henry the Navigator in Portugal in the 15th century and an expedition of the Chinese Flotilla led by General He calling on Africa centuries before European colonial hegemony, it was clearly not until James Watt's redesign of the steam engine, which made the Industrial Revolution possible, that colonial designs began to be justified in Europe. Leopold II of Belgium signalled Europe's scramble for Africa. The German Chancellor Otto von Bismarck would eventually call the Berlin conference of 1884 to partition the continent to contending European powers (Mackenzie, 1983).

Colonialism would not only exploit Africa on the negative side, but would also introduce more modern economic ways, which became the heritage of the nationalists who were invariably fathers of independent new nations following the wind of change proclaimed by then-British Prime Minister Harold MacMillan.

The education of colonized peoples, in the thesis of Brazilian educator Paulo Freire's *Pedagogy of the Oppressed*, eschewed creative thinking, with the minds of the colonized treated as piggy banks into which idea deposits were made (Freire, 1996). This deposited knowledge was designed to be enough only to maintain the system, but inadequate to enable the colonized to creatively seek a new order in which they could break out of their underdevelopment.

The effect of this colonial education paradigm, which carried into the independence era, in our observation significantly froze entrepreneurship and created contradictions in economic management that resulted in one crisis after the other. That state of crisis is effectively captured in the title of van de Walle's (2001) book: *African Economies and the Politics of Permanent Crisis, 1979–1999.*

The outcome of these crises, marked significantly by the Structural Adjustment Programmes of the mid-1980s, was not without some wins. One of them is in the financial sector entrepreneurship that followed reforms in that sector in Nigeria: for example, systemic crisis in the banking sector in the 1920s and 1950s resulted in high entry barriers, which limited ventures into banking to mainly governments and multinational banks. Reforms led to the lowering of regulator-created barriers to entry. The rapid growth of those banks, and the intensity of rivalry in the banking sector in Nigeria, have given rise to the internationalizing of several banks.

In developments similar to Michael Porter's analysis in *The Competitive Advantage of Nations*, intensity of competition in Nigerian banking led to quite a few banks acquiring local banks around the continent or seeking the license to operate in such countries as Ghana, Kenya, Gambia, and as far south as Namibia. In several other African countries where the business environment and economy is government- or public sector-dominated, a Small-to-Medium Enterprise (SME) sector dominated by aliens from Asia and the Middle East has emerged. In some countries, such as Uganda, those conditions resulted in the expulsion of Asians during Idi Amin's strongman rule. In countries like Nigeria, where indigenization laws were enacted to shift control of the economy to indigenes, it dramatically changed the economic context in terms of enterprise ownership culture and disposition of foreigners to invest. In the face of such a variegated domain, it is important to determine the different levels of analysis of drivers of change and how best to respond, as a manager, to change stimuli.

Levels of analysis

The drivers of change come principally at three different levels: global, national, and corporate. It should be helpful therefore to show how frameworks at these levels determine pressures for change, with consequences for frameworks of analysis. Even though factors at the individual and idiosyncratic level can affect change, it is not a critical level for our purpose.

At the level of globalization the convergence of three streams of technology (computing), telecommunications, and broadcasting –now manifested in the internet of things, with its social media subscript – have produced the global village that Ben Bagdikian wrote about 40 years ago and it seemed like science fiction. Equally driving globalization are labour costs and the new currency, knowledge. China's ascendance on the back of cheap labour in manufacturing gave new meaning to globalization.

Technology now enables both the small and big to be equally able to compete in a global marketplace. Technology made it easy for securitization vehicles that enabled US financiers to create bundles of bad and OK risks to be sold around the world. When, in 2008, it turned out that subprime mortgage lending, which comprised very bad risks, dominated those portfolios, the speed of contagion was so fast in being transmitted through the globe it was clear that both business leaders and political leaders, who were used to a different pace before this new globalization, were caught off guard. A global financial crisis required Main Street (government) to bail out Wall Street (the private sector), and prescriptions for stronger corporate governance went global. They were required for both the perpetrators of bad banking practice and their victims. The South African judge Mervyn King, who had chaired a commission that produced one of the strictest codes of corporate governance, became a household name. Stress tests were ordered for banks in the US. Nigeria, which was significantly insulated because its banks invested little in such securities and because its foreign reserves provided buffer for the economy, also ordered similar tests.

The arbitrary choice in implementing the stress tests triggered a systemic crisis. This was a classic example of globalization producing a mimicking of practices from elsewhere with little reflection of different local enterprises. The result, as a global financial consultant said at the Wharton

Africa business club conference in Philadelphia the year after, was that Nigeria achieved the halving of the value of its financial system unprovoked. The lasting lesson for the business leader in a highly regulated industry where popular culture is prideful with power, often at the expense of purpose, is the need to cooperate with competitors to build institutions that set the boundaries of conduct. The alternative is to build capacity for hedging against the predatory conduct of regulators and public officials. Long before the 2009 stress tests, these risks were highlighted in Utomi (1998) titled *Managing Uncertainty, Competition and Strategy in Emerging Economies* in which the author recommended that careful psychographic studies of officials appointed to regulatory agencies, and shrewd deployment of tools for building sustained goodwill with such actors, can be critical. Equally, smart public relations that is strategic in the planning and programming of engagement with stakeholders is of high value in such unstable business environments.

The developments in the UK and US with Brexit and the Trump ascendancy were clear evidence that the degree of globalization many in Africa consider inevitable is not fully shared. It meant that the discontents of globalization, which Joseph Stiglitz had pointed to for poor countries, was shared by even some apparent beneficiary economies. A tool for analysis to produce coping and adapting logic for action for managers needs to be generated within contending paradigms. If the world is flat, as Friedman (2005) argues, you would require decision-making patterns that ignore boundaries, cultures, and differences. The choices of a Hegelian end of history that Francis Fukuyama had advocated after the Berlin Wall came down paving the way for what would have been the American age should have made globalization the grundnorm (Fukuyama, 1992). But a clash of civilizations (Huntington, 1996) soon manifested as radical Islam changed the world with the 9/11 terrorist attack on the United States of America. Perhaps then, it is the paradigm of a semi-globalized world that Pankaj Ghemawat (2007) prefers that decision makers should rely on.

In *Redefining Global Strategy*, Ghemawat (2007) offers decision-making frameworks for this semi-globalized world in which the received wisdom of thinking global and acting local remains valid. He offers a template for crossing borders in a world where differences still matter. He challenges Levitt's (1983) declaration that "the multinational commercial world nears its end and so does the multinational corporation." Ghemawat provides evidence that Levitt's notion of the global corporation "which sells the same things in the same way everywhere" is an incomplete explication of extant reality. He uses the example of a truly global company – Coca Cola's swings in managing similarities and differences through leadership regimes of Roberto Goizueta, Douglas Ivester, Douglas Daft and Neville Isdell – to illustrate his point. He then offers a framework for thinking about these differences across borders along dimensions that are Cultural, Administrative/political, Geographic, and Economic (CAGE). He also offers the AAA triangle:Adaptations to adjust to differences, Aggregation to overcome differences, and Arbitrage to profit from the inevitable imbalances between markets.

That African governments and business leaders are affected by globalization and global strategies of the corporation comes through in the case of nationalizing banks in Nigeria in 1976, and continues to come through in observation of trends in Nigerian banks expanding to new African destinations in the second decade of the 21st century.

Gamaliel Onosode was CEO of a Lagos-based Merchant Bank, NAL. The bank had two foreign banks as major shareholders and technical partners, Grindlays and American Express Bank. In 1975, he participated in a global strategy session of one of the partner banks which took place in India. During the offsite, it occurred to him that the strategy of a global bank could actually conflict with the development strategy of a host country. On his return to Nigeria, he met with Nigeria's Finance Minister and suggested that a good way to guard against that would be for Nigeria to insist that every bank ensure a Nigerian be appointed to the boards of all banks. This, he suggested, would bring a Nigerian perspective to the domestication of the firm's global strategy. The government chose to go further than the counsel, deciding instead that all banks with less than 60% Nigerian ownership should sell 60%, or what was required for 60% Nigerian control by Nigeria and Nigerians, within 90 days of the order.

In the case of First National Bank of Chicago, which was a commercial bank in the United States but adapted to being a Merchant bank in Nigeria, to avoid the risks of exposure which faced commercial banks from regulatory requirements in Nigeria, the track from global to local was quite evident. First, the nationalization completely changed both the culture of the bank and industry structure. The outcomes would lead to a change of name from First Chicago to International Merchant Bank, and a progressive shift of focus from the asset to the liability side of the ledger.

First Chicago had entered Nigeria primarily to serve the Central Bank, which was witnessing burgeoning reserves with the oil boom of the 1970s. It could have done so from offices outside of Nigeria, but Central Bank policies required that banks servicing the apex bank have formal presence in Nigeria. It chose therefore to enter as a merchant bank not subject to rural banking and sectoral lending requirements which ballooned operating risks for commercial banks.

Government had also failed to anticipate the effect of nationalization on banking and the economy. The abuse consequent on government being a dominant shareholder, and the tragedy of absence of accountability on the part of leaders of banks as agents of the political order on behalf of the citizen is besy left to the imagination. It would take wholesale privatization, less than a decade after, to save the banks.

Another important global factor is the flow of Foreign Direct Investment (FDI), which has become not only a powerful instrument for growth and development, but also accounts for systemic changes in the economy, business, and work environment. Singapore offers a vivid example of the impact FDI can have on a country. With a population of just 1.6 million at independence in 1960, the poor former British crown colony, with no natural resources except a natural deep harbour, enacted a series of policies that attracted FDIs that transformed it from a poor to a developed country in just over three decades.

From the days when FDIs flowed mainly among rich OECD countries, the trend has now changed as investors chase opportunities in developing countries. Consequently, countries with strong economic growth potentials attract more FDIs than those battling recession. This largely explained why FDI inflow into Africa, despite many promises, remained quite low until the "Africa Rising" narrative began. At the peak of Africa's economic growth, in 2014, it attracted a record $87 billion FDI – making it one of the world's fastest-growing destinations for FDI (The Financial Times, 2015). However, as the growth declined, FDI inflows also declined. Figures released by UNCTAD (2017) show that FDI inflow into Africa for 2016 was $59 billion. The majority of investors, besides the security of their investments, cite domestic growth market potentials as the main motivation for investing in Africa.

A major drawback, however, is that almost one-third of capital investment in Africa is resource-seeking, targeting mainly commodities, and rising and diminishing with the vagaries of commodity prices. Although China and India have ramped up investments in other sectors in Africa, they too tend to be resource-seeking, with little technology transfer or collaboration involved.

Regardless, countries like Botswana, Morocco, Egypt, and a host of others who top the FDI chart in Africa, have continued to improve their competitiveness to encourage stronger FDI flows and diversify their economies away from just dealing in commodities. The results are now evident in a much more skilled workforce, improved Human Development Index, and a much more stable political environment that is particularly liked by prospective investors.

In summary, although globalization, with its most potent tools of technology, telecommunication, broadcasting, and the internet has broken down barriers and revolutionized business practices and impacts, discontents (even from direct beneficiaries) with the epochal changes have seen the old order make a furious comeback. Now, just as the social media and technological changes could lead to rapid changes with global effects, cultural/geographic differences are also forcefully asserting themselves. To better understand the changes of our semi-globalized world, Ghemawat (2007) has provided suitable frameworks for thinking about these differences across borders along dimensions that are Cultural, Administrative/political, Geographic and Economic (CAGE) and the triple A triangle:Adaptations to adjust to differences, Aggregation to overcome differences, and Arbitrage to profit from the inevitable imbalances between markets.

Beyond global trends affecting and changing the environment, national-level issues also affect the terrain of competition.

National-level change drivers

In many ways, supranational institutions, especially the multilaterals, have set the agenda for public choice and action of private sector managers at national levels. Two classic examples include the Washington consensus and the events that led to nationalization of banks in Nigeria in the 1970s, and the impact of attempts to override election outcomes in Gambia in 2016 and in Cote d'Ivoire under Laurent Gbagbo.

When oil price shocks of the 1970s and terms of trade challenges resulted in an unsustainable balance of payments crisis for many African countries already in a debt trap (Payer, 1974), Adjustment Programmes, beginning in Senegal, became the familiar road. The playbook from which the Structural Adjustment Programme prescriptions were drawn came to be known as the Washington consensus. It is generally believed that the Washington consensus was first conceptualized in 1989 by John Williamson, who thought the Bretton Woods Institutions based in Washington and the US Treasury Department forged a template that became the prescription for the troubled economies of Latin America at the time. Among the components of this Washington consensus are fiscal discipline, focus on the social sectors and pro-poor policies without the subsidies that were rampant, and the retrenchment of regimes of controls, from prices to exchange rates, to a market-driven approach to economic management. It also involves trade liberalization, deregulation of financial markets, and lowering of entry barriers into banking to engender the competition that would break banking oligopolies which made access to finance very difficult for wannabe entrepreneurs.

Dan Rodrik goes on to suggest that the Washington consensus agenda was augmented with such entries as corporate governance, anti-corruption, flexible labour and standards, prudent capital account management, independent central banks, inflation targeting, and targeted poverty reduction (Babb, 2009).

Where did this body of ideas,which shaped the context in which public and private sector managers had to orient and transform organizations lest they die, come from? Joseph Stanislaw and Daniel Yergin suggest that the policy prescriptions came from Latin America and were developed by Latin Americans in response to their own challenges. Still, it became a template and a global yardstick.

Many African political leaders were frustrated with the promise of the Washington consensus and adjustment reforms. At a World Economic Forum in Durban, South Africa in 2000, one of the heads of government, in graphic humour, lamented that investments were promised as the reward for belt-tightening and showing good track record, but that promised investment failed to materialize after African countries adopted Washington consensus policies.

A response to the expressed frustrations resulted in a search for a more holistic framework, different from the universal analysis that dominates explanations of development failure. The

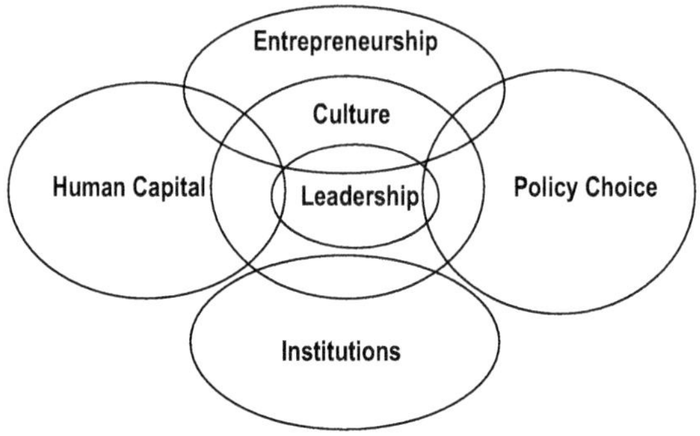

Figure 2.1 Growth Drivers Framework

proposed framework includes such variables as policy choice, institutions, human capital, and entrepreneurship. The result was a framework for evaluating factors that should determine economic performance.

The sets of interdependent variables of the "Growth Drivers Framework" – policy choice, institutions, human capital, entrepreneurship, culture and leadership, as seen in Figure 2.1 – would be the basis for analysis of "Why nations are poor" in a book by that title. This framework has proved fruitful in the evaluation of the environment and its impact on strategy in organization (Utomi, 2006).

To make strategic choices, managers need tools for analyzing trends driving the rapid changes taking place in the environment. The Growth Drivers Framework notes that these variables do not only impact the effects of the decisions directly, but also interact with and influence other variables that affect decision outcomes.

An example is how policy decisions in many adjusting countries resulted in the import substitution manufacturing companies becoming unviable, because tariff walls behind which they thrived had to be removed; or how rigid, managed foreign-exchange regimes that made imported inputs artificially low gave way to market-determined exchange rates. The need for the manufacturing ventures to become more efficient and competitive meant letting go significant numbers of the labour force. The sometimes-discontinuous retrenchments caused a morale crisis. This triggered a deeper culture problem of corruption. There were also other human-capital issues flowing from reduced investments into the education and healthcare sectors. On the positive side, those retrenchments may be producing a ready pool of new entrepreneurs who have management experience, if institutions that inspire and support venturing are given a boost to convert the new unemployed into an army of entrepreneurs.

The effective manager would have to understand these variables, how they are interdependent and make decisions that take advantage of the dynamics, or circumnavigate them to achieve clearly set goals of the organization.

A cursory review of the variables of the framework should highlight the learning points from them on how a skilled manager can navigate the environment for greater effectiveness.

Policy choices

Paul Collier has, for years, canvassed the point that growth was slow because of the policy choices of African leaders. The more statist and command-oriented policy choice-making was, the more challenged the structural impediments tended to be. Ethiopia provides, in a longitudinal frame, the effects of such choice orientation. Centralized East German-type policies under Mengistu Haile Mariam left it one of the poorest countries in the world, and vulnerable to the vagaries of drought. Today it is one of the exemplar economies in Africa, along with a Rwanda that survived genocide and a Botswana which was Africa's example of how to manage Dutch disease with its surge of earnings from diamond exports through the 1970s, just as Norway has been for oil- and gas-producing countries. In a similar manner, Mauritius, with marked competitiveness and winning with windows such as the United States African Growth Opportunities Act (AGOA), shows the benefit of policy choices.

Surely policy matters, but examples of thriving against the tide of policy exist, and can be useful lessons for the apparently trapped manager. During the Mengistu years in Ethiopia, for example, Ethiopian Airlines managed to thrive and be the leading airline in Africa. Policies to bring about growth continue to be central to the essence of modern government.

While ideas of an open economy, as advanced by Rudiger Dornbusch and others as being against more statist policies, define the debate, the range of policy options is quite broad. The community of practice and researchers like William Easterly have lamented the elusive quest for growth in spite of going from one dose of policies to another. Even perspective from within multilateral agencies like the World Bank, which have travelled from the planning era of the Mahbub ul Haqs through seasons of more liberal tones with Larry Summers, to a time with China's Justin Yefu Lin as Chief Economist arguing from the new structural economics for latent comparative advantage-driven industrial policy.

The making of policy choice, while critical, does not come without its constraints. Many countries are forced by limited capacity or lack of power, because of poverty, to accept policies literally forced on them by donors and foreign powers. A good analysis of the ability to make policies, and therefore the future policy trends, would enable the business leaders to determine whether the course will have lasting impact and have consequence for strategy.

Institutions

Former US President Barack Obama, in his first speech as US President on African soil, in Accra, Ghana, was emphatic in saying that what Africa needs is strong institutions, not strong men. His point is clearly justified by the recursive nature of Nigeria's economy. What has happened through the years is that crises produce reforms and gains, but business growing on the back of the new, more attractive policies run into the headwind of weak institutions and are pushed back in the face of predatory actions of public officials and bureaucrats. The pattern can therefore be one of two steps forward and three steps backward, leaving a recursive sketch.

What are these institutions that push back gains from policy? Acemoglu and Robinson (2012) in the influential volume *Why Nations Fail*, explore the origins of power, prosperity, and poverty, and identify institutions as key. More than a decade earlier, Douglas North (1990), in the definitive discussion of how institutions evolve, points out that the main characteristic of poor nations is weak institutions.

Essentially, institutions set boundaries to acceptable conduct. Where they are strong, consequences come for acting outside of the boundaries. This then makes it easier to anticipate outcomes. What is more, weak institutions, as suggested in the book *Managing Uncertainty: Competition and Strategy in Emerging Economies*, lead the risk-averse man to either avoid economic action that could result in loss, or to hedge against that unsavoury outcome. The latter results in higher transaction costs, which make for uncompetitive situations (Utomi, 1998).

In a similar vein,de Soto (2000) proved quite eloquent in separating the prosperous West from the poor South. The main difference between the West and the poor is posited to be how assets, like land, take on a fungible property because of institutions of representational systems, like land registries, that make them readily able to secure access to capital to start ventures. On the other hand, the assets of the poor stay on as dead capital, as they cannot be collateral security because of the absence of land title and markets for the assets. This, which he calls the Mystery of Capital, is key to wealth creation. It is a logic that is taken further by Raghuram Rajan and Luigi Zingales (2003) in the book *Saving Capitalism from the Capitalists*.If there is a paradigm which has emerged in development and economic growth in the past two decades, it is, as Dani Rodrik and Arvind Subramanian (2002) have posited, that institutions determine progress.

To deal with change in Africa is to understand institutions. It is difficult, if not impossible, to apply the strategy models from the Structure-Conduct-Performance paradigm in structural economics, like Michael Porter's Five Forces Model, in the volatile, high-uncertainty contexts of many emerging or underdeveloped economies, because the predatory conduct of public officials could dramatically alter the playing field of the Five Forces. One ready example that comes to mind was that of the flour-milling industry in Nigeria. The terrain of competition was marked by the ban on the importation of flour. This was to protect the local industry and drive growth. It led to significant levels of investment by Flour Mills of Nigeria, which then integrated forward and backward into manufacturing sacks for bagging flour and importation and storage of wheat. At a point the Apapa, Lagos, flour-milling plant of Flour Mills of Nigeria became the biggest single-locationflour mill in the world.

Discretion in the issue of waivers for imports, however, meant that a powerful person could get permission to bring in a ship load of flour, which was not allowed by the fiscal regime of the time. It was an avenue for extracting significant economic rent by the powerful. As the then-Chief Executive of Flour Mills of Nigeria, Babatunde Amosun, told a class at the Lagos Business School when the FMN case was first used for study, a powerful Army General had promised business partners he would obtain a waiver. Assuring them the waiver would be ready before the ship arrived in Nigerian waters, he caused the ship to set sail for Nigeria. Millers got wind of the arrangement and protested to the government, who frustrated the issuance of a waiver. The ship had to turn back. Months later there was a coup d'état. Those whose waiver deal was stopped were now at the top of government. In retaliation, the new government caused the importation of wheat to be banned, citing opinion editorials in newspapers by academics, pointing to a "Wheat Trap." The result was a near crippling of the flour milling industry from January 1st, 1987, when the wheat ban took effect. After losses of tens of millions of dollars and an effort to grow wheat locally, often unsuccessfully, at competitive prices, the ban on wheat imports was lifted.

Dozens of examples of this nature across the continent – including extant populist decisions by evidently well-meaning Tanzanian President John Magufuli, which has challenged strategies of investor groups like Dangote – affirm the view that one of the biggest risks to manage in the environment of business in Africa is regulatory risk.

Weak institutions around the electoral process have also become a source of new uncertainties. In the 1970s these uncertainties came from military coups, but as we can see with disputed electoral outcomes in Gambia in 2016 and Kenya in 2017, severe disruptions to business decision-making can result from how well elections and their outcomes are managed. In Gambia, Yahya Jammeh, who had accepted election results and congratulated his opponent, changed his mind. Fear of the experience in Cote d'Ivoire triggered flight towards and across the borders, disrupting economic activities and challenging the strategy of many a firm.

As Douglas North (1990) has suggested, the action of interested parties acting through business associations, for example, can lead to institutions which set boundaries that checkmate the predatory acts of public officials.

Human capital

In this age of the knowledge worker,so much has been written elsewhere about human capital and the competitiveness of both firms and countries that repeating it is unnecessary. The Human Development Index and other indicators of investment in education and health care both indicate opportunity and sources of competitiveness for companies, as well as whether a demographic dividend or a "Coming Anarchy" vision is the outcome of the youth bulge in most of Africa (Kaplan, 2000). The education and healthcare of citizens is central to economic growth. This is why early UN efforts prescribed as much as 26% of the annual budget go to education. Suffice to say, again, that the strong relationship between human capital and economic/organization growth will compel the business leader to prioritize the acquisition and development of knowledge and skills sets in the organization.

Entrepreneurship

Economic growth depends very much on value creation. Creating value without the resources ordinarily needed to bring about such creation, as the Harvard Business School defines entrepreneurship, is key to economic growth and brings a range of benefits.

In the main a quantum leap in value creation, entrepreneurship is, in Schumpeter's (1983) terms, "creative destruction" that brings about discontinuous change, and replaces yesterday's major value with a higher order value.Yesterday's typewriter, a major leap from writing with pen on paper parchment, is replaced with the desktop and now laptop computer. This process is made easier or more challenging by factors such as Rajan and Zingales (2003) point out in the Institutions that support venturing, such as property rights, institutional arrangements which make access to capital easier for disadvantaged people like the Bumiputra banks in Malaysia and small business administrations in many emerging countries.

The manager who has to develop a supply pipeline to make his production more competitive would need to gauge the spirit of enterprise and the institutions that support it.

Culture

Culture matters. As values help shape human progress, it is hard to agree with Hernando De Soto, who says institutions are the peg of progress but that culture does not matter. Surely values matter. Where corruption is low, the work ethic high, social trust strong, and the sense of personal responsibility very strong, uncertainty will be lower and economic transaction more widespread than where the converse is the case. Certainly, both culture and institutions matter (Utomi, 2015). The Harvard Colloquium on how values shape human progress and the volume that summarized the presentations, *Culture Matters: How Values Shape Human Progress*, edited by Harrison and Huntington Jnr (2000), capture well the importance of culture. Perhaps there is some truth in Daniel Patrick Moynihan's (cited in Huntington 1996)assertion that culture, not politics, determines the success of a society, even if politics can change a culture and save it from itself.

At the level of the firm, the importance of culture comes through even more robustly in the work of Jim Collins and Jerry Porras's (1994) *Built to Last*. They showed how successful companies go to great length to build organizational culture and ensure all employees adapt and embrace those values. Corporate culture, therefore, is not just a prime instrument in sustained superior performance significantly affecting how firms seek to gain advantage over others, but is key to sustainability of the firm.

Leadership

Leadership also matters. But the evidence from the work of Jim Collins in the prequel to *Built to Last*, as with the evidence in *The Art of Leading*,suggest that the principal value of leaders is that they set the tone of culture. Leadership is so critical that without it, all other organizational elements lie dormant. But many people have written enough on the subject that we need not spend more time on it here. What is important is for managers to understand how leadership capacity in stakeholder groups affects the possibilities of choices that impact performance. All these influence how firms craft and implement strategy (Utomi, 2015).

We have seen how the interdependent variables of the "Growth Drivers Framework" – policy choice, institutions, human capital, entrepreneurship, culture and leadership – and other variables, like the instability in the polity and in policies and the predatory behaviour of regulators, help in understanding and explaining change at the national level and its impact on the organization. Deploying these tools will better equip the manager in his strategy formulation, and enable him to carefully navigate the challenges of the environment in pursuit of organizational goals and competitive advantage.

Change and corporatestrategy

The third level of analysis is the firm level. If the national level environment of business can be modelled with such a framework, managers would need to manage transitions in the context of change by aligning their strengths and weaknesses in a way that navigates the opportunities and threats in the tumultuous environment of doing business in Africa.

In making choices about what business they are in (corporate strategy), how to establish advantage over rivals (basic strategy), and how to align the strategy of the functional units to the basic strategy (functional strategy), managers have to stay sensitive to the entrenched reluctance to change. Few thoughts have been more profound than Machiavelli's view in *The Prince* that nothing is more difficult to bring about than a new order of things, because those who profit from the old order would do what is in their power to prevent a new order from coming about (Bowman, 1990). But they have a fourth level of strategy, institutional strategy, which deals with building corporate culture as the basis for competing and as a tool for continuous alignment of the levels of strategy and dynamics in the global, national, and internal contexts of choice.

When structural problems and SAP triggered de-industrialization, and many companies struggled to transform themselves across the continent in the years of Afro-pessimism, many firms embarked on programmatic or culture change programmes; most invariably had to lay off staff and had to implement discontinuous change. Many turned to professional services firms. Leading diversified conglomerates like the UACN group, the SCOA group, and others in Nigeria found that struggling to save one division after the other stretched them close to a state of corporate surrender. They then began to be more focused as the UACN retreated into foods, where the importation of inputs was limited, and into real estate development.

Just like IBM's Louis Gerstner Jr (2002) shows with his IBM story in *Who Says Elephants Can't Dance*, and Rosabeth Moss Kanter (1989) does in *When Giants Learn to Dance*and her earlier volume *The Change Masters*, the executives at UACN learned from the "Change Masters" of the challenge of organizational transitions. But they had, in addition, to take into account the predatory acts of public officials and regulatory risk resulting from weak institutions. Firm-level strategy, national strategy, and the role of institutions are incorporated into a frame of analysis in the Strategy Interface model. The flow of the relations and action suggest that where national strategy is clear and institutions are strong, competitive strategy for firms incline towards commitment with greater likelihood of top performance at firm and national levels.

Conclusion

The foregoing provides much evidence of trends that provoke change. The discussion has also pointed to quite a number of examples of consequences of these changes for firm strategy and performance. The discussion has also offered a number of tools such as the 3E Framework, the Growth Drivers Framework, and Pankaj Ghemawat's CAGE.

These tools of analysis should help managers evaluate consequences from change pressures coming from globalization of products and services as well as management organization; shifts in inflows of Foreign Direct Investment; and technology trends. Other drivers of change across the continent include the rise in entrepreneurship, challenges to stability in the polity, new policy orientations (including regional integration efforts), and the pace of institution building.

The use of the tools offered to the manager would significantly improve his capacity to construct strategy that can enable him to circumnavigate the challenges in the environment in order to deliver superior performance over rivals. We know, for example, that in the face of instability, the choice of generic strategy will more often be flexibility than commitment. But if one considers the example of how one chief executive in not-so-stable, statist Ethiopia could find enough headroom for strong commitment that grew Ethiopian Airlines into a formidable competitor on the continent, it could be possible to imitate that in similar circumstances. Understanding how Ethiopian Airlines became the dominant airline on the continent, despite being in a more adverse environment than both state and private airlines on the continent, should deepen capacity for managing change.

The changes derived from globalization also lead to transmission of culture across boundaries. Firms with strong cultures significantly affected values in the investment recipient countries. In Ghana, for example, the trademark long working hours of Nigeria's Access Bank, which moved into the market, came to be seen as affecting Ghana's banking culture. The bank would be a veritable recruiting ground for rival banks in Ghana in 2015 in the manner that Nigeria's Unilever subsidiary, Lever Brothers, was considered the training school for marketing people in Nigeria in the 1970s.

In his presentation at the 2017 Afriexim Annual General Meeting in Kigali, Rwanda, Justin Yifu Lin, former Chief Economist of the World Bank, pointed to examples of light manufacturing industrial parks in Ethiopia and Rwanda. Each of those showcased business models different from traditional management traditions from the colonial era, especially in frugal, high-discipline work environments. As an example in Nigeria, Chinese business models like the Lea group which was manufacturing flip flops in Nigeria and successfully exporting into Europe in a time of de-industrialization, can seem a traumatic engagement for the indigenes coming from more hierarchical cultures. The idea of managers sleeping in bunk beds right inside the factory was considered extremely unusual, and demanded skills of a particular nature in managing the interface between such Chinese leaders of operations and the casual local labourers. Managing these culture clashes and drawing new business models from them have become part of the remit of today's HR leader in Africa.

In addition to the corporate culture issues derived from increasing Foreign Direct Investment (FDI), quite a number of the multinational corporations began to structure their businesses along continental lines. Major professional services firms like Deloitte consolidated their companies into one continental practice with one board headquartered in South Africa.

This response to change pressures is also evident in the approaches of an emerging generation of African entrepreneurs. Gambian affordable housing developer Mustapha Njie, of TAF Africa Homes, moved the base of his operations to Nigeria because of the market size and discomfort with political conditions under the long rule of President Yahya Jammeh. But his strategy remained Pan-African. His continental ambitions influenced strategies such as selling villas built in Gambia to Nigerian investors who pay in Naira, the Nigeria currency, but were assured US dollar returns. Within months of the demise of the Jammeh regime, he would commit to building two major hotels and 10,000 housing units in his native Gambia, as he was in a position to evaluate new prospects and to seek first-mover advantage.

These case studies show that the change drivers identified are impacting the environment of business. But they are also bringing in technology that allows for higher effectiveness in managing the change. The entrepreneur, manager in business enterprise,or public sector leader who is informed about these change trends, and can use the tools offered here to evaluate the change and the appropriate response to such change stimuli, is more likely to be more effective and to deliver superior performance relative to rivals.

The central issue in the changing context of the environment of governing and enterprise in Africa is one regarding the transitional challenges in Africa's quest for modernity. The dilemmas of the transition are captured well by US-based Nigerian academic Taiwo (2011), who, after much analysis of why progress is slow and misery endemic in Africa, came to the conclusion that the problems of Africa have to do with its not being modern. Taiwo thus argues, as the title of his book suggests, that Africa must be modern. The quest for modernity will include strengthening of the public sphere with more rigor, openness, and civility in public conversation. Many African countries have graduated from military rule to electoral democracies, but public conversation is yet to meet Jurgen Habermas's (1989) idea of democracy as requiring a robust public sphere. Such a public sphere provides the manager a barometer both of the thrust of policy and the boundaries of acceptable conduct. Where this is at a low level, the manager has to develop proxies for barometers of gauging shifts in policy that can impact the performance of the organization.

With the striving to modernity also comes the need for reforming the civil service. A wide range of indiscretion by civil servants,which has engendered corruption and increased uncertainty, has produced widespread calls for reform of the civil service. In Nigeria, academic and senior civil servant Tunji Olaopa has written much about innovation and best practice in public sector reforms, as well as led federal government efforts to implement service compacts with stakeholders. The manager, unable to track the efforts he outlines and drawing both opportunities and threats from them, could be surprised, as in the case when the Federal Ministry of Health implemented a law requiring the ban on distribution of medicines in favour of generics on an Essential Drugs List (EDL). By the time implementation was started, most pharmaceutical companies had lost half their value, and several exited the market before policies were reformed (Olaopa, 2012).

Modernity requires sensitivity to variables which the historian Niall Ferguson has called the Six Killer Apps of Western power in his book, *Civilization*. These include Competition, Science, Property, Medicine, Consumption, and Work Ethic. Ferguson (2011) attributed the dominance of the West over the rest of the world to these "winning tools." As the disposition to walk down the path of these Apps progresses, managers will require a learning agility to ensure continuous alignment of the strengths and weakness outside with opportunities and threats in the environment.

In the main, an African approach to managing change recognizes a number of factors such as weak institutions, young democracies (which tend to mean a ubiquitous state and the dominance of politicians in the environment), and a clash between traditional ways and new ways in transition societies. As a Kenyan writer suggests, the decision maker in Africa is "a child of two worlds." What world dominates the context of choice? Is it the world of Ubuntu (I am because we are), or a world of bruising competition? The typical African would, for example, find US President Donald Trump's manner of referring to opponents offensive and impolite, but in the American context it may be more acceptable. So perhaps in the context of Africa, competition and cooperation can be a collective action for the common good. Competing bodies collaborating to erect institutions that provide a level ground for all may be an attractive option. These factors give a unique African flavour to managing change in a globalised world.

Note

1 Where L is learning and C is change.

References

Acemoglu, D., and Robinson, J. A. (2012) *Why Nations Fail: The Origins of Power, Prosperity and Poverty.* New York, NY: Crown Publishers.

Adebayo, O. (1998) *The Elusive Prince of Denmark: Structural Adjustment and the Crisis of Governance in Africa.* Uppsala: Nordiska Afrikainstitutet.

Asiodu, P. (1993) *Essays in Nigerian Political Economy.* Lagos: Sankore Publishers.

Ayida, A. (1987) *Reflections on Nigerian Development.* Ibadan: Malthouse Press.

Babb, S. (2009) *Behind the Development Bank: Washington Politics, World Poverty, and the Wealth of Nations.* Chicago, IL: The University of Chicago Press.

Bowman, C. (1990) *The Essence of Strategic Management.* New York, NY: Prentice Hall.

Bright, J., and Hruby, A. (2015) *The Next Africa – An Emerging Continent Becomes a Global Power House.* New York, NY: Though Dunne Book.

Collins, J., and Porras, J. I. (1994) *Built to Last – Successful Habits of Visionary Companies.* New York, NY: Harper Business.

Crook, R. C., and Manor, J. (1998) *Democracy and Decentralization in South Asia and West Africa: Participation, Accountability and Performance.* Cambridge: Cambridge University Press.

Deaton, A. (2013) *The Great Escape – Health, Wealth, and the Origin of Inequality.* Princeton, NJ: Princeton University Press.

De Soto, H. (2000) *Mystery of Capital: Why Capitalism Triumphs in the West and Fails Everywhere Else.* London: Black Swan.

Ferguson, N. (2011) *Civilization: The Six Killer Apps of Western Power.* London: Penguin Books.

The Financial Times of London, May 19, 2015.Retrieved from www.ft.com/content/79ee41b6-fd84-11e4-b824-00144feabdc0

Freire, P.(1996) *The Pedagogy of the Oppressed.* New York, NY: Continuum.

Fukuyama, F. (1992) *The End of History and the Last Man.* New York, NY: Free Press.

Gerstner, Jr., L. (2002) *Who Says Elephants Can't Dance.* New York, NY: Harper Business.

Ghemawat, P. (2007) *Redefining Global Strategy – Crossing Borders in a World Where Difference Still Matters.* Boston, MA: Harvard Business School Press.

Habermas, J. (1989) *The Structural Transformation of the Public Sphere: An Inquiry Into a Category of Bourgeois Society.* Cambridge, MA: MIT Press.

Harrison, L., and Huntington, S. P. (Eds.). (2000) *Culture Matters – How Values Shape Human Progress.* New York, NY: Basic Books.

Huntington, S. P. (1996) *The Clash of Civilizations and the Remarking of World Order.* New York, NY: Simon & Schuster.

Kaplan, R. D. (2000) *The Coming Anarchy.* New York, NY: Vintage Books.

Levitt, T. (1983) The globalization of markets. *Harvard Business Review*, 61(3): 92–102Mackenzie, J. M. (1983) *The Partition of Africa 1880–1900 and European Imperialism in the Nineteenth Century.* London: Methuen.

Mahajan, V. (2009) *Africa Rising: How 900 Million African Consumers Offer More than You Think.* Upper Saddle River, NJ: Pearson Education Inc.

North, D. C. (1990) *Institutions, Institutional Change and Economic Performance.* Cambridge: Cambridge University Press.

Okigbo, P. (1987) *Essays in the Public Philosophy of Development.* Enugu: Fourth Dimension Publishing.

Olaopa, T. (2012) *Innovation and Best Practices in Public Sector Reforms: Ideas, Strategies and Conditions.* Ibadan: Bookcraft.

Payer, C. (1974) *The Debt Trap – The IMF and the Third World.* New York, NY: Monthly Review Press.

Rajan, R., and Zingales, L. (2003) *Saving Capitalism From the Capitalists.* New York, NY: Crown Publishers.
Reader, J. (1997) *Africa – A Biography of the Continent.* London: Penguin.
Rodrik, D., Subramanian, A., and Trebbi, F. (2002) *Institutions Rule: The Primacy of Institutions over Integration and Geography in Economic Development.* IMF Working Paper, P/02/189.
Rosabeth Moss Kanter, R. M. (1989) *When Giants Learn to Dance.* New York, NY: Simon & Schuster.
Schumpeter, J. A. (1983) *The Theory of Economic Development.* New Brunswick, NJ: Transaction Publishers.
Taiwo, O. (2014) *Africa Must be Modern: A Manifesto.* Indiana: Indiana University Press.
UNCTAD World Investment Report. (2017) *Investment and the Digital Economy.*
Utomi, P. (1998) *Managing Uncertainty: Competition and Strategy in Emerging Economies.* Ibadan: Spectrum Books.
Utomi, P. (2006) *Why Nations Are Poor.* Lagos: BusinessDay Press.
Utomi, P. (2015) *The Art of Leading.* London and Lagos: Makeway and CVL.
Van de Walle, N. (2001) *African Economies and the Politics of Permanent Crisis.* Cambridge: Cambridge University Press.

3

Firm internationalization as a driver of organizational change

Chris Ogbechie, Franklin N. Ngwu and Godson Ikiebey

Introduction

With the increasing inter-connectedness of the global economy, the localized structures and processes associated with enterprises are changing to more globalized forms (Dicken, 2015). Enhanced by rapid technological advancements and consumer mobility, many companies are now increasingly producing goods and services outside their home countries. This can be attributed to factors such as profit advantage, technology advantage, economies of scale and scope, tax benefits, competitive pressure, excess capacity and proximity to customers and markets (Machado-da-Silva, Casali, and Fernandes, 2001; Czinkota, Ronkainen, and Ortiz-Buonafina, 2004; Dicken, 2015).

While some have argued that African economies are improving and becoming relevant in the international business arena (Marco and Patterson, 2010), some also argue that Africa is still unable to contribute meaningfully to the global economy, given the dominance of commodities and raw materials in Africa's international trade activities (Henson, Masakure, and Cranfield, 2011). While the debate rages on, evidence is emerging to suggest that the speed, scope and scale at which African firms have been investing in the global economy is growing (McNamee, Pearson, and Boer, 2015). For example, in the financial services industry, African banks have emerged to become relevant international players (Beck, Fuchs, Singer, and Witte, 2014). Many "homegrown" African firms are expanding and successfully competing and contributing to intra-regional flow of foreign direct investment. One such example is an African bank: the United Bank for Africa (UBA), a Nigerian-owned bank. Intra-African foreign direct investment (FDI) is growing faster than FDI from any other region and has increased over 30% since 2007 (Ernst and Young, 2013).

The aim of this chapter is to demonstrate that internationalization is a driver of organizational change, specifically in Africa. As internationalization affects the size, structure, operations, culture, value and revenue of an organization, which are elements of organizational change, it is important to explore the role of these elements in organizational change through the internationalization process. Therefore, we try to ask if African firms are internationalizing and what are the challenges faced in the process. We shall also look at the implications for organizational changes of the internationalizing firm and the competitors in the host countries. For instance, it is said that

UBA changed the banking landscape in Ghana. UBA had to respond to international change in its operation, which in turn challenged local banks in Ghana to also adjust their operations to retain their customers.

The remaining sections of the chapter will proceed as follows: The second section captures the essence of internationalization as it concerns the purposes, motives and processes that drive the internationalization of firms. The third section, which evolves from the work of Ghemawat (2001), examines the relationship between internationalization and organizational change. It also examines the fit between organizational culture and cultural distance for a successful organizational change. The last section is the conclusion and implications.

The concept of internationalization

The classics in the field of internationalization have emphasized potential gains and benefits from global trade, notably Adam Smith's absolute advantage, David Ricardo's comparative advantage and other relevant international trade theories. The actions of multinational corporations which underlie internationalization are strongly supported by economic liberalism and free-market systems in a globalized international society. They argue that in such a system, the pursuit of self-interest by all economic agents will maximize global welfare.

Internationalization can be seen as a business strategy and as an environmental pressure leading to strategic changes in organizations (Machado-da-Silva et al., 2001). Internationalization often means that the whole organization will have to go through a structural change, and this is usually challenging. A firm becomes increasingly internationalized as it becomes more involved in and committed to serving markets outside its home country, which can be in the form of exports, franchising, joint ventures, production, mergers and acquisitions. Internationalization contributes to the growth of economies through the development of national industries, improved productivity and employment opportunities. For instance, a study by Hessels and van Stel (2011) found that export-oriented entrepreneurship more strongly contributes to macro-economic growth than localized entrepreneurial activities in both transitional and developed economies.

Those entrepreneurs who are interested in the field of internationalization need to possess the ability to think globally and have an understanding of international cultures. By appreciating and understanding different beliefs, values, behaviors and business strategies operative in other countries, entrepreneurs will be able to internationalize successfully. Entrepreneurs (Firms) must also have an ongoing concern for innovation, maintain a high level of quality and drive their strategy from a sustainability standpoint and cultural approach, while adapting to different countries and cultural contexts. These considerations influenced the strategies adopted by UBA in their internationalization process, one of which included the need to have nationals of the country in the organization since they had better understanding of the country's culture and service needs. It also necessitated their translation of the banking software from English to French in francophone countries, to mitigate the language barrier.

Internationalization may require a company to review its business model, which in turn will require new ideas, technologies and capital, but also changes in culture and in the ways things are done within the company. It may also drive standardization through the demands to meet international best practices. For firms in markets where regulation is weak and standards not effectively enforced, internationalization can help such firms to perform better in the area of compliance (Machado-da-Silva et al., 2001). For UBA, there was no bank-wide employee policy. The bank's employee policy was customized in line with labor laws of the internationalized market. These actions in the internationalization process serve as necessary elements for organizational change.

Why organizations internationalize (motives for internationalization)

Firms internationalize for a variety of reasons such as access to basic inputs, diversification into new markets, searching for new customers and revenue etc., (Pananond, 2015). In fact, presence in foreign markets is an important growth tool for companies, especially where the home market is limited (Amal, Baffour Awuah, Raboch, and Andersson, 2013). Firms also internationalize to augment existing strategic assets or obtain new ones that contribute to long-term competitiveness (Pananond, 2015). Firms internationalize to explore new markets, expand existing markets, find cost-effective labor and to be more competitive. Czinkota et al. (2004) classified the motivations of firms to internationalize into proactive and reactive, or what is simply known as pull and push factors.

Proactive

This approach, according to Czinkota et al. (2004), entails profit advantage, unique products, technical advantage, exclusive market information, tax benefits and economies of scale. As profitability is often considered the core objective of most firms (Onkelinx and Sleuwaegen, 2008), a firm's management is induced to go international when they see international sales as a potential source of reaping higher income or profit. Empirical evidence indicates that higher income and market size are important drivers of internationalization because they attract FDI (Ekholm and Midelfart, 2004; Blonigen, 2005; Jensen, 2008).

A firm is also motivated to go abroad if it has a unique technological advantage over its competitors. The main question here is how long this technological advantage will be sustained in the face of rapid increase in the pace of innovation, both in products and technologies, as well as the firms' lack of intellectual property rights protection (Ekholm and Midelfart, 2004; Blonigen, 2005; Jensen, 2008).

Another proactive factor that induces firms' internationalization is exclusive market information. A firm can go international to take advantage of knowledge about foreign customers, marketplaces or situations that is not known by other firms. For instance, UBA took advantage of the financial service needs of Nigerians in diaspora by going into countries where Nigerians want to do or are already doing business, in order to provide financial services that they need. This first-mover advantage could be very beneficial to such a firm if positively exploited.

Tax benefits also constitute a source of motivation to firms. Companies' management can decide to go international in a bid to take advantage of tax benefits. Some countries do grant tax relief or holidays to encourage or attract international marketing activities. For instance, the Federal Government of Nigeria established free trade zones that confer complete tax holidays on investors operating in the zones in order to attract FDI (Ekholm and Midelfart, 2004; Blonigen, 2005; Jensen, 2008).

A final proactive motivation is economies of scale. Firms participate in exporting activities in a bid to increase their outputs. Increased production for the international market can help the firm to reduce the cost of production.

Reactive

The reactive motivations, on the other hand, include competitive pressure, overproduction, declining domestic sales, excess capacity, saturated domestic markets and proximity to customers and port (Czinkota et al., 2004). A firm may be induced to internationalize for fear of losing its market share to competing firms that are enjoying economies of scale as a result of their exporting activities.

Also, a firm's management can decide to go international for fear of permanently losing foreign markets to domestic competitors that choose to concentrate on these markets. Firms usually move into foreign markets when they observe that domestic competitors are beginning to internationalize and knowing that the first firms that obtain significant market share are most likely to retain it.

Overproduction is another reactive motivating factor for firms to go international. Firms usually perceive foreign markets as ideal channels for excess inventories during downturns in the domestic business cycle. They (firms) access the foreign markets by cutting down their prices to sell excess inventories, then withdraw from foreign markets when the domestic market rebounds (Czinkota et al., 2004). Declining domestic sales of products that are in the declining stage of the product cycle is also a source of motivation to going international. A firm's management can decide to prolong the life of the product by expanding the market rather than attempting to push back the life cycle process at the domestic market by adding a cosmetic innovation to the products (Czinkota et al., 2004; Cassiman and Golovko, 2011).

Under-utilized capacity can also be a motivation to go international. If a firm's production equipment is under-utilized, the firm's management can see internationalization as a strategy for achieving wider distribution of fixed costs. Proximity to customers and port is also considered a reactive motivation. Physical nearness to the foreign market can play a major role in the export activities of a firm. A firm's management can opt to engage in export activities simply because it is established at the border of a neighboring country (Czinkota et al., 2004). The available evidence suggests that firms that go international for reactive or defensive reasons generally under-perform as compared to proactively motivated counterparts (Calof and Viviers, 1995; Ramaseshan and Soutar, 1996; Roberts and Thoburn, 2003).

Motives for internationalization by African firms

Since no country or organization is self-sufficient, it is no longer a serious debate about whether African firms should engage in global economy, as public opinion and policy makers were largely in favor of engagement. The challenge that remains is how best they should internationalize given the risks posed by globalization. Thus, whether to internationalize and how to internationalize have become two of the most burning strategy issues for managers around the world.

There is little available literature with respect to internationalization of African firms (Marco and Patterson, 2010; Boojihawon and Acholonu, 2013; Bakunda, 2003; Ibeh, Wilson, and Chizema, 2012; Nwankwo, 2012; Rolfe et al., 2015. In the financial services industry, more than 70 African banks have emerged to become dominant international players (Beck et al., 2014): Ecobank, Standard Bank and First National Bank individually hold over 30% of banking assets in nine countries. Beyond banking, African multinationals have emerged in the telecommunications, manufacturing, energy, agribusiness, aviation and technology sectors (Adeleye, White, Ibeh, and Kinoti, 2015). Several reasons have been adduced for this development. Many African firms and other emerging economies seek to internationalize for the purpose of establishing global brands which further consolidate their competitive positions in the domestic market (where they have to compete with leading global brands). Since Nigeria has a large domestic population, we expect that Nigerian firms crossing national boundaries in Africa will do so, not so much in search of markets, but to strengthen their competitive position in the domestic market and to establish global (regional) brand.

Not surprisingly, the preponderant motive for international engagements by African firms observed was exporting. Most literature on African internationalization identifies export adoption as the driving force for most African firms to internationalize in view of the proportion of their overall business contributed by exporting. For example, 38% of firms sampled by Azam and colleagues in Cote d' Ivoire get over 75% turnover from their export (Ibeh et.al., 2012); 25% of

South African sample exported over 75% of turnover (Soontiens, 2003); 20% of Tanzanian sample exported 50% or more of output (Grenier, McKay, and Morrissey, 1999) ; 11% of Nigerian sample had an export ratio of 50% and above (Ibeh et al., 2012); and sample of Ghanaian wood firms exported nearly 60% of output (Söderbom and Teal's, 2003).

It is instructive to note that internationalization is a strategic decision among African firms as they proactively plan these moves (Ibeh et al., 2012). Even though their primary motive is export-driven, most Nigerian firms' exports are triggered by growth aspiration and proactive opportunity search (Ibeh et al., 2012). In addition, the nature of African domestic markets pushes to internationalize: the small size of African markets forces local companies to either internationalize or diversify their products in order to obtain sufficient turnover (Kuada, 2006). Similarly, some African firms internationalize in order to escape the difficult local market environment (Ibeh et al., 2012). For example, many indigenous firms in Nigeria move to neighboring countries because of poor infrastructure at home, e.g., Globacom Nigeria, etc. Bakunda (2003) identified upstream internationalization, such as the import of technology and other inputs, as another motive for African internalization. This is because most studies have focused only on downstream internationalization, i.e., export. However, in Africa, this one-sided contemplation of internationalization is misleading. The establishment of business activities with foreign suppliers provides African firms with information, which facilitates downstream internationalization (Kuada, 2006, 2007). "Upstream resource leveraging is therefore a necessary requirement for downstream international expansion" (Kuada, 2007: p.10)

The current trend in the internationalization of African firms reveals a picture of a unique variety of factors propelling African firms to internationalize: reliance on formal and informal networking ties; the tendency to serve regional African markets; the dominance of the service sector; the rising number of early stage and minority entrepreneurs; and others. In the ICT sector, the follow-your-client motive is the driving force behind internationalization of many African ICT firms (Ovadje, 2016). This is aimed at continuing the relationship across borders and may not necessarily be motivated by market, efficiency, resource or strategic considerations. This assures the customers that their providers can service them in any location. Therefore, in organizations where the client values competence, timely delivery and peace of mind, like in the telecommunications sector, internationalization often helps to achieve this.

Given the rising number of African firms on the international stage, Africa has recently been captured in the global press for being at the receiving end of burgeoning international business and politics (Schwarz and Yellin, 2013). For instance, Dangote Cement, a Nigerian company, has increased access to the cement market in Africa through internationalization, and this has led to huge investment outside Nigeria (Ibeh, 2015). A recent Ernst and Young business attractiveness survey concluded that

> While skeptics still abound [. . .] a critical mass of African economies have grown at high and sustained rates; so much so that, despite the impact of the ongoing global economic situation, the size of the African economy has more than tripled since 2000.
>
> *(Ernst and Young, 2013)*

How organizations internationalize

The internationalization approach of firms is mostly traced to the works of Johanson and Wiedersheim-Paul (1975) and Johanson and Vahlne (1977, 1990). There are four stages involved in entering the international market. These stages include no regular export activities; export via independent representatives; establishment of an overseas sales subsidiary; and overseas production/

manufacturing units. Each successive stage represents a higher degree of international involvement (Figure 3.1). Johanson and Wiedersheim-Paul (1975) argued that firms would enter new markets based on the level of knowledge of psychic distance of the market possessed by the firm. Psychic distance refers to those factors that could impede the flow of information between the firm and market; these include differences in culture, language, political systems, level of education and level of industrial development. Realizing the significant cultural difference of North Africa from the rest of Africa influenced UBA's internationalization efforts in the region. This demonstrates that a firm going international would prefer a market about which it has a greater level of knowledge of its psychic distance, than a market about which it has a lower level of knowledge (Johanson and Wiedersheim-Paul, 1975).

Johanson and Vahlne (1977) improved on the work of Johanson and Wiedersheim-Paul (1975) and formulated a dynamic model in which the outcome of one cycle of events forms the input to the next (Figure 3.2). The major structure of the model distinguishes between the state and change aspect of internationalization variables. The state aspects entail market knowledge and market commitment. Market knowledge refers to knowledge about the international markets and operations while the market commitment refers to resources committed to international

Figure 3.1 Stages of entering the international market

Source: Johanson and Wiedersheim-Paul (1975: 307).

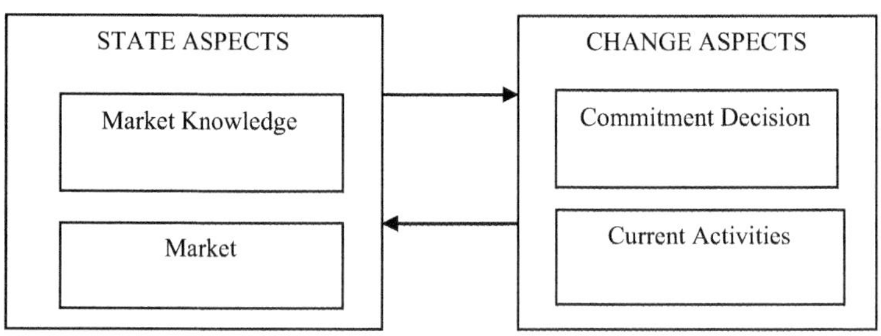

Figure 3.2 The internationalization process of the firm

Source: Johanson and Vahlne (1977: 26)

markets. In internationalization, market knowledge and market commitment influence commitment decisions, the current activities of the firm, and changes the market knowledge and commitment (Johanson and Vahlne, 1977).

Summarily, psychic distance formed the bedrock of most African internationalization strategy. Companies initially export their products to countries that they understand, then build acquired experience to explore opportunities further afield; i.e., firms enter new markets where they are able to identify opportunities with low market uncertainty, then enter markets at successively greater psychic distance (Johanson and Vahlene, 1990). For instance, owing mainly to historical ties, Europe has remained the foremost market for African products (Ibeh et al., 2012; Fafchamps et al., 2008). Fafchamps et al. (2008), for example, found that most Moroccan manufacturing exports go to two countries alone: France and Spain. Moodley (2003) similarly reported the main export destinations for South African wood furniture products to be the United Kingdom and Germany, and to a lesser extent Australia, the Middle East, the United States and other countries in Western Europe. South African telecommunication companies such as MTN took advantage of the growing population of Nigerians who transact one form of business or another to develop telecommunication services for effective and speedy completion of business transactions. It was therefore not surprising that within a few years of operation in Nigeria, the number of MTN subscribers had risen to several million.

In the case of Shoprite, another South African firm, the understanding of the Nigerian market played a significant role in their internationalization success in Nigeria. The desire of the Nigerian consumer to have access to goods at affordable prices, coupled with a conducive environment for a good customer experience provided by Shoprite, made it attractive to many Nigerians. Unlike the traditional market that is rough, rowdy and untidy, Shoprite provided an atmosphere to make purchases with pleasure, and has risen to the point where it gives consumers a prestigious feeling to buy goods from the firm.

Studies of African internationalization strategy suggest that firms initially internationalize to countries with closer characteristic distance. This is reflected in the decision reached by UBA management who decided to enter those countries which had attractiveness in terms of market size, similarity of regulatory environment to Nigeria, ease of entry and similarities of the financial service needs of the market to the needs of the Nigerian market. South African companies such as MTN, SABMiller, Standard Bank, Shoprite etc. internationalized by initially exploring their neighboring markets such as Zimbabwe, Mauritius and Swaziland and then to other markets (Klein and Wöcke, 2007). Ngwu, Adeleye, and Ogbechie (2015), when identifying the internationalization strategies of Nigerian banks, listed amongst other things psychic distance, customer and market-driven opportunities and follow-your-leader strategy (herd behavior). They observed in their study that Nigerian banks tended to initially focus on Anglophone West Africa, then Francophone West Africa, and then other countries (Ngwu et al., 2015).

Exports of Nigerian firms, for instance, are mostly triggered by growth aspirations and proactive opportunity search (Ibeh, Ibrahim, and Ezepue, 2007). Moreover, African firms prefer to export (Ibeh et al., 2012), as it involves less resource commitment than other entry modes, which mitigates the risk and uncertainties of foreign market entry (Demeke and Chiloane-Tsoka, 2015; Rutashobya and Jaensson, 2004). Even though exporting is the preferred entry mode of many African companies, they only have a low export intensity, and Sub-Saharan Africa's share of global exports remains low (Bakunda, 2003; Ibeh et al., 2012; Seyoum, 2007). However, there are large differences between countries and industries: South African firms, for instance, export more than their Nigerian (Söderbom and Teal, 2003) or Tanzanian counterparts (Grenier et al., 1999).

Internationalization among African firms is more pronounced in regional expansion, or what is called Africa-2-Africa (A2A) internationalization. This is because of the size and resource ownership of many African firms (Ngwu et al., 2015), which prevent them from competing with foreign ones. Ibeh et al. (2012) posited that international expansions require considerable ownership of resources – managerial and corporate resources and learning & entrepreneurial skills – which are often scarce and difficult to access in most African countries. Nevertheless, internationalization has evolved more strongly in A2A internationalization through the banking sector. South Africa's "big four" have a considerable presence across the region, with Standard Bank aggressively leading the pack with operations in 18 countries. Nedbank has a presence in six African countries and recently entered into a strategic alliance with Togo-based Ecobank, the regional banking giant with operations in 33 African countries, whose subsidiaries have at least 10% of total bank credit or deposits in 11 francophone countries (IMF, 2015). Equity Bank of Kenya has expanded to four countries, while Mali-based Bank of Africa operates in 14 countries. Nigerian banks have ambitious regional aspirations. The United Bank for Africa, for instance, now has operations in 19 African countries; Guaranty Trust Bank has operations in six, Zenith Bank in three, and Access Bank in eight African countries. This phenomenal increase in internationalization activities of financial institutions provides an interesting opportunity to explore the patterns, strategies, barriers and outcomes of the intra-African internationalization process. South African companies such as MTN, SABMiller, Standard Bank, Telkom, Dimensions Data, Massmart, Nampak and Shoprite now have a presence in at least a dozen African markets (IMF, 2012). Some of these South African multinationals, like SABMiller, Sappi and Barloworld, have even become global contenders (Klein and Wöcke, 2007).

Internationalization as a driver of organizational change

Internationalization can simultaneously be perceived as a strategy and strategic process (Melin, 1992), while also as a process that fundamentally alters the environment when organizations bring new foreign operations within their boundaries (Hitt, Hoskisson, and Kim, 1997). Internationalization has been a key driver of different segments of African economic activities, but the sector which perhaps has the highest level of Africa-2-Africa internationalization (A2A) is the banking sector (Ngwu et al., 2015). With banks establishing branches in different parts of the region, internationalization has also been a major driver of financial inclusion in many parts of Africa, which has led to the financial deepening in the region (Ngwu et al., 2015).

As a result of underdevelopment of the capital markets in developing economies, it has been observed that changes in capital markets do not significantly cause changes in organizations, because senior managers in this context are not under pressure like their counterparts in developed economies to affect stock prices within the shortest possible time (Ovadje, 2014). Hence it is important to look at drivers of change in African firms outside of capital market influences. Ovadje (2014) showed that the major driver of change in developing economies is government and its regulations.

Internationalization and organizational change

Organizational change refers to the transition an organization is going through by continuously renewing its direction, structure and capabilities (Todnem, 2005). Burnes (2004) argued that change is a consistent feature of organizational life. Organizational and strategic changes tend to increase as firms experience international operations (Garri and Konstantopoulos, 2013). Calof and Beamish (1995) argue that firms' international operations impact organizational change through the creation of new departments and hiring of international skilled executives.

The process by which companies move from the current state to some desired future state in order to maintain and even increase organizational effectiveness can be referred to as "organizational change." As organizations internationalize, they tend to reconcile challenges of local relevance, global strategy and organizational learning (Machado-da-Silva et al., 2001), and reconciling these implies organizational change. For change to take place, someone or something within the firm (change agent) must initiate it and steer it through to implementation. Managing the changes needed to accomplish new goals is fundamentally about building and deploying organizational capabilities. It is therefore important to note that internationalization plays an important role in organizational change.

Deductively, internationalization usually means significant changes in the structure of the organization. New organizational levels and units are introduced to handle the new international operations. This is a huge change management process that must be well managed. The challenges concerning the management of this change are resource management, cultural management and environment management. This will require good leadership and management.

Distance, internationalization and organizational change

Four very important factors that could constitute an impediment to successful internationalization are captured by Ghemawat (2001). To drive a concrete understanding of these impediments, the author conceptualizes the CAGE (C = Cultural distance; A = Administrative distance; G = Geographic distance; E = Economic distance) framework: a framework that explains what he called the four dimensions of distance in internationalization (Figure 3.3). For each dimension, the framework identified attributes that could propel internationalization. For culture, it identified language, religion, ethnicity and multiplicity of social norms as possible attributes driving cultural impediment or evolution. For administrative distance, it identified absence of colonial ties, absence of shared monetary and political association, political hostility, government policies and institutional weakness as impediments. For geographic distance, physical remoteness, lack of a common border, lack of sea or river access, size of country, weak transportation or communication links and difference in climate were identified as possible impediments (Ghemawat, 2001). For example, due to the dearth of skilled employees in most developing countries, firms from developed economies have to make plans for training of new entrant, but when a company is internationalizing from a less developed country, the need for such training is minimized. It went further to identify differences in consumer incomes and differences in costs and quality of natural resources, financial resources, human resources, infrastructure, intermediate inputs and knowledge as attributes of economic distance. Furthermore, the framework identified industries or products that could be affected by distance, and situating such industries and products within each distance dimension. For example, for culture it identified products with high linguistic content, such as TV programs; for administrative distance it identified products in which government involvement is high, like the power industry. For geographic distance, it identified products that have a low value to weight or bulk ratio, and for economic distance it identified economies of standardization or scale. Ghemawat (2001) argued that these dimensions cannot be ignored by companies seeking to internationalize because they could serve as hindrances. Organizations that take into account these factors in their internationalization drive could successfully ensure proper management of its internationalization process for change.

Though the essence of culture as it relates to the core functional areas of a firm was initially seen as minimal, academic research and businesses have started paying more attention to cultural differences due to internationalization. This is so as organizations develop business strategies that adapt to different cultural environments (Suarez, 2015). Culture cannot be separated from

<table>
<tr><td rowspan="7">Attributes creating distance</td><td>Cultural Distance</td><td>Administrative Distance</td><td>Geographic Distance</td><td>Economic Distance</td></tr>
<tr><td>Different languages</td><td>Absence of colonial ties</td><td>Physical remoteness</td><td>Differences in consumer incomes</td></tr>
<tr><td rowspan="2">Different ethnicities; lack of connective ethnic or social networks</td><td rowspan="2">Absence of shared monetary or political association</td><td>Lack of a common border</td><td rowspan="5">Differences in costs and quality of:
• Natural resources
• Financial resources
• Human resources
• Infrastructure
• Intermediate inputs
• Information or knowledge</td></tr>
<tr><td>Lack of sea or river access</td></tr>
<tr><td>Different religions</td><td>Political hostility</td><td>Size of country</td></tr>
<tr><td>Different social norms</td><td>Government policies</td><td>Weak transportation or communication links</td></tr>
<tr><td></td><td>Institutional weakness</td><td>Differences in climates</td></tr>
<tr><td rowspan="5">Industries or products affected by distance</td><td>Products have high linguistic content (TV)</td><td rowspan="5">Government involvement is high in industries that are:
• Producers of staple goods (electricity)
• Producers of other entitlements (drugs)
• Large employers (farming)
• Large suppliers to government (mass transportation)
• National champions (aerospace)
• Vital to national security (telecommunications)
• Exploiters of natural resources (oil, mining)
• Subject to high sunk costs (infrastructure)</td><td>Products have a low value-to-weight or bulk ratio (cement)</td><td>Nature of demand varies with income level (cars)</td></tr>
<tr><td>Products affect cultural or national identity of consumers (foods)</td><td>Products are fragile or perishable (glass, fruit)</td><td>Economies of standardization or scale are important (mobile phones)</td></tr>
<tr><td>Product features vary in terms of:
• Size (cars)
• Standards (electrical appliances)
• Packaging</td><td>Communications and connectivity are important (financial services)</td><td>Labour and other factor cost differences are salient (garments)</td></tr>
<tr><td>Products carry country-specific quality associations (wines)</td><td>Local supervision and operational requirements are high (many services)</td><td>Distribution or business systems are different (insurance)</td></tr>
<tr><td></td><td></td><td>Companies need to be responsive and agile (home appliances)</td></tr>
</table>

Figure 3.3 The CAGE Distance Framework

Source: Ghemawat (2001)

business operation, as it lays the ground norm of business philosophy (Suarez, 2015). The importance of culture in an organization was emphasized by Katzenbach, Steffen, and Kronley when they argued that culture supersedes strategy. "A strategy that is at odds with a company's culture is doomed" (Katzenbach et al., 2012. p. 5).

This argument cannot be discountenanced in the internationalization process of an organization. How culture is understood, managed and integrated in the organization, considering the culture of the international market, is important for successful organizational change. To achieve this, organizations must be culture oriented and understand the importance of culture in contemporary business environment (Suarez, 2015). A good example of cultural integration in the internationalization process is the case of UBA. In its internationalization process, new hires in the foreign market were usually brought to Nigeria for training and, in the process, were exposed and integrated to the company's culture.

Africa is often considered to have cultural unity (Wanasika, Howell, Littrel and Dorfman, 2011). As African countries have cultural and historical similarities (Wanasika et al., 2011), it is not surprising that cultural difference (not geographical distance) is ignored by managers and researchers in internationalization discourse within Africa. Ghemawat (2001) argues that it is not enough to consider physical remoteness in making decisions about global expansion. Other dimensions must be considered as well. It has been argued that while African countries are close in many cultural dimensions (that is the norms, values and beliefs of African countries may be similar), they may vary in some dimensions. A lack of sensitivity to this cultural nuance may affect the performance of a foreign subsidiary (Ovadje, 2016). In particular, cultural or psychic distance is assumed to deter investment in remote, culturally distant countries. It is presumed to help shape an ink-stain pattern, with internationalization deeper in culturally similar, neighboring countries, e.g., Southern African countries. Applying the Ghemawat (2001) semi-globalization model to African internationalization, it is apparent that different types of distance matter to different industries' internationalization. Cultural distance affects consumers' product preferences more, which explains why it must be an important consideration for consumer goods or media companies but it is much less important for a cement or steel business. One area where cultural distance is important in internationalization is staffing decisions – whether to use parent country staffs or to develop indigenous ones (Ovadje, 2016). This is because high cultural differences may lead to intra-organizational conflicts and poor implementation of organizational actions, given inconsistencies in values and institutions between home and foreign market operations.

In a bid to avoid some of the cultural conflicts that arise from merging local workers with managers from headquarters who have another cultural perspective, some firms decide to go the route of greenfield entry – using home country nationals as managers. It must be noted, however, that there are cases where the greenfield strategy cannot be applicable because of the stringent regulations around acquiring licenses; in such cases, the firms develop flexible approaches to managing cultural difference. The seeming impossibility of using the same entry strategy in different economies explains why UBA could not adopt the greenfield approach in countries like Burkina Faso and Benin Republic, unlike the other 16 African countries where they operate. Ovadje (2014) argue that such flexibility might lead to changes in leadership style adopted, pace at which things or process get carried out and the means of communication adopted. For instance, UBA had problems operating in countries like DR Congo, Congo-Brazzaville and Chad because the style of leadership adopted was not a fit for the cultural perspective of the citizens. Typical problems include people issues, because the bank had people from Cote d'Ivoire, Burkina Faso, Benin, etc. who were generally considered to have a less aggressive posturing than people from countries like the Central African Republic, Cameroon and Guinea.

Organizational culture vis-à-vis cultural distance

In the course of internationalization, the complexity of cultural distance must be seen as essential to the survival of the firm. Managing the distance between the culture of the organization and the foreign market must be a priority. For Hofstede (1984: 82), culture is the "collective programming of the mind that differentiates the members of a group of people from another." This is very true of organizations, as culture is what differentiates one organization from another. This process requires members of an organization to share norms and values peculiar to that organization. Internationalization enables skills integration in the foreign market. This implies integrating people of diverse cultures different from the organization's culture.

One important factor in internationalization is cultural diversity, as people with distinct cultures are employed into the organization. In a culturally diverse organization, managers would have more options, consider several possibilities and solutions to solving critical business problems and advance a holistic approach to decision making (Reus and Lamont, 2009). In this sense, cultural diversity within the organization can promote a new and innovative way of doing business, and expand the efficient exploration of new resources and capabilities (Reus and Lamont, 2009). This cultural heterogeneity would also encourage employees to be more creative and innovative (Cox, 1991) and would help in strengthening and advancing the organizational culture. Effective communication will help organizations attain this benefit. Through communication, organizations can promote the importance of cultural heterogeneity in the workplace and the benefits of such to the individual employee and to the organization. This is so as communication is an important driver of trust between groups (Reus and Lamont, 2009). To help drive the importance of effective communication at Equity Bank, the Bank's Chief Operating Officer saw himself more as a trainer and coach in order to instill a culture of customer-oriented service, hard work and dedication to local workers in new subsidiaries, thereby institutionalizing organizational culture across the board (Ogbechie and Iheanachor, 2016).

The concept of cultural distance is very important for African firms that are internationalizing. This is because it has a significant role in shaping the culture and norms of the internationalizing firm. National culture almost certainly plays a role, as suggested by the findings that national patterns exist in the propensity of firms to engage in one type of entry mode as opposed to others (Kogut and Singh, 1988). Critically, the African continent is not homogeneous and comprises 55 countries, each with different peoples, tongues, tribes and cultures. For example, Nigeria, the most populous country on the continent with almost 175 million people (July 2013 est.), has over 250 ethnic groups and over 500 indigenous languages. South Africa, the most economically developed country in Sub-Saharan Africa, has a population of almost 49 million (July 2013 est.) who speak 11 official languages. Ghana, described as a beacon of growth in Africa, has a population of over 24 million people (July, 2013 est.) with close to 20 ethnic groups and languages (World Fact Book, 2013).

The fact that Africa is not homogenous and that Chinese firms seem to be doing exceptionally well across the various countries raises questions about the importance and limitations of culture in specific contexts; nonetheless, the same cannot be said of African firms that are internationalizing. Emerging studies on internationalizations from developing countries are of the view that it might be inadequate for firms from the developing world to use the same "Western-oriented" strategies due to differences in institutional environment, socio-economic and cultural structures and types (Hofstede, 2007; Thite, Wilkinson, and Shah, 2012). Using Hofstede's four national culture dimensions as a measure of cultural difference (individualism versus collectivism, power distance, uncertainty avoidance and masculinity versus femininity), Ovadje (2016) compared organizational performance of IT companies between Nigeria, Ghana and Uganda.

She submitted that while the three countries are culturally similar in terms of individualism, power distance and uncertainty avoidance, they differed in masculinity and femininity. This dissimilarity was significant enough to affect the organizational performance of the IT firms in these countries.

Conclusion and implication

There is no doubt that internationalization is a growth strategy that could stimulate change. But how this strategy is driven is important to how successful or how effective it can be in ensuring change. Moving from a local market to a foreign market requires a strategically defined approach. It also requires the knowledge of the market by the company. Organizations should understand that change management is a process that should be properly managed to achieve the desired outcomes. How organizations implement their internationalization strategy is very important within the context of change management. Organizations must be able to define clearly why they are interested in going international. Going international should not be a fad, but a strategic intent that fits into the organization's mission. This is imperative, because the non-alignment of a firm's internationalization strategy with its mission is a recipe for failure. This understanding would help organizations overcome barriers and effectively manage issues around culture, government, society and market that could pop up in the foreign market. Organizations that align and integrate their internationalization strategy with their mission would continuously evolve within the context of the change management process.

The most challenging aspect of managing growth is getting and integrating the right people. Managing cost and cash flow could also ensure success. Therefore, as an organization expands in size due to business expansion, managing growth becomes more and more challenging. How growth is managed in this essence determines the longevity of the organization. Managing growth becomes more and more complex as organizations internationalize and grow. This complexity arises from the expected management of people of diverse cultures, people with different knowledge and skills, and integrating new structures along with changing processes in the organization. In the internationalization process of a firm, these must be aligned to ensure the strategic and responsible management of growth, and how growth is managed is an important determinant to organizational change. An organization must handle success properly to ensure sustainable long-term growth. Business expansion and moving into a new market might advance success, but if the organizational structure and process are not aligned to the business, they might have an adverse effect on change in the organization.

The implication of this study is that African firms should be encouraged to participate in relevant private sector (collaborative and cooperation-based) organizations, and to proactively explore and develop links with strategically relevant actors in local, regional and international markets. Such relationships might provide privileged access to advantage-generating technologies, market intelligence, internationalization support resources, overseas networks and target markets (Asafu-Adjaye, 2004; Moodley, 2003; Roberts and Thoburn, 2003). Challenges and obstacles to their internationalization drive are inevitable but not insurmountable, as new and existing African internationalizing firms will have to build their resilience to be successful in the global market through cost-cutting strategies, long-term investment, managerial quality, mindset technology access, technical learning and access to international business networks. They could also offer an effective platform for lobbying or mobilizing resources for strategically important projects: for example, the provision of support infrastructure for e-internationalization (Moodley, 2002, 2003), which the authors believe will strengthen the organizational performance of many African firms.

We recommend that there should be policy interventions to encourage entrepreneurial thinking and expansive international orientations among the key decision makers of African firms, which will allow them to develop requisite skills and competencies (in product/process technologies, relationship and marketing management, etc.) which might enhance their ability to compete in the domestic and international market. Also, African firms that already internationalize must be encouraged to deepen their level of international investment. Such a level of investment will enhance social and economic development in Africa and encourage FDI within and into Africa.

Finally, emerging African firms should learn from the failure of local and international firms who had attempted internationalization but failed. Some of their failures have been attributed to managerial and strategic factors. African governments should therefore emphasize openness, industry competition, market development and good corporate governance, in addition to the earlier mentioned upgrading of infrastructure and the institutional environment. These may create an enabling environment and encourage better-managed companies to internationalize more quickly and easily.

References

Adeleye, I., White, L., Ibeh, K., and Kinoti, A. (2015) The changing dynamics of international business in Africa: Emerging trends and key issues. In *The Changing Dynamics of International Business in Africa* (pp. 1–12). Palgrave Macmillan, London.

Amal, M., Baffour Awuah, G., Raboch, H., and Andersson, S. (2013) Differences and similarities of the internationalization processes of multinational companies from developed and emerging countries. *European Business Review*, 25(5): 41–428.

Amal, M., and Tomio, B. T. (2015) Institutional determinants of outward foreign direct investment from emerging economies: A home-country perspective. In *Institutional Impacts on Firm Internationalization* (pp. 40–64). London: Palgrave Macmillan.

Asafu-Adjaye, J. (2004) Income inequality and health: A multi-country analysis. *International Journal of Social Economics*, 31(1/2): 195–207.

Bakunda, G. (2003) Explaining firm internationalization in Africa using the competence approach. *Journal of African Business*, 4(1): 57–85.

Beck, T., Fuchs, M., Singer, D., and Witte, M. (2014) *Making Cross-border Banking Work for Africa*. Eschborn, Germany: GIZ.

Blonigen, B. A. (2005) A review of the empirical literature on FDI determinants. *Atlantic Economic Journal*, 33(4): 383–403.

Boojihawon, D. K., and Acholonu, K. K. (2013). Internationalisation process of African banks: an exploratory study. *African Journal of Economic and Management Studies*, 4(2), 244–266.

Burnes, B. (2004) *Managing Change: A Strategic Approach to Organisational Dynamics*. London: Pearson Education.

Calof, J. L., and Beamish, P. W. (1995) Adapting to foreign markets: Explaining internationalization. *International Business Review*, 4(2): 115–131.

Calof, J. L., and Viviers, W. (1995) Internationalization behavior of small-and medium-sized South African enterprises. *Journal of Small Business Management*, 33(4): 71–79.

Cassiman, B., and Golovko, E. (2011) Innovation and internationalization through exports. *Journal of International Business Studies*, 42(1): 56–75.

Cox, T. (1991) The multicultural organization. *The Executive*, 5(2): 34–47.

Czinkota, M., Ronkainen, I. A., and Ortiz-Buonafina, M. (2004) *The Export Marketing Imperative*. Mason, OH: South-Western Educational Publishing.

Demeke, Y., and Chiloane-Tsoka, G. E. (2015) Internationalization drivers of small and medium-sized manufacturing enterprises in Ethiopia. *Problems and Perspectives in Management*, 13(4): 32–42.

Dicken, P. (2015) *Global Shift* (7 Eds) *: Mapping the Changing Contours of the World Economy*. New York, NY: Guilford Publications.

Ekholm, K., and Midelfart, K. H. (2004) Determinants of FDI: The evidence. In G. Barba Navaretti and A. J. Venables (Eds.), *Multinational Firms in the World Economy*. Princeton, NJ and Oxford: Princeton University Press, 127–150.

Ernst and Young. (2013) *Africa 2013: Getting Down to Business.* Ernst and Young's Attractiveness Survey.
Fafchamps, M., El Hamine, S., and Zeufack, A., 2008. Learning to Export: Evidence from Moroccan Manufacturing. *Journal of African Economies*, 17(2): 305–355.
Garri, M., and Konstantopoulos, N. (2013) The management of internationalization: Structural modifications and inter-organizational significance. *Economics and Management: Current Issues and Perspectives Journal*, 29(1): 126–135.
Ghemawat, P. (2001) Distance still matters. *Harvard Business Review*, 79(8): 137–147.
Grenier, L., McKay, A., and Morrissey, O. (1999) Exporting, ownership and confidence in Tanzanian enterprises. *The World Economy*, 22(7): 995–1011.
Henson, S., Masakure, O., and Cranfield, J. (2011) Do fresh produce exporters in sub-Saharan Africa benefit from Global GAP certification? *World Development*, 39(3): 375–386.
Hessels, J., and van Stel, A. (2011) Entrepreneurship, export orientation, and economic growth. *Small Business Economics*, 37(2): 255–268.
Hitt, M. A., Hoskisson, R. E., and Kim, H. (1997) International diversification: Effects on innovation and firm performance in product-diversified firms. *Academy of Management Journal*, 40(4): 767–798.
Hofstede, G. (1984) Cultural dimensions in management and planning. *Asia Pacific Journal of Management*, 1(2): 81–99.
Hofstede, G. (2007) Asian management in the 21st century. *Asia Pacific Journal of Management*, 24(4): 411–420.
House, R. J., Hanges, P. J., Javidan, M., Dorfman, P. W., and Gupta, V. (Eds.). (2004) *Culture, Leadership, and Organizations: The GLOBE Study of 62 Societies.* Thousand Oaks, CA: Sage Publications.
Ibeh, K. I. (2015) Rising Africa and its nascent multinational corporations. In *The Changing Dynamics of International Business in Africa* (pp. 123–147). London: Palgrave Macmillan.
Ibeh, K. I., Ibrahim, E., and Ezepue, P. O. (2007) Factors stimulating initial export activity: Any difference for Nigerian firms? *Journal of African Business*, 8(2): 7–26.
Ibeh, K. I., Wilson, J., and Chizema, A. (2012) The internationalization of African firms 1995–2011: Review and implications. *Thunderbird International Business Review*, 54(4): 411–427.
Ibeh, K. I., and Young, S. (2001) Exporting as an entrepreneurial act-An empirical study of Nigerian firms. *European Journal of Marketing*, 35(5/6): 566–586.
International Monetary Fund, 2015. *Pan-African Banks: Opportunities and Challenges for Cross Border Oversight*, Washington, D.C.: International Monetary Fund.
Jensen, N. M. (2008) *Nation-states and the Multinational Corporation: A Political Economy of Foreign Direct Investment.* Princeton, NJ: Princeton University Press.
Johanson, J., and Vahlne, J. E. (1977) The internationalization process of the firm-a model of knowledge development and increasing foreign market commitments. *Journal of International Business Studies*, 8(1): 23–32.
Johanson, J., and Vahlne, J. E. (1990). The mechanism of internationalisation. *International Marketing Review*, 7(4), 10–24.
Johanson, J., and Wiedersheim-Paul, F. (1975) The internationalization of the firm – Four Swedish cases. *Journal of Management Studies*, 12(3): 305–323.
Katzenbach, J. R., Steffen, I., and Kronley, C. (2012) Cultural change that sticks. *Harvard Business Review*, 90(7): 1–9.
Klein, S., and Wöcke, A. (2007) Emerging global contenders: The South African experience. *Journal of International Management*, 13(3): 319–337.
Kogut, B., and Singh, H. (1988) The effect of national culture on the choice of entry mode. *Journal of International Business Studies*, 19(3): 411–432.
Kuada, J. (2006, August) *Internationalisation of Firms in Developing Countries: Towards an Integrated Conceptual Framework.* International Conference on Globalization, Internationalization of Companies and Cross-cultural Management, Aalborg.
Kuada, J. (2007) Internationalisation, regionalisation and Africa's economic growth strategies. *African Journal of Business and Economic Research*, 2(1): 92–114.
Machado-da-Silva, C. L., Casali, A. M., and Rocha Fernandes, B. H. (2001) Internationalization and organizational change: A multi case study of Brazilian organizations. *Latin American Business Review*, 2(3–4): 61–96.
Marco, F., and Patterson, S. (2010) Africa's outlook. *Organisation for Economic Cooperation and Development. The OECD Observer*, 279: 64–65.
McNamee, T., Pearson, M., and Boer, W. (Eds.). (2015) *Africans Investing in Africa: Understanding Business and Trade, Sector by Sector.* London: Palgrave Macmillan.
Melin, L. (1992) Internationalization as a strategy process. *Strategic Management Journal*, 13(S2): 99–118.

Moodley, S. (2002) Global market access in the Internet era: South Africa's wood furniture industry. *Internet Research*, 12(1): 31–42.
Moodley, S. (2003) The challenge of e-business for the South African apparel sector. *Technovation*, 23(7): 557–570.
Ngwu, F., Adeleye, I., and Ogbechie, C. (2015) Africa-to-Africa internationalization: Rhetoric, reality and risks of intra-African regional expansion. *The Routledge Companion to Business in Africa*, 9–31.
Nwankwo, S. (2012). Renascent Africa: Rescoping the landscape of international business. *Thunderbird International Business Review*, 54(4), 405–409.
Ogbechie, C., and Iheanachor, N. (2016). Equity bank's internationalization: building an African multinational. In *Africa to Africa Internationalization: Key Issues and Outcomes* (pp. 211–268). London: Palgrave Macmillan.
Onkelinx, J., and Sleuwaegen, L. (2008) Internationalization of SMEs. *Flanders DC.*
Ovadje, F. (2014) *Change Leadership in Developing Countries.* New York, NY: Routledge.
Ovadje, F. (2016) The internationalization of African firms: Effects of cultural differences on the management of subsidiaries. *Africa Journal of Management*, 2(2): 117–137.
Pananond, P. (2015) Motives for foreign direct investment: A view from emerging market multinationals. *The Multinational Business Review*, 23(1): 77–86.
Ramaseshan, B., and Soutar, G. N. (1996) Combined effects of incentives and barriers on firms' export decisions. *International Business Review*, 5(1): 53–65.
Reus, T. H., and Lamont, B. T. (2009) The double-edged sword of cultural distance in international acquisitions. *Journal of International Business Studies*, 40(8): 1298–1316.
Roberts, S., and Thoburn, J. (2003) Adjusting to trade liberalisation: The case of firms in the South African textile sector. *Journal of African Economies*, 12(1): 74–103.
Rolfe, R., Perri, A., and Woodward, D. (2015) Patterns and determinants of intra-African foreign direct investment. In *The Changing Dynamics of International Business in Africa* (pp. 101–122). London: Palgrave Macmillan.
Rutashobya, L., and Jaensson, J. E. (2004) Small firms' internationalization for development in Tanzania: Exploring the network phenomenon. *International Journal of Social Economics*, 31(1/2): 159–172.
Schwarz, G., and Yellin, J. (2013) *Obama in Tanzania, Sees Africa as Next Global Economic Success.* Retrieved from http://edition.cnn.com/2013/07/01/world/africa/tanzania-obama/index.html.
Seyoum, B. (2007) Revealed comparative advantage and competitiveness in services: A study with special emphasis on developing countries. *Journal of Economic Studies*, 34(5): 376–388.
Söderbom, M., and Teal, F. (2003) Are manufacturing exports the key to economic success in Africa? *Journal of African Economies*, 12(1): 1–29.
Soontiens, W. (2003) The relevance of non-tariff barriers to regional trade: Experiences of South African exporters. *Global Business Review*, 4(1): 1–13.
Suarez, J. L. (2015) The business of culture. *Ivey Business Journal*, 1–5.
Thite, M., Wilkinson, A., and Shah, D. (2012) Internationalization and HRM strategies across subsidiaries in multinational corporations from emerging economies – A conceptual framework. *Journal of World Business*, 47(2): 251–258.
Todnem By, R. (2005) Organisational change management: A critical review. *Journal of Change Management*, 5(4): 369–380.
Wanasika, I., Howell, J. P., Littrell, R., and Dorfman, P. (2011) Managerial leadership and culture in Sub-Saharan Africa. *Journal of World Business*, 46(2): 234–241.

4

Responsible management education as a catalyst for change

Ijeoma Nwagwu

This chapter makes the case for responsible management education (RME), especially in Africa. The RME narrative will be explored from various perspectives: 1) RME as an imperative to restore the legitimacy of business schools and ensure they play a vital role as key change agents in the advancement of an inclusive and sustainable global economy; 2) The role of the UN Principles for Responsible Management Education; and 3) RME as an organizational change catalyst, equipping managers serving in any type of organization with the skills, competencies, and general knowledge to successfully manage their organizations. The chapter tackles these issues systematically, and provides practical examples.

A note on language: In the following chapter the terms 'business school' and 'management education' will refer to all undergraduate, graduate, and executive business and management education providing institutions.

The global context

The world is ever changing. A decade into the 21st century, the most urgent global challenge was how to navigate the architecture of the international economic crises. However, immediately beyond lay wider and connected developments: increasing shortage of natural resources; the degradation of forests, climate, and water systems; growing inequality; and systemic abuse of human rights (ABIS, 2010). Not only is our world rapidly changing, but how we understand our world is also changing. To a great extent, many economies around the world still function on suppositions from the Industrial Revolution era – an era when there was an abundance of natural resources. The present reality is one in which natural resources are in short supply, bionetworks are more delicate, and not only are humans an integral part of the ecosystems, we are realizing we depend on them far more than we considered (ABIS, 2010).

The World Business Council for Sustainable Development (WBCSD) identifies within its Vision 2050 the desire that some 9 billion people will be able to live well and 'within the limits of the planet' (Muff, 2013: 488). To achieve this, there is the need to rebuild the global economy with new rules such as moving from economic growth that rests on resource consumption and biodiversity degradation, to markets based on long-term value creation and the ability of business to make sustainability an easier choice for consumers and partner companies (Muff, 2013: 488).

The African context

An ongoing debate exists with regard to the development of Africa. Africa is no longer regarded as a hopeless continent beset by wars and famine (Abdulai, 2016; AMI, 2016), but scholars are still divided with regards the level of progress Africa has achieved. Some scholars argue that Africa has reached a turning point, outpacing many other regions in terms of economic development over the last decade, and a new narrative has emerged of the continent as the next frontier of opportunity and investment. However, some other scholars (e.g., Gyimah-Brempong, 2002) believe that Africa has made the least progress in terms of human development among the developing regions of the world.

A recurring theme in the literature is that the development of African nations has generally been stunted by corruption and poor leadership (Gichure, 2006; Gyimah-Brempong, 2002; Harsch, 1993; Houngnikpo, 2006; Hope Sr and Chikulo, 2000; Lawal, 2007; Olivier de Sardan, 1999; Pillay, 2004). Corruption, as seen by these scholars, has reached cancerous proportions within the public and private spheres and is costing most countries on the continent growth and stability of trade and financial systems holding their populations in grinding poverty. Not only is Africa suffering from endemic corruption, the continent seems to be plagued with poor leaders (Goldsmith, 2001; Hope Sr and Chikulo, 2000; Rotberg, 2004). These leaders, described as malevolent, lacking accountability or responsibility, and corrupt and unethical in their behaviours, have too often been known to reject sound policy advice and refuse to take a long and broad view of their jobs. Hence Africa has become a necropolis of many failed reforms (Goldsmith, 2001; Hope Sr and Chikulo, 2000; Rotberg, 2004). While scholars (e.g., Goldsmith, 2001) do not believe that better leadership is the panacea for Africa's stagnated development, they believe it is an important step in the right direction.

Sustainable development and management education

Business schools are increasingly charged with responsibility for creating a more sustainable world by preparing leaders and managers to develop and drive a restructured economy (ABIS, 2010; Dyllick, 2015; Haski-Leventhal, 2014, Muff, 2013; Rasche and Escudero, 2009). There is growing recognition of the vital role that businesses can and should play in cultivating not just economic value, but also environmental sustainability, social justice, and peace in a troubled world. However, questions abound on whether current approaches to management education can fully prepare leaders and managers to meet the emerging needs of businesses and the world (Hockerts, Borgbo, Srkoc, Goldberg, and Chaudry, 2015; Waddock, Rasche, Werhane, and Unruh, 2011). A huge share of blame for the last economic crisis, and unsustainable capitalism in general, is placed squarely upon the shoulders of management education, and to certain scholars (e.g., Visser, 2016), this blame is highly justified. Among many reasons, Visser (2016) believes that management education is to blame because MBA programmes churn out tens of thousands of graduates every year who are trained in a climate reinforcing traditional understandings of business as existing to only make profits.

Traditional business school education (Rasche and Escudero, 2009) has been partly blamed for the economic crisis that began in 2007 (because many of the people who contributed to the crisis had been educated in one way or the other by business schools). It is argued that business school education does not adequately prepare students for the ethical challenges they face in their later careers. Furthermore, there is a general suspicion that business schools cannot deliver what they promise (Rasche and Escudero, 2009). In Africa, management education is believed to have failed to contribute to the continent's growth and development as it has failed to create context-specific solutions to Africa's developmental challenges (Abdulai, 2016).

This has led scholars to pay increasing attention to the role management education has to play in fostering responsible business. According to this understanding, business has a social responsibility to behave in an ethical manner. It is based on the philosophy that business ought to impact society in ways that transcend the objective of profit maximization (Erondu, Sharland, and Okpara, 2004). Some scholars (e.g., Erondu et al., 2004) argue that when business organizations behave ethically, they are helping to create a society that is imbued with such virtues as honesty, integrity, and fairness, which will ultimately benefit them in many important ways. Attention to developing human capital in this direction is essential to eradicating corruption, poverty, and tackling poor leadership in Africa. (Abdulai, 2016; AMI, 2016). In other words, there is a belief that business organizations have a moral obligation to establish an ethical culture which strengthens the social fabric. African scholars (e.g. Erero and Oladoyin, 2000; Hope Sr and Chikulo, 2000) posit that only by creating a moral and ethical culture based on integrity and loyalty, can the foundations for good governance and a corruption-free society be laid.

According to Abdulai (2016), "Management education can contribute to the prosperity of African countries. It will produce the requisite management teams to contribute to the development of innovative products and processes that will enable African countries to be competitive. It will also produce entrepreneurs who will be equipped to run businesses that will provide much-needed employment to Africa's populace." The rapid economic growth of Africa requires well-trained managers in both private and public sphere institutions (Abdulai, 2016; AMI, 2016; Gyimah-Brempong, 2002). These managers are the very people who are vital for translating opportunities into tangible results and generating increased competitiveness towards a better life for all.

To facilitate this change, business schools and management institutions need to embrace an all-encompassing and radical change themselves (Dyllick, 2015; Muff, 2013; Rasche and Escudero, 2009; Shetty, 2017). Change in management education institutions can be understood as spanning actions and decisions in the areas of curriculum development, teaching, research, and public engagement (Dyllick, 2015; Haski-Leventhal, 2014). This new brand of management education would involve grounding "traditional business functions in ethics and accountability" (Haski-Leventhal, 2014: 29). Further, this understanding of management education suggests an understanding of management education saddled with the responsibility of "finding credible ways to question, re-assess, re-imagine, and redirect the purpose of business" (Visser, 2016: ix). This new brand of management education is popularly branded (e.g., Haski-Leventhal, 2014; Rasche and Escudero, 2009) as responsible management education. The tenets of responsible management education seem to be the components missing and much needed in Africa to ensure sustainable development on the continent.

Evolution of management education

In theory, management education passes through several stages in the journey to the responsible management education phase (Visser, 2016), the stage at which it serves as a most effective foundation for transforming broader institutional and societal cultures. Table 4.1 is a visualization of the evolution of business schools in Africa in terms of adopting responsible management education.

Responsible management education

As stated earlier, motivated by debates about whether business schools contributed to (and to what extent) the 2007–2009 financial crises, and whether management education is capable of making positive contributions to economic growth, sustainable development, responsible leadership, and ethical awareness, the calls for more responsible management education have

Table 4.1 Stages of evolution in management education

S/No	*Stage of maturity*	*Keywords*	*Typical practices*
1	Defensive	Compliance, risk	Links ethics to corporate governance or legal context
2	Charitable	Voluntary, philanthropic	Offers optional business ethics module
3	Promotional	Marketing, branding	Offers optional CSR or sustainability module
4	Strategic	Management, codes	Has CSR or sustainability as a core, compulsory module
5	Transformative	Integration, innovation	Has integrated social, ethical, and environmental considerations into all management subjects; emphasizes systemic leadership, futurethinking, eco-innovation, social entrepreneurship, inclusive business and circular economy

Source: Visser (2016: vii)

increased and continue to gain traction (Rasche and Gilbert, 2015; Shetty, 2017). Certain scholars (e.g., ABIS, 2010; Weybrecht, 2013) claim that management institutions as well as their students had taken some initiative in the quest to be more responsible and do social good while making money (e.g., Net Impact, Beyond Grey Pinstripes, The Academy of Business in Society, Globally Responsible Leadership Initiative, European Foundation for Management Development, and UN Principles for Responsible Management Education). These organizations argue against traditional management education and call on business schools to adapt to new realities which can translate to ethically renewed boardrooms and management floors (ABIS, 2010; Rasche and Gilbert, 2015).

Hayes et al. (2016) provide a distinction between the traditional management education and responsible management education, as seen in Table 4.2. Table 4.2 suggests that there is need for a guiding philosophical standpoint that recognizes that business and management are not separate from the global challenges confronting humanity today, the intricacy of global issues, and the opportunity for business to help with many social issues. Indeed, initial adopters of PRME and the RME schema have acknowledged the flaw with the traditional management education by proposing responsible forms of management education.

Burchell, Kennedy, and Murray (2015) describe this shift as the re-evaluation of management education to infuse into management education notions of morality, social responsibility, business ethics, sustainability, and the role of business in environmental deterioration and human rights abuses. With relation to the African context, Abdulai (2016) not only proposes responsible management education, but an African-centred management education. This African-centred management education will be one where programmes and pedagogy design and delivery will take into consideration the African environment, African context, African challenges, and African culture.

Table 4.2 Difference between traditional and responsible forms of management pedagogy

Area of Pedagogy	*Traditional management pedagogy*	*Responsible management pedagogy*
Course content	Textbook learning Key values: profit maximization, individualism, greed is acceptable, competition	Experiential learning Key values: stakeholder view of business, ethical compass, collaboration
Curriculum	Hard skills Teacher-centred Disciplinary Descriptive and prescriptive	Hard and soft skills Student-centred Inter-/intra- and multi-disciplinary Reflective and reflexive
Teaching methods	Passive	Active
Underlying philosophy	Positivist view of management	Emancipatory/critical view of management
Intended outcome	Focused on improving position of a small number of elites Orthodox	Outcome of education is focused on improving society for all Transformational

Source: Hayes, Parkes, and Murray (2016: 23)

RME as a catalyst for organizational change: PRME and the Pradini, Vervoort, and Berthelmess five-element model

As highlighted earlier, business schools need to reconsider their role in society. Aside from being institutions where competencies and skills needed for effective management are delivered, they could also be hubs for aligning business with societal interests. Business schools have an extensive reach and profound impact on the financial and commercial domains (Weybrecht, 2013). In addition, business school students are seen as future initiators of sustainable value for business and society, influencing the organizations and teams they work with (Prandini, Vervoort, and Barthelmess, 2012). Therefore, business schools need to create learning environments to foster responsible management knowledge, skills, and attitudes. Furthermore, beyond training business students, management education institutions afford, through their faculty and diverse student groups, an environment to create much-needed knowledge, craft and test inventive ideas and solutions, and present a space to have conversations about company-tailored and global challenges (Weybrecht, 2013). These can be priceless resources for organizations of all sizes in their change journeys.

In July of 2007, a new framework for responsible management education was established. This spelt the first organized relationship between the United Nations and management education institutions (Kell and Haertle, 2011; Perry and Win, 2013; Waddock et al., 2011). These beliefs are collectively known as Principles for Management Education (PRME, pronounced "prime") (Kell and Haertle, 2011; Perry and Win, 2013; Waddock et al., 2011). As of January 2017, the initiative had grown to more than 650 leading academic institutions from over 85 countries across the globe. "The level of support obtained has been judged a remarkable achievement given the speed with which institutions have been recruited and the worldwide interest in the initiative" (Perry and Win, 2013: 51).

The PRME embodies a set of voluntary ideals which management institutions and programs agree to abide by in the interest of nurturing future leaders with the needed awareness, skills, and proficiencies to deal with matters that business and other organizations are facing (Rasche and Escudero, 2009; Waddock et al., 2011). The PRME is an initiative that intends to motivate and support responsible management education through "research, engagement, and thought leadership" (Haski-Leventhal, 2014: 29). The PRME were set up to amass the backing of business schools and their programs for the advancement of corporate citizenship through infusing their activities with values of global social responsibility, ethics, and sustainability. Furthermore, the PRME are intended to help instruct future managers and leaders, who can quite clearly link social and environmental concerns directly to business issues, to nurture a more cohesive and inclusive global economy (Waddock et al., 2011). That is, it aims to develop future managers and leaders who can combine profitability with sustainability, ethics, and social responsibility (Alcaraz and Thiruvattal, 2010; Kell and Haertle, 2011; Perry and Win, 2013).

The UN PRME comprises of a "six-point value based agenda" (Perry and Win, 2013: 51) known as the six principles of PRME. They are:

Principle 1: Purpose: Signatory business schools ensure that their purpose aligns with the development of students' capabilities to be future generators of sustainable value for business and society at large and to work for an inclusive and sustainable global economy.

Principle 2: Values: Signatory business schools should be able to incorporate the values of global social responsibilities as portrayed in international initiatives such as the United Global Compact in their activities and curricula.

Principle 3: Method: Management institution pedagogical frameworks, materials, processes, and environments should be such that facilitate the creation of responsible global leaders through effective learning experiences.

Principle 4: Research: Management education institutions who are signatories to the PRME should engage in theoretical and conceptual research that propagates understanding about the role, dynamics, and impacts of corporations in the creation of sustainable social, environmental, and economic value.

Principle 5: Partnership: Management education institutions who are signatories to PRME should interact with managers of business corporations to broaden knowledge of their challenges in meeting social and environmental responsibilities and to jointly discover effective approaches to meeting these challenges.

Principle 6: Dialogue: Management education institutions signed to PRME should serve as hubs where dialogue and debate among educators, students, business, government, consumers, media, civil society organizations, and other interested groups and stakeholders are facilitated and supported on critical issues related to global social responsibility and sustainability.

Prandini et al. (2012) suggest a five-element model to realize responsible management education at business schools, as shown in Figure 4.1. This five-element model shares similarities with the Principles of Responsible Management Education.

This model includes, as seen in Figure 4.1:

Goal: the goal of RME as supporting and facilitating the propagation of sustainability, ethics, and responsibility in business and society.

Content: RME consists of an understanding of the role, dynamics, and impacts of corporations in sustainability, ethics, and responsibility.

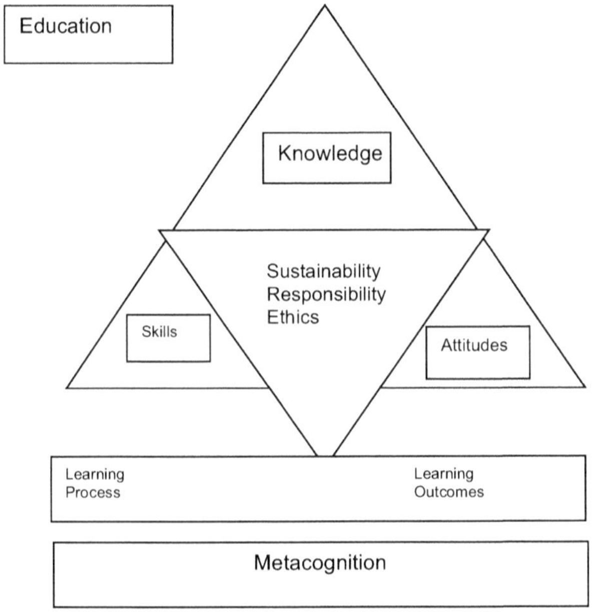

Figure 4.1 Didactic model for responsible management education

Source: Prandini et al. (2012: 18) with adjustments by author

Outcome: it is expected that the understanding and implementation of RME should result in business leaders and businesses who live and practice sustainability, ethics, and responsibility.

Process: the learning process of RME should take place within environments and learning scenarios that allow students construct the relevant knowledge, competencies, and attitudes they need to realize sustainability, ethics, and responsibility as future business leaders.

Normative basis: the standard for evaluating RME is responsibility, sustainability and ethics.

Even as academic institutions differ to a large extent among themselves, the extent to which they incorporate responsible management education into their activities also varies greatly. According to Weybrecht (2013), some institutions have put in place new courses and electives, established student clubs, and organized a series of events and conferences around RME. Others are establishing research centres that focus on ethics, responsible leadership, and sustainability, and their individual faculties publish papers with some reference to RME. 'More engaged' schools are developing a growing elective and core course collection on RME in their curricula. Audits and surveys are conducted to determine where their institutions stand. A number of business schools are making changes to their mission statements and core values to reflect the importance of training students in the area of RME. Sustainability-focused degrees, certificate and specialization programmes, and a rebranding of business degrees to be 'sustainable' are ways other business schools are engaging in RME (Weybrecht, 2013). Table 4.3 highlights a range of ways business schools are engaging in RME and provides a guide to evaluate the engagement of African business schools/management education.

Table 4.3 Spectrum of business school engagement

Basic	*Engaged*	*Advanced*
• Core or elective course on ethics or CSR • At least one student club focused on sustainability-related topics in most cases associated with Net Impact or SIFE • Sustainability conferences and events that bring together students and the academic and business communities • Relevant research centres • Individual faculty research • Campus greening initiatives • Individual staff responsible for sustainability related topics	• Rewrite values/mission statement to include developing responsible leaders • Core courses on ethics/CSR and sustainability topics • Range of electives exploring different sustainability-related topics • Develop new modules and programmes specifically focused on sustainability, including minors, majors, and certificates • Put in place audits and surveys to identify and better understand where the school currently stands • More comprehensive campus sustainability strategy that explores environmental and social issues • Develop an integrative strategy around sustainability with high level support • Working groups, task forces, and committees responsible for implementing sustainability or responsible management education • Stakeholder engagement • Engaging with other schools around this topic	• Put in place, measure, and report on goals and targets • Integrate sustainability across the curriculum and within a dedicated course • Facilitate and develop opportunities for inter- and multidisciplinary teaching and research • Put in place structural changes to enable sustainability integration • Continuous engagement • Transform campus into a living laboratory • Identify sustainability as a focus for research activities and partnerships • Show leadership in this field and share knowledge/lessons with others • Measure the impact of the school's activities on society and business • Collaborate with range of stakeholders, including business
These schools often take a very bottom-up approach: initiatives started and led by individual faculty, staff, and/or students and alumni	These schools take a top-down/bottom-up approach: initiatives are coming from and supported by leadership as well as the faculty, staff, and/or students and alumni	Initiatives are both top-down and bottom-up, and connected by an on-going strategy as well as resources to support them
The terms ethics and CSR are often used	The term ethics, sustainability, responsible management, and responsible business are often used	Schools begin breaking sustainability into its individual parts for targeted response

Source: (Weybrecht, 2013)

Issues in RME implementation within business schools

There is a growing strain between business schools' open pledge to responsible management education and the complexities around its implementation (Rasche and Gilbert, 2015). That is, it is easy to define the principles of responsible management education on an abstract level; however, there is the need for these principles to be broken down into concrete instruction and learning scenarios (Prandini et al., 2012; Weybrecht, 2013). Studies (e.g., Rasche and Gilbert, 2015) reveal that while several deans and faculty of business schools believe that relevant discussions on RME have been fully integrated into their organizations (e.g., through RME courses in their curriculum), about 75 percent of these courses remain electives detached from business school courses. Further, while existing research has boosted knowledge about changes in educational methods, course content, and curriculum design to reflect RME, little is known about whether management schools' commitment to responsible management education affects business schools core organizational practices (Rasche and Gilbert, 2015). The authors believe an understanding of this is important to understand the implementation of RME at institutional levels. Their study postulates that responsible management education continues to expose business schools to institutional pressures that cannot be overlooked. These pressures may come through coercion, need to mimic practices in other institutions, and normative basis.

According to Rasche and Gilbert (2015), coercive pressures are placed on business schools to embed RME into their formal structures by placing sanctions against non-compliance (e.g., The European Quality Improvement System (EQUIS) accreditation guidelines devoting an entire chapter to RME, and the PRME delisting 43 schools in 2014 that failed to comply with the mandatory reporting requirements and nine that had to withdraw from the initiative in 2014). Pressures in mimetic forms can occur when business schools are forced to model their commitment to RME on what changes other well-recognized 'advanced' PRME signatories have implemented. Normative pressures can occur when RME is seen to mirror a suitable line of action and student organizations as Net Impact, publications in trusted media, and professional networks such as GRLI (Global Responsible Leadership Initiative) back such notions (Rasche and Gilbert, 2015).

These pressures have led to certain management institutions resorting to deceptive acts such as not redesigning their curriculum substantially, or ensuring that modifications to curriculum are not embedded in classroom practice, and sometimes preventing the integration of RME into their organizational culture (Rasche and Gilbert, 2015). While this decoupling in the implementation of RME can be problematic by causing a dissonance of legitimacy among external and internal stakeholders of the business schools, it may lead to positive organizational change in some business schools. That is, while external audiences may grant legitimacy based on decoupled formal structures, internal audiences are more likely to respond disdainfully if there is an inconsistency between talk and action that is sustained over a long period of time. On the other hand, the public communication of ambitions (aspirational talk) can help actors rethink and redefine selected practices, "particularly if the communicated aspirations create expectations among students or faculty that cannot be ignored in the long run" (Rasche and Gilbert, 2015: 240).

To counter these RME implementation pressures that may lead to negative outcomes, Sobczak and Mukhi (2016) propose six stages that the integration and implementation of RME in management education institutions should go through. First, there must be recognition of the need and willingness to integrate RME into their organizational structure by business schools and their leaders. Second, relevant knowledge must be acquired in the field of RME. Third, the knowledge acquired must be distributed throughout the management education institution. Fourth, there must be a shared interpretation of the RME implementation policy of a specific business school among its internal and external stakeholders. Fifth, the business school and its stakeholders must be willing to act on the principles of RME. Sixth, there should be storage of RME memory through consistent implementation via reports and events. These stages do not have to occur in a linear sequence. Former stages may need to be revisited in order to deepen or revise certain aspects (Sobczak and Mukhi, 2016).

Shetty (2017) provides certain practical manners in which RME may be integrated into the curriculum, teaching practice and organizational culture of business schools. Examples include: (a) classroom discussions on leadership problems and case studies on ethical conflicts in corporations in different sectors of the economy (e.g., discussions of corporate scandals and scams); (b) industry-academia association and training at the scene of action to bring awareness on practical business conflicts; and (c) periodical ethical surveys, audits.

In 2008, Ashridge, EABIS and their other partners examined global CEOs' perspectives on the most effective learning approaches of senior managers in their companies. Findings revealed that senior executives believe the most effective learning and competence development stems from practical experience. Therefore, they recommended on-the-job learning, project-based learning, and experiential learning. Further, they proposed the enhancement of these learning situations through action learning, appreciative inquiry, and coaching (ABIS, 2010). Mason (2016) provides a practical scenario of responsible management education learning approaches. Using poverty as an object lesson, Mason (2016) posits that to promote the understanding and theorizing of poverty by business students, a good way is for them to experience poverty first-hand – that is, through a study abroad, internship, or service trip that is structured to enable students encounter and engage with poor populations. The author also recommends the use of business cases that deal with poverty alleviation (Mason, 2016).

RME as a catalyst for organizational change: faculty perspective

Even as the calls for RME compliant business schools gain traction, there is a call for RME-competent faculty (e.g., Hockerts et al., 2015; Shetty, 2017). In a 2015 study by Hockerts et al., respondents stressed the vital role RME-competent faculty play in the integration of RME within business schools because of their continued contact with students. Shetty (2017) believe that faculty should act as mentors and role models to business school students since their compliance with the principles of RME can have influence on the students.

Top faculty in business schools all over the world are discovering an extensive collection of ingenious methods, within and outside the classroom, to enable the development of RME-competent students. Not only are they using case studies, guest speakers, and lectures to instruct management students, they are continually engaging along with their students in reflection papers, blogs, simulations, site visits, case competitions, and consulting (Weybrecht, 2013). These top-notch faculty are also developing new courses that 'explore problem solving, systems thinking, and design thinking' (Weybrecht, 2013).

In implementing and integrating RME in management education institutions and ensuring RME-competent faculty that will be able to guide and mentor management students, 'formal faculty development activities are necessary' (Hockerts et al., 2015). These activities will ensure that there is an increased awareness amongst faculty about the new dimensions of teaching management and business. The capacity of faculty to integrate responsible management principles in their students will also be built through these faculty development activities.

Table 4.4 Generic Competency Framework for a responsible manager

Knowledge
- Understanding the competing demands of different stakeholder groups
- Understanding how the core business activities create opportunities for other actors in society and how the company can make a contribution to society
- Understanding the social and environmental risks and opportunities of the company and its industry sector
- Understanding the institutional debate on the role and legitimacy of the firm

Skills
- Well-founded and balanced judgment
- Critical thinking
- Team player
- Creativity, innovation, and original thinking
- Communicating with credibility
- Business acumen
- Listening skills
- Managing stakeholder network relationships
- Emotional intelligence

Attitudes
- Honesty and integrity
- Long-term perspective
- Open-mindedness
- Appreciating and embracing diversity
- Conviction and courage
- The drive to contest resistance
- The capacity to think outside the box

Source: (Prandini et al., 2012: 19)

RME as a catalyst for organizational change: a competence perspective

As earlier stated, for a while, it was widely believed that management education institutions did more harm than good. The global financial crisis that rocked the world was said to have been caused by insatiable bankers, many of whom were trained at prominent management education institutions. Further, these management education program graduates have been regularly described as 'cold-blooded technocrats lacking interpersonal skills, intercultural abilities, emotional and ecological intelligence, trustworthiness or social responsibility' (Prandini et al., 2012: 16).

What, then, differentiates a responsible manager from a traditional business manager? Which competencies does such a manager need to acquire from an education at a business school? How does a responsible manager influence the organization and teams he or she will work with in the course of his or her career? 'How does the responsible manager plan, organize, lead, and control responsible business performance?' (Laasch and Conaway, 2015: 24). According to Prandini et al. (2012), the competency base of a business manager is divided into knowledge, skills, and attitudes, as shown in Table 4.4.

Conceptualizing competencies for RME managers, Laasch and Conaway (2015) proffer four competence pillars. These pillars are: domain competencies (to know), methodological competencies (to do), social competencies (to live together or interact), and self-competencies (to be). Table 4.5 explains in detail these four competence pillars. Expanding on the self-competencies,

Table 4.5 Competencies for RME managers

Competence group	*Mainstream management competences*	*Prime management competencies*
Domain (to know)	Technical (knowledge of and proficiency in a certain specialized field)	Responsible management background domains: sustainability (triple bottom line), responsibility (stakeholders), ethics (morally right decisions) Responsible management tools (for manager's sphere of influence)
Procedural (to do)	Conceptual and diagnostic (analyzing complex situations and providing an adequate response)	System thinking Interdisciplinary work Ethical, sustainable, and responsible decision making
Social (to interact)	Political (exerting influence) Communication Leadership Delegation	Stakeholder networking and communication Change agency skills (leadership) Critical skills
Self (to be)	Toughness (endurance of high workload and high-stress situations) Efficiency Effectiveness Loyalty (to the company)	Meta-perspective Empathy (for responsibility issues and stakeholders) Embracing attitude (toward responsible management practices) Problem awareness Sense of urgency Self-perception (especially about power)

Brewis (1996) calls them personal effectiveness and involves competencies such as communication and presentation skills, conflict handling, creativity, objective setting, decision making, action planning, and creativity.

Another outcome of the study by Ashbridge, EABIS in 2008 of CEOs on the learning needs of their senior managers was that these CEOs believe that senior managers must be equipped with an understanding of their external environments and be able to appropriately respond to changes that occur in such environments. They also put forward the capacity to understand players in the wider political setting, so they are able to engage and build successful connections with new external stakeholders, and connect with a variety of social groups and communities. The ability to survive and flourish in low-certainty and low-agreement situations was highly recommended by the CEOs that were polled in this study (ABIS, 2010).

Mason (2016) provides a practical object lesson on the issue of poverty. The author highlights that certain skills will be necessary for business managers to be equipped with to deal with poor or low income populations. These skills include 'critical thinking and the ability to recognize assumptions and generalizations, an understanding of statistical methods, detailed knowledge of the context into which the enterprise wishes to apply the results, familiarity with current research on poverty alleviation, and a sensitivity to the context' (Mason, 2016: 81, 87, 88). Ways to achieve this understanding are through action learning, experiential learning, coaching/mentoring case studies, and service learning through community service/volunteering secondments to external organizations.

Responsible management as a catalyst for organizational change in Africa

The above narratives on responsible management education are exemplified in lessons drawn from six African management education institutions. As of January 2017, there were more than 27 PRME signatories from Africa. However, only 27 observed the mandatory reporting established by the UN PRME body. These 27 business schools fall into three categories: Basic PRME signatories, advanced PRME signatories, and PRME Champions.

'Basic signatories comply with the SIP (Sharing Information on Progress) policy. Advanced signatories comply with the SIP policy and contribute to the annual service fee. PRME champions are invited group of signatories that contribute to thought and action leadership on responsible management education in the context of the UN Sustainable Development Goals'. Using two advanced signatory institutions in Africa and one PRME champion institution in Africa highlighted in Table 4.6 as object lessons, this section will explore the following questions:

Table 4.6 Communicating PRME signatories in Africa

S/No	*Name*	*Type of signatory*	*Parent organization*	*Type*	*Country*
1	AAA School of Advertising	Basic Signatory		Higher Education Institute offering undergraduate.	South Africa
2	ADALIA School of Business	Basic Signatory		Business School	Morocco
3	Ain Shams University Faculty of Commerce	Basic Signatory	Ain Shams University	Business School	Egypt
4	Al Akhawayn University School of Business Administration	Basic Signatory	Al Akjawayn University in Ifrane	Business School	Morocco
5	American University of Nigeria	Basic Signatory		University	Nigeria
6	Deraya University	Basic Signatory		University	Egypt
7	EUCLID (Euclid University)	Basic Signatory	Treaty-based organization UNTS	University	Gambia
8	Faculty of Business Administration, Economics & Political Science	Basic Signatory	The British University in Egypt (BUE)	Business School	Egypt
9	Faculty of Management Technology/ German University in Cairo	Basic Signatory	German University in Cairo	University	Egypt
10	Gordon Institute of Business Science (GIBS)	Advanced Signatory	University of Pretoria	Business School	South Africa

(Continued)

Table 4.6 (Continued)

S/No	*Name*	*Type of signatory*	*Parent organization*	*Type*	*Country*
11	Graduate School of Business	PRME Champion	University of Cape Town	Business School	South Africa
12	HEM (Institute of Higher Education of Management)	Basic Signatory		Business School	Morocco
13	KCA University	Basic Signatory		University	Kenya
14	Lagos Business School	Advanced Signatory	Pan-Atlantic University	Business School	Nigeria
15	MANCOSA	Basic Signatory	Management College of Southern Africa	Business school	South Africa
16	Milpark Education (Pty.) Ltd.	Advanced Signatory		Business school	South Africa
17	Multitech Business School	Basic Signatory	Makerere Business School	Business School	Uganda
18	Mzumbe University	Basic Signatory		Business School	Tanzania (United Republic of)
19	Nelson Mandela Metropolitan Business School	Advanced Signatory	Nelson Mandela Metropolitan University	Business School	South Africa
20	October 6 University	Basic Signatory		University	Egypt
21	Onitsha Business School	Basic Signatory		Business School	Nigeria
22	Regenesys Business School	Basic Signatory	Stand-alone private Business School	Business School	South Africa
23	Rhodes Business School	Basic Signatory	Rhodes University	Business School	South Africa
24	School of Business, the American University in Cairo	Basic Signatory	The American University in Cairo	Business School	Egypt
25	School of Management, IT and Governance, University of KwaZulu-Natal	Basic Signatory	University of KwaZulu-Natal	Business School	South Africa
26	University of Stellenbosch Business School	Advanced Signatory	University of Stellenbosch	Business School	South Africa
27	Zimbabwe Ezekiel Guti University	Basic Signatory		University	Zimbabwe

How are business schools in Africa changing because of responsible management education? What is the stage of evolution of these management education institutions? How are business schools in Africa integrating ethics and responsibility into their purpose, values, methods, research, partnerships, and dialogue? What spectrum of RME engagement can be found in these institutions, and what prospects does this phenomenon present for contexts of organizational change?

Lagos Business School, Nigeria

The six principles for responsible management education are aligned to the institution's mission and strategy. It is evident in its research objective for 2017 to 2020 to pursue 'practitioner and applied research that addresses and solves social and institutional business problems in Africa'. Lagos Business School's students engage in Personal Social Responsibility projects, which are collaborative student-led community service projects designed and implemented in partnership with corporate organizations and civil society bodies. LBS is home to the Centre for Sustainability as well as the Centre for Research in Leadership and Ethics. Its in-class and online courses contain a large amount of responsibility, ethics, and sustainability components. It is also home to the Sustainability Centre which encourages strategic corporate engagement in sustainable development through innovative research and capacity-building. LBS provides a platform on which its alumni, through their class groups or corporate organizations, can participate in collaborative community service projects informed by knowledge of corporate citizenship and sustainable development issues emanating from the Sustainability Centre.

School of Business, the American University in Cairo

The School of Business, the American University in Cairo (AUC) has integrated responsible business into the School's new 2030 Vision, which includes the creation 'of focus areas relevant to Arab and African regions: entrepreneurship, family business, economic development, and responsible business'. As one of the three themes for the school in its 2015–2019 Strategic Plan, the school incorporated responsible business, ethics, and responsible business practices across all the courses offered by the school. Through its John D. Gerhardt Center for Philanthropy and Civic Engagement and Responsible Business in AUC School of Business, the academic community conducts research and stakeholder consultations around effective giving and civic responsibility to promote social change in the Arab region. This exposure to multisectoral interactions and social issues is atypical of standard business school curricula, and provides students and scholars the opportunity to develop social, political, and cultural understandings which are key to managerial competence and judgment in complex business environments.

Graduate School of Business, University of Cape Town, South Africa (PRME champion)

Its commitment to responsibility, ethics, and sustainability is reflected majorly through its students and alumni. Key changes have been made in its MBA curriculum stream-lined to social innovation, which is the school's major reflection of responsible management. Research within GSB revolves around three themes: emerging markets, finance and trade; social innovation and entrepreneurship; and value-based leadership and sustainable partnership. Its principles and methods of instruction reflect responsible management in its teaching of sustainable entrepreneurship, innovative and blended learning, integration of academia and business, social innovation and leadership, globally oriented programmes, and experience-based learning, flexible learning, and programme design. The school hosts the Bertha Centre for Social Innovation and Entrepreneurship, which hosts practical entrepreneurship leadership programmes, develops indigenous case studies in RME to support capacity-building, and joins civil society and business actors in social change. For business education on the continent, this is a revolutionary approach to understanding business leaders and managers in their interaction with society.

Conclusion

With a growing body of literature and empirical studies on responsible management education, this field is full of opportunities for further studies. In addition, much has been written on the principles themselves; however, not many empirical studies exist in the area of how the responsible management education principles have been practically applied in business schools, and the benefits and differences that has made to the practice of management. Studies can also be carried out with regard to testimonials from employers who have worked with employees who were once management education students who studied in institutions where the principles of management education were upheld. The tension between business schools' increased public commitment toward responsible management education and the difficulties surrounding implementation remains under-theorized (Rasche and Gilbert, 2015: 239). However, the research and teaching methods, content, and structures of responsible management provide the foundation for generating the competencies, skills, and attitudes essential to successful organizational change.

For business leaders and managers, developments around RME present the opportunity for strategic engagement around encouraging volunteerism within the organization, transparency initiatives such as a sustainability reporting, and internship opportunities inviting young business leaders to engage in experiential learning within existing organizations. Other possibilities include making broad stakeholder engagement a routine part of the organization so that the institution emerges as a corporate citizen of the kind that is most beneficial to the society in which it is based. Businesses can also support research on responsible business as a basis for expanding platforms of collaboration with other businesses interested in positive social impact. For the manager leading change, the possibility for engaging RME within and beyond the organization are limitless.

References

Abdulai, D. N. (2016) *African-centred Management Education: A New Paradigm for an Emerging Continent.* Oxon: Routledge.

ABIS. (2010) *Adapting to a Changing Context: The Role of Management Education CEO Perspectives on the Role of Management Education in Helping Organisations Adapt to a Changing Context.* ABIS Global. Retrieved from www.abis-global.org/content/adaptingtoachangingcontext.pdf

Alcaraz, J. M., and Thiruvattal, E. (2010) An interview with Manuel Escudero the United Nations' Principles for Responsible Management Education: A global call for sustainability. *Academy of Management Learning & Education*, 9(3): 542–550.

AMI. (2016) *Catalysing Management Development in Africa: Identifying Areas for Impact.* Johannesburg: African Management Initiative.

Brewis, J. (1996) The 'making' of the 'competent' manager: Competency development, personal effectiveness and foucault. *Management Learning*, 27(1): 65–86.

Burchell, J., Kennedy, S., and Murray, A. (2015) Responsible management education in UK business schools: Critically examining the role of the United Nations Principles for Responsible Management Education as a driver for change. *Management Learning*, 46(4): 479–497.

Dyllick, T. (2015) Responsible management education for a sustainable world. *Journal Management Development*, 34(1): 16–33.

Erero, J., and Oladoyin, T. (2000) Tackling the corruption epidemic in Nigeria. In K. R. Hope Sr and B. C. Chikulo (Eds.), *Corruption and Development in Africa: Lessons From Country Case Studies.* London: Palgrave Macmillan, 280–287.

Erondu, E. A., Sharland, A., and Okpara, J. O. (2004) Corporate ethics in Nigeria: A test of the concept of an ethical climate. *Journal of Business Ethics*, 51: 349–357.

Gichure, W. (2006) Teaching business ethics in Africa: What ethical orientation? The case of East and Central Africa. *Journal of Business Ethics*, 63: 39–52.

Goldsmith, A. A. (2001) Risk, rule, and reason: Leadership in Africa. *Public Administration and Development*, 21: 77–87.

Gyimah-Brempong, K. (2002) Corruption, economic growth, and income inequality in Africa. *Economics of Governance*, 3: 183–209.

Harsch, E. (1993) Accumulators and democrats: Challenging state corruption in Africa. *The Journal of Modern African Studies*, 31(1): 31–48.

Haski-Leventhal, D. (2014) MBA student values, attitudes and behaviors: A cross-cultural comparison of PRME signatory schools. *SAM Advanced Management Journal*, Autumn: 29–41.

Hayes, R., Parkes, C., and Murray, A. (2016) Development of responsible management education and the principles for responsible management education in context. In R. Sunley and J. Leigh (Eds.), *Educating for Responsible Management: Putting Theory Into Practice*, 1st ed. Sheffield, UK: Greenleaf Publishing Limited, 13–27.

Hockerts, K., Borgbo, P., Srkoc, T., Goldberg, E., and Chaudry, R. (2015) *Faculty Development for Responsible Management Education: Results From a Survey Among PRME Signatories*. PRME Secretariat. Retrieved from www.unprme.org/resource-docs/FDReportFinalWeb.pdf

Hope Sr, K. R., and Chikulo, B. C. (2000) Introduction. In K. R. Hope Sr and B. C. Chikulo (Eds.), *Corruption and Development in Africa: Lessons From Country Case-studies*. London: Palgrave Macmillan.

Houngnikpo, M. C. (2006) *Africa's Elusive Quest for Development*. Hampshire: Palgrave Macmillan.

Kell, G., and Haertle, J. (2011) UN global compact and principles for responsible management education: The next decades. *EFMD Global Focus*, 5(2): 15–16.

Laasch, O., and Conaway, R. (2015) *Principles of Responsible Management: Global Sustainability, Responsibility, and Ethics*, 1st ed. Stamford, CT: Cengage Learning.

Lawal, G. (2007) Corruption and development in Africa: Challenges for political and economic change. *Humanity & Social Science Journal*, 2(1): 1–7.

Mason, G. (2016) Strategies for the integration of poverty alleviation into management curriculum: Poverty: How can business help? In M. Gudic, C. Parkes and A. Rosenbloom (Eds.), *Responsible Management Education and the Challenge of Poverty: A Teaching Perspective*. Sheffield, UK: Greenleaf Publishing Limited.

Muff, K. (2013) Developing globally responsible leaders in business schools: A vision and transformational practice for the journey ahead. *The Journal of Management Development*, 32(5): 487–507.

Olivier de Sardan, J. P. (1999) A moral economy of corruption in Africa? *The Journal of Modern African Studies*, 37(1): 25–52.

Perry, M., and Win, S. (2013) An evaluation of PRME's contribution to responsibility in higher education. *JCC*, 49: 48–70.

Pillay, S. (2004) Corruption- the challenge of good governance: A South African perspective. *The International Journal of Public Sector Management*, 17(7): 586–605.

Prandini, M., Vervoort, P., and Barthelmess, P. (2012) Responsible management education for 21st century leadership. *Central European Business Review*, 1(2): 16–22.

Rasche, A., and Escudero, M. (2009) Leading change: The role of the Principles for Responsible Management Education. *Zfwu*, 10(2): 244–250.

Rasche, A., and Gilbert, D. (2015) Decoupling responsible management education: Why business schools may not walk their talk. *Journal of Management Inquiry*, 24(3): 239–252.

Rotberg, R. I. (2004) Strengthening African leadership: There is another way. *Foregin Affairs*, 83(4): 14–18.

Shetty, K. (2017) Responsible global leadership: Ethical challenges in management education. In N. Baporikar (Ed.), *Innovation and Shifting Perspectives in Management Education*. Hershey, PA: IGI Global.

Sobczak, A., and Mukhi, U. (2016) The role of UN principles for responsible management education in stimulating organizational learning for global responsibility within business schools: An interview with Jonas Haertle. *Journal of Management Inquiry*, 25(4): 431–437.

Visser, W. (2016) Foreword. In R. Sunley and J. Leigh (Eds.), *Educating for Responsible Management: Putting Theory Into Practice*. Sheffield, UK: Greenleaf Publishing Limited.

Waddock, S., Rasche, A., Werhane, P. H., and Unruh, G. (2011) The principles for responsible management education: Implications for implementation and assessment. In D. L. Swanson and D. G. Fisher (Eds.), *Towards Assessing Business Ethics Education*. Charlotte, NC: Information Age Publishing, Inc.

Weybrecht, G. (2013) *The Sustainable MBA: The Business Guide to Sustainability*. Chichester: Wiley.

5

A murmuration model of change in Africa

David B. Zoogah

A murmuration model of change in Africa

Since the beginning of the 21st century, academics and practitioners have observed that Africa is changing. Indeed, terms such as "Africa rising" (Economist, 2011); "Lions on the move" (McKinsey Global Institute, 2010); "Africa emerges" (Rotberg, 2013); and "Africa unchained" (Ayittey, 2006) all suggest transformation of African countries.[1] A search of change terms – Africa is changing, Africa rising, transformation in Africa, etc. – in twenty-four magazines and internet sources with a core or peripheral focus on Africa from 2000 to 2015 shows the frequency of change increasing between 2000 and 2015 (see Appendix for terms). These observations indicate that the "old ways of doing business" are giving way to "new ways". Over two decades ago, Jones and Blunt (1993) observed that "there is a need to develop concepts and approaches to organizational development and change which are effective and sensitive to African contexts" because "immense changes have taken place on the African continent during that time" (p. 1735). They observed that a number of changes across multiple levels, including government, education, health, and organizational arrangements, were taking place as a result of independence from colonial masters. Using Mintzberg's (1989) organizational culture model and the observation that "the single most commonly asked question – the virtual obsession of today's managers – is, how can I help bureaucracies to change?" – they argued that the observation is "an overwhelmingly urgent question for many African countries" (p. 1739).

I assert that that observation is even truer today than then: not only have there been many radical government changes across all the regions of Africa and more dramatic changes in education, health, and bureaucracies, but also other tectonic shifts – elimination of apartheid, globalization, technological innovations – have manifested. The question that arises then is: what model effectively captures all the visible and invisible dynamics and dialectics? In this chapter, I present a murmuration model that attempts to answer this question. I explain its attributes – nature, process, drivers, and outcomes. The explanations not only provide an update, but also show the way that the change of today differs from that of yesterday. First, I discuss the contextual characteristics of Africa that provide a background to the change I observe across the continent. Second, I review models of change in general and specifically in Africa. Third, I present the model of change that is unique to Africa – a murmuration model. I then propose some antecedents, contingencies, and outcomes of the model. I conclude with a discussion of how to test the model.

Contextual characteristics of Africa

In order to understand change in Africa, it is important to identify the features of the external environment within which organizations function. I draw from Zoogah, Peng, and Woldu's (2015) contextual characteristics of Africa. They indicate that Africa has two nominal contexts – modern and traditional. The modern context is mostly associated with urban locations which have industrial or manufacturing systems (Mbaku, 2004); relative openness and individualistic tendencies; banks providing finance and credit to many organizations (Collier, 2007); and metropolitan attributes similar to those observed in Western contexts. The traditional context is represented by rural areas with chieftaincy and councils of elders, agrarian forms of living, lineage-based (rather than property rights-based) inheritance, autarkic markets, ethnic and tribal identities (Michalopoulos and Papaioannou, 2015), social institutions that revolve around the family and communal activities, interpersonal funding for economic activities, social rather than scientific learning, high illiteracy rates, low human capital base, and the practice of collectivism. In short, the characteristics of Africa can be summarized in the triadic complex, the triple heritages, religions, geographies, and influences that suggest intricacy on the one hand, and psychological ailment on the other. These complexes include the local-traditional complex, local-modern complex, and foreign-mixed complex. The sets of factors in these complexes integrate to determine manifestations of states, processes, and activities.

These contextual attributes have implications for change in Africa. First, the dual context suggests differences in economic activities, institutional, psychological, sociocultural systems, levels of environmental uncertainty, and change tendencies. It also fits with the concept of dual authority and mixed governance view of African states, where national and ethnic institutions and policies coexist, sometimes in harmony and other times in conflict (Herbst, 2000; Michalopoulos and Papaioannou, 2015; Sklar, 1993). Furthermore, since colonization, Africa has had a modern system originating in the colonial state and a customary one rooted at the ethnic level (Mamdani, 1996). Second, as Zoogah et al. (2015) indicate, "Africa's seeming unresponsiveness to exogenous influence is a product of historical and traditional experiences, which suggests that the African context is a configuration or bundle of exogenous and endogenous stimuli that interactively influence management of organizations" (p. 12). Third, this context suggests that cultural dexterity that involves internalized alternations between collectivistic and individualistic orientations due to the colonial and extant western influences, as well as dual cultural identity arising from the mobility of people between urban and rural areas, affect the change orientations. Lastly, these configurations shape the meanings, underlying behaviors, and attitudes of employees, groups, and organizations (Ugwuegbu, 2001; Zoogah et al., 2015).

Another significant characteristic of Africa is that sometimes things that on the surface seem not to be moving are indeed moving at the bottom, and other times, things that are moving on the surface are indeed not moving at the bottom. This way of thinking about movement, the act or instance of making or becoming different, and transformation is different from what seems to be in the literature (Chia, 1999). It contrasts with Van de Ven's (1987) assertion that change necessarily implicates an "object" of change, but complements Chia's (1999: 218) view that: "there are underneath the change no things which change: change has no need of a support. There are movements, but there is no inert or invariable object which moves: movement does not imply a mobile" (Bergson, 1992). This view derives from the principle of immanence, which stipulates that the past unfolds in the present, and implies that each outcome, each situation or state, always necessarily incorporates and absorbs the events of its past. As Chia (1999) indicates in his rhizomic model, each happening or "event" represents the actual realizing of one of the many possibilities presented by the past configuration of events. Movement ensures manifestations of multiple configurations that, if segmented, can be discerned linearly as suggested in complex adaptive system models. In that process, dualities, complexities, stasis, and equilibria which combine in murmurations can be identified.

Models of change

Across the social sciences – sociology, anthropology, economics, political science, and business – there have been diverse studies of change within and across organizations (see Poole and Van de Ven, 2004). As a result, there are diverse definitions, dimensions, attributes, and typologies of organizational change. Poole and Van de Ven (2004: xi) define organizational change "as a difference in form, quality, or state over time in an organizational entity". The definition seems comprehensive in levels – individuals and organizations; dimensions – content and way of change; types – episodic versus continuous; and attributes – motors, frameworks, and agency. However, as Barnett and Carroll (1995) indicate, it is a "difference" perspective, where the content of change in one period is compared with that of another period. In this chapter I adopt a "flow" perspective where I look at the configuration of factors that "move" countries, organizations, groups, and even individuals, not from one state to another, but across a series of states. In that regard, my model is continuous.

The literature has identified various types of change in relation to organizations. Using the mode of change and unit of change dimensions, Van de Ven and Poole (1995) identify life-cycle, teleological, dialectical, and evolutionary models. Life-cycle models depict organizational change as progressing through a sequence or stages or phases consistent with prescriptions of institutional, natural, or logical programs. Jones and Blunt (1993) proposed a life-cycle model of change and development in Africa. Teleological models view changes as a cycle of goal formation, implementation, evaluation, and modification of actions or goals based on what is learned or intended by the organization. In dialectical models, change is viewed as emergence of conflicts between organizations espousing an opposing thesis and antithesis that collide to produce a synthesis. Evolutionary models involve a repetitive series of variation, selection, and retention events among organizations in a designated population. In addition to these, Chia (1999) proposed a rhizomic model of change that, in contrast to the other models that are based on stasis and equilibrium, focuses on "the inherent dynamic complexities and intrinsic indeterminacy of (organization) transformational processes" (p. 209). His model is based on "the precarious, tentative and heterogeneous network-strengthening features of actor-alliances" (p. 211). This idea is similar to Seo, Putnam, and Bartunek's (2004) model of dualities and tensions of planned organizational change. Even though these models are framed relative to organizations, they are general and can be applied to societies and groups in Africa.

Models of change in Africa

There have been a number of models of change and development in Africa. While some are general, others are specific. Jones and Blunt's (1993) model identifies factors that limit organizational change. They argue that a configuration of factors – mechanistic structures of organizations, emphasis on control rather than performance, the "cult of the generalist" (i.e., preference for individuals with no specialization), political realities and our lack of real knowledge about African administrative systems and practices, misallocation of skills, computerized personnel systems, inter-sectoral mobility, and wage differentiation – limits the development of organizations in the private sector. Abdulraheem, Mordi, Ojo, and Ajonbadi (2013) examined planned change in higher educational institutions of Nigeria. They focus on outcomes and find that the change differed according to the values of each organization. The observation about differences in values seems intuitive and probably not too insightful, partly because it is consistent with previous efforts (see Jones and Blunt, 1993).

However, Adeniji, Osibanjo, and Abiodun (2013) focus on the private sector, particularly the banking industry. They find that human resource management determined the interventionist strategies of the one hundred and twenty-three banks studied. Like the previous one, this model is also country-specific; it focuses on only Nigeria. Burchardt (2012) focuses on South Africa and faith-based organizations using a similar approach. He argues that the asymmetrical power relations between mostly Northern donors and local churches, within which these organizational dynamics unfold, engender two interlocked processes. On the one hand, institutional isomorphism is reflected in the adoption by local actors of the technocratic and official templates promoted by the dominant discourse on civil society and its main protagonist, the nongovernmental organization. On the other hand, local actors deploy strategies of extraversion that contradict the "paper versions" of faith-based development. The author analyzes how the resulting contradictions are played out and shows how both the compliance with, and the strategic refractions of, organizational templates depend on one another.

Yaeger and Sorensen (2011) present case histories of organizational development (OD) in Africa using illustrations from Western, Southern, and Eastern Africa. The cases suggest that Africa is challenging because of the continent's high diversity of cultural traditions, colonial experiences, nation-creation histories that ignore the tribal boundaries, and modern dictatorships. Focusing on South Africa, Sulamoyo (2011) suggests that Ubuntu can be a cultural strategy for OD and change in Sub-Saharan Africa because of the collectivistic attributes of Ubuntu as a cultural value and the promotive tendency of OD. Kudonoo (2013) also focuses on the West African region but centers her arguments on the profession of OD consulting. She argues that the local cultures should be included in the design and implementation of change programs; that the opinion of informal leaders as well as other resources, including employees, should be considered in order to facilitate effective involvement of all key stakeholders. In sum, the literature suggests that change in Africa seems different. There is a multiplex of factors influencing the initiation, flow, and trajectories of change. The process by which the change manifests is similar to a murmuration.

A murmuration model of organizational change in Africa

How do the acts or instances of entities becoming different (i.e., change) manifest in Africa? I contend that change is a function of (a) drivers across different levels, (b) outcomes across the same levels, and (c) contingency factors. I term it a murmuration model of change because it shows complex, dynamic, and flow patterns of multiple factors across multiple levels. These factors seem to manifest in synchrony in change initiatives. A murmuration refers to thousands of the birds that fly in "a dazzling cloud, swirling, pulsating, drawing together to the thinnest of waists, then wildly twisting in pulses of enlargement and diminution" (Hunt, 2013).

I begin by discussing the drivers of change before focusing on the process by which murmuration manifests. I then discuss the outcomes and contingencies. Figure 5.1 shows the overall model.

Environment of change

In models of change, the environment is a central element. Typically, researchers focus on the environment's degree of stability, the interconnections between its various elements, and changes which are occurring (Jones and Blunt, 1993; see also Poole and Van de Ven, 2004). In examining

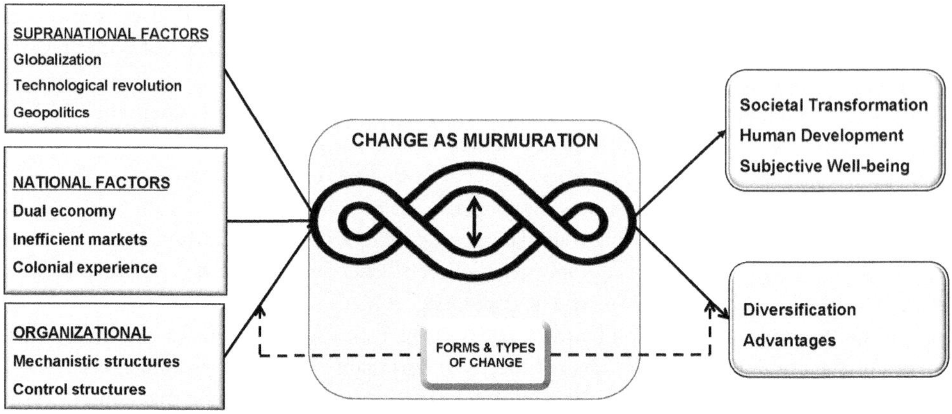

Figure 5.1 Drivers, process, and outcomes of change as murmuration

organizational change and development in Africa, a number of researchers have identified several environmental factors that not only influence the initiation and progress of change, but also acceptance and resistance to that change (see Table 5.1). While some factors focus on the internal environment, others focus on the external environment. They operate at different levels – individual, organizational, national, and even supranational. Jones and Blunt (1993) observe that "some of these factors, and others, lie outside the control of African governments", suggesting that there are supranational factors that influence organizational change in Africa. With regard to complexity, some factors are more suited for alignment, while others are for separation and still others are for cohesion. I also code the factors into configurations as I discuss below.

Models of change in Africa have typically considered these factors as having linear effects, probably for empirical or positivistic reasons. I argue that such an approach is inappropriate. Research shows Africa is "one of the most difficult administrative settings to be found anywhere in the world" (Montgomery, 1989: 11), partly because of African formal organizations' demonstration of tremendous resistance to different forms of bureaucratic reorientation and reform (Kiggundu, 1989), political realities that tend to undermine the appearance of grand scope for administrative modernization (Montgomery, 1989), and the relatively new African nations which inherited from their colonial masters the bureaucratic forms that were designed primarily for the maintenance of law and order, but which have proved extraordinarily resistant to change (Jones, 1991). Furthermore, organizational factors such as mechanistic structures ignore the complex reality of organizations as well as the political, social, psychological, and irrational characteristics of organizational life. There is also an emphasis on control rather than performance (i.e., emphasizing inputs and internal procedures, and neglecting measures of output). In the public sectors, there is overstaffing of the public sectors, resulting in inflated wage bills and a "cult of the generalist" ethos which reflects the customary British and French mistrust of the professional and admiration of the notion of wellroundedness. In addition, there is a lack of real knowledge about African administrative systems and practices as well as a misallocation of skills. These factors neither affect organizations linearly nor discretely; rather, they do so in a complex manner or, more specifically, in synchrony.

Dooley (2004) proposed complex models of organizational change arguing that "organizations can be thought of as examples of a general class of complex systems called complex adaptive systems or CAS" (p. 357). Models in complexity science tend to combine linear and nonlinear

Table 5.1 Characteristics of environmental factors

Factor	*Source*	*Level*	*Dimension*	*Complexity*
Tribal identities	Yaeger and Sorensen (2011); Zoogah et al. (2015)	Individual	Internal	Separation
Cult of generalists	Jones and Blunt (1993)	Individual	Internal	Alignment
Lack of commitment & dynamism	Jones and Blunt (1993)	Individual	Internal	Cohesion
Ethical challenges	Jones and Blunt (1993)	Individual	Internal	Alignment
Ethnos oblige	Zoogah et al. (2015)	Individual	Internal	Separation
Westernism	Zoogah et al. (2015)	Individual	Internal	Alignment
Local cultures	Kudonoo (2013)	National	External	Alignment
Colonial experience	Yaeger and Sorensen (2011); Jones (1991)	National	External	Separation
Dictatorships	Yaeger and Sorensen (2011)	National	External	Separation
Diverse cultural traditions	Zoogah et al. (2015)	National	External	Separation
Political transformations	Yaeger and Sorensen (2011)	National	External	Alignment
Conflict with neighbors	Jones and Blunt (1993)	National	External	Cohesion
National boundaries	Yaeger and Sorensen (2011)	National	External	Separation
Dual economies	Zoogah et al. (2015)	National	External	Alignment
Inefficient markets/ autarky	Kiggundu (1989)	National	External	Alignment
Misaligned educational systems	Collier (2007)	National	External	Alignment
Brain deficit	Zoogah et al. (2015)	National	External	Cohesion
"Stuckness"	Sulamoyo (2011)	Organizational	Internal	Cohesion
Western administrative systems	Montgomery (1989)	Organizational	External	Alignment
Technological evolution	Jones and Blunt (1993)	Organizational	External	Alignment
Shortage of skilled manpower	Jones and Blunt (1993)	Organizational	External	Alignment
Mechanistic structures	Jones and Blunt (1993)	Organizational	Internal	Alignment
Control-focus	Jones and Blunt (1993)	Organizational	Internal	Alignment
Skill misallocation	Jones and Blunt (1993)	Organizational	Internal	Alignment

(*Continued*)

Table 5.1 (Continued)

Factor	*Source*	*Level*	*Dimension*	*Complexity*
Telecommunication	Jones and Blunt (1993)	Organizational	External	Cohesion
Geopolitics	Zoogah et al. (2015)	Supranational	External	Separation
Globalization	Ugwuegbu (2001)	Supranational	External	Cohesion
Dysfunctional systems	Yaeger and Sorensen (2011)	National	External	Separation
Resource deprivation	Jones and Blunt (1993)	National	External	Alignment
Poor infrastructure	Jones and Blunt (1993)	National	External	Separation

causalities; describe both entities and variables with the system; and can be both "top-down" and "bottom-up" (Dooley, 2004). The elements of complex systems include *agents*, which refer to "semi-autonomous units that seek to maximize their fitness by evolving over time" (p. 357); *fitness* of the agent, which is modeled as a complex aggregate of many factors, both local and global; *tags*, which help identify what other agents are capable of interacting with the focal agent; and *boundary*, which defines the specific confines of the system (Anderson, 1999; Holland, 1995; Gell-Mann, 1994). These attributes suggest that CAS tend to be dynamic. Complex dynamical systems exhibit three key characteristics (Gallagher and Appenzeller, 1999). First, they consist of a number of interacting components or agents. These components can be homogeneous or heterogeneous. Second, they exhibit emergent behavior in that their collective behavior exhibits a coherent pattern that could not be predicted from the behavior of the components separately. Third, and most importantly, the emergent behavior is self-organized in that it does not result from a controlling component agent. These three characteristics can be seen clearly in murmuration phenomena, such as bird flocking, which have been modeled as complex dynamical systems (Cavagna et al., 2010). Murmurations are coordination phenomena in which interactions between individual units (birds mostly) produce collective, large-scale patterns. In other words, there seems to be a cooperative generative mechanism.

Murmurations depict different patterns of complex dynamics and flow.[2] Their swirling and pulsating movement where the birds draw together, then wildly twist in pulses of enlargement and diminution, exhibits synchronous behavior. Cavagna et al. (2010) found that starling flocks model a complex physical phenomenon, seldom observed in physical and biological systems, known as scale-free correlation. The fluidity of the flock's motion is such that "the group responds as one" and "cannot be divided into independent subparts". When one starling changes direction or speed, each of the other birds in the flock responds to the change, and they do so nearly simultaneously regardless of the size of the flock. In essence, information moves across the flock very quickly and with nearly no degradation. Cavagna et al. (2010) describe it as a high signal-to-noise ratio.

The scale-free correlation allows starlings to greatly enhance what the researchers call "effective perceptive range", which is another way of saying that a starling on one side of the flock can respond to what others are sensing all the way across the flock – a huge benefit for a starling trying to avoid a predator. Young, Ferguson, Brault, and Craig (2011) determined that in murmurations starlings consistently coordinate their movements with their seven nearest neighbors, and the shape of the flock, rather than the size, has the largest effect on this number;

seven seems optimal for the tightly connected flocks that starlings are known for (www.wired.com/2011/11/starling-flock/). Murmurations are thus described with equations of "critical transitions" – systems that are poised to tip, to be almost instantly and completely transformed, like metals becoming magnetized or liquid turning to gas. Each starling in a flock is connected to every other. When a flock turns in unison, it's a phase transition. In order to model the physiological mechanisms that allow for the almost simultaneous transitions, some studies suggest that the flocking behavior is driven by three simple rules: separation – avoid crowding neighbors (short-range repulsion); alignment – steer towards average heading of neighbors; and cohesion – steer towards average position of neighbors (long-range attraction). These rules explain how the flock moves in a highly realistic way, creating complex motion and interaction that would be extremely hard to create otherwise.

These elements of murmuration fit with the notion of change that I contemplate. First, the drivers seem to move in synchrony when triggered. These complex movements are similar to the complex of social, economic, political, cultural, and legal factors that impinge upon individuals, organizations, and societies. They seem to match the scale-free correlations observed in murmurations. As Chia (1999) observed in his rhizomic model of change, the dominant models of change in general and organizational change in particular are "couched in the language of stasis and equilibrium" (p. 209).[3] The factors that drive organizational change in Africa are not only too numerous, as in a flock, but they encompass multiple levels and seem to move in tandem or synchrony with regard to their effect on change targets. When supranational factors such as globalization and technological systems change, almost simultaneously dual economic attributes and inefficient markets change, and structures and competency systems of entities change along with identities and commitment levels of individual employees. As shown in Figure 5.3, the flow of factors seems ordered, fluid, and so synchronous that it is difficult to identify the specific ones that drive the changes. Rather, it is the multitude of factors that propel the act or instance of becoming different. In addition to movement, separation, alignment, and cohesion seem to define change in Africa. Higher-level factors are separated from lower-level factors, but they align in pace and direction (see Figure 5.3). Those in the same level seem to bind together tightly in their

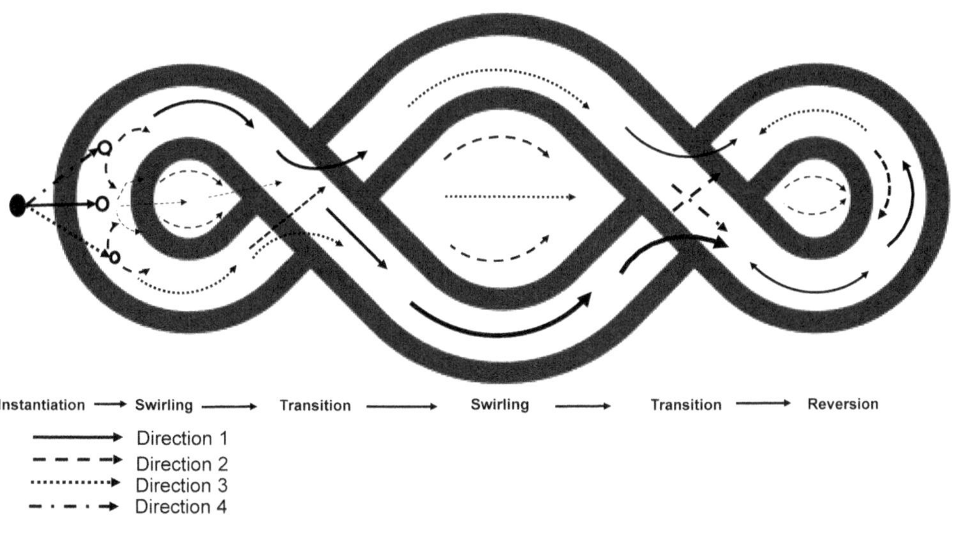

Figure 5.2 Process of change as murmuration

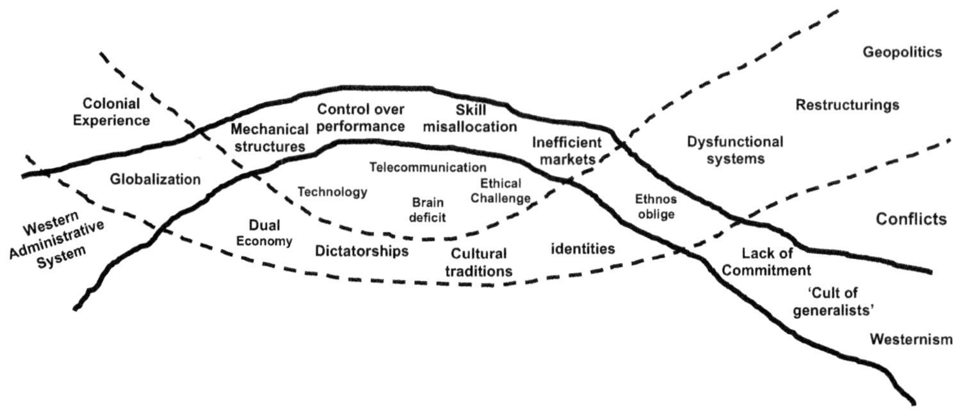

Figure 5.3 Factors of change as murmuration

movement. The model also suggests different forms of configurations of murmurations (see section on forms of change). There are displacements, overlays, grafting, and appendages.

Process of change

Our fundamental contention is that change in Africa is not a function of discrete unitary elements but a complex set of factors. I further contend that those factors do not manifest linearly, but rather nonlinearly or dynamically, like a murmuration. What then is the process by which murmuration change manifests? First, there is a trigger that almost simultaneously instantiates movement of multiple factors across diverse levels. The interlinkages of the social, economic, political, cultural, and organizational contexts suggest that the instantiation of a single factor inextricably triggers other factors across other levels (Zoogah et al., 2015). Second, there are swirlings. As shown in Figure 5.3, swirlings refer to the dynamic and emergent movement of the change elements. There are upward swirlings, where the change elements encompass systems and operations at the upper levels of the organization, as well as downward swirlings which encompass operations at the lower levels. The upward and downward swirlings could also refer to national and supranational factors that move in tandem with organizational and individual factors. The initial swirlings lead to transitions, points of inflection at which different alternative directions (up, down, reversion) can be pursued. Even though two transition areas are identified in Figure 5.2, fewer or greater number of transition areas may be manifest. The critical transitions mark the "stuckness" of organizations in Africa (Malunga, 2004). Effective transitioning requires clarification of the vision and unifying different perspectives undergirding the change. The third sub-process is reversion. A review of murmuration patterns suggests reversion which is similar to feedbacks. Reversion is the dynamic that often attracts the attention of foreigners about the progression of Africa. It also accounts for the challenges of the "Africa dummy" experienced by economists (Collier and Hoeffler, 2002; Englebert, 2000) or the "Africa problem", "the stereotypical intractable challenge of enhancing socio-cultural, economic, political, and scientific development" (Zoogah, Zoogah, and Dalaba-Roohi, 2015: 2).[4] Lastly, it fits the unique contours of Africa – the boom-burst-boom-burst cycles.

Common to all these sub-processes are propulsion, direction, and coordination. The speed at which the change manifests depends on the change agents, champions, resources, and technologies underlying the change initiative. It also depends on the number and type of factors instantiating the change. To the extent that drag factors (i.e., constraints) are harnessed in the change process, propulsion is likely to be slow. The second element is the direction. As shown in Figure 5.2, there are diverse directions – up, down, forward, backward, and diagonal – which could be pursued, adopted, and modified. In other words, a change that has an upward trajectory might revert downward at the transition area depending on the constraints encountered at that point or the leader of the change. Such changes are shown by the thick arrows and the double arrows. Both propulsion and direction are a function of coordination. Just as in murmuration where the flock members coordinate their movements, change in organizations and countries also results from coordination (Poole and Van de Ven, 2004) particularly in Africa (Jones and Blunt, 1993).

The model also suggests that change in Africa is characterized by not only dualities (up and down) involving the dialectic of static and dynamic processes, but also configurations. The dynamics are underneath but sometimes surge up, while the static processes sometimes submerge. There is also the duality of discrete and interlinked forces that, like a murmuration, moves African countries and organizations, but with a cooperative generative mechanism. The cooperative generative mechanism in a murmuration model of change refers to an agency that reflects a particular flow pattern on another pattern. The new pattern is generated from the old pattern. For example, an upward flow pattern that transforms to a downward flow pattern is transformed by the generative mechanism. It is generative in the sense that a new form or pattern emerges after the transformation. That transformation results from "tacit consent" by the agents in the change process.

It fits with the three principles of process espoused in metaphysics – heterogeneous becoming of things, otherness, and immanence (Bergson, 1992; Deleuze and Guattari, 1988; Serres, 1982; Whitehead, 1985). Briefly, the becoming of things is based on process epistemology which begins with the fundamental assertion that the actual world is a "process, and that that process is the becoming of actual entities" (Whitehead, 1929: 26). Second, otherness is based on the insistence that terms do not and cannot stand alone in and of their own right. Instead, the very platform on which things, identities, and situations emerge is predicated upon the suppression and backgrounding of the other that has given rise to it. Third, immanence is based on the idea that

> the past is immanent in the present and this fact implies that each outcome, each situation or state, always necessarily incorporates and absorbs the events of its past. Thus, the present is not merely the linear successor of the past but a novel outcome of it. Each moment of duration absorbs the preceding one, transforming it and with it the whole, constituting at each stage of the process a novel and never-to-be-repeated occasion necessarily grounded in its past, but always projected towards a not-yet knowable future. Each happening or "event" represents the actual realizing of one of the many possibilities presented by the past configuration of events.
>
> *(Chia, 1999: 220)*

Forms of change

The overall model in Figure 5.1 suggests that the effects of the multilevel drivers on change murmurations, and the latter on the outcomes, varies at different levels of change form. The change attributes discussed above do not manifest in the same manner across all African countries and organizations. Even though the organizing processes that undergird business are similar in the context of both developed and developing countries, two major factors differentiate those of Africa, resulting in distinct forms of change. Given that change generally occurs when the experience of an entity no longer facilitates achievement of its goals, the experiences of entities in Africa may be profuse or limited with regard to effectiveness. In other words, entities differ in the degree to which they have been consistently successful in achieving their strategic outcomes. Those with profuse success differ from those with limited success. The differential outcomes arise from different administrative legacies from colonialism, in the case of organizations, or experiences with colonial masters, in the case of nations. The French administrative systems differ from those of the English, German, Spanish, and Dutch. Further, a number of countries encountered multiple colonial experiences (Mazrui, 1993). Togo, for example, has German and French legacies. How companies in these countries experience change may thus differ.

Change may also occur when the foundation that undergirds the entity's activities seems incapable of doing so in the foreseeable future. Some entities may have strong foundations due to ethnic integration or segmentation,[5] etc., while others have weak foundations. To the extent that the foundation is weak or strong, the form of change likely to be experienced by an entity may vary. Those historical (colonial) experiences and cultural (tribal) characteristics suggest that change models take diverse forms. One major distinguishing feature of African countries is tribal heterogeneity; there are more tribal groups in Africa than any other continent (Michalopoulos and Papaioannou, 2015). The heterogeneity suggests intertribal conflicts, which not only affect interactions of employees but also effective functioning of systems and processes, since tribal rivalries may lead to negative deviant behavior (e.g., undermining). Other countries are characterized by homogeneous tribal groups, which suggest that they are unlikely to experience ethnic fractionalization and negative deviant behavior to the same degree. Combining the two dimensions – foundation and experience – I identify four forms of change based on these two dimensions: displacement, appendage, grafting, and overlay (see Figure 5.4).

Change by *overlay* occurs when a new practice, system, or process is mapped onto an old system. It is defined by limited experience and weak foundation of the change agent. During the 1970s when African countries were gaining independence, governments overlaid the new systems they were developing with the old ones they had inherited from the colonial masters because they did not comprehend fully the new ones being proposed and/or the old ones were not too ineffective to be jettisoned. The overlay enabled them to "trim" the old system while the new one expanded. In Ghana, for example, educational instructional methods (e.g., local languages) are overlaid with English instructional methods which are the official and inherited systems.

In contrast to the overlay, change by *appendage* manifests when a new practice is attached to an existing system. The new practice is expected to develop from the "nutrients" of the existing system. It arises in situations defined by strong foundations and limited experience. Curtin (1975) suggests that the internal market systems that prevailed in Africa prior to colonialism were appended to the external market systems in the post-colonial and modern era. The strong foundation underlying internal Afro-Arabic trade that predated colonialism was also characterized by limited experience with Western economic exchange processes.

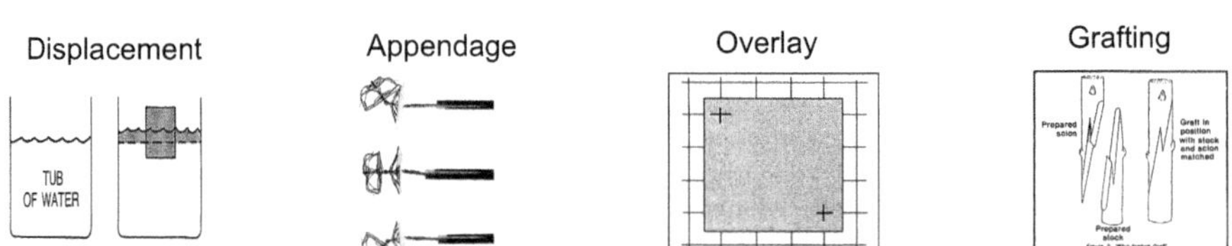

Figure 5.4 Forms of change

Change by *displacement* occurs when historical systems are overturned and new practices and processes consistent with the cultural context are institutionalized. It arises from the profuse experience of the agents (i.e., individuals, organizations, and national actors) and their recognition that the cultural foundation is too tenuous to sustain the entity for a long time into the future. Rwanda, which had a lot of experience with the French traditions, replaced its systems – language, education, market systems, etc., with those of the English mainly because of the awareness that the French system was feeble in supporting the kind of economic development the country envisioned.

The fourth form is change by *grafting*. It occurs when a replica is attached to an existing model and both fuse to be one. The new system fuses into the old system with little to no problems. Grafting arises from situations of profuse experience and strong foundations. Both old and new systems are not only viewed as important, but compatible enough to buttress or feed off of each other. The in-depth knowledge garnered from the experience and the relatively fortified underpinnings provide a basis for the grafting. Ashanti Goldfields, a relatively small mining organization in Africa, was grafted onto AngloGold of South Africa, a large company, as Ashanti Gold, even though it was presented as a merger.[6]

Types of change

Another moderator in Figure 5.1 is type of change. I distinguish the type of change from the form of change by their dimensions. In the latter, the experience (profuse versus limited) and foundation (weak versus strong) of change define the forms as discussed above. In this section it is the source of change (endogenous versus exogenous) and effect of change (minor versus major) that define the types of change. With regard to change, several studies (see Poole and Van de Ven, 2004), including those of Africa (Jones and Blunt, 1993), suggest that changes emerge from different sources. I classify them as endogenous – change arising from the internal structures, systems, processes, operations, employees, etc. of organizations and countries – and exogenous, which refers to change arising from the external agencies such as international supranational entities (e.g., World Bank and International Labor Organization) and international agencies (e.g., multinational corporations). In addition to sources, the effect of the change – minor versus major – can define the type of change (see Figure 5.5).

By combining the two dimensions, I classify the types of change as Types I, II, III, and IV change. Type I change results from endogenous sources with minor effects. The effort, resources, attention, and dedication to change are likely to be lower because of the minimal effects of

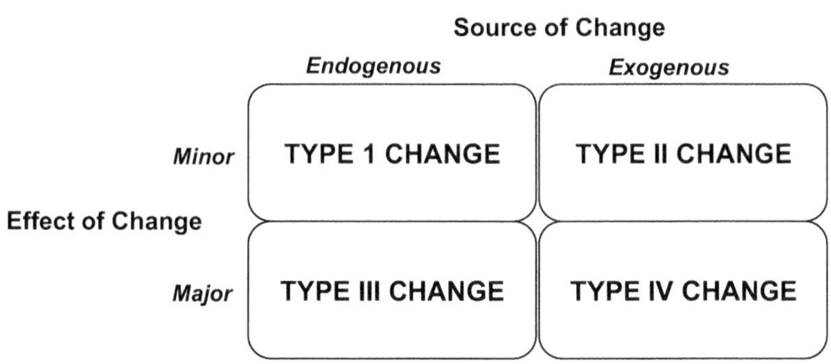

Figure 5.5 Types of change

change. The minimalism is likely to be exacerbated by the source – controllable factors within the organization. Type II change also has minor effects, but derived from exogenous sources. Consequently, tangible and intangible resources directed toward change are likely to be relatively greater than those in Type I change because of the greater visibility from external stakeholders to whom the organization, for example, seeks legitimacy. Type III change combines endogenous sources and major effects. This type of change also involves a lot more resources and effort than in the previous two because its effects are greater, even though the organization has relatively greater control. Lastly, Type IV change combines exogenous sources with major effects. It draws the most attention, resources, effort, and dedication of organizations because of the magnitude of its effects and the legitimacy concerns associated with external agencies.

The forms and types of changes alter the effect of the antecedents on change and the effect of the latter on its outcomes (see Figure 5.1). With regard to changes, appendages, for example, establish weak links at the transition points while grafting establish fissures that may over time weaken. Type IV changes also differ from Type I changes in terms of their effects.

Drivers of change

Why do entities change? This is a fundamental question in studies of change and development (see Poole and Van de Ven, 2004). Generally, the research shows that certain factors drive change. In this section, I identify a number of factors across individual, organizational, national, and supranational levels (see Figure 5.1) and explain why entities change in Africa. Implicit in our discussion of the murmuration model of change in Africa is the notion that multiple factors simultaneously drive change. I explicitly discuss how those factors drive the change process I have conceived. Figure 5.1 guides our discussion.

The factors span individual, organizational, national, and supranational levels. However, just as in murmuration where the movement of big and small starlings is not only parallel but also synchronous, these factors may manifest in tandem. Further, a number of studies show that the complexity of Africa suggests that individual, organizational, national and supranational factors can align as parallel forces driving change in a particular entity (Blunt and Jones, 1991b; Kiggundu, 1991; Zoogah et al., 2015). That view is evident in Figure 5.1. First, the colonial experiences of African countries (Yaeger and Sorensen, 2011; Kiggundu, 1989), as well as inherited western administrative structural systems (Montgomery, 1989), and the "cult of generalists" left behind as a result of those experiences (Jones and Blunt, 1993), instantiate changes. However, the paths of the factors differ as they move along. While the administrative systems are oriented upward (i.e., improving management or organizations), the colonial experience is oriented downward. The latter is an inhibitor while the former is a facilitator. Second, other factors – mechanistic structures (Jones and Blunt, 1993), focus on control rather than performance (Jones and Blunt, 1993), skills misallocation (Jones and Blunt, 1993), and inefficient markets (Kiggundu, 1989) – also seem to be on the upward trajectory. Dual economy (Lewis, 1954), dictatorships (Yaeger and Sorensen, 2011), diverse cultural traditions (Zoogah et al., 2015), and tribal identities (Yaeger and Sorensen, 2011), however, are at the bottom and on a downward trajectory.

Third, technology (Jones and Blunt, 1993), brain deficit (Zoogah et al., 2015), telecommunication (Jones and Blunt, 1993), and ethical challenges (Blunt and Jones, 1991) are in the middle. At the critical transition areas are factors which determine whether an entity in the process of change follows an upward path or a downward one. In our illustrative model, globalization is at one critical transition area. It is a supranational factor that affects not only national and organizational courses, but also individual ones. Another transition factor is ethnos oblige, defined as the obligation of those from a particular ethnic group to act with honor, kindliness, generosity, and forethought toward the group (Zoogah, 2018). Even though it is conceptualized as an individual factor, it has organizational and national implications that can inhibit or facilitate the pace, flow, and propulsion of the other factors. For example, it contributed to the elimination of one dysfunctional system – apartheid – in South Africa, which led to transformational organizational changes (Nkomo and Kriek, 2011). Factors in the reversion area include lack of commitment (Jones and Blunt, 1993), westernism (Zoogah et al., 2015), conflicts (Collier, 2007), geopolitics (Zoogah et al., 2015), and economic restructurings (UNCTAD, 1996). Conflicts, for example, turn change trajectories around. Organizations in Rwanda had to start all over after the genocidal conflict in that country in 1994 (Verwimp, 2003). Geopolitics which contributed to the non-intervention of the French in the conflict (Charles, 1995; Hintjens, 1999) indirectly affected the reversion of organizational change in that country.

In sum, several factors influence the initiation, trajectory, transitioning, and reversion of change in Africa. These multilevel factors determine different interlinked paths that sometimes overlap and other times hang in parallel forms. They either unilaterally or multilaterally affect macro processes which spill over to the micro level to influence change.

Outcomes of change

The rate of change in Africa is accelerating and in many ways becoming increasingly turbulent particularly for organizations (Chironga, Leke, Lund, and van Wamelen, 2011; Jones and Blunt, 1993; Zoogah and Nkomo, 2013). As a result, managers of systems in Africa have a responsibility to anticipate, initiate, monitor, interpret, and manage change. This responsibility is even more critical given that the change I describe here involves not just discrete but multiplex factors that are associated with greater uncertainty, and frequently involve confusion, disturbance, and turbulence (Torrington, Weightman, and Johns, 1989). The change is aggravated by the failure of organizational leaders, for example, to articulate a clear vision of the proposed change and its intended outcomes.

Several outcomes are associated with the change I describe (see Figure 5.1). I must point out that the discussion in this section uses organizations as exemplars, and the specific outcomes I identify are no different from those experienced by systems in other contexts for three reasons. First, systems in Africa have similar effectiveness expectations as those in other contexts. Second, the actors in the change initiative – individuals, organizations, and societies – function as change agents or champions in much the same way: to ensure the change is successful in terms of the desired outcomes. Third, the outcomes of change depend on the degree to which tangible and intangible resources are deployed to facilitate the change.

What differentiates African systems from those in other contexts are the levels, viability, and magnitude of the outcomes. Change outcomes in Africa do not affect only individual systems (e.g., organizations) but also others (e.g., individuals and societies) for two reasons. First, most organizations (e.g., state-owned enterprises) have governments as significant stakeholders (Jones and Blunt, 1993; Montgomery, 1989). Governments are agents, representing the interests of the principals, the citizens. As a result, whatever outcomes accrue to them revert to the citizens. Change outcomes also affect individuals because of the interlinkages of individuals to organizations. Remember that African countries are collectivistic where individuals are inextricably linked to their workplaces. With regard to viability, change outcomes do not last because of the vicissitude of exogenous and endogenous forces buffeting organizations. It is not uncommon in Africa for change that results in leadership replacement to be supplanted by another leadership change due to exogenous influences (e.g., political appointment) (Montgomery, 1989; Zoogah et al., 2015).

Recently Zoogah et al. (2015) presented a typology of organizational effectiveness indicators that emerge from two dimensions – period (short-term versus long-term) and context (internal versus external). Those outcomes do result from organizational change. For example, productivity, innovation, and profitability, which are short-term outcomes, can result from the change model I have described. In addition, growth, competitive advantage, and viability result from change initiatives. Besides these internal outcomes, organizational change leads to external outcomes such as customer satisfaction in the short-term, as well as investor attraction, supplier welfare, and societal transformation in the long-term. Even though all the outcomes identified by Zoogah et al. (2015) are important, I highlight four outcomes (see Figure 5.1) that I consider more significant.

First, the change I discuss has the potential to increase innovation. It cannot be gainsaid that innovation is vital for the transformation of African societies, organizations, and individuals (Ekekwe, 2015). Research shows that management of companies contributes to national development (Bloom, Genakos, Sadun, and Van Reenen, 2012). Innovation is often the desiderated outcome underlying change initiatives (Poole and Van de Ven, 2004). In Africa "innovation combines smart, economical responses with bold high-tech solutions" (Anderson et al., 2016: 22) because innovative systems that are adopted to transform organizational operations invariably spill across to other sectors, up to governments and nations and down to individuals (Adesida, Karuri-Sebina, and Resende-Santos, 2016). For example, cellphone technology system M-Pesa, which was initially used to enable Safaricom to effectively engage its operations, has resulted in the spread of the innovation to farming (harnessing earth, wind, and fire), health (fighting back against HIV/AIDS and Ebola), education (learning partnerships), finance (transfer or payment of money), employment (information about job availability), culture (filmmaking on a shoestring budget), and media (video and news dissemination) (Anderson et al., 2016). It has also transformed the lives of individuals through income generation, employment, and education (Gikunda, Abura, and Njeru, 2014; Prashaant and Sharma, 2015).

Second, organizational change leads to a number of advantages. In this chapter, I focus on two – competitive and cooperative. For a long time competitive advantage was prominent among organization scholars, beginning with Porter's (1980) five forces model and Barney's (1991) extension to sustained competitive advantage via the resource-based view. However, since the beginning of the 21st century, competitive advantage has been viewed as insufficient for optimizing outcomes (Lei, Slocum, and Pitts, 1997; Skrabec, 1999). This is because of the increasing use of cooperative ventures or strategic alliances by companies to minimize cost, increase learning, and improve innovation (Zoogah, 2012). In other words, cooperative advantage is equally important as competitive advantage Studies show that collaboration yields more gains for the actors in the endeavor than competition (Zaheer and Venkatraman, 1994). Zoogah (2012) defines "cooperative advantage as the advantage that is associated with working in concert with others and developing capacities to connect individual efforts which harness resources and yield outcomes beyond what individual organizations could achieve" (p. 116). Further, Zoogah (2008) contends that the focus on competitive advantage which grew out of an individualistic culture in which actors (i.e., individuals, groups, and organizations) are socialized to compete for advantages (i.e., gain outcomes, dominance, and power) has to be substituted for cooperative advantage in collectivist cultures, such as those in Africa, where actors are socialized to cooperate for advantage. African organizations can harness both competitive and cooperative advantages consistent with the environment dynamics – influence of foreign companies from Western individualist cultures and the cultural attributes of Africa – to provide them superior positions.

Third, I propose that organizational change leads to diversification outcomes. Diversification generally refers to the expansion of a company outside a specific industry and has several components, including customer, product, location, system, and technology (Ramanujam, 1987). While the first three are within the control of African organizations, the latter two seem to be uncontrollable because of the limited capabilities and resource deprivation (Jones and Blunt, 1993). Some companies can diversify internationally by ensuring that a share of foreign operations (sales, assets, subsidiaries, or profit) is included within their business portfolio. Of course, this is limited to medium and large companies. For small companies, customer diversification is possible, particularly for those in the public sector. Diversification by product seems to be the easiest in Africa because of the low sophistication of clientele and markets. Customers tend not to discriminate purchases based on product attributes such as quality, price, etc. (Arnold and Quelch, 1998).

In addition to organizational outcomes, societal outcomes often result from change, particularly in state-owned enterprises (Jones and Blunt, 1993). In arguing for high-impact management research in Africa, Zoogah et al. (2015) argued that meaningful research can solve social and technical problems in Africa. Consistent with that view, I argue that change can contribute to societal transformation, human development, and subjective well-being. Given that innovations seep into society (Anderson et al., 2016), change that yields exemplary or best practices can be adopted to transform society. More generally, change can help resolve the "African problem" manifested in the multitude of challenges that range from socio-cultural, regulatory, technological, and governance (The Economist, 2011) to transform African societies.

Social problems which arise from the social environment – the patterns of normative interactions among individuals and groups (Blumer, 1971; Spector, 1987) – can be resolved with resultant change initiatives. Initiatives by organizations to root out or neutralize corruption may be transferred to the national level to resolve societal corruption, which is deeply entrenched or cancerous in Africa in the public sector (Mbaku, 2004, 2007; Dia, 1996). In addition, technical problems which arise from the technological environment, the context in which novel processes, improvements in techniques, and technical developments and knowledge manifest (Chang, Kim, Song, and Lee, 2015), can also be resolved through change initiatives. Some scholars contend that the African dummy is partly a function of technological constraints (Collier, 2007). The extant innovations in cell phones which have contributed to improvement in health, education, farming, finance, and culture attests to the positive influence of change initiatives. The M-Pesa technology platform has revolutionized lending and funding in the informal sectors of Africa; it emerged from a change initiative of Vodafone through its Safaricom operations in 2007 (Anderson et al., 2016).

Human development manifests through educational structures, training, internships, and continuous learning. Wilson and Gapsiso (2014) suggest that achievement of the millennium development goals (MDG), which were designed to promote socio-economic well-being, requires not only knowledge and skills, which can be achieved through e-learning, for example, but also organizational systems such as best practices. Further, by developing their employees through change initiatives, organizations indirectly contribute to human development at the national level because the skills and competencies from change initiatives improve the capabilities of the employees as citizens.

Subjective well-being (SWB), the degree to which individuals experience the "right things to do" for a happy, fulfilling, satisfactory, and high-quality life (Diener, Scollon,and Lucas, 2009), is the third national outcome. Since the beginning of the 21st century, there has been increased research examining subjective well-being across cultures. Research distinguishes individual subjective well-being from collective well-being (Diener, Lucas, Oishi, and Suh, 2002). Consequently, they have different predictors. At the societal level, improved human rights (e.g., civil and political rights), more equality (e.g., equality of income and educational access for both sexes), higher incomes, and individualism rather than collectivism (orientation towards personal versus group goals and desires) have been shown to affect people's ability to reach their goals, and thus predict a higher SWB across nations (Diener, Diener, and Diener, 1995; Oishi, Diener, Lucas, and Suh, 1999). In this chapter, I argue that change is another predictor of subjective well-being. Quality of life often results from economic well-being, which derives from meaningful employment. Given that change initiatives are intended to improve not only working conditions, it is likely they could result in improved productivity that emerges at the national level to affect quality of life. The high level of economic deprivation in Africa suggest that changes that result in improved employment outcomes can also improve the quality of life of not only the individual employees, but their extended relations and family members. These outcomes are likely in state parastatals which tend to dominate industries in African economies (Kiggundu, 1989). Further, productive well-being, which contributes to subjective well-being, also results from organizational changes that lead to human capital development. Research shows that African countries with high human resources development tend to have high productive well-being (Zoogah, 2016).

In sum, change depends on factors at the organizational, national, and supranational levels. To the extent that the change manifests in a pattern consistent with a murmuration, it is likely to lead to outcomes for the organization and the society in which the organization is based.

Discussion

Less than a decade ago Africa was believed to be the next center of global focus because of the growth trajectories of vibrant economies such as Botswana, Mauritius, and Rwanda. Underneath the foundation, however, were several major problems that impeded sustainable individual, organizational, and national development. The portrait is one where change is driven by a multiplex of factors and functions more like a murmuration than a discrete event characterized by one factor. As I argued above, change in Africa fits more of a complex system that combines dualities, dialectics, and flows. While some dynamics are underneath but sometimes surge up, others stay on the surface but sometimes submerge. Thus, I present a model of change termed a murmuration model. It is a complex systems model of change (Dooley, 2004) that not only differs from others in the literature, but also seems consistent with the boom-burst-boom-burst cycles of Africa.

How can this model be empiricalized? Because it is based on the CAS platform, complexity techniques have to be used to study the model. Dooley (2004) discusses various methods and approaches to study complex changes. Such techniques can be applied to this model. In addition, murmuration techniques such as the scale-free correlation (Young et al., 2011) I mentioned earlier can also be used. One could also study the different aspects of the model (e.g., forms) using emergent and/or mapping techniques such as those in the business process literature (Biazzo, 2002; Kettinger, Teng, and Guha, 1997; Kuhn and Corman, 2003; Weber and Manning, 2001). For example, one could use mapping to investigate specific cases of change experienced by specific organizations or countries. Other methods include qualitative approaches such as descriptions or historical portrayals of the past, present, and future trajectories of the entities experiencing the change to provide meaningful insight. Nkomo and Kriek (2011), for example, use "leaders' life stories and the case research method to understand the leadership of change in 14 South African organizations" (p. 453). They "describe how leaders led the changes required to balance the imperatives emanating from South Africa's socio-political changes and return the country to the international business arena, as well as the challenges created by years of inequality and neglect of the socio-economic development of the majority of its population". Evident in their study is the multiplexity of factors influencing the change in organizations. Furthermore, network techniques are useful methods to investigate the murmuration model I describe. Networks are useful in complex, patterned events, situations, behaviors, attributes, etc. (Poole, 2004).

They are sometimes considered maps of interlinkages. In that regard, they can show not only the flow of the factors as the network shape changes but also the composition (dropping and joining behavior observed in murmurations).

The availability of all these techniques to study murmurations as complex phenomena suggests that the model I describe is not only meaningful, but also has practical relevance. It is meaningful to the extent that I can empirically demonstrate the triggers to change and the flow of change. Such knowledge will enable systems in Africa to improve. It will also help policy makers

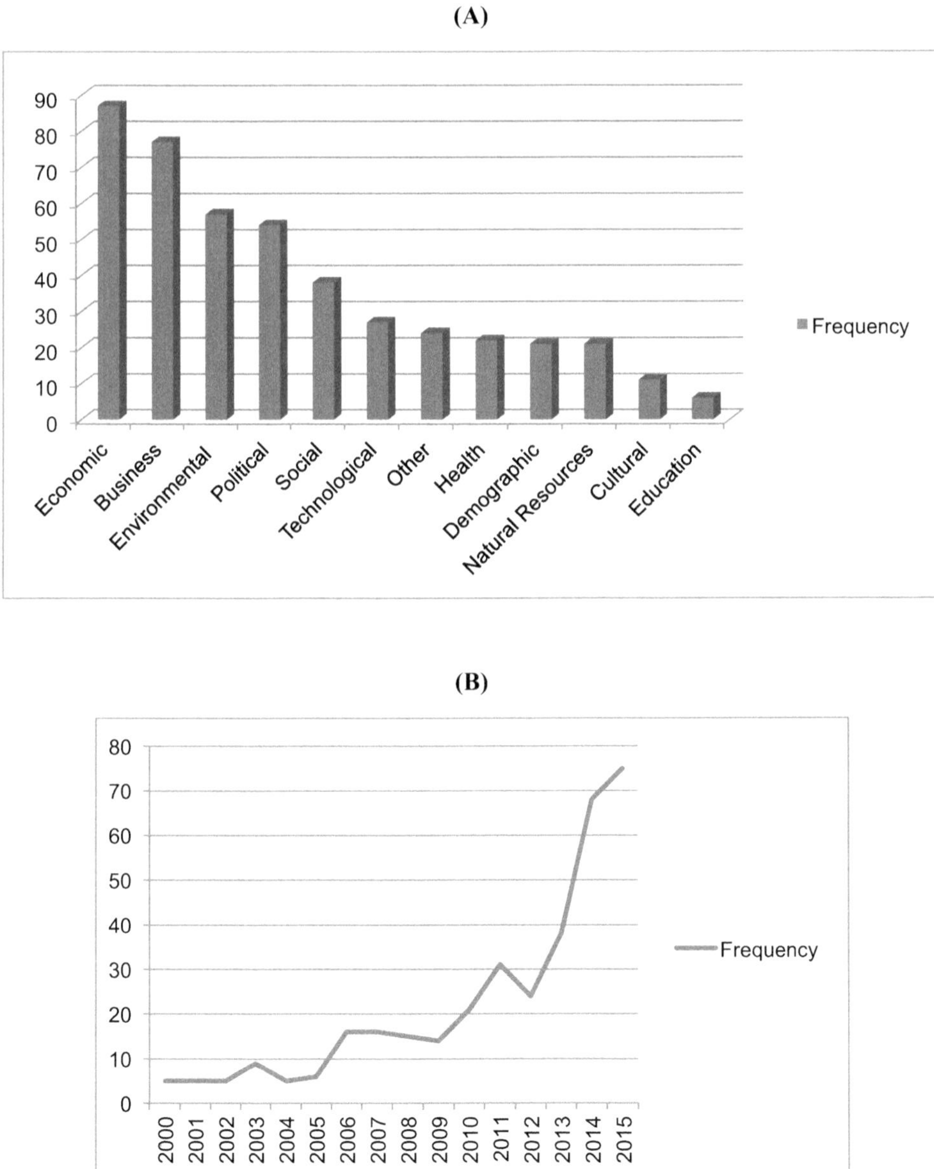

Figure Appendix 5.1 Results of change terms in the popular press by (a) dimension and (b) period

to facilitate industrial growth. In conclusion, I present a model that is unique to Africa. I hope future research will generate insight that helps improve systems in Africa.

Notes

1 We conducted a search of the change terms – Africa is changing, Africa rising, transformation in Africa, etc. – in twenty-four magazines and internet sources with a core or peripheral focus on Africa from 2000 to 2015 (see Appendix for terms). We found that the frequency of change increased between 2000 and 2015.
2 In the original version I had an illustration of several murmurations, but the publisher requested that I take them out due to copyright concerns.
3 However, since Poole and Van de Ven's (2004) edited book on organizational change and innovation, models depicting movement flux, movement, change, and transformation have been proposed.
4 Zoogah et al., (2015) note that the term "the Africa problem" has evolved with different meanings. The evolution of the term is similar to the murmuration depicted in this chapter.
5 Other factors that may account for the strength or weakness of the foundation include colonial network ties, founders' value systems, and cultural orientations. For simplicity of the typology, we focus on only the two dimensions – historical experience and tribal integration or segmentation.
6 http://mg.co.za/article/2004-03-12-the-difficult-birth-of-anglogold-ashanti

References

Abdulraheem, I., Mordi, C., Ojo, I. S., and Ajonbadi, H. (2013) Outcomes of planned organisational change in the Nigerian public sector: Insights from the Nigerian higher education institutions. *Economic Insights – Trends and Challenges*, 2(1): 26–37.
Adeniji, A. A., Osibanjo, O. A., and Abiodun, A. J. (2013) Organizational change and human resource management interventions: An investigation of the Nigerian banking industry. *Serbian Journal of Management*, 8(2): 139–154.
Adesida, O., Karuri-Sebina, G., and Resende-Santos, J. (2016). Innovation Africa—Looking Forward. In Innovation Africa: Emerging Hubs of Excellence (pp. 427-449). Emerald Group Publishing Limited. London, UK.
Anderson et al. (2016). Frontline: Innovative Africa. *The Africa Report.* Retrieved from http://www.theafricareport.com/North-Africa/frontline-innovative-africa.html. Accessed on April 9, 2017.
Anderson, P. (1999) Perspective: Complexity theory and organization science. *Organization Science*, 10(3): 216–232.
Arnold, D. J., and Quelch, J. A. (1998) New strategies in emerging economies. *Sloan Management Review*, 40(1): 7–20.
Ayittey, G. B. N. (2006) *Indigenous African Institutions.* NY: Transnational Publishers,Inc.
Barnett, W. P., and Carroll, G. R. (1995) Modeling internal organizational change. *Annual Review of Sociology*, 217–236.
Barney, J. (1991) Firm resources and sustained competitive advantage. *Journal of Management*, 17(1): 99–120.
Bergson, A. (1992) Communist economic efficiency revisited. *The American Economic Review*, 82(2): 27–30.
Biazzo, S. (2002) Process mapping techniques and Organisational analysis: Lessons from sociotechnical system theory. *Business Process Management Journal*, 8(1): 42–52.
Bloom, N., Genakos, C., Sadun, R., and Van Reenen, J. (2012) Management practices across firms and countries. *The Academy of Management Perspectives*, 26(1): 12–33.
Blumer, H. (1971) Social problems as collective behavior. *Social Problems*, 18(3): 298–306.
Blunt, P., and Jones, M. L. (1991a) Editorial: Human resource management in developing countries. *Journal of the History of Economic Thought*, 2(1): 3–5.
Blunt, P., and Jones, M. L. (1991b) Management development in the third world. *The Journal of Management Development*, 10(6): 4–6.
Burchardt, M. (2012) Faith-based humanitarianism: Organizational change and everyday meanings in South Africa. *Sociology of Religion*, srs068.
Cavagna, A., Cimarelli, A., Giardina, I., Parisi, G., Santagati, R., Stefanini, F., and Viale, M. (2010) Scale-free correlations in starling flocks. *Proceedings of the National Academy of Sciences*, 107(26): 11865–11870.

Chang, H., Kim, J., Song, K., and Lee, K. (2015, April 26) *Imitation to Innovation: Late Movers' Catch-up Strategy and Technological Leadership Change*. Columbia Business School Research Paper No. 15–51. Retrieved from SSRN http://ssrn.com/abstract=2599140 or http://dx.doi.org/10.2139/ssrn.2599140

Charles, S. D. (1995) The geopolitics of Rwandan resettlement: Uganda and Tanzania. *A Journal of Opinion*, 23(2): 54.

Chia, R. (1999) A 'rhizomic' model of organizational change and transformation: Perspective from a metaphysics of change. *British Journal of Management*, 10(3): 209–227.

Chironga, M., Leke, A., Lund, S., and van Wamelen, A. (2011) Cracking the next growth market: Africa. *Harvard Business Review*, 89(5): 1–7.

Collier, P. (2007) The bottom billion. *Economic Review Deddington*, 25(1): 17.

Collier, P., and Hoeffler, A. (2002) On the incidence of civil war in Africa. *Journal of Conflict Resolution*, 46(1): 13–28.

Curtin, P. (1975) *Economic Change in Pre-Colonial Africa*. Madison, WI: University Wisconsin Press, 375.

Diener, E., Lucas, R. E., Oishi, S., and Suh, E. M. (2002). Looking up and looking down: Weighting good and bad information in life satisfaction judgments. *Personality and Social Psychology Bulletin*, 28(4), 437–445.

Deleuze, G., and Guattari, F. (1988) *A Thousand Plateaus: Capitalism and Schizophrenia*. New York: Bloomsbury Publishing

Dia, M. (1996) *Africa's Management in the 1990s and Beyond: Reconciling Indigenous and Transplanted Institutions*. Washington DC: World Bank Publications.

Diener, E., Diener, M., and Diener, C. (1995) Factors predicting the subjective well-being of nations. *Journal of Personality and Social Psychology*, 69(5): 851.

Diener, E., Scollon, C. N., and Lucas, R. E. (2009). The evolving concept of subjective well-being: The multifaceted nature of happiness. In Assessing well-being (pp. 67-100). Springer, Dordrecht.

Dooley, K. J. (2004) Complexity science models of organizational change and innovation. *Handbook of Organizational Change and Innovation*, 354–373.

Economist. (2011, December 3) *The Hopeful Continent: Africa Rising*. Retrieved from www.economist.com/node/21541015

Ekekwe, N. (2015) Improving Innovation in Africa. *Harvard Business Review*. Retrieved August 30, 2016 from https://hbr.org/2015/02/improving-innovation-in-africa

Englebert, P. (2000) Pre-colonial institutions, post-colonial states, and economic development in tropical Africa. *Political Research Quarterly*, 53(1): 7–36.

Gallagher, R., and Appenzeller, T. (1999) Complex systems. *Science*, 284(5411): 79–109.

Gikunda, R. M., Abura, G. O., and Njeru, S. G. (2014). Socio-economic effects of MPESA adoption on the livelihoods of people in bureti sub county, Kenya. *International Journal of Academic Research in Business and Social Sciences*, 4(12), 348.

Herbst, J. (2000) Economic incentives, natural resources and conflict in Africa. *Journal of African Economies*, 9(3): 270–294.

Hintjens, H. M. (1999) Explaining the 1994 genocide in Rwanda. *The Journal of Modern African Studies*, 37(2): 241–286.

Holland, J. H. (1995) *Hidden Order: How Adaptation Builds Complexity*. Retrieved from www.wired.com/2011/11/starling-flock/

Hunt, G. (2013) *In Murmurations, Starlings Have a Darwinian Dance Partner*. Retrieved February 9, 2018 from www.allaboutbirds.org/in-murmurations-starlings-have-a-darwinian-dance-partner/

Jones, M. L., and Blunt, P. (1993) Organizational development and change in Africa (1). *International Journal of Public Administration*, 16(11): 1735–1765.

Jones, T. M. (1991) Ethical decision making by individuals in organizations: An issue-contingent model. *Academy of Management Review*, 16(2): 366–395.

Kettinger, W. J., Teng, J. T., and Guha, S. (1997) Business process change: A study of methodologies, techniques, and tools. *MIS Quarterly*, 55–80.

Kiggundu, M. N. (1989) *Managing Organizations in Developing Countries: An Integrative Approach*. Boulder, Colorado: Lynne Rienner Publishers.

Kiggundu, M. N. (1991) The challenges of management development in sub-Saharan Africa. *Journal of Management Development*, 10(6): 32–47.

Kudonoo, E. C. (2013) Organization development consulting in sub-Saharan Africa: The little things that make a big difference. *Organization Development Journal*, 31(1): 9.

Kuhn, T., and Corman, S. R. (2003) The emergence of homogeneity and heterogeneity in knowledge structures during a planned organizational change. *Communication Monographs*, 70(3): 198–229.

Lei, D., Slocum, J. W., and Pitts, R. A. (1997) Building cooperative advantage: Managing strategic alliances to promote organizational learning. *Journal of World Business*, 32(3): 203–223.

Lewis, W. A. (1954) Economic development with unlimited supplies of labour. *The Manchester School*, 22(2): 139–191.

Malunga, C. (2004) Using African proverbs in organisational capacity building. *Cell*, 8: 868624.

Mamdani, M. (1996) *Citizen and Subject: Contemporary Africa and the Legacy of Late Colonialism*. Princeton, NJ: Princeton University Press.

Mazrui, A. A. (ed.) (1993) *General History of Africa, Volume VIII*. New York: UNESCO.

Mbaku, J. M. (2004) *Institutions and Development in Africa*. Trenten, New Jersey: Africa World Press.

Mbaku, J. M. (2007) Institutions and poverty alleviation in Africa. *African and Asian Studies*, 6(1–2): 107–134.

McKinsey Global Institute. (2010) *Lions on the Move: The Progress and Potential of African Economies*. Retrieved from https://www.mckinsey.com/mgi/overview. Accessed on June 25, 2017.

Michalopoulos, S., and Papaioannou, E. (2015) On the ethnic origins of African development: Chiefs and precolonial political centralization. *The Academy of Management Perspectives*, 29(1): 32–71.

Mintzberg, H. (1989) *Mintzberg on Management: Inside Our Strange World of Organizations*. New York: Simon & Schuster.

Montgomery, D. (1989) *The Fall of the House of Labor: The Workplace, the State, and American Labor Activism, 1865–1925*. Cambridge: Cambridge University Press.

Nkomo, S. M., and Kriek, D. (2011) Leading organizational change in the 'new' South Africa. *Journal of Occupational and Organizational Psychology*, 84(3): 453–470.

Oishi, S., Diener, E. F., Lucas, R. E., and Suh, E. M. (1999) Cross-cultural variations in predictors of life satisfaction: Perspectives from needs and values. *Personality and Social Psychology Bulletin*, 25(8): 980–990.

Poole, M. S., and Van de Ven, A. H. (Eds.). (2004) *Handbook of Organizational Change and Innovation*. Oxford: Oxford University Press.

Porter, M. E. (1980) *Competitive Strategy: Techniques for Analyzing Industry and Competitors*. Boston, Massachusetts: Free Press.

Prashaant, A., and Sharma, N. (2015). Vodafone's M-Pesa-A Mobile Wallet Revolution. *FIIB Business Review*, 4(2), 26–29.

Ramanujam, V. (1987) Diversification and performance: A reexamination using a new two-dimensional conceptualization of diversity in firms. *Academy of Management Journal*, 30(2): 380–393.

Rotberg, R. (2013) *Africa Emerges: Consummate Challenges, Abundant Opportunities*. Hoboken, New Jersey: John Wiley & Sons

Seo, M., Putnam, L. L., and Bartunek, J. M. (2004) Dualities and tensions of planned organizational change. *Handbook of Organizational Change and Innovation*, 73–107.

Serres, M. (1982) The origin of language: Biology, information theory and thermodynamics. *Oxford Literary Review*, 5(1\2): 113–124.

Sklar, R. L. (1993) The African frontier for political science. In R. Bates, V.Y. Mudimbe and J. O'Barr (Eds.), *Africa and the Disciplines* (pp. 83–110). Chicago, IL: University of Chicago Press.

Skrabec, Q. R. (1999) Cooperative advantage – A new measure of performance. *National Productivity Review*, 18(2): 69–73.

Spector, P. E. (1987) Method variance as an artifact in self-reported affect and perceptions at work: Myth or significant problem? *Journal of Applied Psychology*, 72(3): 438–443.

Sulamoyo, D. (2011) *Ubuntu as a Cultural Strategy for OD*. Presentation at the Annual Linkage OD Summit, Chicago, IL.

Torrington, D., Weightman, J., and Johns, K. (1989) *Effective Management: People and Organization*. London: Prentice-Hall.

Ugwuegbu, D. C. E. (2001) *The Psychology of Management in African Organizations*. Westport, CT: Quorum Books/Greenwood Publishing Group.

UNCTAD. (1996) *Globalization and Liberalization: Effects of International Economic Relations on Poverty*. New York, NY and Geneva: UNCTAD.

Van de Ven, A. H. (1987) Review essay: Four requirements for processual analysis. In *The Management of Strategic Change*. Oxford: Blackwell, 330–341.

Van de Ven, A. H., and Poole, M. S. (1995) Explaining development and change in organizations. *Academy of Management Review*, 20(3): 510–540.

Verwimp, P. (2003) Testing the double-genocide thesis for central and southern Rwanda. *Journal of Conflict Resolution*, 47(4): 423–442.

Weber, P. S., and Manning, M. R. (2001) Cause maps, sense making, and planned organizational change. *The Journal of Applied Behavioral Science*, 37(2): 227–251.

Whitehead, A. N. (1985) *Symbolism: Its Meaning and Effect.* New York, NY: Fordham University Press.
Whitehead, R. B. (1929) The portrait medals and zodiacal coins of the Emperor Jahāngīr. *The Numismatic Chronicle and Journal of the Royal Numismatic Society*, 9(33): 1–25.
Wilson, J., and Gapsiso, N. D. (2014) Achieving the millennium development goals in Africa: Harnessing e-learning potentials. *Developing Country Studies*, 4(15): 28–34.
Yaeger, T. F., and Sorensen, P. F. (2011) OD in Africa. *OD Practitioner*, 43(3): 50–54.
Young, W., Ferguson, S., Brault, S., and Craig, C. (2011) Assessing and training standing balance in older adults: A novel approach using the 'Nintendo Wii' Balance Board. *Gait & Posture*, 33(2): 303–305.
Zaheer, A., and Venkatraman, N. (1994) Determinants of electronic integration in the insurance industry: An empirical test. *Management Science*, 40(5): 549–566.
Zoogah, D. B. (2008) African business research: A review of studies published in the Journal of African Business and a framework for enhancing future studies. *Journal of African Business*, 9(1): 219–255.
Zoogah, D. B. (2012) A cooperative advantage: An alternative informed by institutional theory. *Industrial and Organizational Psychology*, 5(1): 116–119.
Zoogah, D. B. (2018) Ethnos oblige, inequality, and economic deprivation. Presented at the Africa Academy of Management Biennial Conference Addis Ababa, Ethiopia.
Zoogah, D. B. (2016) Tribal diversity and collective productivity: The intervening mechanisms of social inclusion, human resource development and tribal identity. In A. Klarsfeld, E. S. Ng, L. A. E. Booysen, L. C. Christiansen and B. Kuvaas (Eds.), *Research Handbook of International and Comparative Perspectives on Diversity Management.* London, UK: Edward Elgar.
Zoogah, D. B., and Nkomo, S. (2013). Management research in Africa: Past, present and future possibilities. In Lituchy, T., Punnett, B., Puplampu, B. (Eds.), *Management in Africa: Macro and micro perspectives* (pp. 9–31). New York, NY: Routledge.
Zoogah, D. B., Peng, M. W., and Woldu, H. (2015) Institutions, resources, and organizational effectiveness in Africa. *The Academy of Management Perspectives*, 29(1): 7–31.
Zoogah, D. B., Zoogah, R. B., and Dalaba-Roohi, F. (2015) Riding the tide: Management in Africa and the role of high-impact research. *Africa Journal of Management*, 1(1), 27–53.

6

Ubuntu as essential inspiration for more humanistic organizational management

Mzamo P. Mangaliso, Nomazengele A. Mangaliso, Bradford J. Knipes, Howard Jean-Denis and Leah Z. B. Ndanga

Introduction

Many emerging market countries, particularly in Africa, have experienced low rates of economic development and human progress. These have been attributed to the strategic failure of leadership and management to unlock workforce potential (Bloom, Lemos, Sadun, Scur, and Van Reenen, 2014; Cunha, Fortes, Rodrigues, and Rego, 2015; Zoogah, Peng, and Woldu, 2015; Kamoche, 1997; Walumbwa, Avolio, and Aryee, 2011). Over the years, organizational theorists have noted that the practice of management is largely culture-bound, and that it may be the failure to recognize and adapt corporate strategies to indigenous worldviews and cultures that is the root cause of the problems (Ahiauzu, 1986a; Blunt, 1995 Hofstede, 1980, 1993; Javidan, House, Dorfman, Hanges, and De Luque, 2006; Kras, 1989; Mangaliso, 1992; Ngambi, 2011). As the competitive landscape becomes increasingly global, local (indigenous) values will increasingly play a prominent role in management (Mangaliso, 1993; Ngambi, 2011). Success will require the ability to reel in other cultural points of reference and navigate across the cultural differences (Dayasindhu, 2002; Hofstede, 1980; Javidan et al., 2006; Mangaliso, 1993). The general consensus in the extant literature is that at every stage of the strategy-making process, including the management of change, culture influences the decision-maker's behavior (Hofstede, 1980; Redding, 1980; Schneider, 1989).

Despite acknowledging the importance of the worldviews of indigenous people, until fairly recently, the management discourse has largely been reluctant to incorporate them, allowing managerial thought and practice to be predominantly informed by western[1] theoretical frameworks (Weber, 1947; March and Simon, 1958; Barnard, 1938; Chandler, 1962). This is notwithstanding a number of scholars noting that such theoretical frameworks are, in most cases, inadequate for addressing the cultures and conditions of the developing world (Adler, 1983; Boyacigiller and Adler, 1991; Beugelsdijk, de Groot, Linders, and Slangen, 2004; Korten, 1981; Mithas and Whitaker, 2007; Mudambi and Swift, 2011; Narayanan and Fahey, 2005). In this chapter, we adopt the position that managerial practices must be discursively reconstructed to ensure their contextual relevance to local epistemologies. In other words, they must be made relevant to the social context in which the practices are considered acceptable and desirable, instead of satisfying the mandates of western-based management 'truths' described above (Foucault, 1970; Lincoln and Denzin, 1994). The chapter will be divided as follows. We will first discuss the prerequisites for effective management in Africa. This will be followed by a discussion of Ubuntu as a defining African philosophy. This will be followed by a presentation of a model that shows the connection between selected core values and the management variables that mediate performance outcomes in African organizations. The discussion will lead to a set of propositions linking these variables to desired performance outcomes, followed by a discussion of the implications and our concluding comments.

Prerequisites for effective management in Africa

Effective management is predicated upon the creation of a system that supports the simultaneous fulfillment of both personal and corporate goals (Locke and Latham, 1990). In the era of globalization, another imperative has emerged that presents a challenge to corporations operating in societies that are different from western societies. That imperative is to create an environment where corporate goals and culture are harmonized with the culture and aspirations of the host nation. For instance, western corporate culture emphasizes individualism, competition, and efficiency. But these attributes present potential conflict with many indigenous cultures where the emphasis is on cooperation, familyhood, and equality. Considering that sub-Saharan Africa is predominantly populated by people who uphold these values, the fact that the principles and canons that guide the practice of management in the workplace are still predominantly of western philosophical origin continues to be a challenge to management. There may be many reasons for this. The most dominant of these might be the legacy of colonialism that still hovers like a cloud over Africa. In most anthropological accounts given by western writers, the dominant mode by which the African continent has been comprehended and represented has been nomological, non-reflexive, non-inclusive, and etic, lacking in any serious, systematic dialogue with the Africans themselves (Nyamnjoh, 2012).

Western thought also pervades the practice of management in Africa because the training most managers receive across the continent – from The Gambia in the west, to Kenya in the east, and to South Africa in the south – has largely been based on western philosophical canons (Muwanga-Zake, 2009). Until recently, western scholarly writings have not seriously considered indigenous cultures in relation to how organizations are run. The dominance of western thought is also the result of the orientation programs which new employees undergo upon entrance into an organization. The management literature has either tacitly ignored, or, through editorial oversight, actually suppressed the influence of indigenous value systems and traditions. It is no surprise, therefore, that when one reads the management literature as it relates to Africa, one finds an abundance of writings that apply theories developed in the west to the practice of management in the African context. The main concern seems primarily to be with the instrumentality of western management ideas in Africa, and how well Africa performs against western-conceived metrics of managing. Among the most important reasons that Africa has appeared to lag behind in many measures of performance is that Africans have viewed western organizations as intrusions in their lifestyles, an extension of the original exploitation that westerners became associated with. Obviously, for firms that continue to operate in this mode, even if compliance is there, African employees will still harbor a degree of residual umbrage toward anything associated with those philosophies. To the extent that corporate goals and objectives are not seen to be in sync with the African goals and collective sense of purpose, employees will be reluctant to contribute.

A better approach would be one that seeks to consciously uncover and acknowledge phenomena in the African milieu, understand those phenomena in colloquial terms, and apply them in the daily management of organizations in Africa, in keeping with what Mudimbe (1988) has incisively referred to as the construction of an 'authentic African episteme' (p. 179). Philosophies similar to the ones discussed in this chapter may be manifest in other parts of the world. Our concern in this project is with understanding and explaining management in uniquely African ways and less about generalizability beyond Africa. We leave the issue of their broader generalizability for future study and exploration.

Ubuntu as a defining African philosophy

There is general consensus in the extant management literature that Ubuntu is an embodiment of a worldview and philosophy characteristic of most of sub-Saharan African people (Horwitz, 2009; Inyang, 2008; Kayuni and Tambulasi, 2012; Karsten and Illa, 2005; Khomba and Kangaude-Ulaya, 2013; Khoza, 2005; Mangaliso, 2001; Ncube, 2010; Sigger, Polak, and Pennik, 2010). Ubuntu captures the communality of human life and the collective obligation we all have for the preservation of human dignity. The central tenet of Ubuntu is articulated in the Xhosa aphorism, '*Umntu ngumntu ngabanye abantu*.' Literally the phrase translates to, 'A human being is a human being through other human beings,' which means that sharing the common bond of humanity is what defines us as humans. In fact, among Africans there is no worse ignominy than to be characterized as '*akangomntu*' (not a human being), literally being relegated to the status of a non-human. In recent years, the African worldview represented in Ubuntu has found increasing visibility in the scholarly management discourse. Most of these articles argue that with its emphasis on compassion and communality among actors, Ubuntu benefits the organizations that incorporate its principles and practices. Ubuntu has been discussed in a wide variety of social science disciplines, including human resource management (Blunt and Jones, 1997; Horwitz, 2009, 2015), leadership (Khoza, 2005; Ngambi, 2004; Walumbwa et al., 2011), psychology (Mkhize, 2004; Hanks, 2008; Washington, 2010), philosophy (Gyekye, 1997; Masolo, 2003; Nicolito, 2011; Ramose, 1999), theology (Mbiti, 1969; Mnyaka and Motlhabi, 2005; Setiloane, 1986), and business ethics (Taylor, 2014; Mkhize, 2008). Not surprisingly, Ubuntu is most often cited to understand leadership, ethics, HRM, team dynamics, and potential difficulties with globalization when MNCs operate in African countries in which it is embraced. The Ubuntu worldview has also been contrasted with western as well as Asian worldviews.

In management, Ubuntu is cited to explain the differences between the western and African cultures. However, some have taken issue with the characterization of Ubuntu as a Pan-African philosophy, or even that it is a uniquely African philosophy. They use as evidence the incredibly diverse sociocultural, linguistic, and historical composition of the continent, even if the discussion is limited only to sub-Saharan countries. We concur with the opposing view that it is erroneous and overly discriminatory to interpret this diversity as evidence of the absence of any shared, unifying characteristics of African culture (Gyekye, 1997; Mbiti, 1969). Considerable variation does exist across the countries of Europe, yet we are still able to distinguish a Pan-European character and culture. In the same way, there is an underlying African character, which resulted from its unique geographical, historical, cultural, and political experience (Ahiauzu, 1986a; Gyekye, 1997; Mbiti, 1969; Sithole, 1959). We also concur with these scholars that Africans can be identified by certain common characteristics in their way of life, and that there certainly is a clearly identifiable African thought system. The literature identifies several important attributes of the African thought-system as it relates to organizational behavior. The core values imbedded in the African worldview include the high aspiration for harmonious coexistence, a commitment to unity of the collective, honor and respect, and humility (see Figure 6.1). Their holistic view of life is supported by an ideology that balances the individual human as an integral part of

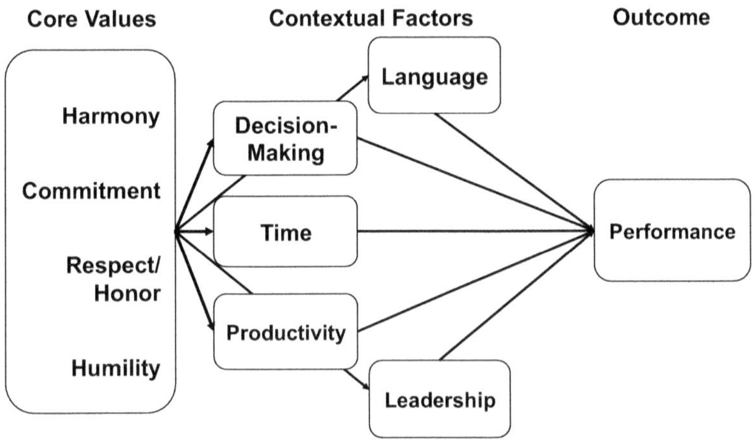

Figure 6.1 Diagram of Ubuntu-inspired change management

the community, connected to the spiritual world of ancestors, and living in harmony with the physical environment. This worldview has been continuously passed on to successive generations mainly through the oral tradition – proverbs, ballads, and legends – rather than through impersonal written histories (Ahiauzu, 1986a). Ubuntu values place a premium on the dignity of the person irrespective of race, gender, or creed. It is not in the purview of this chapter to assemble an exhaustive compendium of the foundations of Ubuntu. Instead, we will discuss a few of the essential characteristics that are regarded as the cardinal defining ideas in Ubuntu. The next section discusses the contextual factors underlying Ubuntu and their potential for influencing organizational performance outcomes. Figure 6.1 is a diagrammatic representation of the core and contextual variables that influence performance in African society.

Core values that drive management practice

Values are concepts or beliefs about desirable end states or behaviors that transcend specific situations, guide selection or evaluation of behavior or events, and are ordered by relative importance (Agle and Caldwell, 1999). The centrality of values under rapidly changing environmental conditions must be acknowledged and recognized, because of the role they play as stabilizing mechanism in the face of uncertainty. In a recent conversation, scholars noted the importance of understanding the role that subconscious goals and implicit attitudes and values must play in understanding the drivers of organizational performance.

This is where the assumption of applicability of values from one social setting to others becomes problematic. On one hand are the Anglo-Saxon organizational values, at the roots of which are the ideas of utilitarianism, market efficiency, innovation, entrepreneurship, individually-based tacit knowledge, and shareholder value maximization (Friedman, 1970; Mill, 1843; Smith, 1937; Schumpeter, 1911). In that context, humans are generally viewed as an individualistic, self-serving, opportunistic, and utility-maximizing species. In particular, in his seminal work, *The Wealth of Nations*, Smith (1937) advanced the notion that it is individual self-interest that ultimately serves the common good. In one of his most widely cited passages he observes that, 'It is not from the benevolence of the butcher, the brewer, or the baker that we expect our dinner, but from their regard to their own self-interest' (Smith, 1937: 14).

On the other hand, there are alternative values based on the centrality of the collective as a prerequisite for corporate success that are commonplace in many other parts of the world, where public discourse has long been very critical of the Euro-American values. In these societies, humans are also seen as prosocial and communal beings, whose choices and preferences are influenced not only by rationality, but also by compassion and emotional ties to others. An example is the lifetime employment commitment that characterized Japanese values for a long time, so that employee layoffs were the last thing to be considered (Ouchi, 1981). A central point of departure in this alternative paradigm is that altruism is the highest form of self-interest. That is, by serving others well, one ultimately serves one's own best interests. It is in that context that Ubuntu is regarded as a distinguishing value in Africa for its distinctive recognition of the common bond that binds all of humanity, and the fact that we can only be human together. The extant literature articulates a number of canons in Ubuntu that serve as guiding principles for the African worldview. These include the primacy of harmony and solidarity, reciprocity, respect for elders, collaboration, mutual concern, compassion, consultation, and consensus (Darley and Blankson, 2008; Khoza, 2011; Ramose, 2002, Mangaliso, 2001; Teffo, 1998). More recently, a great deal of research on Ubuntu has offered positive vantage points for revaluing African philosophies and translating them into management practices, most notably in the field of human relations (Horwitz, Kamoche, and Chew, 2002). For the purposes of this chapter, we will limit our discussion to four of these values: harmony, commitment, respect/honor, and humility.

Harmony

Harmony can be defined as a balanced combination of different parts or perspectives to form a consistent and orderly whole supported by trust, strong ties, a collective identity and commonly shared values (Lewicki and Bunker, 1996). In the African context, harmony is closely associated with the related values of solidarity, synchronicity, and empathy (Mangaliso, 2001; Murithi, 2006). Research has shown that strong within-group ties are actually beneficial to organizational harmony, especially if balanced by a number of strong ties linking the various groups together with external stakeholders (Nelson, 1989). Empirical research has demonstrated that harmony and concern influence the level of employee participation, which suggests that a high level of managerial trust in employees is reflected in high employee participation (Tzafrir, 2005). Recognition of harmony can be acknowledged when the firm's management, employees, and external stakeholders move together cohesively toward similar goals. Within many organizations, power and bureaucracy take precedence over negotiations and important decisions. This prevents the emphasis on harmony, which Ubuntu management helps to establish. When used in connection with human resource management, the concept of Ubuntu (or humanness) means that a person is seen not as an individual, but as part of a collective society (Horwitz et al., 2002). Therefore, by accepting Ubuntu, managers can preserve harmony by bringing key stakeholders from divergent groups together to reconcile various perspectives, in face-to-face, consensus-building meetings. In Africa, a sense of community is critical for managers as they traverse organizational boundaries. Comprehensive humaneness should be embraced throughout, and especially in strategic management, because of its global consequences.

Commitment

Scholars in the past have defined commitment in various ways. Some see it as the willingness of an employee to exert high levels of effort on behalf of the organization, a strong desire to stay with the organization, and an acceptance of its major goals and values (Porter and Lawler, 1968);

some view it as the intention to work toward its goals, and the willingness to give loyalty to the organization (Sheldon, 1971; Kantor, 1968); others perceive it as a coalescence between the individual and the organization that generates a sense of individual conviction and a willingness to devote increased effort to the organization (Barnard, 1938). Mowday, Steers, and Porter (1979: 228) define organizational commitment as 'the relative strength of an individual's identification with and involvement in a particular organization.'

The running theme in these definitions is a conception of commitment as a psychological bond formed between people and the organizations for which they work. It is a normative motivational process clearly distinct from instrumental-utilitarian approaches to the explanation of work behavior (Weiner, 1982). In general, when people see their personal values reflected in organizational values, their identification with the organization, hence their commitment, rises. Organizational commitment also reflects the emotional attachment of the worker with the values, goals, missions, and perceived support received from the employing organization (Landsman, 2008; Jaskyte and Lee, 2009). There is an enormous body of research that has focused on the antecedents of commitment. Most of it has been conducted on private sector companies, and the antecedents studied have largely been job-related factors such as job satisfaction, job scope, rewards, stress, need for achievement, etc. (Reichers, 1985). Relatively few studies have related commitment to group norms, belongingness or identification with the group, personal importance within the group, and group well-being. These are the antecedent factors that we consider most important in African communities. Some western researchers state that African culture is inhospitable to organizational development because the culture itself discourages innovation, individualism, and openness, valued elements.

Respect/honor

In Ubuntu, any human being is regarded as a dignified individual deserving of all the courtesies and respect that should be accorded humans. In Southern African languages respect is characterized as *isithunzi*, which literally means a 'shadow.' But it refers to the quality in humans that invokes the right to be valued and respected. Respect is manifest in all communication – in the choice of words, vocal tone, in name referents, and in body language or gestures. Addressing someone by their clan name is one common way of showing respect, as, for example, the late President Mandela being referred to as 'Madiba,' his clan name, which is supposed to be the name of the forebear who started the clan. An extra amount of respect is expected when dealing with elder members of the community not only because of their seniority, but also due to their familiarity with community traditions and mores, and their temporal proximity to the ancestors. It is worth noting that a similar level of respect can also be found in reverence to figures of authority. This is congruent with what western scholars of organizational bureaucracy have noted, that this respect is directed not necessarily just to the incumbent, but to the position of authority he or she occupies (Barnard, 1938; Weber, 1947). Several scholars have noted respect and civility toward others is a value that sustains human society (Mnyaka and Mothlabi, 2005; Von Bergen et al., 2012). It follows that when employees are treated with civility and dignity, they will respond by showing greater commitment to organizational goals, which will go a long way toward creating an atmosphere of mutual respect and an increased sense of company identity among employees (Mangaliso, 2001).

Humility

Several definitions have been advanced for the term humility. Merriam-Webster's (2011) dictionary defines humility as having a modest or low view of one's own importance. The etymological roots of the term can be traced to the Latin word *humilis*, which means 'from the earth,' 'grounded,' or 'of low rank' (Bhattacharya, Chatterjee, and Basu, 2017). The related Latin word 'humus' means 'earth.' Humility involves modesty about one's accomplishments on issues, and even a denial of the significance of one's contributions to the success of one's team and an ascription of those contributions to other team members. In the African annals, humility is defined as that which, once you say you have, you just lost. In colloquial terms, humility is frequently seen as a weakness and equated with having low regard of oneself. Yet humility is the antithesis of this stereotypical caricature of a stooped-shouldered, self-deprecating, and weak-willed person only too willing to yield to the wishes of others (Tangney, 2000). A humble person can be assertive and yet be without arrogance, capable of keeping her talents and accomplishments in perspective and, at the same time, accepting her own imperfections (Emmons, 1998; Payne, Sandage, Rupert, Devor, and Bronstein, 2015; Tangney, 2000). In the African context humility is an imperative, almost canonical, in leadership efficacy. To adopt an attitude of humility sets a tone to all stakeholders – internal as well as external stakeholders – that management is open to considering their preferences seriously. This canon is an essential link to the creation of harmonious relationships, and to promoting the feelings of belonging which are at the core of Ubuntu (Mangaliso, 2001). Others have argued that, in spite of the consequential impact it has on follower behavior, the extant leadership literature has overlooked the pivotal role of humility (Nielsen, Marrone, and Slay, 2010). Drawing on the extant literature, these authors defined humility as a desirable personal quality that is an understanding of oneself through awareness of personal identities, strengths, and limitations, in addition to having perspective of the self's relationship with others (Nielsen et al., 2010: 34).

Contextual variables underlying Ubuntu

Ubuntu-mediated management operates through a distinctive set of values and beliefs that manifest themselves in a number of contextual factors to affect organizational outcomes. First are what is considered to be generally held Ubuntu core values in which behavior is embedded. Examples in the literature include harmonious relationships, commitment to working together, honor and trust, and humility and kindness (Makgoba, 2016; Mashele, 2013; Masolo, 2003; Mkabela, 2014). These values serve an informative and facilitative function for the contextual factors that drive performance. Because of their performative function, contextual factors strongly influence human agency at all levels – the personal, proxy, and/or collective levels. In the African worldview, the last two are important. Since proxy-level agency relies on the 'other' acting on one's behest to secure desired outcomes, honor and trust provide assurance (Bandura, 2002). In Africa in particular, individuals are part of closely knit collectives, and therefore individual level agency tends to express itself in the expectations of the collective, with a strong reciprocal relationship between the two levels. Socially mediated agency steps in to play a greater role of interceding on behalf of the individual, especially during times of need. Socially mediated agency as described above is different in western societies, which are well-known for the value they place on individual freedoms relatively independently of social constraint (Bandura, 2002; Nisbett, Peng, Choi, and Norenzayan, 2001).

Due to the confines of space and time, we have limited our set of contextual factors to language, decision-making, time, productivity, and leadership. In the normal running of organizations, a deeper understanding of culturally embedded communication is vital. A confluence of the aforementioned core values and contextual factors plays a significant role in the resultant performance outcomes and overall employee satisfaction. Table 6.1 outlines distinctions between African and western philosophies, and shows the implications of the Ubuntu philosophy to managing change in Africa.

Table 6.1 African and western systems: Implications for change in Africa

Element	*African*	*Western*	*Implications*
Language and communication	Preferred communication is based on the oral tradition. Context-specific meaning of words. Oratory valorized.	Reliance on written communication. Content-specific meaning of words. Written communication.	Choice of oral, face-to-face communication is preferred, especially for changes that will have a significant impact on employees.
Decision-making	Humanistic decisions arrived at by consensus. The process is circular. Vision tends to be polyocular. Dissenters compensated for at some future time.	Rationally based decisions, usually by majority. Winner takes all. The process is linear. Unity of vision is typical. Monocular.	Considering multiple perspectives for decisions reached by consensus is more time consuming, but assures long-run commitment.
Time	Not a finite commodity, it is the healer; allow enough of it for important issues before arriving at a decision.	Time is money – a strategic commodity that must be used frugally.	Taking extra time for deliberations and allowing employees to air their views leads to more widely supported decisions.
Age and leadership	An ongoing process of maturing and acquiring wisdom. Older people are respected. Gray hair is a sign of wisdom.	Age beyond a certain point becomes a negative. Senior citizens regarded as 'dead wood.'	The wisdom that comes with maturation and age is venerated. Successful leadership will combine professional knowledge, social skills, and appreciation of African values.
Productivity	Optimal productivity is the goal. Solidarity, working together in social harmony are important. Rewards are shared and so is suffering in times of hardship.	Maximizing productivity is the guiding philosophy. In the workplace economic considerations supersede social considerations.	Harmonious working relations and a positive work environment are predicates for a highly productive workforce.

The next section discusses each of the contextual factors and ends by suggesting propositions that point to researchable areas in which African thought might bring new insights for managing in the African context.

Language, context, and importance of conversation

In the African worldview, language and the context within which communication takes place are essential foundation blocks for establishing a sense of community. It is in this area that major ontological differences have been observed between the philosophical and linguistic worlds of the west and Africa (Mudimbe, 1988, Said, 1978). Whereas in the west, greater emphasis is put on the performative aspects of language and relationships, in Africa the context is more important than the literal meaning of words (Mkhize, 2004). The differences in the two worldviews encompass life at work and beyond. For instance, the nature of employment and the employer-employee relationship have been shown to be different from the perspective of the two worldviews (Kiggundu, Jorgensen, and Hafsi, 1983; Mangaliso, 1991). In Africa, where a history of strong oral tradition dominates, even such activities as conversing have different purposes and significance. Children are socialized from birth in the nuances of conversation and its importance in establishing a sense of community, and shared heritage, and common welfare. In a western context, the utility of conversation is emphasized with primacy given to the efficiency of information transfer, accuracy of translation of ideas onto words, appropriateness of the exchange medium, and receptiveness of the receiver. In the African context, the social effect of conversation is emphasized, with primacy given to establishing and reinforcing relationships. Unity and understanding among affected group members is valued above efficiency and accuracy. In language, words are embedded in semantics and syntactical structures, and enmeshed in dense fans of taken-for-granted associations that can unwittingly be unleashed by mere mention. It is with awareness of that web of communication that the African worldview should be understood (Comaroff and Comaroff, 1989; Masolo, 2003).

Temporal pauses, for example, can present a problem in the manner in which westerners engage in conversation with African indigenes. Sociolinguistics has demonstrated that there is a level of discomfort in the ways that different cultures interpret pauses and silences during conversations (Chick, 1990, 1996; Gal and Irvine, 1995; Lin and Luk, 2002). In work situations where tasks are individually structured with little interaction, western-oriented supervisors who are concerned with efficiency usually discourage conversation and other forms of socializing. However, African workers would find this oppressive and unnatural, in fact, inhuman. It is worth noting that the German social scientist Karl Marx was the first to highlight the importance of human interaction in social life and in the workplace, when he asserted that humans are social beings who perceive work as a productive affirmation of their human community. It is the emergence of modern industrialism, as championed by Frederick W. Taylor, which began to distort the human social fabric by breaking up jobs into individual repetitive tasks with little room for creative input by workers. The ultimate manifestation of division of labor is captured in the saying that workers do the work, and managers do the thinking. Taylorism creates tension among employees and produces social distance between them, which runs counter to the core values of Ubuntu. Thus, in the end, one finds a workforce whose values and beliefs support cooperation, community, and consultation, and yet who are immersed in a work system in which the dominant logic is competitiveness, individualism, and dictum. Specifically, open discussions and conversations are crucial for implementing change, and the greater the magnitude of change, the more important it is to encourage open discussion. Differences and dissentions will no doubt occur. However, they need not be understood as negative – they are simply part of the normal dynamic. The foregoing observations can be summarized in the following proposition:

> *Proposition 1*: In the African workplace, change is facilitated by encouraging open and interactive dialogue with employees. Oral, face-to-face communication is the preferred medium, especially for communicating changes that will have a significant impact on employee life.

The dynamics of decision-making

We next consider the case of decision-making and how differently the process is followed in the African worldview. Decision-making in Ubuntu reflects a similar kind of commitment and loyalty to the social group as seen in communities such as those in Japan (Glisby and Holden, 2003). In traditional western literature, decision-making is defined as the conscious choice of one course of action from the available alternatives. The process is typically linear, with one decision situation setting a precedent for the next, and the parameters being reasonably well-defined, all of which is designed to reach a speedy and meritorious resolution. The process is typically driven by a monocular vision because unity of vision is idealized. A person whose perspective differs markedly from convention is often frowned upon. The goal of decision-making is to arrive at the 'right' choice by selecting the alternative that best satisfies the decision parameters. In the African context, the decision-making process is circular and inclusive, proceeding at a deliberate speed, often allowing deviations in order to allow stakeholders to express their views, however remotely related to the issue at hand. Vision tends to be polyocular, which contrasts sharply with the monocular vision in the west – a legacy of the Fordist CEO-dominated vision (Alrøe and Noe, 2014; Connell, 1996; Ncube, 2010; Maruyama, 2004). The difference is that polyocularity of view operates with conditional truths, i.e., truths that only hold in the context of their perspective; whereas monocularity operates with simple truth claims and works to sharpen observational abilities with a singular focus at a time (Alrøe and Noe, 2014). This may be the reason why some scholars have cast doubt on the feasibility or desirability of singularity of vision in the global context (Zahra and O'Neill, 1998; Hitt, Keats, and DeMarie, 1998). Ubuntu decision-making is about more than just reaching better decisions. It accomplishes two important purposes. The first is to strengthen the relations between workers and managers. Relationships forged in the process of inclusive decision-making have important consequences in the ultimate success of the organization. The second purpose is to foster the broader perspectives and valuable insights brought in by the multiple viewpoints. Before closure is reached, a considerable amount of time is devoted to ensure that all voices have been heard, in order to gain consensus and preserve community togetherness (Mangaliso, 2001; Mqhayi, 1934). While it is acknowledged that some situations will require expedited decision, e.g., in response to competitive pressure, many decisions can be slowed down to provide opportunity for more input and inclusiveness.

An example of inclusive decision-making leading to sustainable decision-making was demonstrated in the negotiations of the Convention for a Democratic South Africa (CODESA) between apartheid government representatives and the various anti-apartheid political organizations. Most of the decisions taken at the CODESA talks that led to the first democratic elections in 1994 were reached by consensus (Mangaliso, 2001). This is not to suggest that speed was not important, but it only shows that a decision that is supported and enthusiastically implemented can achieve superior results to one that is technically the most optimal but that fails to win the buy-in of many stakeholders. The distinction between western and African decision processes suggests that rigidly enforced bureaucratic procedures are likely to be dysfunctional and to result in unpopular decisions in the African context. Wider consultation and listening to stakeholders may initially be costly in time and effort, but will likely result in greater commitment to established goals. The following proposition summarizes these observations.

> *Proposition 2:* While in the African worldview authority is revered, important decisions are preceded by wide consultation with the stakeholders, typically in live open forums. While the process might appear to be time consuming, the advantage comes in valuable insights gained, and in the long-run commitment of employees to the decisions reached, based on the conviction that their voices have been heard.

Conception of time

It is generally acknowledged that different cultures have different conceptions of time, and that the concept of time itself conveys paradigmatically different meanings in different cultures (Sorokin and Merton, 1937). These differences have often resulted in misunderstandings, social *faux pas*, and breakdowns in cross-cultural communication. The story of a western salesman who had secured an hour-long appointment at the home of a customer in KwaZulu-Natal illustrates this (Mangaliso, 2001). The salesman arrived punctually, but he was upset that his host was not ready as expected. It took another half hour before the host was finally ready to meet and discuss business with him. The salesman found out later that in Zulu culture, when you make an appointment at someone's home, the host has control over what happens in that time period. By agreeing to meet in the home of the client, the salesman was agreeing that his host's priorities and family activities were more important than the business discussion. Misunderstandings such as these are a common source of friction in cross-cultural interactions. They arise not because of the differing importance assigned to time commitments, but because of fundamentally different meanings attached to time. The gulf of understanding can only be bridged by understanding the worldview of people from other cultures or, at a minimum, accepting the validity and reasonability of their worldviews.

The value of tolerance also stresses the importance of allowing time for extended discussions where necessary, and not rigidly sticking to meeting time tables (Broodryk, 2006). In the African worldview, time is not a series of deadlines, but rather a series of opportunities to create or reinforce the social bonds among individuals. Unlike in the western context, where time is a strategic commodity to be productively used, in the African context it is not a commodity to be frugally consumed. Time is a reference that locates communities with respect to their collective past and shared future, assigns significance to patterns of events, and orders relationships and affairs. It has symbolic value and is seen as a unifying and integrating construct, a kind of currency that reinforces interdependence, shared heritage, regularity, and congruity. The foregoing discussion is captured in the following proposition.

Proposition 3. In the African worldview, time is a complex construct with several components. Allowing enough of it during deliberations will lead to more inclusive, unifying, and therefore sustainable decisions because of the embrace likely to be received from a majority of the stakeholders, and greater commitment to the agreed-upon direction of change.

Interpretation of productivity and efficiency

The western conception of productivity is understood in terms of obtaining the maximum useful output from a given set of resource inputs. Productivity is assumed to be a critical determinant of organizational viability, with efficiency expressed in terms of maximizing the ratio of outputs to inputs, signifying the primary goal of the enterprise. In the African worldview, greater emphasis is placed on social well-being rather than technical rationality, with efficiency maximization having less of a priority than societal harmony. An empirical study conducted among the baTswana people of Botswana found that they were more concerned with the quality of the relationship with their boss and with internal interpersonal issues than with the organization's performance, its clients, and external issues (Jones, Blunt, and Sharma, 1996). The implications in this case may be that productivity and performance outcomes are predicated on healthy relationships. In other words, taking care of relationships first almost guarantees strong organizational performance, and vice-versa – pushing for increased efficiency at the expense of good working relationships can have negative consequences on organizational performance.

Relationships are important, both when organizations face prosperity and when adversity arrives. Consider times when an organization faces adverse market conditions, demand goes down, and profitability suffers. To a manager trained in the western tradition, the answer to maintaining profits would be what Prahalad and Hamel (1994) call 'denominator' management – the denominator being the input factors. He/she would turn to laying off some employees as the answer to restoring corporate profitability. In Africa, where work is both a social and professional activity, the economic input-output factors cannot be assumed to be acting independently of one another or to be the only contributing factors in performance outcome. The downsizing literature has shown that employee cutbacks can have a significant negative impact on performance outcomes (De Meuse, Bergmann, Vanderheiden, and Roraff, 2004; O'Neill, Pouder, and Buchholtz, 1998). Multinationals often resort to between-country unit productivity comparisons to the total exclusion of the national contexts of the countries being compared. For example, they would state that in one country two fewer operators than in a developing country could run a production line. Logic would suggest that two operators could be removed from the line or laid off. Such a decision might be easily explained in a western context, but not in Africa. In Africa, it carries the risk of alienating the entire workforce and resulting in decreased productivity as well as other disruptions. The highly collectivist (Hofstede, 1980) orientation of the African culture favors a system of spreading the burden (across the board pay-cuts) instead of making one or two individuals suffer the pain or disgrace (layoffs) of management efficiency decisions.

This demonstrates the dilemma of implementing western-originated ideas in firms in developing countries. Some performance criteria that originate in the western worldview – productivity and efficiency – may be in direct conflict with the values structure of African society – solidarity, group well-being, and social harmony. This does not mean they are necessarily incompatible and, with some protocols observed and proper channels of communication followed, even the most difficult change can be implemented effectively. Ironically, however, applying Ubuntu to leadership contributes to changing and transforming the world (Ncube, 2010). The following proposition summarizes this conclusion:

> *Proposition 4:* Some western conceptions of organizational performance may be inappropriate, even contrary to the African worldview. Metrics for calibrating productivity should be checked for relevance and fit with African cultural norms. For any changes in the performance metrics to be fully embraced, wide and inclusive consultation with employee groups is important.

Leadership and experience

Leadership is another key area where reconciling corporate culture and societal culture can make the difference between success and failure in any change effort (Cummings and Worley, 2009). It is important from the onset to state that in the African worldview of Ubuntu, the leader is one of the most revered individuals, someone to whom most people defer, and from whom a lot is expected. In studies of culture, Africans invariably rate among the highest in power distance (Hofstede, 1980; Javidan et al., 2006). Employees look to their leadership to take care of them, not only at work, but to show interest in them personally, and to care for them outside of work. Paternalism is thus not only acceptable in the African workplace, but expected. Hierarchy is accepted as a norm and age is venerated both in social and professional settings (Munene, Schwartz, and Smith, 2000). In traditional African society, age, experience, and leadership are invariably bound together. The wisdom necessary to earn followers' respect and build strong informal networks grows with age and experience. This argues for the time-honored cultural tradition of considering the employee's age and experience among the criteria used for promotion to leadership. In the African milieu it is a lot easier for subordinates to accept leadership from an older, more experienced individual than from a younger person. By contrast, it is unusual and rare for a younger person to be comfortable leading a group of people he/she regards as his/her seniors. Power distance requires the leader to be more directive, a requirement that goes against the grain of African culture if carried out by a junior (age-wise) member of the community. An older person might not necessarily possess the expert knowledge of the task at hand, but through his/her wisdom, vision, and ability to maintain harmonious working relations, he/she can get others to perform well. The role of the leader is not so much to direct but to coordinate consideration, discussion, and implementation of group decisions. Ironically, this approach to managing is gaining increasing acceptance even in the context of more contemporary western thinking, as more successful managers are increasingly being seen acting as coaches, sages, and nurturers, rather than cops, experts, and naysayers (Cummings and Worley, 2009; Peters and Waterman, 1982). The incursion into the African workplace of indigenous African thought systems and relationships has begun to confound the role of leaders and leadership. This requires a manager to balance the demands of both technical and social competence. For instance, how can a manager motivate a group of older workers who refuse to accept his/her technical 'wisdom,' or misinterpret his/her professionalism (Ahiauzu, 1986b)? Leadership is a key factor in Ubuntu because through it, changes and transformation can be achieved that allow organizations to adjust to meet the challenges of a changing global environment (Waldron, 2015). These thoughts are captured in following proposition:

Proposition 5: In the African context, leaders are revered as the most influential people, to whom others will defer for final decision-making. Experience and maturity are closely associated with wisdom, and these are qualities that are venerated and expected of an effective leader. Selection to leadership should be based upon demonstrated professional knowledge, social skills, and on full comprehension of, and empathy toward, the African values and belief systems.

Implications for change management in Africa

From the foregoing discussion, several considerations arise concerning the best way to incorporate Ubuntu philosophy for managing change in contemporary African organizations. The suggestions that follow are offered only as useful starting points for bringing the authentic indigenous African worldview into the way organizations on the continent are managed.

Most of the change management literature references the pioneering work of Kurt Lewin (1951), who is widely considered to be the 'father' of organizational development. Lewin suggested that successful change generally involves three phases, which he labeled the unfreezing, movement, and refreezing stages. While acknowledging that Lewin's (1951) model is not a cure-all for all organizational change, and that, indeed, other researchers have extended, modified, and refined it to address contemporary change, his three phases are still considered foundational to any change process (Burnes, 2004; Dawson, 1994; Hatch, 1997; Kantor, Stein, and Jick, 1992; Schein, 1996). In the discussion that follows, we show how change can be made more successful by engaging some of the principles of Ubuntu covered in this chapter.

Unfreezing stage

This stage requires breaking down and disrupting the established patterns in order to clear the way for the new way of operating. At this stage, research has highlighted the importance of a compelling message intended to convince the employees about urgency of the need for change, with a buy-in of employees as the focus for success (Kotter, 1996). In order for them to accept the change and contribute to making it successful, people need to understand how it will benefit them. Understanding the reason for the change is essential because of the strong reactions that change evokes by challenging people's core assumptions about the existing *status quo*. It is at this stage that the importance of coalition and consensus-building plays a key role. However elusive the ability to relate to people across socio-economic, political, and cultural lines of divide, showing respect for their values is an invaluable asset. Research has shown that one of the most important reasons change fails is the failure to anchor it on the values of those affected by it (Kotter, 1995). In Africa, upholding the values of reciprocity seen in practices such as *shosholoza* – working collaboratively and in synchronicity, and *simunye* – working together as one, is important in consensus decision-making, and is critical in successfully managing change in Africa (Bangura, 2009; Nafukho, 2006; Weir, Mangaliso, and Mangaliso, 2010). Several scholars have noted how understanding and applying these principles may help to lower the communication barriers and facilitates coalition-building (Darley and Blankson, 2008; Khoza, 2011; Mangaliso, 2001; Weir et al., 2010; Washington and Hacker, 2005). This was seen in an empirical study conducted in Botswana, which demonstrated that when individuals understood the change, they were more likely to be committed to supporting it (Washington and Hacker, 2005). Ubuntu not only enhances communication between management and employees, but it provides voice to the employees. In particular, a voice speaking from Ubuntu enables a participatory interaction, where openly conflictual social formation can occur, producing inventive ways of living together. Ubuntu enhances coalition-building as a management tool that gives employees a voice and platform from which consensus can evolve.

Movement stage

In this second stage, incentives are created to 'move' to the desired state. It is the stage at which everyone seeks to find ways to resolve the uncertainties created during the unfreezing stage. The duration of this stage may be long and drawn out, since people have different rates of adjusting to change or embracing it, and some may continue to resist change longer than others. Research has shown that a significant reason for this is often the lack of alignment between the value system upon which the change intervention is based, and of the values of the majority of the majority members of the organization undergoing the change (Bernard and Jackson, 2011). At this stage, the value of the open forum discussions can play a facilitative role. In this regard, dialogue with employees offers them opportunities for expressing their preferences, fears, and hopes in the context of changes being discussed. Open forums such as the *Indaba* among the Nguni, or the *Lekgotla* among the baTswana, come naturally and have been known to take place through the ages as vehicles for the public to air their views out in the open without fear of reprisal (Newenham-Kahindi, 2009; Van de Bunt-Kokhuis, 2011). Whether or not management agrees at the end is not as important as the fact that their feelings have been expressed. Under pressure to rush toward the implementation phase, the temptation is great for management to avoid these open forums for fear of encountering hostilities. But this is not advisable since in the African worldview, few things are more important than being listened to, being given a hearing. Management that shuns such dialogue does so at great risk of extending the resistance to change and causing disruptive work stoppages that could otherwise be avoided. There have been instances when companies following formal western management protocols have suffered major disruptions involving, *inter alia*, work stoppages that could have easily been avoided had local change management approaches been adopted. This was expressed in the words of a spokesperson of the mine workers' union who commented that 'The only thing that the employees wanted was for top management to come and address us. Just to speak to us.' (Mangaliso, 2001: 23). All the workers wanted was a listening ear from senior management, and not necessarily to have all their grievances redressed. In this case, by failing to honor the cardinal Ubuntu belief of respect and honor conveyed, in this case, through face-to-face communication, senior management cost the company millions of dollars in the strike action that ensued.

Refreezing stage

Refreezing is necessary to help the organization internalize or institutionalize the changes and new ways of working. It does so by establishing new patterns so that once the desired state has been reached, there is no return to the previous state. This means making sure that the changes are incorporated into everyday routines, so that a new sense of stability is created. The refreezing stage is still important in contemporary times, even though it is an acknowledged fact that change is constant. Without the stability given by refreezing the new *status quo*, employees may be trapped in the transitional uncertainty, and this might prompt some to resort to the old ways of doing things. In the absence of a new frozen state, it is very difficult to tackle the next change initiative effectively. As part of the refreezing process, the success of the change must be celebrated. The literature suggests that celebrations help people mark milestones of accomplishments, and helps them believe that future change will be successful (Kotter, 1995, 1996). In Africa ceremonies are seen as outlets for joys and/or sorrows in the belief that joy shared is joy multiplied, and pain shared is pain diminished. Hence, it is not uncommon to see people doing the *toi-toi* dance either in celebration or in protest demonstrations. Several high-profile personalities are known to have taken a lead in the singing and dancing to celebrate an important accomplishment, including Nelson Mandela, Desmond Tutu, the late Chris Hani, and Jacob Zuma. Such Ubuntu-style ceremonies tend to leave an iconic imprint in the minds of organization members for cementing the successful implementation of change. In their leadership role, how managers behave toward employees has implications for organizational success. As we noted elsewhere, Africans have a penchant for ceremonial celebrations (Mangaliso, 2001). The continent boasts an extremely rich repertoire of rituals and attending forms of entertainment including drumming, music and singing, dance, and the eloquent verbal expressions of praise singers. Celebrating of accomplishment of important milestones of achievement therefore fittingly satisfy the African allure of ceremony. Not only are celebrations fun, but they also promote a sense of trust and belonging – an essential affirmation of Ubuntu's cardinal values. The best-known African companies that have adopted the principles of Ubuntu include SABMiller, the second-largest beer company in the world; South African Airways, the flagship air carrier of South Africa; and Eskom, the supplier of electricity in South Africa (Broodryk, 2006; Mangaliso and Nkomo, 2001; McFarlin, Coster, and Mogale-Pretorius, 1999; Wolmarans, 2005. Other companies that have taken their Ubuntu practices beyond the South African borders include ABSA (Amalgamated Banks of South Africa), Stanbic (Standard Bank Investment Corporation), and Sanlam in financial services, as well as Vodacom and MTN in telecommunication (Newenham-Kahindi, 2009; Yawson, 2017). One example of a company to pioneer the implementation of the Ubuntu principles is Cashbuild Cash and Carry, which started off as a small entrepreneurial grocery store, but subsequently grew to become a billion-dollar company with operations in several African countries (Koopman, 1991). Even beyond Africa, global companies such as Southwest Airlines, Starbucks, and many others are known to have begun embracing many elements of Ubuntu in their corporate practices (Gittell, 2003; Milliman, Ferguson, Trickett, and Condemi, 1999; Schultz, 2016).

Discussion and conclusion

Over the years the model has come under criticism for several reasons (Burnes, 1996, 2004; By, 2005; Kantor et al., 1992; Wilson, 1992). Among the important reasons stated are its simplicity and emphasis on relatively small-scale and incremental change; its assumption of steady state organizational conditions; its top-down view from the perspective of senior managers; and its neglect of organizational conflict and politics (Bamford and Forrester, 2003; Burnes, 1996; By,

2005; Wilson, 1992). These criticisms are especially true for most organizations operating in Africa. The changes needed in Africa are enormous, most countries are not in steady state conditions socio-politically, the senior management of most large organizations are physically or psychologically removed from local cultures, and the organizations are not buffered from the political upheavals that characterize most countries. Yet, for historical reasons, Africa has not seemed able to completely rid itself of the western foundations of management that have been imposed on it since colonial times (Mkhize, 2004; Nkomo, 2011). In our view, any effort to implement authentic change in African organizations will continue to be unsuccessful until change systems immersed in endogenous African perspectives are acknowledged, embraced, and institutionalized (Khoza, 2005; Ngambi, 2004; Nkomo, 2011; Edoho, 2001). More attention needs to be paid to authentic African ideas of leading change, such as RARE leadership (Ngambi, 2011), attuned leadership (Khoza, 2011), and several more.

We conclude by restating our thesis that in order to be effective in Africa, management principles and practices must first embrace the nuances of their host cultures. Effective management in Africa will hinge on the successful harnessing and harmonizing of the traditional corporate practices with practices that are appropriate in the African worldview. According to many analysts, the world economy has reached the stage of globality (Sirkin, Hemerling, and Bhattacharya, 2008; Yergin and Stanislaw, 2002). This is the end-state of the global economy, in which the process of globalization is complete or nearly so, barriers have fallen, and a new global reality has emerged in which both developed and developing economies compete on an equal basis. With globality has also come a renewed sense of cultural awareness around the world, and this is bound to make people in emerging market countries more assertive about consideration and respect that their ways of life deserve within the corporate setting. In this regard, the philosophy of Ubuntu offers great potential for enlightening organizations about the African worldview.

Our hope is that organization theorists with an interest in Africa will be inspired to develop new research agendas based on the ideas presented in this and other chapters of this handbook. Hopefully, an ensuing discourse will foment a new set of frameworks and theories that are of genuinely African origin, and informed by the realities of the subcontinent. In the long run, we hope that such an Africa-centered perspective on management will infuse management curricula and training programs that are rigorous. The ideal outcome of such an undertaking would be to provide the world with further insights about the benefits and challenges of managing organizations the Ubuntu way. Future research is needed to test the proposition suggested in this chapter, that managing organizational change in sub-Saharan Africa through these principles can result in high levels of performance.

Note

1 We will use the term 'western' or 'west' throughout the text in reference to Western Europe and/or North America. We are aware that there are several differences between the cultures and philosophies of these two regions as there are differences among the cultures that exist within the African continent. But it is the differences between the African and the western contexts that are the main *foci* of this paper.

References

Adler, N. J. (1983) Cross-cultural management research: The ostrich and the trend. *Academy of Management Review*, 8(2): 226–232.

Agle, B. R., and Caldwell, C. B. (1999) Understanding research on values in business. *Business and Society*, 38(3): 326–387.

Ahiauzu, A. I. (1986a) Preface to the special issue on management and organization in Africa. *International Studies of Management and Organization*, 16(2): 3–5.

Ahiauzu, A. I. (1986b) The African thought-system and the work behavior of the African industrial man. *International Studies of Management and Organizations*, 16(2): 37–58.
Alrøe, H. F., and Noe, E. (2014) Second-order science of interdisciplinary research: A polyocular framework for wicked problems. *Constructivist Foundations*, 10(1): 65–95.
Bamford, D. R., and Forrester, P. L. (2003) Managing planned and emergent change within an operations management environment. *International Journal of Operations & Production Management*, 23(5): 546–564.
Bandura, A. (2002) Social cognitive theory in cultural context. *Applied Psychology: International Review*, 51(2): 269–290.
Bangura, A. K. (2009) Federalism, economic development, science and technology for a United States of Africa: An Ubuntu-clustering approach. *Journal of Pan African Studies*, 3(2): 33–71.
Barnard, C. I. (1938/1968) *The Functions of the Executive (30th Anniversary Edition)*. Cambridge, MA: Harvard University Press.
Bernard, B., and Jackson, P. (2011) Success and failure in organizational change: An exploration of the role of values. *Journal of Change Management*, 11(2): 133–162.
Beugelsdijk, S., de Groot, H., Linders, G. J., and Slangen, A. (2004) *Cultural Distance, Institutional Distance and International Trade*. ERSA Conference, Portugal.
Bhattacharya, O., Chatterjee, A., and Basu, J. (2017) Humility: An emerging construct in moral psychology. *Psychological Studies*, 62(1): 1–11.
Bloom, N., Lemos, R., Sadun, R., Scur, D., and Van Reenen, J. (2014). JEEA-FBBVA Lecture 2013: The new empirical economics of management. *Journal of the European Economic Association, 12*(4), 835–876.
Blunt, P. (1995) The cultural limits of process consulting in development assistance. In R. Reineke and R. Sulzer (Eds.), *Management Consultancy in Developing Countries*. Berlin: Gabler, 1–9.
Blunt, P., and Jones, M. L. (1997) Exploring the limits of Western leadership theory in East Asia and Africa. *Personnel Review*, 26(1/2): 6–23.
Boyacigiller, N. A., and Adler, N. J. (1991) The parochial dinosaur: Organizational science in a global context. *Academy of Management Review*, 16(2): 262–290.
Broodryk, J. (2006) The philosophy of Ubuntu: Some management guidelines. *Management Today*, 7(22): 52–55.
Burnes, B. (1996) No such thing as . . . a 'one best way' to manage organizational change. *Management Decision*, 34(10): 11–18.
Burnes, B. (2004) Kurt Lewin and the planned approach to change: A re-appraisal. *Journal of Management Studies*, 41(6): 977–1002.
By, R. T. (2005) Organizational change management: A critical review. *Journal of Change Management*, 5(4): 369–380.
Chandler, A. (1962) *Strategy and Structure: Chapters in the History of the Industrial Enterprise*. Cambridge, MA: MIT Press.
Chick, J. K. (1990) The interaction accomplishment of discrimination in South Africa. In D. Carbaugh (Ed.), *Cultural Communication and Intercultural Contact*. Hillsdale, NJ: Lawrence Erlbaum Associates.
Chick, J. K. (1996) Safe talk: Collusion in apartheid education. In H. Coleman (Ed.), *Society and the Language Classroom*. Cambridge, UK: Cambridge University Press.
Comaroff, J., and Comaroff, J. (1989) The colonization of consciousness in South Africa. *Economy and Society*, 8(3), 267–296.
Connell, I. (1996) Unity of vision: Constructing workplace hegemony. *Javnost-The Public*, 3(4): 49–66.
Cunha, M. P., Fortes, A., Rodrigues, F., and Rego, A. R. (2015) *Leadership Paradoxes in Angolan Organizations: Emic Paradoxes, Etic Paradoxes, and Paradox Work (WP# 1501)*. Retrieved May 9, 2018, from NOVAFRICA: www.novafrica.org
Cummings, T. G., and Worley, C. G. (2009) *Organization Development and Change*. Mason, OH: Cengage Learning.
Darley, W. K., and Blankson, C. (2008) African culture and business markets. *Journal of Business and Industrial Marketing*, 26(3): 374–383.
Dawson, P. (1994) *Organizational Change: A Processual Approach*. London, UK: Paul Chapman Publishing.
Dayasindhu, N. (2002) Embeddness, knowledge transfer, industry clusters and global competitiveness: A case study of the Indian software industry. *Technovation*, 22(9): 551–560.
De Meuse, K. P., Bergmann, T. J., Vanderheiden, P. A., and Roraff, C. E. (2004) New evidence regarding organizational downsizing and a firm's financial performance: A long-term analysis. *Journal of Managerial Issues*, 16(2): 155–177.
Edoho, F. M. (2001) Management in Africa: The quest for a philosophical framework. In F. M. Edoho (Ed.), *Management Challenges for Africa in the Twenty-first Century: Theoretical and Applied Perspectives*. Westport, CT: Praeger.

Emmons, R. A. (1998) *The Psychology of Ultimate Personality, Spirituality, and Intelligence.* Unpublished Manuscript, University of California at Davis.

Foucault, M. (1970) The order of discourse – Inaugural lecture at the College de France – I. McLeod (Transl.). In M. J. Shapiro (Ed.), *Language and Politics.* Oxford: Blackwell.

Friedman, M. (1970) The social responsibility of business is to increase its profits. *New York Times Magazine.* New York, NY.

Friedman, T. L. (2005) *The World is Flat: A Brief History of the Twenty-First Century.* New York: Farrar, Straus and Giroux.

Gal, S., and Irvine, J. T. (1995) The boundaries of languages and disciplines: How ideologies construct difference. *Social Research*, 62(4): 967–1001.

Gittell, J. H. (2003) *The Southwest Airlines Way: Using the Power of Relationships to Achieve High Performance.* New York, NY: McGraw-Hill, Inc.

Glisby, M., and Holden, N. (2003) Contextual constraints in knowledge management theory: The cultural embeddedness of Horako's knowledge-creating company. *Knowledge and Process Management*, 10(1): 29–36.

Gyekye, K. (1997) *Tradition and Modernity: Philosophical Reflections on the African Experience.* New York, NY: Oxford University Press.

Hanks, T. L. (2008). The Ubuntu paradigm: Psychology's next force? *Journal of Humanistic Psychology, 48*(1), 116–135.

Hatch, M. J. (1997) *Organization Theory: Modern, Symbolic and Postmodern Perspectives.* Oxford, UK: Oxford University Press.

Hitt, M. A., Keats, B. W., and DeMarie, S. M. (1998) Navigating in the new competitive landscape: Building strategic flexibility and competitive advantage in the 21st century. *The Academy of Management Executive*, 12(4): 22–42.

Hofstede, G. (1980) Motivation, organization, and leadership: Do American theories apply abroad? *Organizational Dynamics*, 9(1): 42–63.

Hofstede, G. (1993) Cultural constraints in management theories. *Academy of Management Executive*, 7(1): 81–94.

Horwitz, F. M. (2009) Managing human resources in Africa: Emergent market challenges. In *Routledge Companion to Strategic Human Resource Management.* London: Routledge.

Horwitz, F. M. (2015) Human resources management in multinational companies in Africa: A systematic literature review. *International Journal of Human Resource Management*, 26(21): 2786–2809.

Horwitz, F. M., Kamoche, K., and Chew, I. K. (2002) Human resource management in Africa. *International Journal of Human Resource Management*, 13(7): 1019–1041.

Inyang, B. J. (2008) The challenges of evolving and developing management indigenous theories and practices in Africa. *International Journal of Business and Management*, 3(12): 122–132.

Jaskyte, K., and Lee, M. (2009) Organizational commitment of social workers: An exploratory study. *Administration in Social Work*, 33(3): 227–241.

Javidan, M., House, R. J., Dorfman, P. W., Hanges, P. J., and De Luque, M. S. (2006) Conceptualizing and measuring cultures and their consequences: A comparative review of GLOBE's and Hofstede's approaches. *Journal of International Business Studies*, 37(6): 897–914.

Jones, M. L., Blunt, P., and Sharma, K. C. (1996). Managerial perceptions of leadership and management in an African public service organization. *Public Administration and Development*, 16(5), 455–467.

Kamoche, K. (1997) Knowledge creation and learning in international HRM. *International Journal of Human Resources*, 8(2): 213–225.

Kantor, R. M. (1968) Commitment and social organization: A study of commitment mechanisms in utopian communities. *American Sociological Review*, 33: 499–517.

Kantor, R. M., Stein, B. A., and Jick, J. D. (1992) *The Challenge of Organizational Change: How Companies Experience and Leaders Guide It.* New York, NY: The Free Press.

Karsten, L., and Illa, H. (2005) Ubuntu as a key African management concept: Contextual background and practical insights for knowledge application. *Journal of Managerial Psychology*, 20(7): 607–620.

Kayuni, H. M., and Tambulasi, R. I. C. (2012) Ubuntu and corporate social responsibility: The case of selected Malawian organizations. *African Journal of Economic and Management Studies*, 3(1): 64–76.

Khomba, J., and Kangaude-Ulaya, E. (2013) Indigenization of corporate strategies in Africa: Lessons from the African Ubuntu philosophy. *China-USA Business Review*, 12(7): 672–689.

Khoza, R. J. (2005) *Let Africa Lead.* Johannesburg, South Africa: Vezubuntu Publishing.

Khoza, R. J. (2011) *Attuned Leadership: African Humanism as a Compass.* Rosebank, Johannesburg, South Africa: Penguin Books.

Kiggundu, M. N., Jorgensen, J. J., and Hafsi, T. (1983) Administrative theory and practice in developing countries: A synthesis. *Administrative Science Quarterly*, 28: 66–84.

Koopman, A. (1991) Transcultural management: Allowing employees to be enterprising – democratically. *European Journal of Management*, 9(3): 295–300.

Korten, D. C. (1981) The management of social transformation. *Public Administration Review*, 41: 609–618.

Kotter, J. P. (1995) Leading change: Why transformation efforts fail. *Harvard Business Review*, 73(2), 56–67.

Kotter, J. P. (1996) *Leading Change*. Boston, MA: Harvard Business School Press.

Kras, E. (1989) *Management in Two Cultures: Bridging the Gap Between U.S. and Mexican Managers*. Yarmouth, ME: Intercultural Press.

Landsman, M. J. (2008) Pathways to organizational commitment. *Administration in Social Work*, 32(2): 105–132.

Lewicki, R. J., and Bunker, B. B. (1996) Developing and maintaining trust in work relationships. In M. R. Kramer and R. T. Tyler (Eds.), *Trust in Organizations: Frontiers of Theory and Research*. Thousand Oaks, CA: Sage Publications, 114–139.

Lewin, K. (1951). *Field Theory in Social Science*. New York, NY: Harper & Brothers.

Lin, A., and Luk, J. (2002) Beyond progressive liberalism and cultural relativism: Towards critical postmodernist sociohistorically situated perspectives in classroom studies. *Canadian Modern Language Review*, 59(1): 97–124.

Lincoln, Y. S., and Denzin, N. K. (1994) The fifth moment. In N. K. Denzin and Y. S. Lincoln (Eds.), *Handbook of Qualitative Research*. Thousand Oaks, CA: Sage Publishing Company.

Locke, E. A., and Latham, G. P. (1990) *A Theory of Goal Setting and Task Performance*. Englewood Cliffs, NJ: Prentice-Hall.

Makgoba, T. (2016) *Rebuilding South Africa, Recovering Our Vision and Renewing Our Society*. Opening Remarks During the Launch of a National Conversation on the Socio-Economic Future of South Africa, Friday, March 11. Retrieved April 16, 2016 from http://archbishop.anglicanchurchsa.org/2016/03/rebuilding-south-africa-recovering-our.html

Mangaliso, M. P. (1991) Whose knowledge matters? The case for developing multicultural theories of management. In J. D. Jansen (Ed.), *Knowledge and Power in South Africa: Critical Perspectives Across the Disciplines*. Johannesburg, South Africa: Skotaville, 237–247.

Mangaliso, M. P. (1992) Entrepreneurship and innovation in a global context. *Entrepreneurship, Innovation, and Change*, 1(4): 437–450.

Mangaliso, M. P. (1993) Cultural exigencies in management and organizational theory. *Entrepreneurship, Innovation, and Change*, 2(3): 321–334.

Mangaliso, M. P. (2001) Building competitive advantage from Ubuntu: Management lessons from South Africa. *Academy of Management Executive*, 15(3): 23–33.

Mangaliso, M. P., and Nkomo, S. M. (2001). Eskom's Chairman Reuel Khoza on the transformation of South African business. *Academy of Management Executive*, 15(3), 8–15.

March, J. G., and Simon, H. A. (1958) *Organizations*. Oxford: Wiley.

Maruyama, M. (2004) Polyocular vision or sub-understanding. *Organization Studies*, 25(3): 467–480.

Mashele, T. L. (2013) *Improving Relationship Management in South African Construction Project Performance From the Concept of Ubuntu*. Unpublished Doctoral Dissertation. University of Witwatersrand. Johannesburg, SA. Retrieved August 30, 2017 from http://wiredspace.wits.ac.za/bitstream/handle/10539/12821/Final%20Draft%20Rev%203.with%20corrections.pdf?sequence=1

Masolo, D. A. (2003) Philosophy and indigenous knowledge: An African perspective. *Africa Today*, 50(2): 21–38.

Mbiti, J. (1969) *African Philosophy and Religion*. London: Longman.

McFarlin, D. B., Coster, E. A., and Mogale-Pretorius, C. (1999) South African management development in the twenty-first century: Moving toward an Africanized model. *Journal of Management Development*, 18(1), 63–78.

Merriam-Webster. (2011) *Humility*. Retrieved September 11, 2017 from www.merriam- webster.com/dictionary/humility

Mill, J. S. (1843/1906) *A System of Logic*. London: Longman.

Milliman, J., Ferguson, J., Trickett, D., and Condemi, B. (1999) Spirit and community at Southwest Airlines: An investigation of a spiritual values-based model. *Journal of Organizational Change Management*, 12(3): 221–233.

Mithas, S., and Whitaker, J. (2007). Is the world flat or spiky? Information intensity, skills, and global service disaggregation. *Information Systems Research, 18*(3), 237–259.

Mkabela, Q. N. (2014) Ubuntu as an axiological framework for human rights education. *Indilinga African Journal of Indigenous Knowledge Systems*, 13(2): 283–291.
Mkhize, N. (2004) Psychology: An African perspective. In K. Ratele, N. Duncan, D. Hook, N. Mkhize, P. Kiguwa and A. Collins (Eds.), *Self, Community & Psychology*. Lansdowne, South Africa: UCT Press.
Mkhize, N. (2008) Ubuntu and harmony: An African approach to morality and ethics. In R. Nicolson (Ed.), *Persons in Community: African Ethics in Global Culture*. Westville, KZN: University of KwaZulu-Natal.
Mnyaka, M., and Motlhabi, M. (2005) The African concept of Ubuntu/Botho and its socio-moral significance. *Black Theology: An International Journal*, 3(2): 215–237.
Mowday, R. T., Steers, R. M., and Porter, L. W. (1979). The measurement of organizational commitment. *Journal of Vocational Behavior*, 14(5), 224–247.
Mqhayi, S. E. K. (1934) *Ityala Lamawele*. Alice, South Africa: Lovedale Press.
Mudambi, R., and Swift, T. (2011) Leveraging knowledge and competencies across space: The next frontier in international business. *Journal of International Management*, 17(3), 186–189.
Mudimbe, V. Y. (1988) *The Invention of Africa: Gnosis, Philosophy, and the Order of Knowledge*. Bloomington, IN: Indiana University Press.
Munene, J. C., Schwartz, S. H., and Smith, P. B. (2000) Development in sub-Saharan Africa: Cultural influences and managers' decision behavior. *Public Administration and Development*, 20: 339–351.
Murithi, T. (2006) Practical peacemaking wisdom from Africa: Reflections on Ubuntu. *The Journal of Pan African Studies*, 1(4): 25–34.
Muwanga-Zake, J. W. (2009) Building bridges across knowledge systems: Ubuntu and participative research paradigms in Bantu communities. *Discourse: Studies in the Cultural Politics of Education*, 30(4): 413–426.
Nafukho, F. M. (2006) Ubuntu worldview: A traditional African view of adult learning in the workplace. *Advances in Developing Human Resources*, 8(3), 408–415.
Narayanan, V. K., and Fahey, L. (2005). The relevance of the institutional underpinnings of Porter's five forces framework to emerging economies: An epistemological analysis. *Journal of Management Studies*, 42(1), 207–223.
Ncube, L. B. (2010) Ubuntu: A transformative leadership philosophy. *Journal of Leadership Studies*, 4(3): 77–82.
Nelson, R. E. (1989) The strength of strong ties: Social networks and intergroup conflict in organizations. *Academy of Management Journal*, 32(2): 377–401.
Newenham-Kahindi, A. (2009) The transfer of Ubuntu and Indaba business models abroad: A case of South African multinational banks and telecommunication services in Tanzania. *International Journal of Cross Cultural Management*, 9(1): 87–108.
Ngambi, H. C. (2004) African leadership: Lessons from the chiefs. In T. A. Meyer and I. Boninelli (Eds.), *Conversations in Leadership: South African Perspectives*. Johannesburg: Knowledge Resources.
Ngambi, H. C. (2011) *RARE Total Leadership: Leading With the Head, Heart, and Hands*. Claremont, South Africa: Juta and Company, Ltd.
Nicolito, A. G. (2011) Delving into the ethical dimension of Ubuntu philosophy. *Cultura*, 8(1): 63–82.
Nielsen, R., Marrone, J. A., and Slay, H. S. (2010) A new look at humility: Exploring the humility concept and its role in socialized charismatic leadership. *Journal of Leadership & Organizational Studies*, 17(1): 33–43.
Nisbett, R. E., Peng, K., Choi, I., and Norenzayan, A. (2001) Culture and systems of thought: Holistic versus analytic cognition. *Psychological Review*, 108(2): 291–310.
Nkomo, S. M. (2011) A postcolonial and anti-colonial reading of 'African' leadership and management in organization studies: Tensions, contradictions and possibilities. *Organization*, 18(3): 365–386.
Nyamnjoh, F. B. (2012) Blinded by sight: Divining the future of anthropology in Africa. *Africa Spectrum*, 2(3): 63–92.
Ouchi, W. (1981) Theory Z: How American business can meet the Japanese challenge. *Business Horizons*, 24(6), 82–83.
O'Neill, H. M., Pouder, R. W., and Buchholtz, A. K. (1998) Patterns in the diffusion of strategies across organizations: Insights from the innovation diffusion literature. *Academy of Management Review*, 23: 98–114.
Payne, D. R., Sandage, S. J., Rupert, D., Devor, N. G., and Bronstein, M. (2015) Humility as a psychotherapeutic virtue: Spiritual, philosophical, and psychological foundations. *Journal of Spirituality in Mental Health*, 17(1): 3–25.
Peters, T., and Waterman, B. (1982) *In Search of Excellence: Lessons From America's Best-run Companies*. New York, NY: Harper & Row.
Porter, L. W., and Lawler III, E. E. (1968) *Managerial Attitudes and Performance*. Homewood, IL: Irwin Publishers.

Prahalad, C. K., and Hamel, G. (1994) *Competing for the Future.* Boston, MA: Harvard Business School Press.
Ramose, M. B. (1999) *African Philosophy Through Ubuntu.* Harare, Zimbabwe: Mond Books.
Ramose, M. B. (2002). The philosophy of Ubuntu and Ubuntu as a philosophy. In P. H. Coetzee and A. P. Roux (Eds.), *Philosophy from Africa* (pp. 230–238). Cape Town, South Africa: Oxford University Press.
Redding, S. G. (1980) Cognition as an aspect of culture and its relation to management processes: An exploratory view of the Chinese case. *Journal of Management Studies*, 17(2): 127–148.
Reichers, A. E. (1985) A review and reconceptualization of organizational commitment. *Academy of Management Review*, 10(3): 465–476.
Said, E. (1978) *Orientalism.* New York, NY: Pantheon Books.
Schein, E. H. (1996). Culture: The missing concept in organization studies. *Administrative Science Quarterly*, 41(2), 229–240.
Schneider, S. C. (1989) Strategy formulation: The impact of national culture. *Organization Studies*, 10(2): 149–168.
Schultz, H. (2016, December 6) *Howard Schultz Accepts 2016 Ripple of Hope Award.* Starbucks Newsroom. Retrieved November 22, 2017 from https://news.starbucks.com/news/schultz-ripple-of-hope-award
Schumpeter, J. A. (1911) *Theory of Economic Development.* Cambridge, MA: Harvard University Press.
Sirkin, H., Hemerling, J., and Bhattacharya, A. (2008) *Globality: Competing with Everyone from Everywhere for Everything* . Boston, MA: Boston Consulting Group.
Setiloane, G. (1986) *African Theology: An Introduction.* Johannesburg: Skotaville Publishers.
Sheldon, M. E. (1971) Investments and involvements as mechanisms producing commitment to the organization. *Administrative Science Quarterly*, 16: 143–150.
Sigger, D. S., Polak, B. W., and Pennink, B. J. W. (2010) *'Ubuntu' or 'Humanness' as a Management Concept.* CDS Research Report No. 29 ISSN 1385-9218. Retrieved October 7, 2014 from www.rug.nl/research/globalisation-studies-groningen/publications/researchreports/reports/ubuntuorhumanness.pdf
Sithole, N. (1959) African personality. *Voice of Africa*, 1(8): 18–27.
Smith, A. (1937) *An Inquiry Into the Nature and Causes of the Wealth of Nations.* New York, NY: Random House.
Sorokin, P. A., and Merton, R. K. (1937) Social time: A methodological and functional analysis. *American Journal of Sociology*, 42(5): 615–629.
Tangney, J. P. (2000) Humility: Theoretical perspectives, empirical findings and directions for future research. *Journal of Social and Clinical Psychology*, 19(1): 70–82.
Taylor, D. F. P. (2014) Defining Ubuntu for business ethics – A deontological approach. *South African Journal of Philosophy*, 33(3): 331–345.
Teffo, L. J. (1998) Both/ubuntu as a way forward for contemporary South Africa. *Word and Action*, 38(365): 3–5.
Tzafrir, S. S. (2005) The relationship between trust, HRM practices and firm performance. *International Journal of Human Resource Management*, 16(9): 1600–1622.
Van de Bunt-Kokhuis, S. (2011) Servant leadership in a cross-cultural ethical perspective. In D. T. Weir and N. Sultan (Eds.), *From Critique to Action: The Practical Ethics of the Organizational World.* Newcastle upon Tyne, UK: Cambridge Scholars Publishing, 273–294.
Von Bergen, C. W., Von Bergen, B. A., Stubblefield, C., and Bandow, D. (2012) Authentic tolerance: Between forbearance and acceptance. *Journal of Cultural Diversity*, 19(4), 111–117.
Waldron, J. (2015) *Exploring the Differences Between South African and Western Business Management Philosophies: A Multiple Case Study.* Unpublished Dissertation. North Central State University.
Walumbwa, F. O., Avolio, B. J., and Aryee, S. (2011) Leadership and management research in Africa: A synthesis and suggestions for future research. *Journal of Occupational and Organizational Psychology*, 84(3): 425–439.
Washington, K. (2010) Zulu traditional healing, Afrikan worldview and the practice of Ubuntu: Deep thought for Afrikan/Black psychology. *The Journal of Pan African Studies*, 3(8): 24–39.
Washington, M., and Hacker, M. (2005). Why change fails: Knowledge counts. *Leadership & Organization Development Journal*, 26(5), 400–411.
Weber, M. (1947) *The Theory of Social and Economic Organization* (A. M. Henderson and T. Parsons, Trans.). New York, NY: Oxford University Press.
Weiner, Y. (1982) Commitment in organizations: A normative view. *Academy of Management Review*, 7(3): 418–428.
Weir, D. T., Mangaliso, M. P., and Mangaliso, N. A. (2010) Some implications of the intercultural approach to international HRM: Ubuntu and Ummah. In L. Toombs (Ed.), *Academy of Management Proceedings. 2010.* Braircliff Manor, NY: Academy of Management, 1–6.

Wilson, D. C. (1992) *A Strategy of Change*. London: Routledge.

Wolmarans, S. (2005). *Ubuntu Means to SAA What 'Putting People First' Meant to BA*. Retrieved May 9, 2018, from Ubuntu + Psychology: http://www.ubuntupsychology.org/2005/03/

Yawson, R. M. (2017) Leadership development in South Africa. In A. Ardichvili and K. Dirani (Eds.), *Leadership Development in Emerging Market Economies* (pp. 93–109). New York, NY: Palgrave Macmillan.

Yergin, D., and Stanislaw, J. (2002). *The Commanding Heights: The Battle for the World Economy*. New York, NY: Touchstone - Simon and Schuster Publishing.

Zahra, S. A., and O'Neill, H. M. (1998) Charting the landscape of global competition: Reflections on emerging organizational challenges and their implications for senior executives. *Academy of Management Executive (1993–2005)*, 12(4): 13–21.

Zoogah, D. B., Peng, M. W., and Woldu, H. (2015) Institutions, resources, and organizational effectiveness in Africa. *Academy of Management Perspectives*, 29(1): 7–31.

7

A circumstantiated model of change in Africa

David B. Zoogah

There is growing evidence by academics and practitioners that Africa is changing. This change is manifested in terms such as "Africa rising" (Economist, 2011); "Lions on the move" (McKinsey Global Institute, 2010); "Africa emerges" (Rotberg, 2013); and "Africa unchained" (Ayittey, 2006) all of which suggest transformation of African economies. It seems that the "old ways of doing business" are giving way to "new ways." About thirty years ago, Jones and Blunt (1993) observed that "there is a need to develop concepts and approaches to organizational development and change which are effective and sensitive to African contexts" because "immense changes have taken place on the African continent during that time" (p. 1735). The authors observed that changes in diverse sectors - government, education, health, and organizational arrangements – were taking place as a result of independence from colonial masters. Drawing from Mintzberg's (1989) organizational culture model and their observation that "the single most commonly asked question – the virtual obsession of today's managers – is how can we help bureaucracies to change?" – the authors noted that their observation is "an overwhelmingly urgent question for many African countries" (p. 1739).

I assert that that observation is even truer nowadays than then: not only are there many radical government changes across all the regions of Africa and more dramatic changes in several sectors including education, health and bureaucracies, but also there are other tectonic shifts – elimination of apartheid, globalization, technological innovations – which have also affected Africa directly and indirectly.

These contextual dynamics affect organizations in Africa albeit in a different way from those in other contexts (Blunt and Jones, 1991). Consequently, we leverage insights from the organizational development and change literature (see Bartunek and Woodman, 2015) to propose a model that we believe fits the unique contextual attributes of Africa to answer the question: how does organizational change in Africa manifest? We term the model circumstantiated because the drivers, processes, and outcomes of organizational change and development (henceforth, OCD) are based on internal and external circumstances of organizations. Our explanations not only extend the extant model of OCD – the dialogic model – but also show the way that the change of today differs from that of yesterday. First, we discuss the contextual characteristics of Africa that provide a background to OCD in the continent. Second, we review models of change in general and specifically in Africa. Third, we present a model of OCD that is unique to Africa – a circumstantiated model. We conclude with a discussion of how to test the model.

Contextual characteristics of Africa

I have reviewed these characteristics and their implications in Chapter 5. Briefly, research in the social sciences show that the contextual characteristics of Africa differ from those of Europe, America, and Asia (see Collier, 2007; Mbaku, 2004; Michalopoulos and Papaioannou, 2015; Zoogah, Peng, and Woldu's, 2015)

Models of change

Similar to the contextual characteristics, I encourage you to see Chapter 5 of this book for models of change in general and specifically to Africa. Several studies in the social sciences – sociology, anthropology, economics, political science, and business – have examined change within and across organizations (see Poole and Van de Ven, 2004). The studies show diverse definitions, dimensions, attributes, and typologies of organizational change. They also identify various types of change in relation to organizations that range from life-cycle, teleological, and dialectical, to evolutionary models (see Poole and Van de Ven, 2004).

More recently, Bartunek and Woodman (2015) reviewed the literature on planned organizational change, often termed organizational development, and outline not only past reviews but also major models of OCD and approaches. They argue that the majority of OD scholars often use the unfreeze-change-refreeze model developed by Lewin (1947) and expanded by Schein (1996). As Bartunek and Woodman (2015) indicate, planned organizational change, most frequently referred to as organization development (OD), has undergone multiple changes over the course of the sixty-plus years that it has been recognized as a discrete area of focus (e.g., Beckhard, 1969; French and Bell, 1995; Marrow, 1969; Mirvis, 1988, 1990; Seo, Putnam, and Bartunek, 2004). They argue that "the sequential model of change developed by Kurt Lewin in 1947 to characterize how change should unfold – unfreeze-change-refreeze – has remained largely untouched" (p. 158), and show that most scholars ignore the "fundamental temporal dimensions of organizational change" (p. 159) or attempt to replace OD with other concepts such as quality of work life (QWL).

A cursory reading of their article shows a view of the diagnostic model as an approach to change that is based on a positive orientation. As an episodic model, it is functional in environments characterized by clear and controllable attributes; works with some systems; and is based on planned outcomes. In addition, it focuses on technical construction of organizational structures and systems, as well as small group intervention approaches. It relies on differentiated and specific epistemologies because the mode of inquiry is basic given the simplicity of the model. The three stages represent stasis with slow and determined pacing such that the rhythm of change is stage-oriented. Lastly, it is characterized by monophony (i.e., a single chorus or pattern change). In sum, it is a model that is based on organizational diagnosis and problem-solving (French and Bell, 1995).

Attempts to improve the diagnostic model resulted in the dialogic model (Bushe and Marshak, 2009, 2014). It is "an approach to change based on complexity theory, narrative, conversation, and a positive orientation" (Bartunek and Woodman, 2015: 159). However, as Bartunek and Woodman (2015) indicate, "although it is labeled as new (Burnes and Cooke, 2012; Bushe and Marshak, 2009), a dialogic emphasis has actually been evolving since the 1980s, with roots that go back at least to the late 1950s" (p. 159). It combines the positivist and constructivist epistemological perspectives. The constructivist perspective highlights the social construction emphasized by the dialogic model. It also employs conversational approaches, where change agents discuss with change targets, and champions the causes, processes, and outcomes of change. Like the diagnostic model, it functions effectively in relatively predictable or clear and controllable environments, as in western countries. However, it works with entire systems rather than partial ones as proposed by the diagnostic model. It also focuses on desired or planned futures and uses large group interventions. The mode of enquiry is appreciative, which comprises discovery, dreaming, design, and destiny (Cooperrider, 1986). Rather than the positivistic method, the dialogic model relies on action research, a reflective process of progressive problem-solving led by individuals working with others in teams or as part of a "community of practice" to improve the way they address issues and solve problems or changes (Wenger, 1988). Appreciative inquiry is characterized by selection of a focus, clarifying theories, identifying research questions, data collection and analysis, reporting results, and taking informed action. In terms of complexity, the dialogic model is relatively complex but clear. The clarity emerges from the conversation or dialogue with change agents. In terms of timing, the model is sequential and dynamic (Bartunek and Woodman, 2015). The trajectory of the change process can change through dialogue. Pacing is also checkered and moderated by new insights that emerge from the conversation. Consequently, the rhythm of change is repetitive, intense and frequent in variability (Bartunek and Woodman, 2015). Lastly, it is characterized by polyphony (i.e., multiple choruses or patterns of change). In sum, it is a model that is based on dialogue and dynamics (Bartunek and Woodman, 2015; Bushe and Marshak, 2009).

Models of change in Africa

Models of change in Africa are few. They include Jones and Blunt's (1993) model, which identifies factors that limit organizational change; Abdulraheem, Mordi, Ojo, and Ajonbadi (2013)'s model of planned change in higher educational institutions of Nigeria; Adeniji, Osibanjo, and Abiodun's (2013) model of change in the banking industry; Burchardt's (2012) model of faith-based organizations in South Africa; Yaeger and Sorensen's (2011) models of organizational development (OD) in Africa; Sulamoyo's (2011) application of Ubuntu to OD and change in Sub-Saharan Africa; and Kudonoo's (2013) model of OD for OD consulting (see Chapter 5 of this book for details).

A circumstantiated model of organizational change and development in Africa

Given the radical contrast between the cultural, social, political, institutional, economic, and regulatory environments of Africa and western countries, we adapt the dialogic OD model to Africa. We term our model a circumstantiated model of change, because as several authors have pointed out (Adeniji et al., 2013; Jones and Blunt, 1993; Kudonoo, 2013; Yaeger and Sorensen, 2011), the internal and external conditions of Africa often impinge on drivers, processes, and outcomes of organizational change. It is an approach to change based on complexity theory, conversation, positivist, and circumstantiated orientations. It combines the approach of the dialogic model with unique attributes of Africa – exogenous influences on the ecology of change in an unplanned and unexpected manner. How then does change manifest in African organizations? We begin by providing an operational definition of change.

The meaning or definition of change is taken for granted in the literature. A review of the literature (see Bartunek and Woodman, 2015; Van de Ven and Poole, 2004) shows that change is often tied to a particular state (e.g., institution) or process (e.g. innovation) in definitional terms. For example, Van de Ven and Hargrave (2004) define "institutional change as the difference in form, quality, or state over time in an institution" (p. 261). Even though this chapter is not a review of change conceptualization, it is nonetheless important to define what we mean by change. That is significant in developing a general model that is operative across levels and at the same time unique to Africa. Characteristics of such a model are shown in Table 7.1.

Table 7.1 Models of change

Characteristics	*Old OD model*	*New OD model*	*Expanded OD model (Africa)*
	Diagnostic OD	*Dialogic OD*	*Circumstantiated*
Definition	"an approach to change based on a positive orientation"	"an approach to change based on complexity theory, narrative, conversation, and a positive orientation"	"an approach to change based on complexity theory, conversation, positive and circumstantial orientations"
Environment	Clear and controllable	Clear and controllable	Unclear and uncontrollable
Systems	Work with some systems	Work with formal systems	Work with formal and informal systems
Construction	Technical	Social	Social and technical
Epistemologies	Differentiated and specific perspectives	Positivist, variety of perspectives	Integrative & variety of perspectives
Intervention	Small group	Large group	Very large group
Approaches	Rational	Conversational	Conversational + circumstantial
Inquiry	Basic	Appreciative: discovery, dream, design, destiny	Appreciative and non-appreciative
Research	Positivistic	Action	Action + intuition + imposed
Sequence	Linear	Nonlinear	Nonlinear
Complexity	Simple	Complex but clear	Very complex and ambiguous
Timing	Static & staged;	Sequential and dynamic	Moderated dynamism
Pacing	Slow and determined	Checkered and moderated	Checkered and unmoderated
Rhythm of change	Staged	Repetitive, intense and frequent in variability	Repetitive sometimes; variability is indeterminate
Outcomes	Planned	Desired future	Planned and unplanned

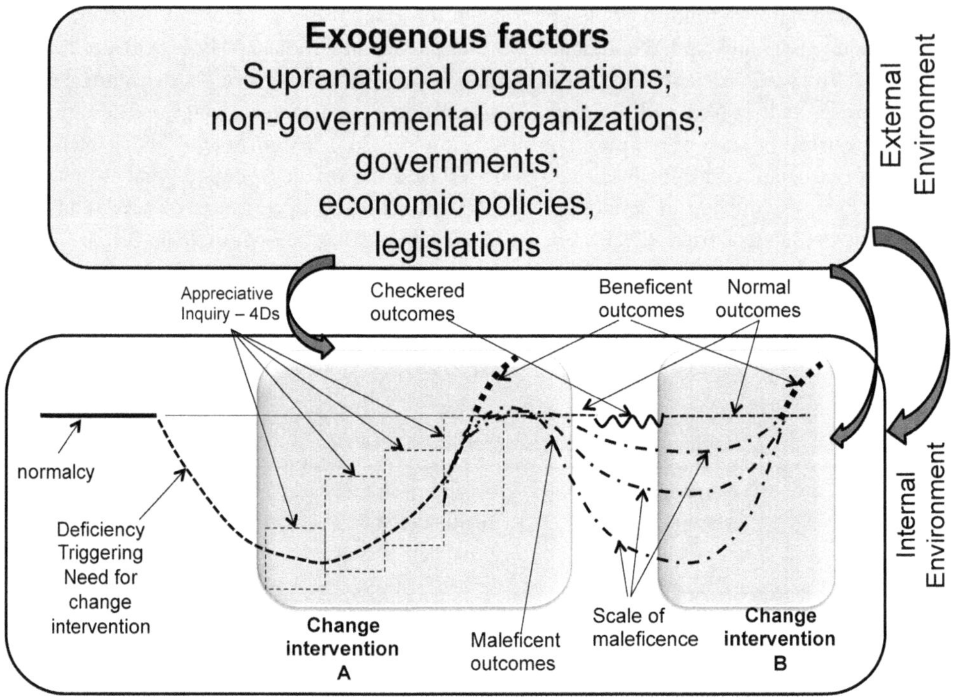

Figure 7.1 Circumstantiated model of change

Circumstantiated model

Characteristics

Environment of change

Circumstantiated change is explained by a number of indicators. The first is the environment of change. In models of change, the environment is a central element. Typically, researchers focus on the environment's degree of stability, the interconnections between its various elements, and changes which are occurring (Jones and Blunt, 1993; see also Poole and Van de Ven, 2004). In examining organizational change and development in Africa, a number of researchers have identified several environmental factors that not only influence the initiation and progress of change but also acceptance and resistance to that change. While some factors focus on the internal environment, others focus on the external environment. They operate at different levels – individual, organizational, national, and even supranational. Jones and Blunt (1993) observe that "some of these factors, and others, lie outside the control of African governments", suggesting that there are supranational factors that influence organizational change in Africa.

In sum, the external environment of organizations in Africa is unclear, unpredictable, and ambiguous (Zoogah et al., 2015). It contrasts with the fairly predictable external environments of organizations in the west. Models of change in Africa have typically considered these factors as having linear effects, probably for empirical or positivistic reasons. We argue that such an approach is inappropriate. Africa is "one of the most difficult administrative settings to be found anywhere in the world" (Montgomery, 1989: 11), partly because of African formal organizations' demonstration of tremendous resistance to different forms of bureaucratic reorientation and reform (Kiggundu, 1989), political realities that tend to undermine the appearance of grand scope for administrative modernization (Montgomery, 1989), and the relatively new African nations which inherited from their colonial masters the bureaucratic forms that were designed primarily for the maintenance of law and order, but which have proved extraordinarily resistant to change (Jones, 1991). Furthermore, organizational factors such as mechanistic structures ignore the complex reality of organizations, as well as the political, social, psychological, and irrational characteristics of organizational life. There is also an emphasis on control rather than performance (i.e., emphasizing inputs and internal procedures, and neglecting measures of output). In the public sectors, there is overstaffing of the public sectors resulting in inflated wage bills, and a "cult of the generalist" ethos which reflects the customary British and French mistrust of the professional and admiration of the notion of wellroundedness. In addition, there is a lack of real knowledge about African administrative systems and practices as well as a misallocation of skills.

Systems

In contrast to the diagnostic model, which focuses on part of the system, the dialogic model works with the whole system (Bartunek and Woodman, 2015; Bunker and Alban (1997, 2014; Pasmore and Fagans, 1992). By whole system, we mean a combination of social, technical, and managerial systems. Specifically, Emery and Trist's (1960) theory of sociotechnical systems emphasizes the importance of work with a whole system to accomplish change. Working with the whole system suggests working in large group interventions which enables a large number of organizational members to work together (Bunker and Alban, 2014).

The types of systems proposed by the diagnostic and dialogic models – technical and socio-technical – are fairly stable, structured, relatively more aligned, and with fairly predictable processes and subsystems than those in Africa (Zoogah et al., 2015). Given that modern organizations are legacies of colonialism and are predicated on cultural assumptions that differ from those in Africa (Mamdani, 1996), it is likely the dialogic model would have to be extended to incorporate unanticipated systems or subsystems that might be imposed or chanced upon organizations during interventions. Jones and Blunt (1993) noted this point in their observation that western models of OD cannot be transplanted in Africa; they have to be adjusted because of different socio-cultural, technological, and economic systems. In Africa, consideration has to be given to both formal and informal systems because Africa is characterized by both formal and informal economies (Godfrey, 2011). The informal systems complement and enhance the formal systems.

Construction

Integrating social elements in OD is the central point of the dialogical model; it advocates social construction of change interventions. Extant research suggests that it has had a profound impact on organizational scholarship and practice (e.g., Avenier, 2010; Van de Ven, 2007). It proposes that there may be different meanings among varying groups and individuals regarding any particular phenomenon (Moch and Bartunek, 1990). As a result, there may not be one objective truth about organizational phenomena, including what a problem is (Burnes and Cooke, 2012; Oswick, 2009) or what a change is (Wiebe, 2010).

Unlike the diagnostic and dialogic models, which emphasize technical and social construction respectively, the circumstantiated model we propose emphasizes a combination of not only the socio-technical construction but an ecological construction. By ecological construction we mean interventions that explore deeply the interactions between organizations in Africa and their environments, which encompass organizational, national, supranational, and global contexts. It incorporates the cultural, economic, and even political ecologies into the socio-technical constructions (Sklar, 1993). That approach is more likely to yield effective outcomes because unknown unknowns will not supervene.

Epistemologies

Organizational change generates knowledge – novel or comparative. The justified beliefs underlying that change – epistemology – do not only provide a basis for action, but also rationale for mobilization of resources to facilitate goals of change. The epistemology underlying the diagnostic model is rooted in mid-20th-century positivist orientations (e.g., Van Nistelrooij and Sminia, 2010) that operated under the illusion that there is an objectively valid reality that can be addressed (Bushe and Marshak, 2009). That might be due to the methods, validity, and scope investigations in the diagnostic model. However, it focuses on specific ways of knowing about transformations. This view contrasts with the dialogic model, which operates out of social constructivist or critical realist perspectives (Bartunek and Woodman, 2015; Burnes and Cooke, 2012; Marshak and Grant, 2008; Oswick, 2009) and uses a variety of ways of knowledge, including positivist and constructivist.

The circumstantiated model builds on the dialogic model epistemology. It proposes that there are circular, nonlinear, and constructivist and positivist ways of knowing. This comprehensive and integrative view of knowing is certainly different from that of western thought. The difference suggests that change processes and outcomes are likely to be different from those in the west. For example, Ubuntu, which is borne out of the philosophy that community strength comes of community support, and that dignity and identity are achieved through mutualism, empathy, generosity and community commitment, may on the one hand mobilize employees toward change initiatives but on the other hand induce them not to take the initiative seriously because of the belief that change process is nonlinear and therefore might be reverted to at another time. Indeed, OD studies in the public sector shows that employees had a lackadaisical attitude toward the change interventions (Torrington, Weightman, and Johns, 1989).

Intervention

Organizational development and change often arises from deficiencies – incompetence, lack of technology, poor performance, etc (Van de Ven and Poole, 1995). As a result, they tend to be considered interventions to resolve the deficiencies. While the diagnostic model uses small group interventions, the dialogic model uses large group interventions. Bunker and Alban (1997: xv) defined large group interventions as "methods for involving the whole system, internal and external, in [a planned] change process". Bartunek and Woodman (2015: 164) add that "in such interventions large numbers of participants in a system, including everyone who has a stake in issues under discussion, gather together for several days of focused and guided conversation about a topic". They are like town halls where there is an intentional search for multiple and differing perspectives, and all participants are given an opportunity to influence deliberations with the hope that a common ground will be reached where participants can agree on ways to effect positive change in their organizations (Bartunek, Balogun, and Do, 2011). Such interventions have become common since the 1980s (Bunker and Alban, 1992, 1997).

The use of large group interventions to search for common goal is similar to consensus decision-making, which is characteristic of societies in Africa. The process of such interventions can be challenging in western cultures which are characterized by high individualism. In contrast, they fit with the collectivistic culture of African societies. As a result, even larger groups are likely to be appropriate in Africa. Such interventions are likely to be easily executed because of the traditional mechanisms that make them effective. Previous studies (Jones and Blunt, 1993; Torrington et al., 1989) did not specify the types of interventions – small, medium, or large – partly because they focused on the diagnostic model. However, we can leverage insight from the dialogic model to argue that if large group interventions are effective in cultures not congruent with them, then even larger group interventions can be more effective in cultures fit for such groups. A second reason for the appropriateness of very large group interventions in Africa is the flexibility of organizational systems and structures. The flexibility may arise inadvertently from incompetence or ineffectiveness, but it nonetheless facilitates interventions that can yield positive outcomes for organizations. Executives, as leaders, are likely to be perceived as traditional regents who are often accorded authority and respect to moderate initiatives and decisions.

Approaches

How are interventions conducted? The diagnostic model suggests a rational approach where one expects to identify the pros and cons of solutions to change need. The dialogic model relies on conversational approaches to change (Bartunek and Woodman, 2015). Those approaches fit with the social construction view of change, which emphasizes discourse and conversation (e.g., Barrett, Thomas, and Hocevar, 1995; Boje, Oswick, and Ford, 2004; Ford and Ford, 1995; Heracleous and Barrett, 2001; Heracleous and Marshak, 2004; Marshak and Grant, 2008; Tsoukas, 2005). The types of conversations held in organizations, as well as the participants in the conversations, are crucial for change. Ford and Ford (1995, 2009), identified four different types of conversations managers may have with employees at particular times during a change initiative and suggested how these types of conversations may affect the initiative. These include *initiative conversations* to introduce a change, *understanding conversations* to engage organizational members in the change, *performance conversations* to support commitment to the change, and *closure conversations* to complete the change. In addition to managers' conversations, conversations that employees have among themselves regarding change (Hardy, Lawrence, and Grant, 2005; Maitlis and Christianson, 2014) are important, because narratives "make things happen" (Buchanan and Dawson, 2007: 671).

In addition to formal conversations, circumstantial narratives and informal conversations can be incorporated in African initiatives. Circumstantial narratives are expectations of unexpected and unplanned happenings that occur during change interventions. These narratives vary from purpose and progression to termination narratives. Some circumstantial narratives often affect communities in a way that cannot be explained by western thought or philosophy (Mbiti, 1969). While purpose narratives focus on the unexpected happenings about the mission of the organization, progression narratives center on the advancement of the intervention. It may be sped up or slowed in an unexpected way. Termination narratives center on how interventions end. Even though they may be conversations about how interventions should end, there are often unplanned termination narratives that complement the conversations and dialogs that are held as a result of the intervention. For example, a state parastatal organization that plans to complete organizational restructuring within three years might not achieve that goal because of the supervention of a governmental change that results in CEO changes.[1]

Inquiry

There are a number of methodological inquiries that are used in OD interventions. The dialogic approach seems to fit with appreciative inquiry, because it builds most explicitly on social constructivism and a conversational approach oriented toward creating a desired future state (Bartunek and Woodman, 2015). Appreciative inquiry (AI) is a technique advanced by Cooperrider and Srivastva (1987). It relies on large group intervention (Ludema, Whitney, Mohr, and Griffin, 2003); explicitly uses the social construction of reality as an epistemological foundation; and fosters "conversation that inquires into the life-generating experiences, core values, and moments of excellence in organizational life" (Barge and Oliver, 2003: 124). AI has four phases – discovery, dream, design, and destiny. Each phase has its own type of conversation (Cooperrider and Whitney, 2005; Gergen, Gergen, and Barrett, 2004). While participants share stories about when they have felt most positive or excited about their work or their organization in the discovery stage, they talk with each other in small groups to develop "what is the world calling for us to become" (Cooperrider and Whitney, 2005: 77) in the dream stage. In the design stage, the small groups identify, on the basis of their prior discussion of the optimal core of their organization, a collective vision of the future they want. The organization then adopts the preferred design in the destiny phase, with the intention of strengthening the "capability of the whole system, enabling it to build hope and sustain momentum for ongoing positive change and high performance" (p. 78).

AI, which is predicated on the whole system working together with a future-oriented positive focus through dialogue to yield positive outcomes (Bartunek and Woodman, 2015), differs from the diagnostic approach that focuses on identification of factors that cause rigidity to be altered. That inquiry can be extended in Africa by combining the basic technique of the diagnostic model with the AI technique of the dialogic model, and with other techniques, or what we call non-AI techniques. In addition to the questions of excitement, future, structure, and choice implied by AI, questions of disquiet, past, process, and benefaction can be asked. These "unappreciative" questions are intended to complement those of AI, because the past and present are often the lived realities of Africans (Mbiti, 1969).

Research

Another significant factor in OD is research. The diagnostic model adopts "positivist assumptions of a fixed, objective external reality with a formulation that emphasized ways that individuals, in interaction with each other, help create what we later come to recognize as real" (Bartunek and Woodman, 2015: 164). The diagnostic OD seeks to collect accurate information (Argyris, 1976; Pasmore and Friedlander, 1982; Nadler, 1977) for problem-solving. This approach contrasts with that of the dialogic model, which assumes that problem-solving approaches are problematic in themselves (Barge and Oliver, 2003) and suggests conversation and dialog (Barge and Oliver, 2003; Ford and Ford, 1995) as a way of initial data gathering that increases "awareness of the variety of experiences contained in the system" (Bushe and Marshak, 2009: 360). In other words, it advocates action research. Coghlan (2011) described how contemporary approaches to action research – a cornerstone of diagnostic OD – are actually more consistent with the dialogic model, but Bartunek and Woodman (2015: 167) contend that "such rethinking may be thought of in terms of freezing the model of the new OD".

The circumstantiated model extends the dialogic model by including intuition with action. There is accumulated evidence in the decision-making literature about the role of intuition in managerial decisions (Burke and Miller, 1999; Dane and Pratt, 2007). Even though we did not find studies exploring the role of intuition in OD, it is easy to see how the dialogic model which relies on conversation can be extended to include intuition. Rather than separating the qualitative from quantitative process, OD in Africa should be informed by both data and intuition in order to drive the desired outcomes. In addition, we believe impositions – ideas, plans, programs, etc. – from external agencies could be included in OD. These impositions might be insightful and helpful for OD interventions, particularly in Africa, where expertise from foreigners tends to be proffered and preferred.

Sequence

OD interventions, particularly those of the diagnostic model, tend to be sequential. Sequence refers to a temporal ordering of events (Albert, 2013; Amis, Slack, and Hinings, 2004; Bluedorn, 2002; Langley, 1999). As Bartunek and Woodman (2015) indicate, a sequence which need not necessarily be linear "may include several dimensions, including recognizable steps and stages, order of events within a particular stage or phase and the effect of this ordering on the overall sequence, interval and duration of each stage, and when events appear within a sequence" (p. 168). The diagnostic model is linear in sequence, but the dialogic model is nonlinear because conversations can cycle back and forth (Greenwood and Hinings, 1988).

The nonlinear sequence of the dialogic model extends to the African context because the sequence of events and time is not linear (Mbiti, 1969). Things can cycle back from where they began. That tendency seems to account for the African problem or African dummy often observed by economists on the inability of African countries and organizations to dramatically improve their performance (The Economist, 2014).

Complexity

Another factor heightened by the dialogic model, in contrast to the diagnostic model, is complexity. The stages – unfreeze, change, refreeze – are simple with regard to complexity. Even though the simplicity has clarity because of the linearity and discreteness of the model, the complexity of the dialogic model fills in the deficit of the diagnostic model. Dooley (2004) proposed complex models of organizational change, arguing that "organizations can be thought of as examples of a general class of complex systems called complex adaptive systems or CAS" (p. 357). Models in complexity science tend to combine linear and nonlinear causalities; describe both entities and variables with the system; and can be both "top-down" and "bottom-up" (Dooley, 2004). The elements of complex systems include *agents* which refer to "semi-autonomous units that seek to maximize their fitness by evolving over time" (p. 357); *fitness* of the agent, which is modeled as a complex aggregate of many factors, both local and global; *tags*, which help identify what other agents are capable of interacting with the focal agent; and *boundary*, which defines the specific confines of the system (Anderson, 1999; Gell-Mann, 1994). These attributes suggest that CAS tend to be dynamic. Complex dynamical systems exhibit three key characteristics (Gallagher and Appenzeller, 1999; Gallagher, Appenzeller, and Normile (1999). First, they consist of a number of interacting components or agents. These components can be homogeneous or heterogeneous. Second, they exhibit emergent behavior in that their collective behavior exhibits a coherent pattern that could not be predicted from the behavior of the components separately. Third, and most importantly, the emergent behavior is self-organized in that it does not result from a controlling component agent. These attributes of complexity apply in the dialogic model where conversation which may be intended to be simple devolves into a complex system.

Even though the complexity may also characterize the circumstantiated model, the difference is that in the dialogic model, the complexity seems to have a clear pattern because of the structured systems and processes. In contrast, the complexity of the circumstantiated model is ambiguous partly because of exogenous influences (Blunt and Jones, 1991).

Timing

The diagnostic and dialogic models centralize time, although in different ways. Time in the former is staged or periodic, while it is continuous in the latter. Time is emphasized at individual and organizational levels. Langley (1999), for example, indicates deadlines, the simultaneity of alternative possibilities for action, and when information is available in comparison with the need to act. Ancona, Goodman, Lawrence, and Tushman (2001) also indicate that not only are there timetables in organizations against which organization members can determine their progress, but also there are timing norms regarding when particular events are appropriate. Further, Ancona and Chong (1996: 252) note that the timing of events in organizations sometimes shifts periodically or in relation to certain types of environmental change (when external contexts shift dramatically). Bartunek and Woodman (2015) also suggest that "an important dimension of timing regarding change is awareness of the best time to act" (p. 170). These views of time are rational and linear, based on western thought. They enable individuals and organizations to capture windows of opportunity (Huy, 2001) or the right time for change (Albert, 2013, Bartunek and Necochea, 2000, Gersick, 1988), occasions when there is readiness for it (Armenakis, Harris, and Mossholder, 1993). Time as linear facilitates predictability of interventions' potential to benefit from receptivity to change and more bountiful resources (Huy, 2001). It also orients actions toward sequence and dynamics of activities.

However, "the linear concept of time in western thought with an indefinite past, present and infinite future, is practically foreign to African thinking" (Mbiti, 1969: 16–17). As Mbiti (1969) indicates, the future is virtually absent because events which lie in it have not taken place, and if realized only represents *potential* time. "Actual time is what is present and what is past. It moves 'backward' rather than 'forward'. Because people set their minds not on future things, but chiefly on what has taken place" (Mbiti, 1969: 17), the idea of interventions for future outcomes may not be appreciated.

This view of time in traditional Africa suggests that planning for the unknown, predicting likely outcomes, and orchestrating a sequence of actions are unlikely to be effective. "This time orientation – present and past dimensions – dominates African understanding of the individual, community, and the universe suggests that time has to be experienced in order to make sense or to become real" (Mbiti, 1969: 17). Thus, time is reckoned as an experience of events or phenomenon calendar, not numerical calendar, and created or produced. In other words, "the traditional concept of time is intimately bound up with the entire life of people and our understanding of it helps to pave the way for comprehending the thinking, attitude, and actions of people in work and nonwork contexts" (Mbiti, 1969: 27). Even though modern organizations in Africa are legacies of colonialism and western design (Mamdani, 1996), their members who are socialized traditionally are likely to behave consistent with the African rather than western conception of time.

A model of change in Africa therefore has to be circumstantiated. Experience of the phenomena is likely to be different across organizations and change interventions. The rationale for the change intervention might not also be fully appreciated. Windows of opportunity might be moderated rather than predicted. Resources in the form of human agents may not be realized due to the time orientation. The "emotional stir up" implied by Lewin (1947) is unlikely to be strong because arousal as a result of future orientation or anticipation seems lacking in Africa.

For example, meetings based on time to meet deadlines associated with change activities may not manifest according to plans. Change is not sequential or linear; rather, it has to be moderated consistent with deviations arising from phenomenon calendars.

Pacing

Change involves pacing, the speed of change (Amis et al., 2004; Ancona and Chong, 1996). Pacing may include overall speed or different pacing at different times in a change process (Bartunek and Woodman, 2015) because change sometimes takes on different speeds as it unfolds (Ancona and Chong, 1996; Bartunek and Woodman, 2015; Gersick, 1988; Huy, 2001; Klarner and Raisch, 2013).

The dialogic model, in contrast to the diagnostic model, suggests that speed is necessary to generate momentum for a change to overcome inertia, especially at the beginning of a radical change (Amis et al., 2004; Bartunek and Woodman, 2015; Jansen, 2004). Given that the sequential linear conception of time is not alien to Africa, pacing of change is likely to be checkered but unmoderated. Moderated pacing is regulatory control based on a sequence of activities. To the extent that sequence is lacking, and participation in change is based on experience or phenomenon, then pacing is likely to be unmoderated because of the inability to determine a priori the sequence of events. Further, macro events which coincide with micro events sometimes align in pace and direction, but most often do not because of the unpredictability of temporal and contextual factors (Mbiti, 1969).

Rhythm

Bartunek and Woodman (2015) note that "there is nothing in Lewin's model that refers to rhythmic patterns" (p. 170) but the dialogic model has such patterns. A rhythm is defined as repetitions of cycles (cf. Ancona and Chong, 1996; Mintzberg and Westley, 1992) that create dominant temporal orderings and often become inertial. Some define rhythm of change as "a pattern of variability in the intensity and frequency of organizational activities, typically characterized by periods of accelerated activity and slowed activity" (Huy, 2001: 613), and others (Klarner and Raisch, 2013: 168) identify four types of rhythms: focused (long periods of change and short periods of stability), punctuated (long periods of stability and short periods of change), temporarily switching (alternating stability and change), and regular (in which intervals between changes are relatively equal), some of which are applicable to the dialogic model. Even though the punctuated rhythm (Gersick, 1988) is the most studied in organizational settings (Bartunek and Woodman, 2015), other types are applicable to the dialogic model and the circumstantiated model.

The intensity and frequency of variability of the dialogic model (Huy, 2001) is expanded in the circumstantiated model. The variability, however, is indeterminate in the latter. The indeterminacy is due to the potential for exogenous factors and processes to be introjected into a change intervention (Jones and Blunt, 1993). The speed at which the change manifests depends on the change agents, champions, resources, and technologies underlying the change initiative. It also depends on the number and type of factors instantiating the change. To the extent that drag factors (i.e., constraints) are harnessed in the change process, propulsion is likely to be slow. The second element is the direction. There are diverse directions – up, down, forward, backward, and diagonal – which could be pursued, adopted, and modified. In other words, a change that has an upward trajectory might revert downward at the transition area depending on constraints that may emerge during the change process (Jones and Blunt, 1993).

Outcomes of change

Change is purposeful in the sense that it seeks to achieve specific outcomes. The major outcome is transformation (Bunker and Alban, 1992; Lindaman and Lippitt, 1979). While it is planned in diagnostic models (Lewin, 1947), it is the specific desired future state in the dialogic model (Bushe and Marshak, 2009, 2014). Thus, both the diagnostic and dialogic models emphasize desired future outcomes but in different ways. In addition to the specific desired future outcome, other ancillary outcomes often emerge from change interventions. It is not uncommon for OD interventions to influence the (dis)satisfaction of employees (Jones and Blunt, 1993). Other outcomes include capability enhancement (Yaeger and Sorensen, 2011).

The circumstantiated model, however, proposes a combination of planned and unexpected or unplanned outcomes. The rate of change in Africa is accelerating and in many ways becoming increasingly turbulent, particularly for organizations (Chironga, Leke, Lund, and van Wamelen, 2011; Jones and Blunt, 1993; Zoogah and Nkomo, 2013). As a result, managers of systems in Africa have a responsibility to anticipate, initiate, monitor, interpret, and manage change. This responsibility is even more critical given that the change we describe here involves not just discrete, but multiple factors that are associated with greater uncertainty, frequently involving confusion, disturbance, and turbulence (Torrington et al., 1989). The change is aggravated by the failure of organizational leaders, for example, to articulate a clear vision of the proposed change and its intended outcomes. First, systems in Africa have similar effectiveness expectations as those in other contexts. Second, the actors in the change initiative – individuals, organizations, and societies – function as change agents or champions in much the same way: to ensure the change is successful in terms of the desired outcomes. Third, the outcomes of change depend on the degree to which tangible and intangible resources are deployed to facilitate the change.

What differentiates African systems from those in other contexts are the levels, viability, and magnitude of the outcomes. Change outcomes in Africa do not affect only individual systems (e.g., organizations) but also others (e.g., individuals and societies) for two reasons. Most organizations (e.g., state-owned enterprises) have governments as significant stakeholders (Jones and Blunt, 1993; Montgomery, 1989). Governments are agents, representing the interests of the principals, the citizens. As a result, whatever outcomes accrue to them revert to the citizens. Change outcomes also affect individuals because of the interlinkages of individuals to organizations. Remember that African countries are collectivistic, where individuals are inextricably linked to their workplaces. With regard to viability, change outcomes do not last because of the vicissitude of exogenous and endogenous forces buffeting organizations. It is not uncommon in Africa for change that results in leadership replacement to be supplanted by another leadership change due to exogenous influences (e.g., political appointment) (Montgomery, 1989; Zoogah et al., 2015).

First, the change we discuss has the potential to increase innovation. It cannot be gainsaid that innovation is vital for the transformation of African societies, organizations, and individuals (Ekekwe, 2015). Research shows that management of companies contributes to national development (Bloom, Genakos, Sadun, and Van Reenen, 2012). Innovation is often the desiderated outcome underlying change initiatives (Poole and Van de Ven, 2004). In Africa "innovation combines smart, economical responses with bold high-tech solutions" (et al., 2016: 22) because innovative systems that are adopted to transform organizational operations invariably spill across to other sectors, up to governments and nations and down to individuals (Adesida, Karuri-Sebina, and Resende-Santos, 2016). For example, cellphone technology system M-Pesa, which was initially used to enable Safaricom to effectively engage its operations, has resulted in the spread of the innovation to farming (harnessing earth, wind, and fire), health (fighting back against HIV/AIDS and Ebola), education (learning partnerships), finance (transfer or payment of money), employment (information about job availability), culture (filmmaking on a shoestring budget), and media (video and news dissemination) (Anderson et al., 2016). It has also transformed the lives of individuals through income generation, employment, and education (Gikunda, Abura, and Njeru, 2014; Prashaant and Sharma, 2015).

Second, organizational change can contribute to growth of systems in Africa. It is no secret that the "African problem" (Zoogah et al., 2015) and the "Africa dummy" (Englebert, 2000), which center on economic growth, spill over to companies. To the extent that inefficiencies pervade the economic system, the external environment of organizations cannot help but be affected by that inefficiency which constrains growth. Resource dissipation, as a consequence of inefficient behaviors such as corruption, constrains growth. In the Ease of Doing Business surveys conducted by the World Bank, African companies rate lack of financial resources or access to loans as a major constraint that limits their growth (World Bank, 2013). Change that results in different funding modes can reverse this situation.

The second set of outcomes manifests at the individual level. We focus on three important ones – competence, performance, and motivation – because research shows they contribute to the relative economic deprivation experienced in Africa (Dia, 1996; Mbaku, 2007). Competence, the individual skill and knowledge attributes that enable work performance, is suboptimal because of the lack of training centers, programs, and initiatives (The Economist, 2014). Change enables individuals to learn new ways of doing work and improves the competence of those people. Such competence is important in Africa; it improves work performance (Jones and Blunt, 1993). Change can also lead to performance improvement. One of the reasons for the ineffectiveness of African organizations, particularly those in the public sector, is the preference of executives for control rather than performance (Jones and Blunt, 1993). There is a neglect of measures of output "while questions of individual and organizational performance receive little attention" (Jones and Blunt, 1993: 1752). Jones and Blunt (1993), along with other scholars (Kiggundu, 1991; Dia, 1996; Yaeger and Sorensen, 2011), advocate for change initiatives that lead to performance improvement. We echo those views because organizational effectiveness is sorely needed in Africa (Zoogah et al., 2015) where there have been calls for measures to move the civil service, for example, towards a more performance-oriented culture (Jones and Blunt, 1993).

Research shows that effective change sometimes result in arousal and persistence of individual employees to achieve high strategic objectives of organizations (see Poole and Van de Ven, 2004). Given the breadth, depth, diversity of motivational agents (i.e., employees), and the variety of motivation mechanisms, it is not clear which motivational mechanism is directly attributed to organizational change. Nevertheless, it is generally recognized in the literature that organizational transformation has the potential to arouse feelings of satisfaction, expectations, and fairness among employees (see Poole and Van de Ven, 2004). Subsumed within motivation are exposure, experience, training, and sheer determination, which affect the persistence and effort directed at achieving the organization's resultant goals.

Process of change

Our fundamental contention is that change in Africa is not simple; rather, its complexity mirrors that of the African environment. As shown in Figure 7.1, the process of change suggested by the circumstantiated model combines the processes of the diagnostic and dialogic models. It also incorporates circumstantial elements. It begins by recognizing that organizations operating in normal states do not need change. Rather, it is when a deviation (primarily a negative one) occurs that the need for change is triggered. That deviation initiates a change intervention

(Intervention A). The intervention involves use of appreciative inquiry techniques – discovery of what caused the deviation and how to correct it; dreaming, designing, and destiny. To the extent that the intervention is successful, it is likely to yield desired outcomes. Three types of outcomes are likely. First, normal outcomes may be obtained. These get the organization back to its normal level. The outcomes may be checkered or not. Second, the outcomes may exceed expectations. These outcomes suggest a beneficent environment. Beneficence refers to the degree to which environments facilitate organizational effectiveness (Godfrey, Hatch, and Hansen, 2010). It centers on environment conditions – munificence or capacity-enhancement, stability, and predictability (Dess and Beard, 1984) – that enable institutions to yield desired outcomes. Studies of innovation and creativity suggest that countries with beneficent business environments attract investors (Doh, Jones, Mudambi, and Teegen, 2005; Zoogah et al., 2015) observed that "to the extent that African countries are beneficent, they enable institutional norms to effect desired organizational outcomes" (p. 20). Beneficent environments are not only devoid of shocks, uncertainties, and chaos, but they also enable organizations to counter transaction costs and institutional voids. Beneficence enables organizations to develop integration systems to amalgamate disparate processes into a harmonious and coherent whole that facilitates effective functioning (Hermann, 1963; Lawrence and Lorsch, 1967). Third, the outcomes might be less than expected, a situation that triggers a depression like the first one. We term these maleficent outcomes because they indicate the ill-fated attribute of the environment. The scale of the maleficence ranges from mild through medium to severe. That maleficence may trigger another intervention (Intervention B).

Discussion

Less than a decade ago, Africa was believed to be the next center of global focus because of the growth trajectories of vibrant economies such as Botswana, Mauritius, and Rwanda. Underneath the foundation, however, were several major problems that impeded sustainable individual, organizational, and national development. As we argued above, change in Africa fits more of a complex system that combines dualities, dialectics, and flows. While some dynamics are underneath but sometimes surge up, others stay on the surface but sometimes submerge. It is a complex system model of change (Dooley, 2004) that not only differs from others in the literature, but also seems consistent with the boom-burst-boom-burst cycles of Africa.

How can this model be empiricalized? Because it is based on the CAS platform, complexity techniques have to be used to study the model. Dooley (2004) discusses various methods and approaches to study complex changes. Such techniques can be applied to this model. One could also study the different aspects of the model (e.g., forms) using emergent and/or mapping techniques such as those in the business process literature (Biazzo, 2002; Kettinger, Teng, and Guha, 1997; Kuhn and Corman, 2003; Weber and Manning, 2001). For example, one could use mapping to investigate specific cases of change experienced by specific organizations or countries. Other methods include qualitative approaches such as descriptions or historical portrayals of the past, present, and future trajectories of the entities experiencing the change to provide meaningful insight. Nkomo and Kriek (2011), for example, use "leaders' life stories and the case research method to understand the leadership of change in 14 South African organizations" (p. 453). They "describe how leaders led the changes required to balance the imperatives emanating from South Africa's socio-political changes and return the country to the international business arena, as well as the challenges created by years of inequality and neglect of the socio-economic development of the majority of its population." Evident in their study is the multiplexity of factors influencing the change in organizations. Networks are useful in complex, patterned events, situations, behaviors, attributes, etc. (Poole, 2004). They are sometimes considered maps of interlinkages.

The availability of all these techniques to study the circumstantiated model that we describe is not only meaningful but also has practical relevance. It is meaningful to the extent that we can empirically demonstrate the triggers to change and the flow of change. Such knowledge will enable systems in Africa to improve. It will also help policy makers to facilitate industrial growth. In conclusion, we present a model that is unique to Africa. We hope future research will generate insight that helps improve systems in Africa.

Note

1 The author worked with a major news organization in Ghana on a labor relations change initiative when, midway through the intervention, a government change resulted in the replacement of the CEO and termination of the intervention.

References

Abdulraheem, I., Mordi, C., Ojo, I. S., and Ajonbadi, H. (2013) Outcomes of planned organisational change in the Nigerian public sector: Insights from the Nigerian higher education institutions. *Economic Insights – Trends and Challenges*, 2(1): 26–37.

Adeniji, A. A., Osibanjo, O. A., and Abiodun, A. J. (2013) Organizational change and human resource management interventions: An investigation of the Nigerian banking industry. *Serbian Journal of Management*, 8(2): 139–154.

Adesida, O., Karuri-Sebina, G., and Resende-Santos, J. (Eds.). (2016) *Innovation Africa: Emerging Hubs of Excellence*. London, UK: Emerald Group Publishing.

Albert, S. (2013) *When: The Art of Perfect Timing*. Hoboken, New Jersey: John Wiley & Sons.

Amis, J., Slack, T., and Hinings, C. R. (2004) The pace, sequence, and linearity of radical change. *Academy of Management Journal*, 47(1): 15–39.

Ancona, D.G.,and Chong, C. (1996) Entrainment: Pace, cycle, and rhythm in organizational behavior. In L. L. Cummings and B. M. Staw (Eds.), *Research in Organizational Behavior* (vol. 18, pp. 251–284). Greenwich, CT: JAI Press.

Ancona, D. G., Goodman, P. S., Lawrence, B. S., and Tushman, M. L. (2001) Time: A new research lens. *Academy of Management Review*, 26(4): 645–663.

Anderson et al., (2016). Frontline: Innovative Africa. The Africa Report. (http://www.theafricareport.com/North-Africa/frontline-innovative-africa.html). Accessed on April 9, 2017.

Anderson, P. (1999) Perspective: Complexity theory and organization science. *Organization Science*, 10(3): 216–232.

Argyris, C. (1976) Single-loop and double-loop models in research on decision making. *Administrative Science Quarterly*, 363–375.

Armenakis, A. A., Harris, S. G., and Mossholder, K. W. (1993) Creating readiness for organizational change. *Human Relations*, 46(6): 681–703.

Avenier, M. J. (2010) Shaping a constructivist view of organizational design science. *Organization Studies*, 31(9–10): 1229–1255.

Ayittey, G. B. N. (2006) *Indigenous African Institutions*. NY: Transnational Publishers,Inc.

Barge, J. K., and Oliver, C. (2003) Working with appreciation in managerial practice. *Academy of Management Review*, 28(1): 124–142.

Barrett, F. J., Thomas, G. F., and Hocevar, S. P. (1995) The central role of discourse in large-scale change: A social construction perspective. *The Journal of Applied Behavioral Science*, 31(3): 352–372.

Bartunek, J. M., Balogun, J., and Do, B. (2011) Considering planned change anew: Stretching large group interventions strategically, emotionally, and meaningfully. *The Academy of Management Annals*, 5(1): 1–52.

Bartunek, J. M., and Necochea, R. A. (2000) Old insights and new times: Kairos, Inca cosmology, and their contributions to contemporary management inquiry. *Journal of Management Inquiry*, 9(2): 103.

Bartunek, J. M., and Woodman, R. W. (2015) Beyond Lewin: Toward a temporal approximation of organization development and change. *Annual Review of Organizational Psychology and Organizational Behavior*, 2: 157–182.

Beckhard, R. (1969) *Organization Development: Strategies and Models*. Reading, MA: Addison-Wesley Publishing Company.

Biazzo, S. (2002) Process mapping techniques and Organisational analysis: Lessons from sociotechnical system theory. *Business Process Management Journal*, 8(1): 42–52.
Bloom, N., Genakos, C., Sadun, R., and Van Reenen, J. (2012) Management practices across firms and countries. *The Academy of Management Perspectives*, 26(1): 12–33.
Bluedorn, A. C. (2002) *The Human Organization of Time: Temporal Realities and Experience*. Stanford, CT: Stanford University Press.
Blunt, P., and Jones, M. (1991) Editorial: Human resource management in developing countries. *Journal of the History of Economic Thought*, 2(1): 3–5.
Boje, D. M., Oswick, C., and Ford, J. D. (2004) Language and organization: The doing of discourse. *Academy of Management Review*, 29(4): 571–577.
Buchanan, D., and Dawson, P. (2007) Discourse and audience: Organizational change as multi-story process. *Journal of Management Studies*, 44(5): 669–686.
Bunker, B. B., and Alban, B. T. (1992) Editors' introduction: The large group intervention – A new social innovation? *The Journal of Applied Behavioral Science*, 28(4): 473–479.
Bunker, B. B., and Alban, B. T. (1997) *Large Group Interventions: Engaging the Whole System for Rapid Change*. San Francisco, CA: Jossey-Bass.
Bunker, B. B., and Alban, A. T. (2014) Large group interventions. In B.B. Jones and M. Brazzel (Eds.), *The NTL Handbook of Organization Development and Change: Principles, Practices, and Perspectives,* 2nd ed. (pp. 407–427). San Francisco: Wiley.
Burchardt, M. (2012) Faith-based humanitarianism: Organizational change and everyday meanings in South Africa. *Sociology of Religion*, srs068.
Burke, L. A., and Miller, M. K. (1999) Taking the mystery out of intuitive decision making. *The Academy of Management Executive*, 13(4): 91–99.
Burnes, B., and Cooke, B. (2012) Review article: The past, present and future of organization development: Taking the long view. *Human Relations*, 65(11): 1395–1429.
Bushe, G. R., and Marshak, R. J. (2009) Revisioning organization development diagnostic and dialogic premises and patterns of practice. *The Journal of Applied Behavioral Science*, 45(3): 348–368.
Bushe, G. R., and Marshak, R. J. (2014) The dialogic mindset in organization development. *Research in Organizational and Change Development*, 22: 55–97.
Chironga, M., Leke, A., Lund, S., and van Wamelen, A. (2011) Cracking the next growth market: Africa. *Harvard Business Review*, 89(5): 117–122.
Coghlan, D. (2011) Action research: Exploring perspectives on a philosophy of practical knowing. *The Academy of Management Annals*, 5(1): 53–87.
Collier, P. (2007) The bottom billion. *Economic Review Deddington*, 25(1): 17.
Cooperrider, D. L. (1986) *Appreciative Inquiry: Toward a Methodology for Understanding and Enhancing Organizational Innovation*. Cleveland, OH: Case Western Reserve University.
Cooperrider DL, Srivastva S. 1987. Appreciative inquiry in organizational life. In R.W. Woodman and W.A. Pasmore (Eds.), *Research in Organizational Change and Development*, Vol. 1 (pp. 129–170). Greenwich, CT: JAI.
Cooperrider, D. L., and Whitney, D. D. (2005) *Appreciative Inquiry: A Positive Revolution in Change*. Oakland, CA: Berrett-Koehler Publishers
Dane, E., and Pratt, M. G. (2007) Exploring intuition and its role in managerial decision making. *Academy of Management Review*, 32(1): 33–54.
Dess, G. G., and Beard, D. W. (1984) Dimensions of organizational task environments. *Administrative Science Quarterly*, 52–73.
Dia, M. (1996) *Africa's Management in the 1990s and Beyond: Reconciling Indigenous and Transplanted Institutions*. Washington, DC: World Bank Publications.
Doh, J. P., Jones, G. K., Mudambi, R., and Teegen, H. (2005) Foreign research and development and host country environment: An empirical examination of US international R&D. *MIR: Management International Review*, 121–154.
Dooley, K. (2004) Complexity science models of organizational change. In S. Poole and A. Van De Ven (Eds.), *Handbook of Organizational Change and Development* (pp. 354–373). Oxford University Press.
Economist. (2011, December 3) *The Hopeful Continent: Africa Rising*. Retrieved from www.economist.com/node/21541015
Economist. (2014) *Science in Africa: On the Rise*. Retrieved September 14, 2014 from www.economist.com/Africa/21611112-scientifc-research-africa-gathering
Ekekwe, N. (2015) Improving innovation in Africa. *Harvard Business Review*. Retrieved Auguat 30, 2016 from https://hbr.org/2015/02/improving-innovation-in-africa

Emery, F. E., and Trist, E. L. (1960) Socio-technical systems. In C. West Churchman and M. Verhubt (Eds.), *Management Science, Models and Techniques*, Vol. 2. New York: Pergamon.

Englebert, P. (2000) Pre-colonial institutions, post-colonial states, and economic development in tropical Africa. *Political Research Quarterly*, 53(1): 7–36.

Ford, J. D., and Ford, L. W. (1995) The role of conversations in producing intentional change in organizations. *Academy of Management Review*, 20(3): 541–570.

Ford, J. D., and Ford, L. W. (2009) Decoding resistance to change. *Harvard Business Review*, 87(4): 99–103.

French, W. L., and Bell, C. H. (1995) *Organization Development: Behavioral Science Interventions for Organization Development*. Englewood Cliffs, NJ: Prentice-Hall.

Gallagher, R., and Appenzeller, T. (1999). Complex systems. *Science*, 284(5411): 79–109.

Gallagher, R., Appenzeller, T., and Normile, D. (1999) Beyond reductionism. *Science*, 284(5411): 79.

Gell-Mann, M. (1994). Complex adaptive systems. In G. Cowan, D. Pines, and D. Meltzer (Eds.), Complexity: Metaphors, models and reality (pp. 17–45). Reading: MA: Addison-Wesley Publishing Company.

Gergen, K. J., Gergen, M. M., and Barrett, F. J. (2004) Dialogue: Life and death of the organization. In D. Grant, C. Hardy, C. Oswick, and L.L. Putnam (Eds.), *The Sage Handbook of Organizational Discourse* (pp. 39–59). London: Sage.

Gersick, C. J. (1988) Time and transition in work teams: Toward a new model of group development. *Academy of Management Journal*, 31(1): 9–41.

Gikunda, R. M., Abura, G. O., and Njeru, S. G. (2014) Socio-economic effects of Mpesa adoption on the livelihoods of people in Bureti Sub County, Kenya. *International Journal of Academic Research in Business and Social Sciences*, 4(12): 348.

Godfrey, P. C. (2011) Toward a theory of the informal economy. *The Academy of Management Annals*, 5(1): 231–277.

Godfrey, P.C., Hatch, N.W. and Hansen, J.M. (2010). Toward a general theory of CSRS: the roles of beneficence, profitability, insurance and industry heterogeneity. *Business and Society*, 49(2): 316–394.

Greenwood, R., and Hinings, C. R. (1988) Organizational design types, tracks and the dynamics of strategic change. *Organization Studies*, 9(3): 293–316.

Hardy, C., Lawrence, T. B., and Grant, D. (2005) Discourse and collaboration: The role of conversations and collective identity. *Academy of Management Review*, 30(1): 58–77.

Heracleous, L., and Barrett, M. (2001) Organizational change as discourse: Communicative actions and deep structures in the context of information technology implementation. *Academy of Management Journal*, 44(4): 755–778.

Heracleous, L., and Marshak, R. J. (2004) Conceptualizing organizational discourse as situated symbolic action. *Human Relations*, 57(10): 1285–1312.

Hermann, C. F. (1963) Some consequences of crisis which limit the viability of organizations. *Administrative Science Quarterly*, 61–82.

Huy, Q. N. (2001) Time, temporal capability, and planned change. *Academy of Management Review*, 26(4): 601–623.

Jansen, K. J. (2004) From persistence to pursuit: A longitudinal examination of momentum during the early stages of strategic change. *Organization Science*, 15(3): 276–294.

Jones, M. L., and Blunt, P. (1993) Organizational development and change in Africa (1). *International Journal of Public Administration*, 16(11): 1735–1765.

Jones, T. M. (1991) Ethical decision making by individuals in organizations: An issue-contingent model. *Academy of Management Review*, 16(2): 366–395.

Kettinger, W. J., Teng, J. T., and Guha, S. (1997) Business process change: A study of methodologies, techniques, and tools. *MIS Quarterly*, 55–80.

Kiggundu, M. N. (1989) *Managing Organizations in Developing Countries: An Integrative Approach*. Boulder, Colorado: Lynne Rienner Publishers.

Kiggundu, M. N. (1991) The challenges of management development in sub-Saharan Africa. *Journal of Management Development*, 10(6): 32–47.

Klarner, P., and Raisch, S. (2013) Move to the beat – Rhythms of change and firm performance. *Academy of Management Journal*, 56(1): 160–184.

Kudonoo, E. C. (2013) Organization development consulting in sub-Saharan Africa: The little things that make a big difference. *Organization Development Journal*, 31(1): 9.

Kuhn, T., and Corman, S. R. (2003) The emergence of homogeneity and heterogeneity in knowledge structures during a planned organizational change. *Communication Monographs*, 70(3): 198–229.

Langley, A. (1999) Strategies for theorizing from process data. *Academy of Management Review*, 24(4): 691–710.

Lawrence, P. R., and Lorsch, J. W. (1967) Differentiation and integration in complex organizations. *Administrative Science Quarterly*, 1–47.
Lewin, K. (1947) Frontiers in group dynamics II. Channels of group life; social planning and action research. *Human Relations*, 1(2): 143–153.
Lindaman, E. B, Lippitt R. O. (1979). Choosing the Future You Prefer: A Goal-Setting Guide. Ann Arbor, MI: Hum. Resource Dev. Assoc.
Ludema, J. D., Whitney, D., Mohr, B. J., and Griffin, T. J. (2003) *The Appreciative Inquiry Summit*. San Francisco, CA: Berrett-Koehler.
Maitlis, S., and Christianson, M. (2014) Sensemaking in organizations: Taking stock and moving forward. *The Academy of Management Annals*, 8(1): 57–125.
Mamdani, M. (1996) *Citizen and Subject: Contemporary Africa and the Legacy of Late Colonialism*. Princeton, NJ: Princeton University Press.
Marrow, A. J. (1969) American Board of professional psychology: New directions and approaches, 1968 annual report. *American Psychologist*, 24(2): 151.
Marshak, R. J., and Grant, D. (2008) Organizational discourse and new organization development practices. *British Journal of Management*, 19(S1): S7–S19.
Mbaku, J. M. (2004) *Institutions and Development in Africa*. Trenten, New Jersey: Africa World Press.
Mbaku, J. M. (2007) Institutions and poverty alleviation in Africa. *African and Asian Studies*, 6(1–2): 107–134.
Mbiti, J. (1969) *African Philosophy and Religion*. The York: Praeger.
McKinsey Global Institute. (2010) *Lions on the Move: The Progress and Potential of African Economies*. Retrieved from https://www.mckinsey.com/mgi/overview. Accessed on June 25, 2017.
Michalopoulos, S., and Papaioannou, E. (2015) On the ethnic origins of African development: Chiefs and precolonial political centralization. *The Academy of Management Perspectives*, 29(1): 32–71.
Mintzberg, H. (1989) *Mintzberg on Management: Inside Our Strange World of Organizations*. New York: Simon & Schuster.
Mintzberg, H., and Westley, F. (1992) Cycles of organizational change. *Strategic Management Journal*, 13(S2): 39–59.
Mirvis, P. H. (1988) Organization development: Part I – An evolutionary perspective. *Research in Organizational Change and Development*, 2: 1–57.
Mirvis, P. H. (1990) Merging of executive heart and mind in crisis management. In S. Srivastva and D. Cooperrider (Eds.), *Appreciative Management and Leadership*. San Francisco, CA: Jossey-Bass.
Moch, M. K., and Bartunek, J. M. (1990) *Creating Alternative Realities at Work: The Quality of Work Life Experiment at FoodCom*. New York: Harper Business.
Montgomery, D. (1989) *The Fall of the House of Labor: The Workplace, the State, and American Labor Activism, 1865–1925*. Cambridge: Cambridge University Press.
Nadler, D. A. (1977) *Feedback and Organization Development: Using Databased Methods*. Boston, MA: Addison-Wesley Longman Publishing Co., Inc.
Nkomo, S. M., and Kriek, D. (2011) Leading organizational change in the 'new' South Africa. *Journal of Occupational and Organizational Psychology*, 84(3): 453–470.
Oswick, C. (2009) Revisioning or re-versioning? A commentary on diagnostic and dialogic forms of organization development. *The Journal of Applied Behavioral Science*, 45(3): 369–374.
Pasmore, W. A., and Fagans, M. R. (1992) Participation, individual development, and organizational change: A review and synthesis. *Journal of Management*, 18(2): 375–397.
Pasmore, W. A., and Friedlander, F. (1982) An action-research program for increasing employee involvement in problem solving. *Administrative Science Quarterly*, 343–362.
Poole, M. S. (2004) Central issues in the study of change and innovation. In M. S. Poole and A. H. Van de Ven (Eds.), *Handbook of Organizational Change and Innovation*. New York, NY: Oxford University Press, 3–31.
Poole, M. S., and Van de Ven, A. H. (Eds.). (2004) *Handbook of Organizational Change and Innovation*. Oxford: Oxford University Press.
Prashaant, A., and Sharma, N. (2015) Vodafone's M-Pesa-a mobile wallet revolution. *FIIB Business Review*, 4(2): 26–29.
Rotberg, R. (2013) *Africa Emerges: Consummate Challenges, Abundant Opportunities*. Hoboken, New Jersey: John Wiley & Sons.
Schein, E. H. (1996) Kurt Lewin's change theory in the field and in the classroom: Notes toward a model of managed learning. *Systems Practice*, 9(1): 27–47.

Seo, M., Putnam, L., Bartunek, J. M. (2004) Dualities and tensions of planned organizational change. In M.S. Poole and A.H. Van de Ven (Eds.), *Handbook of Organizational Change and Innovation* (pp. 73–109). New York: Oxford Univ. Press.

Sklar, R. L. (1993) The African frontier for political science. In R. Bates, V.Y. Mudimbe and J. O'Barr (Eds.), *Africa and the Disciplines* (pp. 83–110). Chicago, IL: University of Chicago Press.

Sulamoyo, D. (2011) *Ubuntu as a Cultural Strategy for OD*. Presentation at the Annual Linkage OD Summit, Chicago, IL.

Torrington, D., Weightman, J., and Johns, K. (1989) *Effective Management: People and Organization*. London: Prentice-Hall.

Tsoukas, H. (2005) *Complex Knowledge: Studies in Organizational Epistemology*. Oxford: Oxford University Press.

Van de Ven, A. H. (2007) *Engaged Scholarship: A Guide for Organizational and Social Research*. Oxford: Oxford University Press on Demand.

Van de Ven, A. H., and Hargrave, T. J. (2004) *Social, Technical, and Institutional Change*. Oxford: Oxford University Press, 259–303.

Van de Ven, A. H., and Poole, M. S. (1995) Explaining development and change in organizations. *Academy of Management Review*, 20(3): 510–540.

Van Nistelrooij, A., and Sminia, H. (2010) Organization development: What's actually happening? *Journal of Change Management*, 10(4): 407–420.

Weber, P. S., and Manning, M. R. (2001) Cause maps, sense making, and planned organizational change. *The Journal of Applied Behavioral Science*, 37(2): 227–251.

Wenger, M. G. (1988) Marxism and social research: The mythology of epistemology. *Science & Society*, 133–162.

Wiebe, E. (2010). Temporal sensemaking: Managers' use of time to frame organizational change. In T. Hernes and S. Maitlis (Eds.), Process, sensemaking, & organizing (pp. 213–241). Oxford: Oxford University Press.

World Bank Group (Ed.). (2013) *Doing Business 2014: Understanding Regulations for Small and Medium-size Enterprises*, Vol. 11. Washington, DC: World Bank Publications.

Yaeger, T. F., and Sorensen, P. F. (2011) OD in Africa. *OD Practitioner*, 43(3): 50–54.

Zoogah, D. B., Nkomo, S. (2013) Management research in Africa: Past, present and future possibilities. In T. Lituchy, B. Punnett, B. Puplampu (Eds.), *Management in Africa: Macro and micro perspectives* (pp. 9–31). New York, NY: Routledge.

Zoogah, D. B., Peng, M. W., and Woldu, H. (2015) Institutions, resources, and organizational effectiveness in Africa. *The Academy of Management Perspectives*, 29(1): 7–31.

8

Authentic leaders as change agents

Everlyne Misati and Fred O. Walumbwa

Introduction

Context matters for organizational change because context influences the choice of the objective, content, drivers, and process of the change (Ovadje, 2014). Africa is a complex and diverse continent, spanning 54 countries, each with its own characteristics. The continent is culturally, administratively, geographically, and economically or CAGE (Ghemawat, 2001) diverse, and this presents a variety of business and policy challenges. Thus, doing business on the African continent can be a daunting experience for organizations. This is because organizations operating in Africa face a myriad of uncertainties and challenges, including under-developed infrastructure, poverty, inequality, high unemployment rates, corruption, inadequate education and legal systems, and violations of human rights (PricewaterhouseCoopers or PwC, 2016). Doing business in Africa also presents great opportunities. This is because the continent is richly endowed with natural resources, which remain relatively underexplored, it has the fastest-growing middle class in the world – estimated at about 120 million and projected to grow steadily to 1.1 billion by 2060 (AfDB, 2014) – and its technology sector is burgeoning, as evidenced by the proliferation of mobile phone technology.

The difficulties and challenges notwithstanding, many organizations in Africa have learnt to brace themselves and adapt quickly, to overcome the challenges, and mitigate risks, thereby turning Africa into the next frontier for growth (PwC, 2016). Admittedly, there are a number of African companies that are leading the charge in terms of creativity and innovation in industries ranging from media and telecommunications, to retail, to restaurants, and food and beverage. For example, Nsehe (2012) listed ten African organizations that continually reinvent themselves, setting industry standards and radically changing their sectors. According to Nsehe (2012), the companies in question create, recreate, innovate, and exploit new ideas, products and services to produce dynamic and lucrative new businesses. These companies include Kenya's Safaricom, Nation Media Group, and East African Breweries; South Africa's Nando's, Mobile Telephone Networks (MTN), Woolworths, Pick n Pay, and Famous Brands; Zimbabwe's Econet; and Nigeria's Iroko TV. Fast Company (2015) also published a list highlighting some of Africa's true innovators, such as Eneza Education, Konga, Ubongo, M-KOPA, Praekelt Foundation, and Jobberman, operating predominantly in the fields of technology applications, education, and the information and communications technology (ICT) sector in a number of technology-driven African countries, led by Kenya and Nigeria.

How can these firms and other African organizations continue on this growth trajectory? By managing change more efficiently, effectively, and sustainably. Although there are a myriad of potential strategies, we suggest that these organizations need leaders who promote positive relationships through transparent and fair disclosures, including openness in terms of information sharing, accountability, and honesty, and leaders who view those they lead as the cornerstone for change management (Walumbwa, Christensen, and Hailey, 2011b).

A survey by PwC (2016) showed that CEOs operating in Africa anticipate that global trends, including technological advances, demographic shifts, shifts in global economic power, urbanization, resource scarcity, and climate change, will transform stakeholders' expectations of business. These CEOs revealed four common priorities, including diversification and innovation leading to sustained growth, addressing greater stakeholder expectations, effectively leveraging growth catalysts like technology, innovation, and talent, and measuring and communicating shared prosperity. Thus, to be well-armed in the war for talent, most of these CEOs in Africa expect to change some aspects of their current talent management strategy. Indeed, about half of those surveyed plan to invest more in their leadership pipeline and to focus on developing their institutional culture (PwC, 2016). Consistent with this survey, Walumbwa, Avolio, and Aryee (2011a) argued that, ultimately, a country's (or organization's) economic performance is contingent on the effectiveness of its leadership and management practices that serve to unlock the potential of its workforce to effectively implement the organization's strategic goals. This is because leaders formulate strategic directions, practices, and policies, and more importantly, as supervisors, these leaders enact practices and policies critical for harnessing employee skills and competencies to implement an organization's strategic directions.

Leadership in the African context

Leadership has been identified as one of the most significant factors that influence change in organizations (Herold, Fedor, Caldwell, and Liu, 2008). In this chapter, we focus on *authentic leaders*, as change agents. This is because we believe that the future of Africa depends on leaders who are willing to rise to the challenge and embrace authenticity as the new normal (Igiehon, 2014). Authentic leaders are said to possess accurate self-knowledge guided by internal moral standards (Walumbwa et al., 2011b). Such leaders are also said to rely on intuition born of formative experience to understand the expectations and concerns of the people they seek to influence (Goffee and Jones, 2005), and thus are more likely to be excellent change agents, especially in the unique African context where organizations are confronted with a myriad of challenges.

George (2003) drew attention to authentic leadership as a call to action for the new generation to learn from negative leadership examples in the wake of the Enron, WorldCom, and Tyco corporate scandals in the United States in the early 2000s. George defined authentic leaders as genuine, moral, and character-based leaders. More specifically, he posited that authentic leaders are people of the highest integrity, who are committed to building enduring organizations, have a deep sense of purpose, are true to their core values, have the courage to build their companies to meet the needs of all their stakeholders, and who recognize the importance of their service to society. He further posited that authentic leaders espouse qualities such as understanding their purpose, practicing solid values, leading with heart, establishing connected relationships, and demonstrating self-discipline. In other words, because authentic leaders understand which personality traits they should reveal to whom and when, and are highly attuned to their environments

(Goffee and Gareth, 2006), such leaders are more likely to win acceptance in strong corporate and social cultures and to use those elements of cultures for radical change and development (Walumbwa et al., 2011b). Importantly, George, Sims, McLean, and Mayer (2007) interviewed 125 business leaders from different racial, religious, national, and socioeconomic backgrounds to understand how leaders become and remain authentic. The interviews showed that one does not have to be born with any particular characteristics or traits to lead, nor does one have to be at the top of one's organization to lead; anyone can learn to be an authentic leader.

Building on the work of George and his colleagues, as well as insights from positive psychology, Avolio, Gardner, Walumbwa, Luthans, and May (2004) conceived of authentic leaders as persons who have achieved high levels of authenticity in that they know who they are and what they believe and value, and they act upon those values and beliefs while transparently interacting with others. These authors suggested that authentic leaders act in accordance with deep personal values and convictions, to build credibility and win the respect and trust of their followers by encouraging diverse viewpoints and building networks of collaborative relationships with followers, and thereby lead in a manner that followers recognize as authentic. According to Avolio and colleagues (2004), the essence of authenticity is to know, accept, and remain true to one's self, even in the face of adversity or extreme challenges. In other words, authentic leaders are those who do not deny responsibility, hide information, and deceive others, but rather lead with authenticity and integrity (Peus, Wesche, Streicher, Braun, and Frey, 2012).

Gardner, Avolio, Luthans, May, and Walumbwa (2005) emphasized the developmental processes of leader and follower self-awareness and self-regulation, arguing that the influence of the leader's and followers' personal histories and trigger events are considered as antecedents of authentic leadership and followership, as well as the reciprocal effects, with an inclusive, ethical, caring, and strength-based organizational climate. These authors viewed positive modeling as a primary means whereby leaders develop authentic followers. They posited that the outcomes of authentic leader-follower relationships include heightened levels of follower trust in the leader, engagement, workplace well-being, and veritable, sustainable performance. Other potential antecedents of authentic leadership may also include leader self-knowledge and self-consistency (Peus et al., 2012). In a review of the literature and research on authentic leadership, Gardner, Cogliser, Davis, and Dickens (2011) concluded that truly authentic leaders must lead in a way that honors their core values, beliefs, strengths, and weaknesses. Thus, a central premise of the authentic leadership theory is that it assumes that people in organizations can effectively lead and follow in a way that enables them to express their own unique identity and style.

Summarizing the work of Avolio, Gardner, Walumbwa, and others, we define authentic leadership as the extent to which leaders are aware of and exhibit a pattern of openness and clarity, and are consistent in their disclosure and enactment of personal values, motives, and sentiments (Hirst, Walumbwa, Aryee, Butarbutar, and Chen, 2016; Walumbwa, Avolio, Gardner, Wernsing, and Peterson, 2008). Authentic leadership is described by four related dimensions: balanced processing, internalized moral perspective, relational transparency, and self-awareness (Avolio and Walumbwa, 2014; Walumbwa et al., 2008). *Balanced processing* refers to the extent to which a leader seeks, analyzes, and objectively considers all available information prior to making decisions. Most notably, this leader behavior invites contrasting viewpoints that challenge his or her own viewpoints (Gardner et al., 2005). *Internalized moral perspective* relates to the extent to which a leader's behavior is congruent with one's personal values and moral standards. *Relational transparency* involves the extent to which followers perceive that leaders express their true thoughts and feelings. Leaders who are relationally transparent are honest, candid, and openly share information (Avolio, Walumbwa, and Weber, 2009). *Self-awareness* involves the extent to which leaders understand their strengths and weaknesses, recognize how their decisions impact others, and are cognizant of how others perceive their leadership. Research and theory suggest that these four unique dimensions additively combine to create an overall authentic leadership construct (Caza, Bagozzi, Woolley, Levy, and Caza, 2010; Moriano, Molero, and Mangin, 2011; see Avolio and Walumbwa, 2014, for a review).

Organizational change management

Increased globalization, defined as the international integration in commodity, capital, and labor markets (Bordo, Taylor, and Williamson, 2003), has resulted in convergence in the ways that businesses operate in Africa and globally. This means that African organizations have to compete against global companies or global standards (PwC, 2016). To achieve a competitive and distinctive edge, organizations have to undertake certain changes, and these changes need to be managed well. Change management is a process of guidance and adjustment aimed at achieving the goals for change (Boonstra, 2008). Thus, change management is a broad discipline that involves ensuring change is implemented efficiently, effectively, and sustainably, by considering its broader impact not only on the organization, but also the people, both individuals and teams, within that organization.

Change may either be planned – in stable and predictable situations where the problems are unambiguous – or developmental – in situations where the problems are vague, where there are several perspectives on the problems and solutions, and where the direction of change is not yet completely clear (Boonstra, 2008). Planned organizational change typically begins with the perception of a need for change. Huy (2001) proposed four ideal types of planned change processes – commanding, engineering, teaching, and socializing – each with distinct temporal and nontemporal assumptions, and each associated with altering a distinct organizational element. Huy (2001) specifically argued that large-scale change involves an alteration of multiple organizational elements, thus requiring the enactment of multiple types of interventions and change agents who display temporal capability skills to effectively sequence, time, pace, and combine the variety of interventions.

Pettigrew, Woodman, and Cameron (2001) argued that the most meaningful approach is to view organizational change processes as continuous rather than as a movement from one state to another, meaning that change processes should be viewed as sequences of individual and collective events, actions, and activities unfolding over time, in context. Additionally, these authors suggested that value comes from exploring the change process in relation to time, history, linkage to action (pacing and sequencing), and linkage to performance. Change may also be driven by forces that are internal or external to the organization. Internal forces may include an organization's leadership mandate, while external forces may include competitors and the institutional context. When an organization undertakes certain projects or initiatives to improve performance, seize market opportunities or to address key strategic issues, changes to processes, job roles, organizational structures as well as the adoption of new technology are always expected.

However, employees are an organization's most valuable resource, and it is the employees who in the end have to change how they perform their tasks. Thus, it is particularly important to pay attention to the people in an organization from the conception of a change process. In support of this argument, research (e.g., Kotter, 1996; McKinsey and Company, 2008; Willis Towers Watson, 2013) has shown that about 70 percent of change programs fail to achieve their goals, largely due to employee resistance and lack of management support in that investments in employee readiness and engagement through critical training, communication and leadership activities, are underfunded or not included at all. Willis Towers Watson (2013) indicated that, for a decade, their surveys showed that organizations that are able to sustain change over time are those that focus on the fundamental levers, such as leadership, communication, involvement, training/learning, and measurement, that are known to drive success. To further explore organizational change management, we define this process in terms of creativity and innovation because these functions encourage the use of imagination to find new ways to rise to dynamic market challenges.

Creativity and innovation

Earlier research (e.g., Woodman, Sawyer, and Griffin, 1993) defined organizational creativity as the creation of a valuable, useful new product, service, idea, procedure, or process by individuals working together in a complex social system. By so doing, these authors framed the definition of organizational creativity as a subset of the broader domain of innovation. These authors then characterized innovation as a subset of an even broader construct of organizational change. This is because, according to these researchers, although organizational change can include innovation, much of organizational change is not innovation, and on a similar vein, even though creativity may produce the new product, service, idea, or process that is implemented through innovation, the latter can also include the adaptation of preexisting products or processes, or those created outside of the organization. Scholars such as Amabile, Conti, Coon, Lazenby, and Herron (1996) have shown that innovation typically involves creativity, but is not identical to it because innovation begins with creative ideas and involves acting on or implementing those creative ideas to make some specific and tangible difference in the domain in which the innovation occurs. Thus, creativity may be displayed by individuals, while innovation occurs only in the organizational context.

Luecke and Katz (2003) defined innovation as the introduction of a new thing or method, that is, the embodiment, combination, or synthesis of knowledge in original, relevant, valued new products, processes, or services. McLean (2005) averred that creativity fuels the innovation pipeline, and that innovation is the process by which creative ideas are captured, filtered, funded, developed, modified, clarified, and eventually commercialized and/or implemented. Davila, Epstein, and Shelton (2006) argued that, like many business functions, innovation is a management process that requires specific tools, rules, and discipline. According to these authors, creativity implies coming up with ideas, while innovation implies bringing ideas to life.

More recently, in their review article, Anderson, Potočnik, and Zhou (2014) conceived of both creativity and innovation as being integral parts of essentially the same process, and they proposed a new, integrative definition. They wrote,

> Creativity and innovation at work are the process, outcomes, and products of attempts to develop and introduce new and improved ways of doing things. The creativity stage of this process refers to idea generation, and innovation refers to the subsequent stage of implementing ideas toward better procedures, practices, or products. Creativity and innovation can occur at the level of the individual, work team, organization, or at more than one of these levels combined, but will invariably result in identifiable benefits at one or more of these levels of analysis.
>
> *(p. 1298)*

Anderson et al. (2014) noted that research into creativity has typically examined the stage of idea generation, whereas innovation studies have commonly also included the latter phase of idea implementation. They concluded that creativity and innovation in any organization are vital to its successful performance, and longer-term survival, and that creativity and innovation are complex, multilevel, and emergent phenomena that pan out over time, and that require skillful leadership in order to maximize the benefits of new and improved ways of working. In an effort to further explicate creativity, Unsworth (2001) developed a matrix of four creativity types including responsive creativity (responding to presented problems because of external drivers), expected creativity (discovering problems because of external drivers), contributory creativity (responding to presented problems because of internal drivers), and proactive creativity (discovering problems because of internal drivers). Innovation, on the other hand, may be radical (revolutionary) or incremental.

Authentic leaders as change agents and facilitators of creativity and innovation

Leadership is one key contextual factor that has a substantial impact on employee creativity and innovation (Anderson et al., 2014; Zhou and Hoever, 2014). Leaders create a conducive work environment for idea generation (Tierney, 2008). Authentic leaders, in particular, actively seek both positive and negative sources of information and feedback (Gardner et al., 2005) through balanced processing. They solicit information and involvement from employees in the decision-making process and expose the employees to diverse informational resources in a supportive context (Ilies, Morgeson, and Nahrgang, 2005). These behaviors facilitate divergent and convergent thinking, creativity-relevant cognitive processes that are instrumental to making unique conceptual connections and generating new ideas (Zhou and Shalley, 2011).

Through self-awareness, authentic leaders are also acutely aware of their personal characteristics, knowledge, skills, and abilities, and apply them in novel ways to motivate group members and ameliorate the group's effectiveness (Gardner et al., 2005). Using both relational transparency and internalized moral perspective, authentic leaders also encourage group members to collectively identify and leverage their unique capabilities for the group's benefit (Ilies et al., 2005). Hence, authentic leaders are adept at identifying and accentuating their own, as well as their followers', unique attributes to generate and implement creative and new ideas. Thus, authentic leaders are likely to have a positive influence on the creativity and innovation of those they lead by encouraging them to share information to generate new knowledge and ideas.

More specifically, we suggest that authentic leaders can model creativity and innovation skills by demonstrating heightened levels of self-knowledge (Peus et al., 2012). In support, recent empirical evidence suggests that authentic leadership influences employee creativity directly and fosters creativity indirectly through positive affective (e.g., positive affect), psychological (e.g., hope and psychological capital), relational (e.g., leader-member exchange or LMX, employee identification, and interactional justice), and contextual (e.g., support for innovation) mechanisms (Cerne, Jaklic, and Skerlavaj, 2013; Hmieleski, Cole, and Baron, 2012; Li, Yu, Yang, Qi, and Fu, 2014; Muceldili, Turan, and Erdil, 2013; Rego, Sousa, Marques, and Pina e Cunha, 2012, 2014). Consistent with this extant research, we anticipate and propose that leaders who demonstrate authentic leadership behaviors will play a pivotal role in enhancing and maintaining creativity and innovation in African organizations.

Barriers or challenges to organizational change

Organizational change agents need to understand and deal with resistance to change. Change agents can achieve this by understanding the cognitive, affective, and behavioral dimensions of individual resistance to change, and how this resistance is influenced by factors such as individual predispositions towards openness and resistance to change, individuals' considerations of threats and benefits of change, communication, understanding, participation, trust in management, management styles, and the nature of individuals' relationships with the change agents (Erwin and Garman, 2010). During the change process, it is important to pay attention to the underlying mindsets and discursive arguments of stakeholder groups as well as the passionate resistance and emotional responses from these stakeholders as they may fear and distrust the system and perceive a loss of control (Heracleous and Barrett, 2001). Change agents should realize that resistance to change is not necessarily always an irrational and dysfunctional reaction located in change recipients and that change agents are not always inherently right and may contribute to (or inadvertently impede change efforts) the occurrence of resistance through their own actions and inactions (Ford, Ford, and D'Amelio, 2008).

Employees may develop a cynical attitude toward change. Recognizing that cynicism about organizational change often combines pessimism about successful change with blame of those responsible for the change as lazy, incompetent, or both, Reichers, Wanous, and Austin (1997) depicted a scenario of how cynicism arises. These authors suggested that cynicism may arise from a history of change programs that are not consistently successful, a lack of adequate information about change, and a predisposition to cynicism. Reichers et al. (1997) concluded that managing cynicism about organizational change involves providing timely, appropriate, and credible information. These authors also observed that cynicism can be minimized by admitting mistakes when they occur, apologizing, and quickly taking appropriate corrective action. Additionally, two-way communication is critical to success, since it enables leaders to become aware of employee perceptions of change and their feelings about it. In sum, according to these authors, addressing people's fears helps them let go of their concerns long enough to give change a chance of succeeding.

Employees' ambivalence may also be evident during the change process. Understanding the nature of ambivalence in employee responses to change might be useful in predicting the mode in which employees will communicate their responses to change agents and in identifying the most appropriate process for addressing those responses (Piderit, 2000). First, these authors illustrated that when employees are experiencing emotional ambivalence rather than uniformly negative responses to a proposed change, they may be more likely to express their responses through humor or other indirect modes of communication; thus, providing them with more data about the change initiative might not be very useful, even if it can be provided efficiently in large-scale rollout meetings. Instead, more impromptu and casual conversations might be more effective in creating an atmosphere in which employees feel safe expressing their negative emotional responses openly. Second, the authors illustrated that when employees are experiencing cognitive ambivalence about a proposed change, but no negative emotional responses, they may be quite direct in expressing their concerns; therefore, change agents might find that their listening ability is more important than their ability to communicate their own perspectives on the change to employees, since overselling the benefits of the change may not be effective in securing employee support, particularly if employees already accept that the change will have some positive outcomes but feel a different perspective is required.

Lastly, employee silence may be observed during the change process. Silence may be caused by powerful forces in organizations that cause widespread withholding of information, by employees, about potential problems or issues (Morrison and Milliken, 2000). According to these authors, silence stems from employees' shared perceptions that speaking up is futile, unwise, or dangerous since the employees fear that there would be negative repercussions for speaking up. Leaders therefore need to actively encourage employee voice, in order to elicit honest upward communication about issues and problems.

Influencing organizational change in Africa

When organizations embark on various changes, they are typically not arbitrary investments but rational responses to the business environment; therefore, strong leadership sets the tone from the top and instils a culture of high productivity (PwC, 2016). Authentic leaders see themselves not as passive observers but as individuals who learn from their experiences; thus, they develop self-awareness by asking for, and listening to, honest feedback, and using formal and informal support networks to help them stay grounded and lead integrated lives (George et al., 2007). These authors further argued that while it may be possible to drive short-term outcomes without being authentic, authentic leadership is the only way to create long-term results. The authors also suggested that achieving business results over a sustained period of time is the ultimate mark of authentic leadership.

Avolio et al. (2004) developed a theoretical framework of how authentic leaders influence follower attitudes, behaviors, and performance by drawing from positive organizational behavior, trust, hope, emotion, identification, and identity theories to describe the processes by which authentic leaders exert their influence on followers' attitudes and behaviors. Gardner et al. (2005) argued that through increased self-awareness, self-regulation, and positive modeling, authentic leaders foster the development of authenticity in followers, and that, in turn, followers' authenticity contributes to their well-being and the attainment of sustainable and veritable performance. Avolio and Gardner (2005) explored the underlying processes and factors by which authentic leaders and their followers can positively impact sustained performance, and they proposed that environments that provide open access to information, resources, support, and equal opportunity for everyone to learn and develop will empower and enable leaders and their associates to accomplish their work more effectively.

Ovadje (2014) argued that the wrong choice of leadership style can demotivate employees who would have otherwise championed the change. To help managers think through the key decisions, including choice of leadership style, which need to be made in planning and executing change, the author presented a decision-making model for leading organizational change in developing countries. This is because, as Ovadje (2014) stated, organizations must be both adaptive and flexible in today's changing world since the macroeconomic environment, technology, globalization, and a host of other factors are driving radical changes in organizations and entire industries. Thus, managers must not only anticipate these changes, but they must also respond quickly and effectively in order to survive and thrive.

Porter and McLaughlin (2006) posited that leadership in organizations does not take place in a vacuum, it takes place in organizational contexts which can represent discrete organizational components, such as culture/climate, goals/purposes, people/composition, processes, state/conditions, structure, and time. Walumbwa et al. (2011a) suggested that effectiveness of leadership and managerial practices are culturally contingent. Organizational contexts in Africa are shaped by such factors as uncertainty, which arises, at least in part, from political upheavals, logistical challenges due to underdeveloped infrastructure, institutional voids (Khanna and Palepu, 1997) resulting from weak governing institutions, underdeveloped educational systems leading to a scarcity of human capital, and limited experience operating in the global economy. Walumbwa et al. (2011a) acknowledged the aforementioned factors, but the authors added that the poor economic performance of African countries may also be attributed to incredibly abusive, unethical, and inept leadership and management of people, leadership challenges that may well stem from the continent's colonial history. These authors, however, called for a forward-looking perspective: *the leadership that Africa needs.*

Authentic leadership and change management in Africa

Change agents are essentially the people who act as catalysts for change. They typically possess favorable attributes, such as credibility, trustworthiness, sincerity, and expertise, all of which bolster their ability to create readiness for change (Armenakis, Harris, and Mossholder, 1993). As change agents, authentic leaders can influence employee readiness – the cognitive precursor to the behaviors of either resistance to, or support for, a change effort – for organizational change through proactive attempts by the change agents to influence the beliefs, attitudes, intentions, and ultimately the employees' behaviors, using the primary mechanism for readiness: the message for change (Armenakis et al., 1993). Armenakis and colleagues (1993) argued that the impact of any message generated by the change agent will be shaped by the social interpretation of that message, and that readiness for change must be maintained throughout the process of large-scale change, particularly since such change is composed of smaller changes which are ongoing. Pettigrew et al. (2001) reiterated that it is imperative that a systematic strategy be developed that tailors communication of change messages to address the differing concerns of different parts of the organization.

Igiehon (2014) averred that in the case of Africa, many inaccuracies still exist on both sides: for the foreign investor, and the local African businessperson or government official. This is because, quite often, the foreign investor explores partnerships with African businesses with the assumptions that corruption only exists in Africa, Africans cannot be trusted, and that as a foreigner, one inherently brings superior knowledge, or one-size-fits-all solutions for Africa. Igiehon (2014) therefore argued that authentic leaders in Africa would create a necessary environment of trust, accountability, and innovation. In agreement, Ovadje (2015) suggested that to lead successful change in Africa, managers need a good change plan and a deep understanding of the socio-cultural context, and that a humane leadership style is likely to engender more commitment to the realization of the change. Avolio et al. (2004) suggested that the behavioral style per se is not what necessarily differentiates the authentic from the inauthentic leader. In support, George (2015) argued that authentic leadership is built on a leader's character, that is, on who one is as a human being, and the forces that shaped the individual, not superficial elements such as one's style, which is the outward manifestation of one's leadership. Based on these arguments, we submit that authentic leaders would be excellent change agents in the African context.

Putting things into context

In spite of the fact that there is a tendency to portray Africans as one homogenous group (Ovadje, 2014; Walumbwa et al., 2011a), it is important to note that Africans are divided along linguistic and ethnic lines, each with different cultural practices and values, and sensitivity to the ethnic diversity of the workforce is required in leading and managing people in Africa (Walumbwa et al., 2011a). With that said, there are underlying commonalities in cultural values, including deference to authority, paternalism, humanism, filial piety, an emphasis on harmony, and a collective ethos, that can inform the practice of leadership and management (Jackson, 2004; Walumbwa et al., 2011a). For example, in Africa, followers recognize those in leadership as knowledgeable, having the right answers, and wise, thus, African employees are not likely to give candid opinions or challenge the views of their bosses even if they think these views are wrong, or have better alternatives (Jackson, 2004; Ovadje, 2015). As change agents, leaders should recognize this and make efforts to encourage openness and candor within their organizations. Hsiung's (2012) study revealed that to initiate employees' sincerity and honesty, organizational leaders should first display their own authenticity and act as role models, this then increases employees' opinion expression since voice behavior may be viewed as a manifestation of authenticity.

We argue that authentic leaders would be best suited to break through this cultural barrier. This is because authentic leaders are real and genuine, they are not perfect, nor do they try to be, they make mistakes, are willing to admit their errors and learn from them, they know how to ask others for help since they are self-confident (George, 2015). This has important implications for change management because if employees see their leaders as trustworthy and willing to learn, they will respond very positively to requests for help in getting through difficult times. Additionally, George (2015) explained that authentic leaders match their behavior to their context, an essential part of emotional intelligence (EQ), they do not burst out with whatever they may be thinking or feeling; rather, they exhibit self-monitoring, understand how they are being perceived, and use EQ to communicate effectively, as one might expect of true and revered African elders.

Africans are also generally sensitive to the needs of others: they are caring (Jackson, 2004). Those who are employed are often under immense pressure to care for their extended families, leaving them with a lot of baggage (Ovadje, 2015). Authentic leaders are sensitive to the needs of others (George, 2015). Therefore, authentic leaders would be well positioned to understand the impact of work-life initiatives, both structural (flexible job design, human resource policies) and cultural (supportive supervisors, climate), designed to foster workplace structures and cultures that are supportive of the interface between work, family, and personal life, geared toward enabling employees to manage work and caregiving (Kossek, Lewis, and Hammer, 2010).

Authentic leaders should not, however, be mistaken for 'pushovers'. These leaders adopt flexible styles that fit the situation and capabilities of their direct reports, At times, authentic leaders are coaches and mentors, inspiring others and empowering their teammates to lead through the most important tasks without a great deal of supervision (George, 2015). At other times, authentic leaders make very difficult decisions, terminating people and going against the will of the majority, as required to meet the situational imperative (George, 2015). Indeed, the organizational context in Africa is constantly evolving, requiring leaders that can adapt quickly to the needs of their organizations. George (2015) noted that authentic leaders are not rigid; they are constantly growing, since becoming authentic is a developmental state that enables leaders to progress through multiple roles, as they learn and grow from their experiences.

Due to high rates of unemployment, and because employees in the African context prioritize stability of employment and predictable income streams (Ovadje, 2015), change may be perceived as a threat to this stability. Jensen and Luthans (2006) found that employees' perception of authentic leadership serves as a strong predictor of employee job satisfaction, organizational commitment, and work happiness. Jackson (2004) observed that almost inevitably within an organization in Africa, there is a dominant ethnic, racial, or cultural group. In-group collectivism is characteristic of the African socio-cultural context in that an African employee is more likely to work hard to achieve the goals of the in-group to which one belongs (Ovadje, 2015), which means that for change management initiatives to be successful, it is very important for employees to feel that they belong not just to their work group, but to the organization at large.

Further evidence of the importance of authentic leadership

Authentic leadership has also been linked to a variety of important outcomes (Avolio and Walumbwa, 2014). For example, this leader behavior has been linked to extra-role and in-role performance, measured in terms of employee proficiency, adaptability and proactivity, performance, and firm performance (Hirst et al., 2016; Hmieleski et al., 2012; Leroy, Anseel, Gardner, and Sels, 2015; Wang, Sui, Luthans, Wang, and Wu, 2014). Other researchers (e.g., Peus et al., 2012) have also demonstrated that followers' satisfaction with supervisor, organizational commitment, and extra effort, as well as perceived team effectiveness, are outcomes of authentic leadership. Importantly, the authors also showed that the relations between authentic leadership and followers' work-related attitudes, as well as perceived team effectiveness, are mediated by perceived predictability of the leader, a particular facet of trust. Similarly, Leroy, Palanski, and Simons (2012) proposed, tested, and found support for the notion that authentic leadership behavior is an antecedent to perceptions of leader behavioral integrity, which in turn, affects follower affective organizational commitment and follower work role performance.

Lastly, while examining the effect of authentic leadership on employee trust and employee engagement, Wang and Hsieh's (2013) results showed that both supervisors' consistency between words and actions as well as their moral perceptions, are positively related to employee engagement. The authors also found that supervisors' consistency between words and actions is positively related to employee trust, which is in turn, positively related to employee engagement, and that employee trust has a partial mediating effect between authentic leadership and employee engagement. Taken together, the above evidence suggests authentic leadership's robust impact on a variety of employee attitudes and behaviors and their work context, providing support that authentic leadership can indeed create an environment amenable for organizational effectiveness and performance. We, therefore, propose and expect that authentic leadership will serve as a crucial leadership behavior in facilitating change management in Africa.

General discussion

Authentic leaders position their organizations to achieve positive outcomes in several ways. First, authentic leaders communicate with their employees. Ford and Ford (1995) argued that leaders may produce intentional organizational change by employing communication as the medium within which change occurs. In other words, these authors suggested considering organizational change as a communication-based and communication-driven phenomenon, and focusing on different types of interactions in the process, including initiative, understanding, performance, and closure, to create, sustain, focus, and complete the change process. Dutton, Ashford, O'Neill, and Lawrence (2001) suggested that leaders may push ideas forward or shape issue-selling microprocesses, including packaging, involvement, and timing, that contribute to organizational change. They defined issue selling as the process by which individuals affect others' attention to and understanding of the events, developments, and trends that have implications for organizational performance. The authors argued that successful issue sellers draw on relational, normative, and strategic contextual knowledge and employ a variety of moves to achieve their objectives, including characterizing their appeal as a rational, incremental step tied to important organizational goals and priorities. Issue sellers also involve a wide range of others early in the process, with a special focus on involving those at their level or above; they keep their bosses informed and they persist in their selling efforts while taking advantage of timing to decide when to sell and when to hold back.

To guide authentic leaders in their communication efforts, Heracleous and Barrett (2001) explored the role of discourse in shaping organizational change processes through its influence on actors' interpretations and actions, in the context of information technology (IT) implementation. These authors' research indicated that leaders should go beyond what multiple stakeholders say about intended implementation of IT and attempt to understand the deeper values and beliefs of these stakeholders that are enshrined in the groups' discursive structures, because these are what persist over time and guide actors' interpretations and actions. The authors argued that this is because, although the mutability (inconsistency) of the content of communicative actions helps in responding to various contextual factors, it is the deep structures that are the main influence on what the stakeholders say and do and therefore on the success or failure of systems' implementation.

Additionally, Lüscher and Lewis (2008) observed that, as change becomes a constant in organizational life, middle managers charged with interpreting, communicating, and implementing the change often struggle for meaning or sensemaking. These authors therefore embarked on a study whose findings demonstrated that leaders can indeed have an effect on how employees think, and this enables the leaders to help employees escape from ingrained ways of thinking by acting as facilitators who alter the frames and knowledge structures from which the employees draw in their sensemaking process. The authors argued that, in this role, leaders assist employees to appreciate the information provided, encourage them to get engaged and contribute by explaining to, training, and involving them in the production of the information provided.

Second, authentic leaders empower their employees. Craig, George, and Snook (2015) argued that authentic leaders empower others to lead, and that by empowering leaders throughout their organizations, authentic leaders create high performance organizations because all members are encouraged and inspired to reach their full potential. These authors suggested that one must be authentic and then foster a climate of mutual respect by treating other people as equals, listening to them, and learning from them. The authors further noted that to empower others, one must create a culture of authenticity, high standards, and shared responsibility through leading by example, and that to be an empowering leader, one must have honest conversations that build trust and engagement in one's team or organization. Zhang and Bartol (2010) found that empowering leadership positively affects psychological empowerment, which in turn influences both intrinsic motivation and creative process engagement. The authors found the latter two variables to have a positive influence on creativity. Additionally, the authors found that empowerment role identity moderates the link between empowering leadership and psychological empowerment, while leader encouragement of creativity moderates the connection between psychological empowerment and creative process engagement.

Lastly, authentic leaders facilitate a favorable organizational culture and climate. Scott and Bruce (1994) hypothesized that leadership, individual problem-solving style, and work group relations affect innovative behavior directly and indirectly through their influence on perceptions of the climate for innovation. They found that task type moderated the relationship between leader role expectations and innovative behavior. Organizational cultures emerge as much from the bottom-up emergent choices made by participants as they do from top-down decisions of leaders (Jassawalla and Sashittal, 2002). These authors further noted that cultural transformation relies on leadership as well as the willingness and the capacity of participants to manage their anxiety about change, trust others, discard old and adopt new value and belief systems, and learn new behaviors.

Avolio et al. (2004) pointed out that authentic leaders lead in a manner that followers recognize as authentic, and that this process then cascades to followers, who may also operate in a similar manner, portraying to leaders, colleagues, customers, and other interested stakeholders their authenticity, which over time may become a basis for the organization's culture. Avolio et al.'s (2004) model proposed that authentic leadership influences followers' attitudes and behaviors through the key psychological processes of identification, hope, positive emotions, optimism, and trust. They also suggested that contextual factors, such as organizational power and politics, organizational structure, gender, and organizational culture and climate, may be relevant to the study of the authentic leadership process. McLean (2005) argued that, besides an individual creator and one's personality, traits, abilities, experiences, and thought processes, the social environment can influence both the level and frequency of creative behavior. McLean (2005) suggested that organizational culture essentially creates the parameters for the behavior that is desirable and will be encouraged, and that which is unacceptable and will be censured.

Concluding remarks and additional insights

It's important to note that every change initiative has its own unique set of objectives and activities, all of which must be coordinated by the change agent, the authentic leader. Changes are more likely to be implemented successfully if they are specific, measurable, attainable, relevant, and timely (SMART), are well communicated, and have the support of senior management and commitment from the employees. Ford et al. (2008) suggested that if change agents have a preconceived expectation that people will resist change, their behaviors can actually influence that resistance negatively. Additionally, change agents tend to be very positive about the direction the organization is headed, and as a result, the message they communicate to others may be tainted with grandiose views rather than being reflective of the amount of work and difficulty it will take to achieve the desired changes. Consequently, these authors observed, when change becomes difficult, employees may feel that their efforts are failing.

Furthermore, Ford et al. (2008) intimated that breaching or breaking agreements, including psychological and implied contracts, before and during the change process, by failing to restore the subsequent loss of trust that may occur when agents of the organization knowingly or unknowingly renege on a promise or an understood and expected pattern of cooperation, failing to legitimize change by providing justification of the change, misrepresenting change by being deceptive or overly optimistic, and failing to call employees to action because of focusing too little on asking for actual behavioral changes, may impede change. Ford et al. (2008) warned that change agents need to carefully listen to the change recipient, because not all criticism is intended as resistance. In fact, the authors argued, criticism and critical thinking can be an important process of sensemaking for the change recipient, and interpreting this sensemaking as resistance can harden the opinion of the change recipient. Ford et al. (2008) suggested that in many cases, initial criticism can serve as an opportunity for the change agent to take charge of or participate in the sensemaking process by justifying the change, and that, if correctly restructured, resistance can be a resource for change.

Based on Ford and colleagues' (2008), and other researchers' suggestions, as change agents, we suggest that authentic leaders should avoid embarking on change efforts with preconceived perceptions that employees will resist change. They should evaluate whether what they observe is truly resistance or a reaction to a situation where alternative action could have been taken. They should also provide their employees with a realistic picture of the change efforts, honor all commitments, and/or explain to their employees when this is not possible. Moreover, the demonstrated influence of authentic leadership on important organizational outcomes across different cultural contexts further highlights the importance of authentic leadership in creating work environments conducive for employee creativity and change. Specifically, these demonstrated positive findings suggests that training programs focusing on positive forms of leadership, such as authentic leadership development, may be important in engendering employee creativity and managing change in Africa. More specifically, we suggest that African organizations and their leaders should also be attentive to creating a work environment that solicits employee feedback and strive to involve employees in decision-making process. Beyond creating a motivating social context, we encourage African managers to foster supportive interpersonal relationships with employees to help develop and share creative ideas without fear of social consequences. A trust-based relationship motivates employees to speak up and share risky, unproven ideas with others (Zhang and Zhou, 2014), and thus encourage effective change management in Africa.

To summarize, leadership is important to the success or failure of the major challenges our society, institutions, or organizations face today. Indeed, we know from decades of research that the quality of leadership can make a significant difference to organizational performance, and thus leadership represents a valuable source of any organizational improvement. In this chapter, we have made what we believe is a persuasive argument for the need for authentic leaders to help African organizations to prosper and to manage change. Note, however, that we are not in any way suggesting that authentic leadership is the only solution. Other leadership styles or behaviors, such as transformational leadership (Herold et al., 2008), may be equally critical in change management in Africa. For example, Oke, Munshi, and Walumbwa (2009) argued that followers of transformational leaders are more likely to respond to leader's change initiatives even in the face of a turbulent environment such as those facing African organizations, because of transformational leaders' understanding, support, and encouragement. Rather, we argue that given the unprecedented challenges African organizations face, we have to move beyond usual leadership characteristics such as charismatic and inspiring leadership behaviors or classic command and control leadership behaviors of the last century to a more broader leadership behavior that empowers others to step up and lead so that people throughout the organization are highly motivated to give their best (Craig et al., 2015).

Authentic leaders also align people around a common purpose that inspires them to peak performance, and such leaders are said to unite people around a common set of values so that everyone knows precisely what is expected (Craig et al., 2015). As succinctly noted by Walumbwa and colleagues (2011b), because authentic leaders are self-aware, 'they are more likely to understand how they influence others and, in turn, they adjust their interactions to create a more positive dynamic to enhance the motivation of those they lead' (p. 113). Indeed, authentic leaders not only demonstrate the ability to translate purpose into action, such leaders also create greater openness in their interactions, where essential information needed by those they lead is readily available (Walumbwa et al., 2011b). Thus, we believe that authentic leaders would drive Africa forward, and that understanding and implementing the suggestions offered in this chapter will enable organizations to more fully realize elevated levels of sustained and veritable growth and performance that a leadership process grounded in authenticity has the potential to provide. However, given the limited research linking authentic leadership and change, especially in the African context, we encourage scholars to invest more effort in exploring the extent to which authentic leadership effects cascade over time and across different levels of the organizational hierarchy, in order to better inform organizations and their leaders regarding how such leadership behaviors can best be developed and sustained over time.

References

African Development Bank. (2014) *Leadership for the Africa We Want.* Retrieved April 2016 from www.afdb.org/en/annual-meetings-2014/programme/leadership-for-the-africa-we-want/

Amabile, T. M., Conti, R., Coon, H., Lazenby, J., and Herron, M. (1996) Assessing the work environment for creativity. *Academy of Management Journal*, 39(5): 1154–1184.

Anderson, N., Potočnik, K., and Zhou, J. (2014) Innovation and creativity in organizations a state-of-the-science review, prospective commentary, and guiding framework. *Journal of Management*, 40(5): 1297–1333.

Armenakis, A. A., Harris, S. G., and Mossholder, K. W. (1993) Creating readiness for organizational change. *Human Relations*, 46(6): 681–703.

Avolio, B. J., and Gardner, W. L. (2005) Authentic leadership development: Getting to the root of positive forms of leadership. *Leadership Quarterly*, 16(3): 315–338.

Avolio, B. J., Gardner, W. L., Walumbwa, F. O., Luthans, F., and May, D. R. (2004) Unlocking the mask: A look at the process by which authentic leaders impact follower attitudes and behaviors. *Leadership Quarterly*, 15(6): 801–823.

Avolio, B. J., and Walumbwa, F. O. (2014) Authentic leadership theory, research and practices: Steps taken and steps that remain. In D. V. Day (Ed.), *The Oxford Handbook of Leadership and Organizations*. Oxford: Oxford University Press, 331–356.
Avolio, B. J., Walumbwa, F. O., and Weber, T. J. (2009) Leadership: Current theories, research, and future directions. *Annual Review of Psychology*, 60: 421–449.
Boonstra, J. (Ed.). (2008) *Dynamics of Organizational Change and Learning*. West Sussex, UK: John Wiley & Sons.
Bordo, M. D., Taylor, A. M., and Williamson, J. G. (Eds.). (2003) *Globalization in Historical Perspective National Bureau of Economic Research Conference Report*. Chicago, IL: University of Chicago Press.
Caza, A., Bagozzi, R. P., Woolley, L., Levy, L., and Caza, B. B. (2010) Psychological capital and authentic leadership: Measurement structure, gender comparison, and cultural extension. *Asia Pacific Journal of Business Administration*, 2(1): 53–70.
Cerne, M., Jaklic, M., and Skerlavaj, M. (2013) Authentic leadership, creativity, and innovation: A multilevel perspective. *Leadership*, 9(1): 63–85.
Craig, N., George, B., and Snook, S. (2015) *The Discover Your True North Field Book: A Personal Guide to Finding Your Authentic Leadership*. Hoboken, NJ: John Wiley & Sons, Inc.
Davila, T., Epstein, M. J., and Shelton, R. (2006) *Making Innovation Work: How to Manage It, Measure It, and Profit From It*. Upper Saddle River, NJ: Wharton School Publishing.
Dutton, J. E., Ashford, S. J., O'Neill, R. M., and Lawrence, K. A. (2001) Moves that matter: Issue selling and organizational change. *Academy of Management Journal*, 44(4): 716–736.
Erwin, D. G., and Garman, A. N. (2010) Resistance to organizational change: Linking research and practice. *Leadership & Organization Development Journal*, 31(1): 39–56.
Fast Company. (2015) *Ranked: Top 10 Most Innovative Companies in Africa*. Retrieved April 15 2016 from www.itnewsafrica.com/2015/02/ranked-top-10-most-innovative-companies-in-africa/
Ford, J. D., and Ford, L. W. (1995) The role of conversations in producing intentional change in organizations. *Academy of Management Review*, 20(3): 541–570.
Ford, J. D., Ford, L. W., and D'Amelio, A. (2008) Resistance to change: The rest of the story. *Academy of Management Review*, 33(2): 362–377.
Gardner, W. L., Avolio, B. J., Luthans, F., May, D. R., and Walumbwa, F. O. (2005) Can you see the real me? A self-based model of authentic leader and follower development. *The Leadership Quarterly*, 16(3): 343–372.
Gardner, W. L., Cogliser, C. C., Davis, K. M., and Dickens, M. P. (2011) Authentic leadership: A review of the literature and research agenda. *The Leadership Quarterly*, 22(6): 1120–1145.
George, B. (2003) *Authentic Leadership: Rediscovering the Secrets to Creating Lasting Value*. San Francisco, CA: Jossey-Bass/John Wiley & Sons.
George, B. (2015, November 10) *Authentic Leadership Rediscovered*. Harvard Business School Working Knowledge. Retrieved April 15, 2016 from http://hbswk.hbs.edu/item/authentic-leadership-rediscovered
George, B., Sims, P., McLean, A. N., and Mayer, D. (2007) Discovering your authentic leadership. *Harvard Business Review*, 85(2): 129.
Ghemawat, P. (2001) Distance still matters: The hard reality of global expansion. *Harvard Business Review*, 79(8): 137–147.
Goffee, R., and Jones, G. (2006) *Why Should Anyone Be Led by You?: What it Takes to Be an Authentic Leader*. Boston, MA: Harvard Business Publishing.
Goffee, R., and Jones, G. (2005) Managing authenticity: The paradox of great leadership. *Harvard Business Review*, 83(12): 87–94.
Heracleous, L., and Barrett, M. (2001) Organizational change as discourse: Communicative actions and deep structures in the context of information technology implementation. *Academy of Management Journal*, 44(4): 755–778.
Herold, D. M., Fedor, D. B., Caldwell, S., and Liu, Y. (2008) The effects of transformational and change leadership on followers' commitment to a change: A multilevel study. *Journal of Applied Psychology*, 93: 346–357.
Hirst, G., Walumbwa, F., Aryee, S., Butarbutar, I., and Chen, C. J. H. (2016) A multilevel investigation of authentic leadership as an antecedent of helping behavior. *Journal of Business Ethics*, 139(3): 485–499.
Hmieleski, K. M., Cole, M. S., and Baron, R. A. (2012) Shared authentic leadership and new venture performance. *Journal of Management*, 38(5): 1476–1499.
Hsiung, H. (2012) Authentic leadership and employee voice behavior: A multi-level psychological process. *Journal of Business Ethics*, 107(3): 349–361.

Huy, Q. N. (2001) Time, temporal capability, and planned change. *Academy of Management Review*, 26(4): 601–623.
Igiehon, O. (2014) *Success in Africa Requires Authentic Leadership*. Retrieved April 15, 2016 from www.newglobalcitizen.com/story/authentic-leadership-requirement-long-term-success-africa
Ilies, R., Morgeson, F. P., and Nahrgang, J. D. (2005) Authentic leadership and eudaemonic well-being: Understanding leader-follower outcomes. *Leadership Quarterly*, 16: 373–394.
Jackson, T. (2004) *Management and Change in Africa: A Cross-cultural Perspective*. London, UK: Routledge.
Jassawalla, A. R., and Sashittal, H. C. (2002) Cultures that support product-innovation processes. *The Academy of Management Executive*, 16(3): 42–54.
Jensen, S. M., and Luthans, F. (2006) Entrepreneurs as authentic leaders: Impact on employees' attitudes. *Leadership & Organization Development Journal*, 27(8): 646–666.
Khanna, T., and Palepu, K. (1997) Why focused strategies may be wrong for emerging markets. *Harvard Business Review*, 75(4): 41–51.
Kossek, E. E., Lewis, S., and Hammer, L. B. (2010) Work – Life initiatives and organizational change: Overcoming mixed messages to move from the margin to the mainstream. *Human Relations*, 63(1): 3–19.
Kotter, J. P. (1996) *Leading Change*. Boston, MA: Harvard Business School Press.
Leroy, H., Anseel, F., Gardner, W. L., and Sels, L. (2015) Authentic leadership, authentic followership, basic need satisfaction, and work role performance: A cross-level study. *Journal of Management*, 41: 1677–1697.
Leroy, H., Palanski, M. E., and Simons, T. (2012) Authentic leadership and behavioral integrity as drivers of follower commitment and performance. *Journal of Business Ethics*, 107(3): 255–264.
Li, F., Yu, K. F., Yang, J., Qi, Z., and Fu, J. H. (2014) Authentic leadership, traditionality, and interactional justice in the Chinese context. *Management and Organization Review*, 10: 249–273.
Luecke, R., and Katz, R. (2003) *Managing Creativity and Innovation*. Boston, MA: Harvard Business School Press.
Lüscher, L. S., and Lewis, M. W. (2008) Organizational change and managerial sensemaking: Working through paradox. *Academy of Management Journal*, 51(2): 221–240.
McKinsey and Company. (2008) *Creating Organizational Transformations*. Retrieved April 15, 2016 from http://gsme.sharif.edu/~change/McKinsey%20Global%20Survey%20Results.pdf
McLean, L. D. (2005) Organizational culture's influence on creativity and innovation: A review of the literature and implications for human resource development. *Advances in Developing Human Resources*, 7(2): 226–246.
Moriano, J. A., Molero, F., and Mangin, J. P. L. (2011) Authentic leadership. Concept and validation of the ALQ in Spain. *Psicothema*, 23(2): 336–341.
Morrison, E. W., and Milliken, F. J. (2000) Organizational silence: A barrier to change and development in a pluralistic world. *Academy of Management Review*, 25(4): 706–725.
Muceldili, B., Turan, H., and Erdil, O. (2013) The influence of authentic leadership on creativity and innovativeness. *Procedia – Social and Behavioral Sciences*, 99: 673–681.
Nsehe, M. (2012) *The Ten Most Innovative Companies in Africa*. Retrieved April 15, 2016 from www.forbes.com/sites/mfonobongnsehe/2012/09/07/the-ten-most-innovative-companies-in-africa/#2d4c710656df
Oke, A., Munshi, N., and Walumbwa, F. O. (2009) The influence of leadership on innovation processes and activities. *Organizational Dynamics*, 38(1): 64–72.
Ovadje, F. (Ed.). (2014) *Change Leadership in Developing Countries*. Abingdon, Oxon: Routledge.
Ovadje, F. (2015) Developing Change Competence for the African Environment. Retrieved April 15, 2016 from www.worldfinancialreview.com/?p=3764
Pettigrew, A., Woodman, R., and Cameron, K. (2001) Studying organizational change and development: Challenges for future research. *The Academy of Management Journal*, 44(4): 697–713.
Peus, C., Wesche, J. S., Streicher, B., Braun, S., and Frey, D. (2012) Authentic leadership: An empirical test of its antecedents, consequences, and mediating mechanisms. *Journal of Business Ethics*, 107(3): 331–348.
Piderit, S. K. (2000) Rethinking resistance and recognizing ambivalence: A multidimensional view of attitudes toward an organizational change. *Academy of Management Review*, 25(4): 783–794.
Porter, L. W., and McLaughlin, G. B. (2006) Leadership and the organizational context: Like the weather? *Leadership Quarterly*, 17(6): 559–576.
PricewaterhouseCoopers. (2016) *Africa Business Agenda*. Retrieved May 25, 2016 from www.pwc.co.za/en/assets/pdf/africa-business-agenda-2016.pdf
Rego, A., Sousa, F., Marques, C., and Pina e Cunha, M. P. (2012) Authentic leadership promoting employees' psychological capital and creativity. *Journal of Business Research*, 65: 429–437.

Rego, A., Sousa, F., Marques, C., and Pina e Cunha, M. P. (2014) Hope and positive affect mediating the authentic leadership and creativity relationship. *Journal of Business Research*, 67: 200–210.
Reichers, A. E., Wanous, J. P., and Austin, J. T. (1997) Understanding and managing cynicism about organizational change. *The Academy of Management Executive*, 11(1): 48–59.
Scott, S. G., and Bruce, R. A. (1994) Determinants of innovative behavior: A path model of individual innovation in the workplace. *Academy of Management Journal*, 37(3): 580–607.
Tierney, P. (2008) Leadership and employee creativity. In J. Zhou and C. E. Shalley (Eds.), *Handbook of Organizational Creativity*. New York, NY: Taylor and Francis, 95–123.
Unsworth, K. (2001) Unpacking creativity. *Academy of Management Review*, 26(2): 289–297.
Walumbwa, F. O., Avolio, B. J., and Aryee, S. (2011a) Leadership and management research in Africa: A synthesis and suggestions for future research. *Journal of Occupational and Organizational Psychology*, 84(3): 425–439.
Walumbwa, F. O., Avolio, B. J., Gardner, W. L., Wernsing, T. S., and Peterson, S. J. (2008) Authentic leadership: Development and validation of a theory-based measure. *Journal of Management*, 34(1): 89–126.
Walumbwa, F. O., Christensen, A. L., and Hailey, F. (2011b) Authentic leadership and the knowledge economy: Sustaining motivation and trust among knowledge workers. *Organizational Dynamics*, 40(2): 110–118.
Wang, D. S., and Hsieh, C. C. (2013) The effect of authentic leadership on employee trust and employee engagement. *Social Behavior and Personality: An International Journal*, 41(4): 613–624.
Wang, H., Sui, Y., Luthans, F., Wang, D., and Wu, Y. (2014) Impact of authentic leadership on performance: Role of followers' positive psychological capital and relational processes. *Journal of Organizational Behavior*, 35: 5–21.
Willis Towers Watson. (2013) *Towers Watson Change and Communication ROI Survey*. Retrieved April 15, 2016 from www.towerswatson.com/en/Press/2013/08/Only-One-Quarter-of-Employers-Are-Sustaining-Gains-From-Change-Management
Woodman, R. W., Sawyer, J. E., and Griffin, R. W. (1993) Toward a theory of organizational creativity. *Academy of Management Review*, 18(2): 293–321.
Zhang, X., and Bartol, K. M. (2010) Linking empowering leadership and employee creativity: The influence of psychological empowerment, intrinsic motivation, and creative process engagement. *Academy of Management Journal*, 53(1): 107–128.
Zhang, X., and Zhou, J. (2014). Empowering leadership, uncertainty avoidance, trust, and employee creativity: Interaction effects and a mediating mechanism. *Organizational Behavior and Human Decision Processes*, 124(2), 150–164.
Zhou, J., and Hoever, I. J. (2014) Research on workplace creativity: A review and redirection. *Annual Review of Organizational Psychology*, 1: 333–359.
Zhou, J., and Shalley, C. E. (2011) Deepening our understanding of creativity in the workplace: A review of different approaches to creativity research. In S. Zedeck (Ed.), *APA Handbook of Industrial and Organizational Psychology*. Washington, DC: American Psychological Association, 275–302.

9

Human resource function as change agent

Samuel Aryee

The dynamic environment in which African organizations operate has placed a premium on marketplace agility (Dyer and Shafer, 2003), thereby making an understanding and management of change an important prerequisite for organizational survival and growth (Jackson, 2004; Ovadje, 2014). Organizations face these challenges at a time when the traditional sources of competitive advantage such as capital and technological advancements have, increasingly, been supplanted by a reliance on employees as competitive resource. Against this background and in light of the premium placed on agility, the HR function's emergence as a strategic partner will have to stem from its contributions to marketplace agility through the development of a capability to manage change (Judge, Naoumova, and Douglas, 2009; Mohrman and Worley, 2009).

There is evidence of a number of African organizations across industrial sectors, such as telecommunications, media, food and beverage, that have embraced change and innovation to foster marketplace agility, and therefore assure their survival and growth in a dynamic environment (Nsehe, 2012). However, these organizations are clearly in the minority, raising concerns about the ability of the vast majority of African organizations to survive and grow in this emergent business environment. The optimistic discourse on Africa's growth potential rests in part on the growth of its population, a rising African middle class, and the implications for an internal market. Indeed, the Africa Competitiveness Report (2017) notes that:

> The working-age population in Africa is expected to grow by close to 70 percent, or by approximately 450 million people between 2015 and 2035. If current trends continue, only about 100 million of them can expect to find stable employment opportunities. Countries that are able to enact policies conducive to job creation are likely to reap significant benefits from this rapid population growth.
>
> *(2017: xiv)*

Although the focus of the report was on countries rather than organizations, African organizations will also have to be agile to survive and grow in order to provide the stable job opportunities that will transform the continent's growing population into an internal market. A PricewaterhouseCoopers' (PwC) survey of African CEOs (2017: 3) revealed that 'while organic growth and cost reduction are important, CEOs recognise that they cannot achieve these and other goals without investment in innovation, technology and people.' The role of people and their effective management in driving innovation, and thereby marketplace agility, places the Human Resource (HR) function in African organizations at the centre of their efforts to adapt to the dynamic business environment. Grounded in an adaptive view of organizations, this chapter examines the HR function's contribution to marketplace agility through the development of a change management capability, as a source of sustained competitive advantage.

Environmental context

An open system view of organizations has long recognized that organizations do not exist in a vacuum but, rather, their survival and growth depend on an active interaction with their environments. While organizations can attempt to control their environments the prevailing view is that organizations are adaptive systems that respond to environmental changes in order to survive and grow (Boisot and Child, 1999). Responding to environmental uncertainty, and therefore change, usually entails organizations having to develop strategies and internal arrangements such as organization design and structure, as well as management practices and policies to match the emergent uncertainty (Utomi, 1998). In this context, doing the right thing (through strategic management) is never constant and must be periodically reviewed to ensure a fit between environmental pressures and the organization's strategic posture. This underlines the temporariness of competitive advantage and the importance of successful organizations changing their business model or initial advantage when this opportunity is exhausted (McGrath, 2013).

The influx of multinationals as well as the openness of African economies has created opportunities and threats for many African organizations (Mohan and Power, 2008). For example, locally based entrepreneurs complain about the flooding of the market with cheap foreign imports, increasingly from China, which puts them at a competitive disadvantage, price-wise. Furthermore, an emergent middle class with high expectations in terms of product and service quality suggest that organizations must be innovative in order to meet the diverse and changing needs and expectations of customers. Although the continent's population explosion and the rate of urbanisation suggest a huge customer base (but with rising expectations), organizations will have to understand and respond to these product-market pressures (PwC, 2017). This suggests that African organizations must proactively manage the change inherent in the effective implementation of new strategies which therefore, requires developing a capability for change management.

The people-intensive nature of strategy implementation underscores the criticality of the HR function in building this change management capability as an essential component of its role as a strategic partner. As Walker (1992: 8–9) observed, 'The capacity to implement changes called for in business strategies is dependent on people. People, not companies, innovate, make decisions, develop and produce new products, penetrate new markets, and serve customers more effectively.'

Understanding (strategic) organizational change

While strategic repositioning is critical to organizational adaptation to an increasingly turbulent and uncertain environment, even more critical is the implementation of the change inherent in such repositioning. Consequently, strategic change has long been considered an important subfield in the field of strategic management (Rajagopalan and Spreitzer, 1997; Zajac, Kraatz, and Bresser, 2000). Although organizational change and strategic change tend to be used interchangeably, organizational change may entail a wider range of changes which may not only be smaller in scope, but crucially, these changes may not be strategic. In contrast, strategic change denotes a fundamental form of change that tends to affect major elements of the organization such as structure, identity, or strategy and typically initiated by top management (Kunisch, Bartunek, Mueller, and Huy, 2017). This may encompass 'changes in product and service domains,' 'an organization's attempt to change current modes of cognition and action' or 'the means through which organizations maintain co-alignment with shifting competitive, technological, and social environment' (Kraatz and Zajac, 2001). In light of the competing definitions of the construct, we adopt Rajagopalan and Spreitzer's (1997) more integrative definition of strategic change as an organization's alignment with its external environment. This alignment entails: (i) changes in the content of the firm's strategy as defined by its scope, resource deployments, competitive advantages and synergy; and (ii) changes in the external environment and organization brought about to initiate and implement changes in the content of strategy (1997: 49).

Their integrative model of strategic change highlights three interrelated themes. First is the view that strategic change is a rational, planned activity whereby managers adapt their organizations to environmental pressures by ensuring a fit between their strategic orientation and opportunities and threats emanating from the environment. Second is the notion of learning which highlights a process view of change that depicts strategic change as 'an iterative process through which managers effect changes through a series of relatively small steps that enable organizations to understand both the environment and the organization leading to changes in the content of the firm's strategy.' Last is a distinction between managerial cognitions and actions, whereby cognitions provide the underlying logic for managerial actions that define the content of strategic change. Rajagopalan and Spreitzer's (1997: 70) integrative model of strategic change is helpful because it provides conceptual guidance to researchers in terms of understanding (i) why different firms respond differently to a similar context (because of different cognitions and actions) and (ii) how firms can maximize the effectiveness of their adaptive responses (through different managerial actions aimed at the environment and/or the organization).

As African organizations increasingly operate in a dynamic environment, Rajagopalan and Spreitzer's (1997) integrative model of strategic change provides a conceptual lens through which to understand this environment, the potential strategic actions in their product/service and market domains and the resource deployments necessary to implement strategic change. In effect, it is not enough to map out strategic change, but equally importantly, organizations and their top management will have to development strategic change capabilities that can create value and promote competitive advantage. We posit marketplace agility as a form of strategic change in response to dynamic conditions, but the question remains as to how African organizations can build a change management capability to ensure their agility, and therefore survival and growth.

Managing strategic change: building adaptive capability

Recognition that organizations must constantly adapt to an ever-changing environment suggests that they must continuously create new capabilities in response to the complexity of their environments or become strategically agile. Weber and Tarba (2014: 7) define strategic agility as 'the ability of management to constantly and rapidly sense and respond to a changing environment by intentionally making strategic moves and consequently adapting the necessary organizational configuration for successful implementation.' The defining attributes of strategic agility include: (i) a set of actions taken by an organization that operates in an environment characterized by rapid and unpredictable change; (ii) changes that are different from regular and routine types of changes are continuous, systematic variations in an organization's products, processes, services and structures; (iii) a high level of flexibility and speed to adequately respond to emergent threats and opportunities emanating from the environment. We posit that Weber and Tarba's (2014) conceptualization of strategic agility culminates in marketplace agility, thereby promoting organizational survival and growth in a dynamic environment. These attributes of strategic agility are consistent with Rajagopalan and Spreitzer's (1997)'s integrative model of strategic change, which depicts it as a rational activity that entails managerial cognitions and actions, as well as learning.

Fostering marketplace agility through strategic change requires developing and leveraging an appropriate capability which may account for the differential performance of organizations in uncertain times. Indeed, Mohrman and Worley (2009) observed that building a dynamic capability and the inherent strategic change is best done during a period of crisis. This is because it enhances 'the organization's capacity to leverage knowledge and employee involvement . . . in finding solutions to the challenge it faces' (p 434). Teece (2007: 1319) define dynamic capabilities as the ability to continuously create, extend, upgrade, protect, and keep relevant an enterprise's unique asset base. Dynamic capabilities therefore constitute change-oriented capabilities that enable organizations to redeploy and reconfigure their resources to respond to changing customer demands and competitor strategies. To that extent, dynamic capabilities operate as firm-level processes that enable organizations to successfully deploy and reconfigure their resources, thereby promoting survival and growth. As discussed in a subsequent section, and given the criticality of employees in change implementation (Walker, 1992), we conceptualized HR intervention to foster agility as a firm-level dynamic capability which enables an organization and its employees to engage in the strategic behaviours (e.g., innovation) that promote marketplace agility.

Weber and Tarba (2014) observed that agile organizations are characterized by a relentless search for new ways of organizational renewal, maintaining a high level of organizational flexibility, developing learning and knowledge transfer skills and developing an adaptive culture, among others. They also posit that these activities are facilitated by managerial and organizational practices that promote 'reconfiguration and transformation,' learning, and coordination and integration (Teece, Pisano, and Shuen, 1997). These managerial and organizational practices provide the framework for an HR change intervention in the form of a change management capability necessary to enhance the marketplace agility and competitiveness of African organizations.

In their discussion of marketplace agility and consistent with the view of employees as a strategic resource, Dyer and colleagues (Dyer and Shafer, 2003; Dyer and Ericksen, 2006) identified three essential competencies needed to reconfigure and enhance an organization's marketplace agility. First is a scalable workforce, which they describe as 'the capacity of an organization to keep its human resources aligned with business needs by transitioning quickly and easily from one human resource configuration to another, ad infinitum' (Dyer and Ericksen, 2006: 3). The second capability is continuous learning and knowledge sharing to foster the creativity and innovation at the core of marketplace agility. In the view of Dyer and Shafer (2003: 14), learning constitutes a capacity to constantly create, adapt, distribute and apply knowledge. The final capability highlights the design of a fluid or adaptable structure that supports workforce scalability. Dimensions of such an organizational infrastructure are not unlike those of an organic structure such as flat structure and horizontal relationships (Burns and Stalker, 1961).

HR as strategic partner

An increasingly dynamic environment has brought into sharp focus the contributions of functional areas to an organization's competitiveness and therefore survival. While the contributions of many of these functional areas are traditionally more observable because they can easily be quantified, until the last two decades or so, the same was not true of the HR function. Consequently, the HR function has been labelled a cost centre and, therefore, a function that could and should be outsourced (Stewart, 1996). This was in large part due to the function's focus on discrete activities which, while contributing to individual performance, was less evident relative to other functions in terms of bottom-line impact. Traditional HR focused on single HR practices such as recruitment and selection, performance appraisal, training and development, and compensation. While these operational activities ensured that organizations attracted, trained, and motivated employees to contribute to organizational goal attainment efforts, they were not necessarily oriented to developing a dynamic capability that contributed to the attainment of an organization's strategic objectives and therefore competitiveness (Lengnick-Hall, Lengnick-Hall, Andrade, and Drake, 2009; Wright, Dunford, and Snell, 2001).

Calls to demonstrate the HR function's contributions to an organization's bottom-line heralded a shift from a focus on operational and discrete HR activities to a focus on the HR function's strategic contributions to organizational competitiveness. Accordingly, Wright and McMahan (1992: 298) defined strategic HRM as 'the pattern of planned human resource deployments and activities intended to enable an organization to achieve its goals.' HR's strategic partnership status received much fillip with the changed understanding of the factors that foster organizational effectiveness as exemplified in the resource-based view of the firm (RBV). RBV highlights three internal resources which are physical (firm's equipment and finances), organizational capital (firm's structure and HR system) and human capital resources (knowledge, skills, and ability of employees). Thus, rather than looking beyond the organization for resources that account for variation in the competitiveness of organizations, the focus shifted to the resources internal to the organization and how they could be combined to execute strategy (Barney, 1991). Indeed, the essence of RBV was distilled into Barney's (1991: 99) observation that organizations 'obtain sustained competitive advantage by implementing strategies that exploit their internal strengths, through responding to environmental opportunities, while neutralizing external threats and avoiding internal weaknesses.' This conceptual lens holds that, when appropriately configured, resources internal to the organization could serve as sources of competitive advantage. However, to constitute a source of competitive advantage, a resource must possess four basic attributes: valuable, inimitable, non-substitutable, and rare. As many of the traditional sources of competitive advantage could easily be imitated, focus turned to employees and their effective management as a competitive resource (Barney, 1991; Barney and Wright, 1998).

The repositioning of the HR function as a strategic partner rather than a cost centre has meant that its principal role is to align HR activities that constitute an HR system with the organization's strategy, and thereby facilitate strategy execution through the effective management of employees (Lado and Wilson, 1994; Wright et al., 2001). An increasingly important HR system is high performance work systems (HPWS), which describes a 'system of HR practices designed to enhance employees' skills, commitment, and productivity in such a way that employees become a source of sustainable competitive advantage' (Datta, Guthrie, and Wright, 2005: 136). Drawing on conceptual models of how an HR system works (Bowen and Ostroff, 2004; Ferris, Arthur, Berkson, Kaplan, Harrell-Cook, and Frink, 1998), more recent research has focused on accounting for the mediating mechanisms that underpin the previously and much documented HPWS-performance relationship in both developed and developing countries (Aryee, Walumbwa, Seidu, and Otaye, 2012; Jiang, Lepak, Hu, and Baer, 2012).

Of particular relevance to this chapter is the use of a strategically appropriate HPWS to develop an internal capability to implement an organization's strategy. For example, an organization that aims to compete on the basis of innovation in services and products will be expected to build an internal capability that ensures employees are equipped with the requisite skills, are motivated, and have opportunities to engage in innovative behaviours. As this internal capability is causally ambiguous and therefore not easily explicable, it enables an organization to effectively implement its strategic objective of creating and sustaining competitive advantage through marketplace agility. However, to constitute a source of internal capability, this HPWS must foster a supportive organizational climate/culture, focus individual attention, reinforce common goals and values, and become a lever which can be used to promote strategic change (Ulrich, 1987: 173). In the next section, we discuss how HR change intervention in the form of HPWS implementation and the internal capability it builds, constitutes a form of strategic change which can be leveraged to foster marketplace agility.

The human resource function as change agent

Implicit in marketplace agility is the recognition that introducing new products and services, and therefore innovation, is fundamental to organizational survival and growth. As a strategic partner and hence change agent, the HR function must ensure an organization's change capability matches or leads the external pace of change. Ulrich, Younger, Brockbank, and Ulrich (2013: 463), identified three levels of change that the HR function should focus on: (i) change patterns at the institutional level; (ii) making things happen (initiative level); and (iii) enabling personal change (individual level). To accomplish change across these levels, they suggested two interrelated steps: First, the function initiates change by building a compelling case for change and involving key stakeholders in the change process. To this end, they must explain why change matters, what should be changed, overcoming resistance to change, and who supports the change. Second, the function must sustain the change process by institutionalizing change through ensuring availability of resources to implement the change, monitoring and communicating progress of change processes and orchestrating continual learning (Brown, Kulik, Cregan, and Metz, 2017).

Consequently, our focus in this section is to highlight how HR change intervention builds the change management capability which can be leveraged to promote marketplace agility. In light of the changed environment and the need for marketplace agility, the HR system must foster flexibility. Wright and Snell (1998: 758) consider fit and flexibility two essential attributes of an HR system. Consequently, in a dynamic environment, HR systems may engender flexibility and therefore fit by 'using organic HR systems that promote the development of a human capital pool possessing a broad range of skills and that are able to engage in a wide variety of behavior.' We propose that such an HR system, and thereby the HR change agent role in building a change management capability, must focus on the three levels Ulrich and colleagues (2013) identified: change initiatives, institutionalization of these initiatives and individual change in terms of the attitudes and behaviours that promote marketplace agility.

Promoting marketplace agility through HR

Marketplace agility constitutes a means through which an organization pursues value in a highly competitive product market. This entails a quest for innovation and customer-focus leading to value generation, and should underpin HR change efforts and the resulting capability to deliver value generation. As noted in a previous section, the defining attributes of an agile organization (fostering marketplace agility) are workforce scalability, learning and organizational infrastructure, which collectively promote the behavioural flexibility needed to marketplace agility. Following Ulrich and colleagues' (2013) three levels of change that the HR change intervention should focus on, we conceptualized change initiative in terms of an HPWS for agility, change institutionalization in terms of climate for agility and learning, and enabling individual level change in terms of employee attitudes and behaviours that support the strategic goal of marketplace agility (developing an agility mindset and behaviours).

HR change intervention: HPWS for agility

As a lynchpin of HR's strategic influence (Becker, Huselid, and Ulrich, 2001), and given the requirements of marketplace agility, we focused in this chapter on the development of an HPWS for agility. This is because HPWS constitutes a strategy implementation system, and for that reason it is embedded within the organization's strategic goal which, in this context, is marketplace agility. Bamberger and Meshoulam (2000) identified three main HR subsystems that are concerned with (i) people flow including staffing, employee mobility, and training; (ii) appraisal and rewards defined in terms of performance-contingent rewards and benefits; and (iii) employment relations including job design and participation. These subsystems align with the increasingly popular ability, motivation, and opportunity (AMO) framework that underpins much HPWS research (Applebaum, Bailey, Berg, and Kalleberg, 2000). We therefore define HPWS for agility as a set of interrelated practices designed to enhance employees' competencies, motivation, and opportunity for agile behaviours such as innovation and improvisation.

Pertaining to people flow or the ability subsystem, the HR intervention should focus on developing a human capital pool with the requisite skills and potential to engage in strategically appropriate behaviours such as innovation. Staffing practices will therefore have to be selective, focusing on such attributes as openness to change, creativity, proactiveness and willingness to learn. These attributes will have to be reinforced with extensive training programmes designed to build the requisite competencies such as cross-functional work assignments and continuous development opportunities, geared to the flexibility of the workforce so that they can accomplish a wide variety of tasks under diverse conditions (Wright and Snell, 1998). This is also consistent with Dyer and Ericksen's (2006) notion of workforce scalability, which consists of HR practices designed to ensure workforce alignment or fit and workforce fluidity or flexibility. Workforce alignment promotes a fit between the strategic goal of marketplace agility and having the right type of employees in terms of skills and competencies in appropriate numbers. This, however, must be constantly monitored to avoid misalignments, especially in a changing organizational context.

The rewards and compensation or motivation component of an HPWS for agility must entail the adoption of practices that motivate or reinforce employee agility-oriented behaviours such as innovation, profit-sharing schemes and group-based incentives to promote teamwork. To complement the people flow component, focus on developing workforce skill flexibility, the motivation component focuses on promoting behavioural flexibility. Behavioural flexibility describes the capacity of employees to adapt to changing situations or to exhibit appropriate behaviours under different situations (Bhattacharya, Gibson, and Doty, 2005; Pulakos, Arad, Donovan, and Plamondon, 2000). These components of an HPWS for agility reflect resource flexibility, in that it enables an organization to acquire and develop human resources for a wide range of alternative uses (Chang, Gong, Way, and Jia, 2012).

The opportunity component of an HPWS for agility should focus on practices that foster a high-quality relationship with employees and provide the organizational infrastructure to support behavioural flexibility. These practices should include broad role definitions, participation in decision-making and information sharing. Such practices recognise the dynamic nature of an organization's environment and the fact that solutions to organizational problems can emanate from different sources in the organization and not only from the top. The opportunity dimension may ultimately create a sense of responsibility for the success of the organization, as well as provide the structure within which to promote behavioural flexibility such as innovation and creativity. In effect, it facilitates coordination flexibility, and therefore enables an organization to deploy its resources quickly and effectively (Chang et al., 2012) thereby promoting marketplace agility.

HR change institutionalization: promoting climate for agility

As a change intervention strategy, HPWS for agility signals an organization's strategic intent and by implication, the normative expectations regarding the strategically appropriate behaviours to ensure marketplace agility (Bowen and Ostroff, 2004). To constitute a capability for change management, strategically appropriate behavioural expectations must be shared and embedded into the fabric of the organization. This can be accomplished through two interrelated process. The first is the selection-attraction-attrition model, which posits that individuals of similar attributes and qualities tend to be attracted to, selected by and retained in the organization (Schneider, Smith, and Goldstein, 2000). In the context of our discussion, this is made possible by the use of an HPWS for agility that ensures the attraction of this group of employees, thereby facilitating a shared perspective of what matters in the organization. The second process is through a social context model of how HPWS works, which posits a shared perception of strategically appropriate behaviours that stem from social interactions (Ferris et al., 1998). Thus, from their social interactions, employees will develop cues or make sense of what matters in their organization through social information processing. An HPWS for agility will lead employees to develop a shared perspective of broad-based and continuous learning and adaptability as behaviours that are encouraged and rewarded in the organization. These behavioural expectations or shared perspective will constitute a climate for agility with learning and innovation as fundamental attributes of such a climate.

Drawing on Schneider's (1990) seminal work on facet-specific climates, climate for agility describes employees' perceptions of events, practices and procedures, and the kinds of behaviours that get rewarded, supported and expected in a setting. This climate ensures the institutionalizing of the practices that define HPWS for agility and fosters a value system that promotes collaborative and continuous learning concerned not only with knowledge creation, but also its adaptation, distribution or sharing and application. These attributes provide the content of the change that must be institutionalized to promote marketplace agility. As the institutionalization may trigger a fundamental change in the way the organization operates, and given the role of employees in manifesting these attributes, we discuss in the next section the individual-level attitudinal and behavioural changes which must be leveraged to promote marketplace agility.

Individual level changes: promoting agility-oriented attitudes and behaviours

As the individual level changes needed to implement HR's change agent role, what are the strategically congruent attitudinal and behavioural changes needed to develop a capability for change management? Griffin, Neal, and Parker (2007) observed that in dynamic environments, work roles emerge in response to changing conditions, especially as work-related behaviours cannot be prescribed. Of the three work roles that Griffin and colleagues (2007) identified, proactivity and adaptivity are consistent with the agility-oriented mindset and behaviours that Dyer and Shafer (2003) identified. Underpinning these behavioural requirements is a focus on innovation as a way to ensure marketplace agility and, ultimately, organizational survival and growth. Change-oriented HPWS has been shown to indirectly promote group innovation through individual proactivity and group-level creative processes (Lee, Pak, Kim, and Li, 2016). Judge and colleagues (2009) reported organizational capacity for change to relate to firm performance in a transition economy, and this relationship is stronger when levels of uncertainty with the task environment are high. Given the need for marketplace agility in a dynamic uncertain environment, our view is that HR intervention should focus on developing change management as a dynamic capability through the implementation of HPWS for agility. In the next section, we draw on the preceding conceptual discussion to propose a contextualized model of how the HR function can contribute to the marketplace agility of African organizations through the development of a change management capability.

HR and change management in an African context

How do African organizations develop the change management capability to foster marketplace agility and, therefore, their survival and growth? We posit HPWS for agility as a primary HR intervention for developing this dynamic capability. However, the effectiveness of this intervention depends on contextual factors as well as the effectiveness of the HR function as change agent. We therefore seek to highlight the facilitative conditions that must be present if the HR function is to effectively serve as change agent. To do so, we start with the question of the differential adoption of HR change interventions or why some organizations adopt HR change interventions while others don't. Implicit in the differential adoption of HR change interventions is the role of top management support as a major driver of these interventions.

Top management support as driver of HR change intervention (HPWS)

Although research has attributed the adoption of management practices to a host of institutional factors (Cooke and Saini, 2010), we adopt the view that the adoption of HPWS for agility is driven by top management's perception of the strategic importance of employees as a competitive resource. This is particularly the case in an African context, where the relative size of organizations and the structure of ownership make the organization a reflection of the strategic emphasis (e.g., values and beliefs) of top management. Drawing on resource management (Sirmon, Hitt, and Ireland, 2007) and upper-echelons (Hambrick and Mason, 1984; Hambrick, 2007) theories, we posit top management's strategic emphasis on employees as a competitive resource is critical in determining not only the implementation of an HPWS for agility as an HR change intervention, but equally important, the extent to which it is embedded across levels in the organization, and therefore becomes institutionalized.

Central to resource management is the notion of value creation, which is said to be contingent upon the manner in which resources are evaluated, manipulated and deployed. More specifically, Sirmon and colleagues (2007: 273) posit that resource management connotes 'a comprehensive process of structuring the firm's resource portfolio, bundling the resources to build capabilities, and leveraging those capabilities with the purpose of creating and maintaining value.' However, to be effective, resource management activities across organizational levels must be prioritized, synchronized and supported; in other words, orchestrated by top management. Integral to resource orchestration is managerial action related to the development and realization of strategic resources. However, this begs the question of how top management then decides on which of these resources are strategic, and therefore must be developed and deployed to create value.

Drawing on upper-echelons theory, we posit that top management's beliefs and values will determine the extent to which employees are considered a strategic resource and their effective management a source of value creation. This theory posits that ambiguity and uncertainty define the strategic context faced by top management, so in order to navigate this context, top management tends to rely on their cognitive structures (cause-effect beliefs) and personal values. Thus, this theory is predicated on the idea that the ambiguity and uncertainty that characterize information-rich environments cannot be objectively known, but can be interpreted through the conceptual lens of top management. Consequently, understanding strategic decisions, and how and why firms perform the way they do, requires an understanding of the cognitive structures and personal values of top management.

In the context of this chapter, we argue that the extent to which top management subscribes to an employee-centred value system will determine whether employees are considered a resource and therefore, warrant investment in their development and deployment to create value (Bamberger and Meshoulam, 2000). Top management's employee-centred value system has been labelled as 'HR cause-effect belief' and reported to influence the adoption of an HPWS (Arthur, Herdman, and Yang, 2016). Indeed, Arthur and colleagues (2016: 415) argued and found support for their view that 'a belief by top managers that investing in HR will yield positive returns for the company would appear to be a basic condition underlying the use of HPWSs.' Operating within a resource management perspective, Chadwick, Super, and Kwon (2015: 363) also argued that 'given their complexity and comprehensiveness, it is exceedingly unlikely that integrated commitment-based HR systems will spring up within a firm of their own accord . . . independent of top manager's emphasis.'

The preceding discussion highlights the importance of top management action not only in terms of how their organizations will adapt to competitive pressures (strategic orientation), but also the development and leveraging of strategic resources to build a dynamic capability to respond to these pressures. In order to foster marketplace agility, and in view of the empirical evidence, it is important that top management of African organizations consider employees as a strategic resource. This should then provide a facilitative context within which the HR function can develop and implement change intervention through the adoption of an HPWS for agility. While the admittedly sparse research on strategic HRM in Africa has documented the influence of HPWS on organizational performance (Aryee et al., 2012; Zoogah and Zoogah, 2014), little is known about the differential adoption of such an HR intervention strategy. The growing recognition of employees as a strategic resource, and drawing on both upper-echelon and resource management theories, should encourage the top management of these organizations to provide a facilitative context for using HR interventions to develop a change management capability.

Enhancing the implementation of HR change interventions

The role of the HR function in developing a change management capability to promote marketplace agility is much contingent upon its effectiveness in implementing, and thereby institutionalizing HPWS for agility as an HR change intervention. While both the RBV and dynamic capabilities perspectives have highlighted the importance of building a dynamic capability, it is increasingly noted that ability to implement intervention strategies should itself constitute a source of competitive advantage. Accordingly, Barney's (2001: 54) observation that 'the ability to implement strategies is, by itself, a resource that can be a source of competitive advantage' has since been embraced in the strategic HRM literature. For example, Becker and Huselid's (2006) observation that implementation is a key mediating variable in the relationship between HR architecture and organizational performance has since received empirical support (Chow, 2012).

In a 10-year longitudinal study within 10 organizations in the UK, Gratton and Truss (2003) proposed a three-dimensional people strategy. These are (i) vertical alignment (linkage between the overall organizational vision held by top management and the philosophy that underpins the organization's approach to managing people), (ii) horizontal alignment (coherent and consistent approach to managing people across HR practices, thereby enabling the organization to communicate consistent messages to employees), and (iii) action dimension. While the two dimensions operate at the policy level, the action dimension is consistent with the focus on the implementation of HR practices that reflect the view that the 'bridging from business goals to employee performance requires not only policies but also a determination to act as seen through actual practices' (Gratton and Truss, 2003: 75). The focus on implementation in the SHRM literature is particularly instructive given the reported discrepancy between intended and perceived HR interventions (Khilji and Wang, 2006). In the rest of this section, we draw on the change readiness literature to discuss how the HR function in African organizations can institutionalize HPWS for agility as an HR change intervention.

HR intervention, contextual clarity and employee change readiness

Although vertical alignment is integral to the effectiveness of HR change intervention, upper-echelons theory suggests that top management must embed the strategic priority assigned to people as a competitive resource throughout the organization (Hambrick and Mason, 1984). This requires that top management takes a proactive role in ensuring that messages conveyed by the implementation of HPWS for agility are not only distinctive, but are clearly, consistently and unambiguously communicated throughout the organization. Indeed, Bowen and Ostroff (2004: 208) observed that 'in order to function effectively in a social context and make accurate attributions about a situation, an employee must have adequate and unambiguous information.' This is particularly important to enhance understanding of the rationale for the change as well the behavioural requirements needed to implement the organization's strategic goals.

This dovetails with the change readiness literature, which Armenakis, Harris, and Mossholder (1993: 681) defined as an individual's beliefs, attitudes and intentions regarding the extent to which changes are needed, and the organization's capacity to successfully undertake those changes. The HR intervention-related communication must address the cognitive and affective components of change readiness. The cognitive component entails addressing the belief that change is needed and the belief that the individual and organization have the capacity to undertake change (Armenakis et al., 1993). In contrast, the affective component of change readiness, though not originally discussed by Armenakis and colleagues (1993), is thought to describe receptivity to change based on its positive consequences. Rafferty, Jimmieson, and Armenakis (2013: 116) conceived of the change readiness construct in terms of (i) the individual's beliefs (a) that change is needed, (b) that he or she has the capacity to successfully undertake change and (c) that change will have positive outcomes for his/her job/role, and by (ii) the individual's current and future-oriented positive affective emotional responses to a specific change event.

To enhance change readiness, adoption and institutionalization of change, Armenakis and Harris (2002) identified three message-conveying strategies that change agents may utilize. The first is persuasive communication, in which HR as change agent directly communicates the change message. The second is active participation, which with its self-discovery component focuses on enactive mastery, vicarious learning and participation in decision-making. The last is management of information by which external sources in particular provide information regarding the necessity of the change programme in light of industry trends. These communication strategies should enhance the effectiveness of the change message and create a facilitative context for implementing HR change intervention in the form of HPWS for agility. Indeed, research has shown that when the HR function undertakes a strategic change agent role by promoting the change intervention and helping employees to construe the meaning of change events, employees are more likely to feel valued and have lower levels of uncertainty, thereby reducing the likelihood that experience of change will lead to change cynicism (Brown et al., 2017: 9).

Line management and implementation of HPWS for agility

The strategic HR partner role has been accompanied by the devolution of HR roles and responsibilities to line managers. Consequently, line managers have become critical linking-pins in the implementation of HR change interventions (Gratton and Truss, 2003; Purcell and Hutchinson, 2007; Sikora and Ferris, 2014). As Purcell and Hutchinson (2007: 3) observed, 'HR practices perceived or experienced by employees will, to a large extent, be those delivered or enacted by line managers, especially front-line managers (FLMs) with direct supervisory responsibility.' The widely documented gap between actual and enacted HR interventions has therefore been partly attributed to line managers (Khilji and Wang, 2006). There is some evidence that line managers are committed to implementing HR interventions and believe that effectively discharging the HR responsibilities contributes to firm performance (Renwick, 2003; Wright, McMahan, Snell, and Gerhart, 2001). However, the general consensus in the literature is that line managers are either unable or unwilling to implement HR interventions (Sikora and Ferris, 2014). Regardless of the rationale for line managers' non-implementation of HR interventions, it is imperative that they are taught implementation skills and motivated to do so. This is because, as Bowen and Ostroff (2004) noted, for HR interventions such as adoption of HPWS for agility to have their desired effect, they must be implemented in a coordinated and consistent manner.

We are unaware of research that has specifically investigated line management involvement in HR change implementation in African organizations. This is deserving of research attention, because as African organizations implement a variety of strategic changes to adapt to the dynamic environment, they need to draw on actionable knowledge from such a research stream to inform their implantation decisions. Recent research has reported line manager implementation competencies (defined in terms of line manager HR competency and line manager political skill) to relate to employees' work outcomes through the mediating influence of line manager implementation perceptions (Sikora, Ferris, and van Iddenkinge, 2015). Accordingly, it will be helpful to engage line managers in a change dialogue highlighting the overarching objective of promoting organizational survival and growth with the HR change intervention an important plank in this process. This should enable the HR function to understand the concerns of line managers (and increased provision of line manager HR training), build a trusting relationship and provide the resources to mitigate these concerns, as well as motivate their adoption of a change agent mindset.

Our discussion relating to enhancing implementation of HR change intervention underscores Bowen and Ostroff's (2004) call for a strong HR system, whereby HR practices create an unambiguous social structure integrating HR content and process. This integration creates a consistent message for all organizational participants, thereby engendering virtuous organizational goals and practices leading to strategically relevant behaviours.

Discussion

In their seminal article on the future of the HR profession, Roehling et al. (2005: 208) observed that 'since organizational capabilities are deeply rooted in human resource capabilities (e.g., employee attitudes and social networks), HR is best positioned to deliver these outcomes.' They therefore urged researchers to examine HR deliverables in the form of organizational capabilities, as well as how the HR function can be designed and practiced to promote these capabilities. In light of the competitive pressures consequent upon the openness of African economies, African organizations have to become agile not only to survive and grow, but also generate stable employment opportunities for the continent's ever-increasing population. As a strategic partner, the HR function in African organizations, like their counterparts elsewhere, will have to develop a dynamic change management capability to motivate the innovative behaviours that are critical to marketplace agility. Drawing on RBV and the related dynamic capability perspectives, this chapter proposed a model in which HPWS for agility is conceptualized as an HR change intervention geared to the development of a change management capability. As a strategic resource, a change management capability can be leveraged to promote the survival and growth of African organizations.

This model extends extant research that either examined the HR change role as a moderator in the relationship between HR social capital (defined in terms of structural, relational and cognitive) and the function's effectiveness (Kim and Ryu, 2011) or in the relationship between quantity of change and employee change cynicism (Brown et al., 2017), as well as a mediator in the relationship between HR competencies and organizational performance (Long, Ismail, and Amin, 2013). However, the model depicted in Figure 9.1 is consistent with extant research that specifically conceives of organizational change capacity as a dynamic capability (Judge and Elenkov, 2005; Shipton, Budhwar, and Crawshaw, 2012) and reports this capability to relate to firm performance in a transitional economy (Judge et al., 2009). Indeed, Judge and Elenkov (2005: 893) defined organizational change capability as 'a dynamic organizational capability that allows the enterprise to adapt old capabilities to new threats and opportunities, as well as create new opportunities.'

In their discussion of a capability development system through rough times, Mohrman and Worley (2009) noted that top management must, among other things, engage the organization in identifying and capturing new opportunities, flexibly leverage knowledge and resources across the organization to achieve more with shrinking resources, and innovate. Particularly germane to our purposes is the need to leverage knowledge and resources, which is not dissimilar from the dynamic capabilities view of reconfiguring resources. In order to foster the marketplace agility of African organizations through the HR deliverable of change management capability, Figure 9.1 depicts top management of these organizations as primary drivers. Specifically, top management

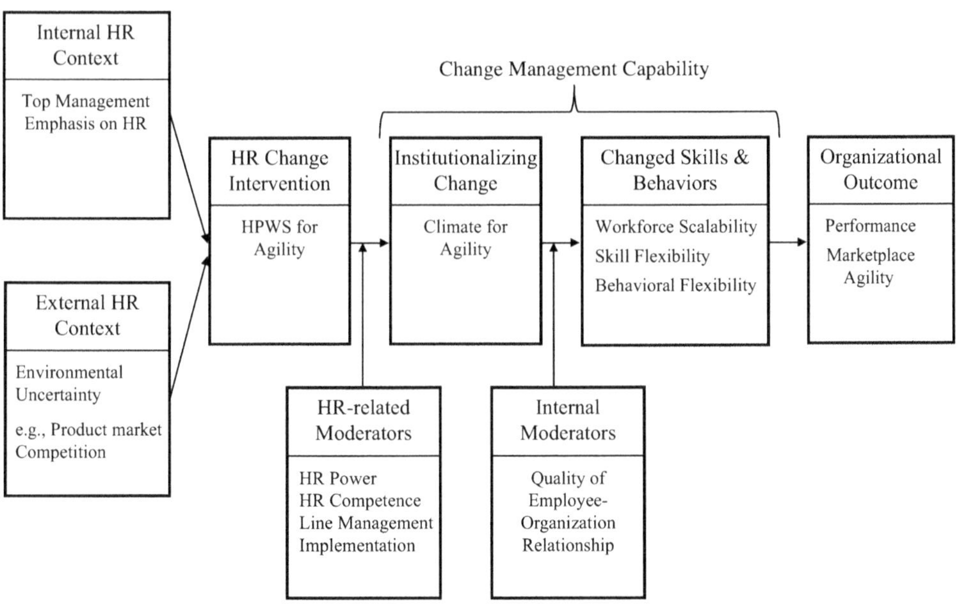

Figure 9.1 HR change agent role content and process

must emphasise employees and their effective management as a source of competitive advantage. This view appears to have been recognized in the PwC survey of African CEOs (2017), which revealed a high degree of importance attached to investment in innovation, technology and people. Within this context, the HR function can meaningfully adopt a strategic partner role by implementing an HPWS for agility, as a change management capability intervention to promote the marketplace agility of African organizations.

As shown in Figure 9.1, this process entails institutionalizing a climate/culture of agility. However, the extent to which such a climate can be institutionalized or embedded in the organization is heavily dependent on the effectiveness of the HR function (defined in terms of power and competencies) and line management implementation of competencies. Once institutionalized, a climate of agility promotes the development of flexible skills and behaviours (such as innovation and creativity), as well as normative expectations in the form of coordination flexibility. However, the outcomes of climate for agility are very much dependent on the quality of the employment relationship, whether it's one of an economic or social exchange. An employment relationship grounded in ubuntu principles, which encourage a sense of organizational familism, fosters a collective sense of responsibility for the survival and growth of the organization. As these path-dependent elements are causally ambiguous firm-level processes, they cannot be easily imitated, and will therefore constitute a competitive resource in the quest of African organizations for marketplace agility.

HR change agent role and marketplace agility in Africa: two contingencies

Perhaps because of the cost involved in the adoption of HR interventions such as HPWS for agility, research has shown these interventions to be mainly adopted by large organizations. Although the vast majority of African organizations can be described as small-to-medium-sized, it is precisely because of their size that the survival and growth of these organizations is contingent upon their ability to be agile in a dynamic environment. This is because small firms have been noted to be prone to greater competitive threats because of the liability of smallness which constrains their resources and capabilities making them vulnerable to product-market competition (Patel and Cardon, 2010). Additionally, such firms tend to be labour intensive, making their survival and growth dependent on effective management of employees if they are to respond to market conditions. For these reasons, it is imperative that African organizations focus on enhancing the effectiveness of the HR role, as well as the quality of the employee-organization relationship, as critical contingencies.

Enhancing the effectiveness of the HR function in African organizations

> Over the long run, the influence of human resources management in organizations rises and falls depending on how well they anticipate and respond to changing external and internal forces that shape employment relationships.
>
> *(Kochan, 1997: 1)*

A steady stream of research has empirically documented the power of the HR function as a critical boundary condition of its effectiveness. Zupan and Kase (2005), for example, conceptualized HR power in terms of both the presence and quality of the HR strategy development and the efficiency and effectiveness of strategy execution. They operationalized the construct in terms of

HR competencies, as well as status and role of HR manager and HR department. Although we are not aware of research that has examined HR power in African organizations, it is probably safe to assume that it is rather weak, with some not even having a formal HR department, especially in small- and medium-sized organizations. Consequently, a major challenge in assuming the emergent strategic partner status role has to do with HR professionals' range of competencies necessary to fulfil this new mandate. Ulrich and Brockbank (2005) proposed a competency model for the HR value proposition entailing five specific competencies, which collectively enhance the function's strategic contribution such as change management capability. First is business knowledge in terms of understanding not only the company, but also its industry. This knowledge should enable HR professionals to ask meaningful questions about the business strategy as well as having a vision of the future of the business. Second is HR delivery in terms of the ability to design and deliver basic and innovative HR practices such as HPWS for agility, as well as ensuring a fit with the organization's culture. Third is HR technology, such as HR information systems, to improve the effectiveness of its operational activities. Lastly is personal credibility, defined in terms of a reputation for meeting their commitments, and effective interpersonal and communication skills in order to work collaboratively with internal stakeholders. It is therefore important that African HR professionals invest in these competencies if they are to effectively serve as capability developers through their role as change agent.

Employee-organization relationship and workplace familism

High levels of unemployment across the continent and the inherent job insecurity that plagues many employees could tempt organizations into treating employees not as an asset to be developed, but rather as cost to be exploited. Although family motivation (the desire to provide for a family's economic sustenance) may constitute a major driver of employee work-related behaviours, it may be related primarily to role-prescribed but not discretionary behaviours. However, the innovative behaviours that sustain marketplace agility can mainly be motivated through the quality of the treatment that employees experience at the hands of their organizations. For this reason, it is imperative that organizations are reminded of the social and not only the economic exchange basis of the employment relationship. Consequently, and to signal their commitment to employees, organizations will have to provide inducements which may include not only intangible development components such as career development opportunities and respectful treatment of employees, but also concrete, materialistic components (such as competitive salaries, good healthcare and medical benefits) if they are to promote a sense of organizational familism. Such a social exchange or high-quality employee-organization relationship will promote relational ties (Sun, Aryee, and Law, 2007) and obligate employees to reciprocate in terms of discretionary behaviours such as exploratory learning and innovative behaviours. In the context of organizational change, Shin, Taylor, and Seo (2012) reported organizational inducements to relate to behavioural support for change through employees' perceived social exchange relationship with their organization. Such a relationship is particularly important in an African context, as it chimes with the ubuntu notion regarding the reciprocal nature of relationships and the idea of an individual belonging to a collective (Mangaliso, 2001), which in this context becomes an organizational family.

Conclusion

Marketplace agility constitutes a strategic response to the efforts of organizations to adapt to an increasingly dynamic environment through innovative products and services. How, then, do African organizations develop the dynamic capabilities to become agile and, ultimately, provide the employment opportunities that are needed to accommodate the continent's ever-increasing population? Uncovering responses to this question is particularly important, as the private sector constitutes the continent's engine of growth and therefore employment generation. Judge and colleagues (2009) observed a dearth of research on how human systems and resources can be configured to enhance organizational change processes and outcomes. While this has since been addressed in both developed and transitional economies, the same cannot be said of the African context. Given its emergent strategic partner status and the role of employees in strategy implementation, the HR function in African organizations should develop the firm-level capabilities to help organizations achieve the strategic objective of marketplace agility.

Grounded in the SHRM literature and drawing on RBV and dynamic capability perspective, this chapter examined the HR change agent role and proposed a model which can be used to promote this role across African organizations. The model recognizes the importance of top management's emphasis on employees as strategic resource to be developed and leveraged to promote marketplace agility. As a change intervention strategy, HPWS for agility must be institutionalized through fostering a climate/culture of agility leading to individual level changes (e.g., KSA) in terms of promoting agility-oriented behaviours such as innovation. It is argued that these firm-level processes are causally ambiguous, which make then non-imitable as change management capability, and therefore a competitive resource. The chapter ends by highlighting two contingencies critical to the ability of African organizations to develop and leverage change management capability to create marketplace agility: (i) the competencies of HR professionals and (ii) consistent with ubuntu, promotion of organizational familism, a form of a high-quality employee-organization relationship necessary to motivate agility-oriented behaviours such as innovation.

References

Africa Competitiveness Report. (2017) *Addressing Africa's Demogrpahic Dividend.* Geneva: World Economic Forum.

Applebaum, E., Bailey, T., Berg, P., and Kalleberg, A. (2000) *Manufacturing Advantage: Whyhigh-performance Work Systems Pay-off.* Ithaca, NY: Cornell University Press.

Armenakis, A. A., and Harris, S. G. (2002) Crafting a change message to create transformational readiness. *Journal of Organizational Change Management*, 15: 169–183.

Armenakis, A. A., Harris, S. G., and Mossholder, K. W. (1993) Creating readiness for organizational change. *Human Relations*, 46: 681–703.

Arthur, J., Herdman, A. O., and Yang, J. (2016) How top management HR beliefs and values affect high-performance work system adoption and implementation effectiveness. *Human Resource Management*, 55: 413–435.

Aryee, S., Walumbwa, F. O., Seidu, E., and Otaye, L. E. (2012) Impact of high performance work systems on individual-and branch level performance: Test of a multilevel model. *Journal of Applied Psychology*, 97: 287–300.

Bamberger, P., and Meshoulam, I. (2000) *Human Resource Strategy.* Thousand Oaks, CA: Sage.

Barney, J. B. (1991) Firm resources and sustained competitive advantage. *Journal of Management*, 17: 99–120.

Barney, J. B. (2001) Resource-based theories of competitive advantage: A ten-year retrospective on the resource-based view. *Journal of Management*, 27: 643–650.

Barney, J. B., and Wright, P. M. (1998) On becoming a strategic partner: The role of human resources in gaining competitive advantage. *Human Resource Management*, 37: 31–46.

Becker, B. E., and Huselid, M. A. (2006) Strategic human resource management: Where do we go from here? *Journal of Management*, 32: 898–925.

Becker, B. E., Huselid, M. A., and Ulrich, D. (2001) *The HR Scorecard: Linking People, Strategy, and Performance.* Boston, MA: Harvard Business Press.

Bhattacharya, M., Gibson, D. E., and Doty, H. D. (2005) The effects of flexibility in employee skills, employee behaviours, and human resource practices on firm performance. *Journal of Management*, 31: 622–640.

Boisot, M., and Child, J. (1999) Organizations as adaptive systems in complex environments: The case of China. *Organization Science*, 10: 237–252.
Bowen, D. E., and Ostroff, C. (2004) Understanding HRM-firm performance linkages: The role of the 'strength' of the HRM system. *Academy of Management Review*, 29: 203–221.
Brown, M., Kulik, C. T., Cregan, C., and Metz, I. (2017) Understanding the change-cynicism cycle: The role of HR. *Human Resource Management*, 56: 5–24.
Burns, T. G., and Stalker, G. M. (1961) *The Management of Innovation*. London: Tavistock.
Chadwick, C.,Super, J. F.,and Kwon,K. (2015) Resource orchestration in practice: CEO emphasis on SHRM, commitment-based HR systems, and firm performance. *Strategic Management Journal*, 36: 360–376.
Chang,S.,Gong,Y.,Way,S. A.,and Jia,L. (2012) Flexibility-oriented HRM systems, absorptive capacity, and market responsiveness and firm innovativeness. *Journal of Management*, 39: 1924–1951.
Chow, I. H. S. (2012) The roles of implementation and organizational culture in the HR-performance link. *International Journal of Human Resource Management*, 23: 3114–3132.
Cooke, F. L., and Saini, D. S. (2010) (How) does the HR strategy support an innovation-oriented business strategy? An investigation of institutional context and organizational practices in Indian firms. *Human Resource Management*, 49: 377–400.
Datta, D. K., Guthrie, J., and Wright, P. M. (2005) Human resource management and labor productivity: Does industry matter? *Academy of Management Journal*, 48: 135–145.
Dyer, L., and Ericksen, J. (2006) *Dynamic Organizations: Achieving Marketplace Agility Through Workforce Scalability*. CAHRS Working Paper Series, 06–12.
Dyer, L., and Shafer, R. (2003) Dynamic organizations: Achieving marketplace and organizational agility with people. In R. S. Peterson and E. A. Mannix (Eds.), *Leading Andmanaging People in the Dynamic Organization*. Mahwah, NJ: Lawrence Erlbaum, 7–40.
Ferris, G. R., Arthur, M. H., Berkson, H. M., Kaplan, D. M., Harrell-Cook, G., and Frink, D. D. (1998) Toward a social context theory of the human resource management-organization effectiveness relationship. *Human Resource Management Review*, 8: 235–264.
Gratton, L., and Truss, C. (2003) The three-dimensional people strategy: Putting human resources policies into action. *Academy of Management Executive*, 17: 74–86.
Griffin, M. A., Neal, A., and Parker, S. K. (2007) A new model of work role performance: Positive behaviour in uncertain and interdependent contexts. *Academy of Management Journal*, 50: 327–347.
Hambrick, D. C. (2007) Upper echelons theory: An update. *Academy of ManagementReview*, 32: 334–343.
Hambrick, D. C., and Mason, P. A. (1984) Upper echelons: The organization as a reflection of its top managers. *Academy of Management Review*, 9: 193–206.
Jackson, T. (2004) *Management and Change in Africa: A Cross-cultural Perspective*. London: Routledge.
Jiang, K., Lepak, D., Hu, J., and Baer, J. (2012) How does human resource management influence organizational outcomes? A meta-analytic investigation of mediating mechanisms. *Academy of Management Journal*, 55: 1264–1294.
Judge, W. Q., and Elenkov, D. (2005) Organizational capacity for change and environmental performance: Empirical assessment of Bulgarian firms. *Journal of Business Research*, 58: 893–901.
Judge, W. Q., Naoumova, I., and Douglas, T. (2009) Organizational capacity for change and firm performance in a transition economy. *International Journal of Human Resource Management*, 20: 1737–1752.
Khilji, S. E., and Wang, X. (2006) 'Intended' and 'implemented' HRM: The missing linchpin in strategic human resource management research. *International Journal of Human Resource Management*, 17: 1171–1189.
Kim, S., and Ryu, S. (2011) Social capital of the HR department, HR's change agent role, and HR effectiveness: Evidence from South Korean firms. *International Journal of Human Resource Management*, 22: 1638–1653.
Kochan, T. (1997) *Human Resources and the Changing Social Contract*. Paper presented at the Conference on Research and Theory in Strategic Human Resource Management: An Agenda for the 21st Century, Ithaca, NY.
Kraatz, M. S., and Zajac, E. J. (2001) How organizational resources affect strategic change and performance in turbulent environments: *Theory and Evidence: Organization Science*, 12: 632–657.
Kunisch, S., Bartunek, J., Mueller, J., and Huy, Q. (2017) Time in strategic management research. *Academy of Management Annals*, 11: 1005–1064.
Lado, A. A., and Wilson, M. C. (1994) Human resource systems and sustained competitive advantage: A competency-based perspective. *Academy of Management Review*, 19: 699–727.
Lee, H. W., Pak, J., Kim, S., and Li, L. Z. (2016) Effects of human resource management systems on employee proactivity and group innovation. *Journal of Management*. doi:10.1177/014920636680029.

Lengnick-Hall, M. L., Lengnick-Hall, C. A., Andrade, L. S., and Drake, B. (2009) Strategic human resource management: The evolution of the field. *Human Resource Management Review*, 19: 64–85.
Long, C. S., Ismail, W. K., and Amin, S. M. (2013) The role change agent as mediator in the relationship between HR competencies and organizational performance. *International Journal of Human Resource Management*, 24: 2019–2033.
Mangaliso, M. P. (2001) Building competitive advantage from ubuntu: Management lessons from South Africa. *Academy of Management Executive*, 15: 23–33.
McGrath, R. G. (2013) *The End of Competitive Advantage: How to Keep Your Strategy Movingas Fast as Your Business.* Boston, MA: Harvard Business Review Press.
Mohan, G., and Power, M. (2008) New African choices? The politics of Chinese engagement. *Review of African Political Economy*, 35: 23–42.
Mohrman, S. A., and Worley, C. G. (2009) Dealing with rough times: A capabilities development approach to surviving and thriving. *Human Resource Management*, 48: 433–445.
Nsehe, M. (2012) *The Ten Most Innovative Companies in Africa.* Retrieved April 14, 2016 from www.forbes.com/sites/mfonobongnsehe/2012/09/07/the ten-most-innovative- companies-in-africa/££2d4c7106756df
Ovadje, F. (2014) *Change Leadership in Developing Countries.* Abingdon and Oxford: Routledge.
Patel, P. C., and Cardon, M. S. (2010) Adopting HRM practices and their effectiveness in small firms facing product-market competition. *Human Resource Management*, 49: 265–290.
Pulakos, E. D., Arad, S., Donovan, M. A., and Plamondon, K. E. (2000) Adaptability in the workplace: Development of a taxonomy of adaptive performance. *Journal of Applied Psychology*, 85: 612–624.
Purcell, J., and Hutchinson, S. (2007) Front-line managers as agents in the HRM-performance causal chains: Theory, analysis, and evidence. *Human Resource Management Journal*, 17: 3–20.
PwC. (2017) *The Africa Business Agenda: Changing Gear.* Retrieved December 28, 2017 from www.pwc./the agenda
Rafferty, A. E., Jimmieson, N. L., and Armenakis, A. A. (2013) Change readiness: A multilevel review. *Journal of Management*, 39: 110–135.
Rajagopalan, N., and Spreitzer, G. M. (1997) Toward a theory of strategic change: A multi-lens perspective and integrative framework. *Academy of Management Review*, 22: 48–79.
Renwick, D. (2003) Line manager involvement in HRM: An inside view. *Employee Relations*, 25: 262–280.
Roehling, M. V., Boswell, W. R., Caliguiri, P., Feldman, D., Graham, M. E., Guthrie, J. R., Morishima, M., and Tansky, J. W. (2005) The future of HR management: Research needs and directions. *Human Resource Management*, 44: 207–216.
Schneider, B. (1990) The climate for service: An application of the climate construct. In B. Schneider (Ed.), *Organizational Climate and Culture.* San Francisco, CA: Jossey-Bass, 383–412.
Schneider, B., Smith, D. B., and Goldstein, H. W. (2000) Attraction-selection-attrition: Toward a person-environment psychology of organizations. In W. B. Walsh, K. H. Crait and R. H. Price (Eds.), *Person-environment Psychology: New Directions and Perspectives*, 2nd ed. Mahwah, NJ: Erlbaum, 61–85.
Shin, J., Taylor, M. S., and Seo, M. G. (2012) Resources for change: The relationships of organizational inducements and psychological resilience to employees' attitudes and behaviors toward organizational change. *Academy of Management Journal*, 55: 727–748.
Shipton, H., Budhwar, P. S., and Crawshaw, J. (2012) HRM, organizational capacity for change, and performance: A global perspective. *Thunderbird International Business Review*, 54: 777–790.
Sikora, D. M., and Ferris, G. (2014) Strategic human resource practice implementation: The critical role of line management. *Human Resource Management Review*, 24: 271–281.
Sikora, D. M., Ferris, G., and van Iddenkinge, C. H. (2015) Line manager implementation perceptions as a mediator of relations between high-performance work practices and employee outcomes. *Journal of Applied Psychology*, 100: 1908–1918.
Sirmon, D. G., Hitt, M. A., and Ireland, R. D. (2007) Managing firm resources in dynamic environments to create value: Looking inside the black box. *Academy of Management Journal*, 32: 273–292.
Stewart, T. A. (1996) Taking on the last bureaucracy. *Fortune*, 15 January: 105–107.
Sun, L. Y., Aryee, S., and Law, K. S. (2007) High-performance human resource practices, citizenship behaviour, and organizational performance: A relational perspective. *Academy of Management Journal*, 50: 558–577.
Teece, D. J. (2007) Explicating dynamic capabilities: The nature and microfoundations of (sustainable) enterprise performance. *Strategic Management Journal*, 28: 1319–1350.
Teece, D. J., Pisano, G., and Shuen, A. (1997) Dynamic capabilities and strategic management. *Strategic Management Journal*, 18: 509–534.

Ulrich, D. (1987) Organizational capability as a competitive advantage: Human resource professionals as strategic partners. *Human Resource Planning*, 10: 169–184.
Ulrich, D., and Brockbank, W. (2005) *The HR Value Proposition*. Boston, MA: Harvard Business School Press.
Ulrich, D., Younger, J., Brockbank, W., and Ulrich, M. D. (2013) The state of the HR profession. *Human Resource Management*, 52: 457–471.
Utomi, P. (1998) *Managing Uncertainty: Competition and Strategy in Emerging Economies*. Ibadan: Spectrum Books.
Walker, J. W. (1992) *Human Resource Strategy*. Boston, MA: McGraw-Hill.
Weber, Y., and Tarba, S. Y. (2014) Strategic agility: A state of the art. *California Management Review*, 56: 5–12.
Wright, P. M., Dunford, B. B., and Snell, S. A. (2001) Human resources and the resource-based view of the firm. *Journal of Management*, 27: 701–721.
Wright, P. M., and McMahan, G. C. (1992) Theoretical perspectives for strategic human resource management. *Journal of Management*, 18: 295–320.
Wright, P. M., McMahan, G. C., Snell, S. C., and Gerhart, B. (2001) Comparing line and HR executives' perceptions of HR effectiveness: Services, roles, and contributions. *Human Resource Management*, 40: 111–123.
Wright, P. M., and Snell, S. A. (1998) Toward a unifying framework for exploring fit and flexibility in strategic human resource management. *Academy of Management Review*, 23: 756–772.
Zajac, E. J., Kraatz, M. S., and Bresser, R. K. F. (2000) Modeling the dynamics of strategic fit: A normative approach to strategic change. *Strategic Management Journal*, 21: 429–453.
Zoogah, D. B., and Zoogah, R. B. (2014) Experimenting with resource strategy: Experimental analysis and strategic human resources management research in Africa. *Research Methodology in Strategy and Management*, 10: 21–53.
Zupan, N., and Kase, R. (2005) Strategic human resource management in European transition economies: Building a conceptual model on the case of Slovenia. *International Journal of Human Resource Management*, 16: 882–906.

10

Rethinking African business elites as change agents

George Ferns and Kenneth Amaeshi

Introduction

It is widely recognised that business elites play an important role in stimulating economic development (Amsden, DiCaprio, and Robinson, 2012; Walder, 2003). Not only do elites have significant economic capital, but they are increasingly influential as political actors (Clemens, 2015). However, appreciation of business elites' role as positive change agents has become challenged in recent years. This stems from a variety of factors related to, amongst others, increasing concerns about inequality (Piketty, 2014), several scandals involving corporate executives (Ailon, 2013; Rhodes, 2016), and the recent financial crisis – the blame of which is often directed toward those in positions of power (Riaz, Buchanan, and Ruebottom, 2016). Of course, the advent of such critique is not novel. Elites have long been accused of undermining democratic virtues (Seekings and Nattrass, 2011), and acting as greed-lusted capitalists (Domhoff, 1967). As the Edelman Trust Barometer (2016) suitably evidences, trust in CEOs continues hovering just below the 50% rate.

Given this increased scrutiny, it comes as no surprise that management and organisation scholars have also expressed a need to critically explore elite power. In this vein, Morgan, Quack, and Hirsch (2015: 7) recently proposed to "put elites on trial [. . .] for their role in the development of a neo-liberal regime which has resulted in fundamental changes in power and inequality; for their role in the financial crisis and in rebuilding the system post-2008." Elites in the developing world have not been spared from critique, where they are often charged with stimulating corruption, cronyism, and rent-seeking behaviour (Acemoglu and Robinson, 2008). As such, since Mills (1956, 2000) first conceptualised the idea of elite power, researchers have predominantly concerned themselves with why elites *are not* the answer to many of the ills that plague the developing world.

However, whilst these above studies certainly provide interesting insights, they neglect that elites are "not all cast from the same mould." Rather, as several scholars (e.g., Scott, 2008; Maclean, Harvey, and Kling, 2014) have alluded to, elites are increasingly fragmented, culturally divided, and spread across class, gender, and race; distinguishing between elite and non-elite has become less straightforward (Spence, Carter, Husillos, and Archel, 2016). Drawing on this understanding of elite composition as a heterogeneous group, we examine instances where business elites purposefully stimulate pro-social forms of economic development. These elites are unique in the sense that they do not shy away from critique, but, to varying degrees, address capitalism's deficiencies head-on, placing themselves and their business operations in the spotlight (Amaeshi and Idemudia, 2015). In developing-country contexts this often involves business elites assuming the role of an apparently absent state, providing basic needs such as healthcare to citizens (Scherer and Palazzo, 2011).

We base our study in the African context, which is often regarded as a sort of exemplar case for the rising role of elites in economic development (Taylor and Nel, 2002). Of particular interest is how to interpret the disparate swath of business elite activity in relation to their increasingly blurred role as pro-social change agents. To do so, we draw from two literatures that together help inform our inquiry. First, to conceptualise elites as change agents, we draw from social consciousness theory (de Swaan, 1988) and other work that addresses different levels of change that elites engage in (Green and Hulme, 2005). Second, we engage broadly with literature on business-society relations to make the distinction between integrative vs. separated strategies (Weaver, Treviño, and Cochran, 1999; Berger, Cunningham, and Drumwright, 2007; Gao and Bansal, 2013).

From this, we devise our typology of business elites as change agents (see Figure 10.1). On the one hand, the level of proposed change regards whether business elites propose large-scale systemic change or small-scale change. On the other hand, the level of integration refers to whether business elites use their own business operations to further change activities – in other words, their business drives change from within – or whether they separate their business activities from their intended change programme. Depending on the configuration of these two dimensions, business elites are categorised as one of four change agents: *Visionary* (systems-scale change, separated change strategy); *Philanthropist* (small-scale change, separated change strategy); *Corporate* (small-scale change, integrated change strategy); and *Change Leader* (systems-scale change, integrated change strategy).

This typology contributes to the current literature on elites and economic development, not only by highlighting the variations that exist amongst business elites, but also by stressing the lack of *Change Leaders* within the African context. In addition, we identify the ways by which business elites could potentially stimulate economic development – based on their categorisation within our typology – including the areas which might still be lacking.

This chapter is structured as follows. We first engage with the concept of elite power in relation to economic development and make the case for business elites as change agents. Next, we theorise our typology by discussing the twofold distinction between levels of change (systemic vs. small-scale) and strategies for change (integrative vs. separated). Thereafter, we illustrate four change agent types, using various examples from African business elites. Finally, we conclude with a discussion of our findings, including propositions in terms of promoting more *Change Leaders*.

Elites, power, and economic development

Before delving into an exploration of elites' role in economic development, it is important to lay a theoretical foundation and provide clarification regarding important concepts used in this article. Firstly, we assume that majority rule does not exist (Michels, 1915; Morgan, 2015). Rather, the elite are the ruling minority "in positions to make decisions having major consequences" (Mills, 1956: 3). Secondly, due to their sheer pervasiveness and social capital (Maclean et al., 2014), elites have a significant impact on economic development (Amsden et al., 2012). Third, elites may, due to a variety of reasons we shall discuss later, seek to proactively stimulate socially inclusive and sustainable forms of economic development (De Swaan, Manor, Øyen, and Reis, 2000; Reis and Moore, 2005). Fourth, in general, elite power in developing-country contexts differs from that of developed-country contexts mainly because of a weaker state, often resulting in an especially concentrated and thus powerful business elite group (DFID, 2010; Scherer and Palazzo, 2011). We now proceed by discussing concepts of power, elites, and their role in stimulating economic development.

The study of elite power is by no means alien to social science. Plato, Aristotle, Machiavelli, Hobbs, Marx, and Weber all considered the role of elite power and its effects within society (Clegg, 2013). Importantly, these thinkers argued that power is not always based on majority rule, but that power is often centralised – as demonstrated by the classical elite theories of Pareto (1901), Mosca (1896), and Michels (1915) that examine elite power structures, the organisation of political elites, and the moral/intellectual superiority of elites. Based on this perspective, elites are the organised minority that rule an unorganised majority, or the masses (Scott, 2008) – they are privileged, and have the ability to exert their ideas on the unprivileged (Amsden et al., 2012: 4). Elites are also diverse as, according to Morgan, Hirsch, and Quack (2015), elites have various channels of influence including: control over the allocation of resources and the political process; occupation of social institutions (e.g., legislative); and manipulation of the distribution of information (e.g., through control of the media). Nevertheless, how exactly elites utilise their power remains subject to debate, as the effects of elite behaviour are often indirect and thus difficult to measure. This results in confusion as who exactly should be classified as an elite, as Scott (2008) remarks:

> To label superior or advantaged groups indiscriminately as 'elites' is to make it more difficult to study them, as it implies spurious similarities among them and with other groups. Such an approach masks their specific features and destroys all distinctiveness that the elite concept can have.
>
> *Scott (2008: 28)*

This mystification surrounding elites arguably contributes to the pejorative misconception regarding their power. For example, elitism is frequently considered a feature of society that jeopardises the virtues of democracy, since power held by elites usually outweighs that of democratically elected representatives (Reed and Wallace, 2015). However, could elite power also be productive for society?

A growing literature explores this possibility with a specific focus on the role of business elites in economic development (Amsden et al., 2012). Here, scholars argue that, given the prevalence of market-based capitalism as the dominant economic paradigm, the private sector has become remarkably impactful on society as well as the natural environment (Gurley and Shaw, 1955; Porter, 2000). Certainly, the decisions of those in charge of the private sector are crucial regarding the economy, and ultimately in terms of wealth creation and economic growth. This point is emphasised by UN Secretary General Kofi Annan's (2002) statement:

> We are realizing that it is only by mobilizing the corporate sector that we can make significant progress. The corporate sector has the finances, the technology and the management to make economic development happen. The corporate sector need not wait for governments to take decisions for them to take initiatives.

Therefore, business elites are particularly important to the UN's vision. This is also evidenced by their involvement in contributing to the construction of concepts such as sustainable development

(Ferns and Amaeshi, 2017). Though their prime interest may stem from a business logic, business elites are often inseparable from the political process and are able to stimulate large-scale social and economic change, a notion explained through transnational capital class theory, and, relatedly, the concept of interlocking directorships (Carroll, Carson, and Fennema, 2010; Useem, 1980). As such, elites may define development objectives, execute development policy, and steer national discourse on development issues (Scherer and Palazzo, 2011). For example, business elites utilise international business networking platforms such as the World Business Council for Sustainable Development or the UN's Global Compact, both of which have a substantial effect on the global development paradigm (Kell, 2012). It is thus apparent that business elites, through their position and network, play a critical role in determining a firm's role within society and its responsibility toward social and environmental well-being.

Interestingly, the effect of an elite's behaviour on economic development is rather paradoxical. Although many suggest that elite behaviour is predominantly motivated by self-interest (Meglino and Korsgaard, 2004), their actions often have beneficial spill-over consequences for economic development. Based on the concept of enlightened self-interest (Keim, 1978), scholars increasingly posit that elites and non-elites share a mutual dependency and therefore elites sometimes engage in pro-development initiatives to ultimately benefit themselves – i.e., "doing good for society, by doing well for yourself." For example, an elite may proactively stimulate development outcomes such as education or healthcare provisions to benefit from a skilled and healthy workforce. Likewise, research on poverty reduction in Brazil (Reis and Moore, 2005) and Bangladesh (Green and Hulme, 2005) shows that elites recognise the "interdependence of social groups in society and the potential impact poverty might have on elite welfare – an impact from which they might be unable to insulate themselves" (Hossain and Moore, 1999: 22). Some researchers have also argued that economic development in Botswana, one of Africa's most successful democracies according to the UN (Good and Taylor, 2008), heavily relies on systematic elite intervention (Acemoglu, Johnson, and Robinson, 2001).

De Swaan's (1988) theory of social consciousness is key to this phenomenon (Clarke and Sison, 2003). De Swaan explains how Europe's social welfare systems were created during the mid-19th century by elites engaging in pro-social development efforts to avoid being affected by a cholera outbreak. For example, elites in Edinburgh and London were involved in the construction of sewage systems to improve sanitation and provide clean water, which, despite being intended for their own needs, provided the infrastructure for extended systems that would benefit non-elites (Thomas, 2015). In other words, elites engaged in self-interested behaviour, to the point of becoming, at least indirectly, altruistic (Anderson, 2007). De Swaan's theory draws from the enlightened self-interest argument, which is based on the principle of reciprocity and states that individuals sometimes engage in "good" deeds whilst profiting from their outcomes – resulting in a win-win situation (Porter and Kramer, 2011). Whilst de Swaan's work is very much based on poverty and income inequality, his theory can be expanded to encompass broader notions of economic development. In doing so, we aim to better conceptualise business elites' motivations for engaging in economic development. This, however, raises the question of why business elites in the first place, and importantly, why now?

Business elites, saviours of the world?

Increasingly, business elites are taking part in a variety of pro-social and environmentally conscious activities (Qobo, 2016). Yet such endeavours, and the elites that promote and implement them, remain heterogeneous. Some prefer setting up their own foundations or charities, and propose large-scale systems change. Others encourage a minimal level of intervention, but propose using their own businesses to implement their change activities. Whether George Soros's age-old proposition to reconfigure our capitalist society into an *open society*; Al Gore's call for paradigmatic market reforms towards *sustainable capitalism*; John Mackey's higher-purpose approach to business through *conscious capitalism*; Tony Elumelu's recent vision of *Africapitalism*; or Bill Gates and Warren Buffet's pledge to donate half of their wealth. These elites argue that the negative effects of capitalism must be reconsidered. To varying degrees, they want to change the world and the societies they live in by transforming how wealth is generated and (re)distributed. But instead of aiming to overthrow capitalism, these elites either propose *redirecting* capitalism and initiating change from within, or using the power of capitalism to further social good (Bishop and Green, 2010). To make sense of the varied approaches and proposals, we present a typology of business elites as change agents as depicted in Figure 10.1.

The matrix is divided into two dimensions: the level of proposed change, and the level of integration with their business activities. First, the level of proposed change (vertical axis) regards whether elites either propose large-scale systemic changes, for example to economic, social, or political systems, or whether they advocate small-scale changes, which often involve pro-social projects with specific objectives, such as bulling a school or certain philanthropic programmes. Here we base our observation that more equitable and sustainable forms of development operate on a systems-level: "organizations themselves become sustainable: individual organizations simply contribute to the large system in which sustainability may or may not be achieved" (Jennings and Zandbergen, 1995: 1023). In addressing economic development on a systemic level, business elites engage in a much wider debate that is often held on national and transnational levels (Zald and Lounsbury, 2010). In addition, systems-level change involves consideration for multiple

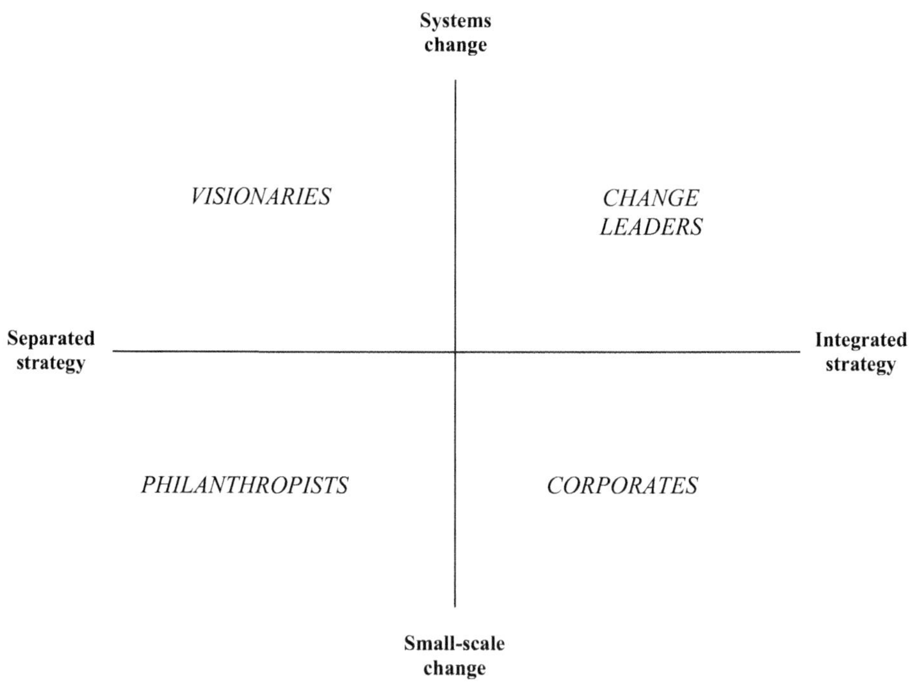

Figure 10.1 Typology of business elites as change agents for economic development

stakeholder views that might be in contention, leading to higher levels of complexity (Hahn, Pinkse, Preuss, and Figge, 2014). Conversely, engaging in small-scale change involves operating on a local level where change projects often have start-end dates, with clearly defined stakeholders and objectives (Cranenburgh and Arenas, 2013).

Secondly, the level of integration (horizontal axis) refers to whether elites use their own business operations to further their change activities – in other words, that their business drives change from within – or whether they have separated their business from their intentions to stimulate change, for example by creating an external organisation such as a foundation. We base our conceptualisation here on the often-discussed distinction between separated vs. integrative perspectives on business-society relations (Carroll, 1991; Kolk and Pinkse, 2010; Weaver et al., 1999). On the one hand, integrative strategies embed ethics, sustainability, and pro-social thinking into their organisations, almost to the point where alternatives become unthinkable. On the other hand, a separated strategy involves decoupling business activity from change endeavours, whether in form of philanthropy or CSR programmes. Depending on the configuration of these two dimensions, business elites are categorised as one of four change agents: *Visionary* (systems-change, separated change strategy); *Philanthropist* (small-scale change, separated change strategy); *Corporate* (small-scale change, integrated change strategy); and *Change Leader* (systems-change, integrated change strategy).

Visionary change agents

Visionary change agents express a need to reform economic and social systems that are often highly institutionalised and therefore difficult to change. Commonly, visionary change agents propose changing certain aspects of capitalism, including, amongst others, short-termism and focusing solely on profits. They execute their ideas through a separated strategy. As such, visionary change agents refrain from using their own business operations, opting instead to use entities that are disconnected from their core business.

Tony Elumelu – the Nigerian banker and entrepreneur – is an exemplar visionary change agent. Elumelu certainly has grand ideas regarding changing approaches to economic development in Africa. His vision is called *Africapitalism*, which references an economic philosophy that hinges on the power of the private sector as a vehicle for long-term, sustainable value creation (Elumelu, 2013). Africapitalism is therefore a call for business people across Africa to instil a mentality of "doing well as a business, by doing good within the community" (Nurse and Dougherty, 2013). Elumelu, who is also one of Africa's wealthiest individuals (Forbes, 2015), coined the term in 2011 and has spearheaded the movement through high-profile media engagements, participation at transnational summits such as the World Economic Forum, and through a self-created pan-African think-tank, The Africapitalism Institute, which was founded in 2014.

Elumelu (2013: 7) suggests that for businesses to "break free from the historical tendencies of exploitation and extraction of wealth," they must realise their own potential: "Africans themselves need to build the kinds of companies that make the products we buy, adding value within the continent for Africa's own benefit." Elumelu has, in addition, founded The Tony Elumelu Entrepreneurship Programme, which promotes Africapitalism by furthering young entrepreneurs' business ideas through seed capital. A unique emphasis is placed on the transformative potential of Africans investing in Africa (Edwards, 2013; Elumelu, 2013). Africapitalism therefore incorporates a sense of economic patriotism – designed to motivate and incite a sense of entrepreneurialism "that generate[s] both economic prosperity and social wealth" (Amaeshi and Idemudia, 2015: 210). Moreover, Africapitalism seeks to combine both financial and social benefits that stem from business activity. Per the Africapitalism manifesto (Elumelu, 2013), the philosophy is based on three principles:

- *Wealth Creation*: The private sector in Africa – both foreign multinationals as well as African business leaders – must break free from the historical tendencies of exploitation and extraction of wealth (i.e., rent-seeking), and instead focus on generating profit through wealth creation.
- *Funding Entrepreneurship*: Leveraging private enterprise to solve problems must be a core area of focus not just for investors, but also for NGOs and philanthropists.
- *Transparent Competitive Markets:* Governments are not responsible for running industries; they are responsible for providing a supportive environment for businesses to thrive, in markets that are fair, transparent, and open.

Overall, it is evident that whilst large-scale change is proposed, Elumelu's main business ventures, which primarily involve the financial industries, do not directly drive his change initiatives. This does not mean that his core business is totally detached from the Africapitalism vision, but rather the driving force behind stimulating change, as attributed, falls directly under the management of external organisations, such as the Tony Elumelu Foundation. This is an important feature of visionary change agents, as they often indirectly work through their business holdings – in other words, have their businesses adopt their vision.

The effectiveness of visionary change agents is evidenced by their ability to shape the norms of society (see Sjöström, 2009), as well as to drive change within their own businesses. In this regard, visionary change agents typify the classical definition of a charismatic leader (Shamir and Howell, 1999). This is particularly useful for driving organisational change, as members of an organisation internalise the ethical values of charismatic leaders. Drawing from the example presented above, Elumelu's leadership style, coupled with the Africapitalism message, may thus inspire his employees to transcend their own immediate interests for a larger, collective purpose (Carter, Armenakis, Feild, and Mossholder, 2013).

Philanthropic change agents

This group of business elites propose small-scale social change and seek to do so by separating their business activities from their change initiatives. Philanthropic change agents therefore rarely promote systemic change or see something necessarily "wrong" with business or capitalism. They also do not explicitly utilise their own business as a vehicle for pro-social change. Separating business from non-business activities allows them to donate their money to specific social projects. A notable example includes South African billionaire Patrice Motsepe, who set up the Motsepe Foundation and signed the Giving Pledge (started by Bill Gates and Warren Buffet) which commits Motsepe to donate half his fortune to charity. As Motsepe states:

> I decided quite some time ago to give at least half of the funds generated by our family assets to uplift poor and other disadvantaged and marginalised South Africans, but was also duty-bound and committed to ensuring that it would be done in a way that protects the interests and retains the confidence of our shareholders and investors.
>
> *(Nsehe, 2013)*

Business elites as philanthropic change agents date back to the 18th century, when elites such as J.P. Morgan and John D. Rockefeller famously donated significant amounts of money to various projects across the US and globally. However, since then, philanthropic change agents have moved away from the engaging in narrowly defined charity work. Today, philanthropic change agents prefer using foundations to fund a variety of projects that have positive impacts on society, either as completely separated entities, or as an offshoot to their actual business. With regard to the latter, corporate foundations have become especially popular as a mechanism for philanthropic change agents to stimulate change in Africa. According to Anheier and Daly (2006), corporate foundations have the following characteristics that set them apart from other charities and commercial organisations:

- *Private entity:* Corporate foundations are institutionally separate from government, and are 'nongovernmental' in the sense of being structurally separate from public agencies.
- *Self-governing entity:* Corporate foundations are equipped to control their own activities. Self-governance implies that foundations must have their own internal governance procedures and enjoy a meaningful degree of autonomy.
- *Non-profit-distributing entity:* Corporate foundations are not to return profits generated by either use of assets or the conduct of commercial activities to their owners, members, trustees, or directors.
- *Serving a public purpose:* Corporate foundations should do more than serve the needs of a narrowly defined social group or category, such as members of a family or a closed circle of beneficiaries.

The Dangote Foundation is an example of such a foundation, and vividly illustrates the role of business elites in furthering economic development as a philanthropic change agent. The Dangote Foundation is primarily responsible for administering and implementing CSR activities of the Dangote Group, which is led by a Nigerian billionaire businessman, Aliko Dangote – Africa's richest and most generous philanthropist, according to Forbes (2016). Dangote Group's vision is framed both in social and commercial goals, highlighting their separated change strategy: "to be a world-class enterprise that is passionate about the standard of living of the general populace and giving high returns to stakeholders." And in its vision the company states: "To touch the lives of people by providing their basic needs."

The effectiveness of philanthropic change agents is underscored when considering the scale and speed at which they are able to affect change. Regarding organisational change, philanthropic change agents' separated approach allows for greater control over strategic change. For example, the Dangote Foundation can – at the discretion of its chairman Aliko Dangote – engage in its own internal change processes. Relatedly, the Foundation can independently allocate financial resources and decide on which organisations it wishes to partner with. The Dangote Foundation has, for instance, donated to the World Food programme (US$ 2 million) and works in partnership with other foundations such as the Bill and Melinda Gates Foundation. In this regard, the Foundation focuses mostly on healthcare, having also constructed several state-of-the-art hospitals, contributed to stopping the recent Ebola catastrophe in West Africa, and donating substantial amount to polio vaccines. Dangote himself speaks emphatically about the mission of his Foundation:

> I believe that the single most important intervention I can support through my foundation, to help build human capital in my country, is to support better nutrition in Nigeria. From the first 1,000 days of a person's life and throughout their life span, we now understand how ending malnutrition will help address myriad other issues, including health, education, and the ability to sustain a livelihood. Everyone's involvement is required, especially political commitment from our countries.
>
> *(International Food Policy Research Institute, 2015, p.ii)*

It is important to note, however, that the Dangote Foundation, and the activities it engages in, remains removed from the core business of the Dangote Group, which focuses on the construction and manufacturing business. Because his business and social activities are decoupled, Dangote mostly engages as a philanthropic change agent, as Dangote himself remarks: "About this philanthropy, I think from this year, I personally want to take it very seriously. I want to be much more aggressive than what we have had in the past." (Dangote in Daily Post, 2014).

Corporate change agents

Corporate change agents rely principally on stimulating social change from within their own organisations. As such, their change initiatives often take the form of corporate social responsibility (CSR) endeavours as they adopt an integrative strategy – seeking to embed sustainability within their daily business practices. Indeed, business elites that fall into this category are on the lookout for "win-wins," or instances where they can find mutually beneficial situations where both their company and society benefit (e.g., Porter and Kramer, 2011). The level of change these individuals seek to entice is relatively small-scale, as they believe that if their own companies are run more sustainably and ethically, this will "trickle down" to their employees and wider society (McWilliams and Siegel, 2000). This is also one of the key ways corporate change agents drive organisational change – i.e., using corporate capitalism to legitimate change initiatives. Since organisational change endeavours are justified by an underlying business logic, success depends principally on whether change is "good for business." Whilst this approach has not evaded critique (Banerjee, 2009), it does offer a less complex approach to both social and organisational change.

A case that resembles a corporate change agent concerns that of Nicky Oppenheimer – heir of the De Beers diamond company and Africa's second-richest elite. Despite having sold his 40% stake in De Beers to Anglo American for $5.1 billion in 2012, Oppenheimer was instrumental in De Beers's CSR strategy (Claasen and Roloff, 2012). Currently De Beers's CSR initiatives are expansive, including a company-wide HIV/AIDS programme, the construction of several primary and secondary schools, and large-scale infrastructure projects such as roads (De Beers, 2016). This was in direct response to global pressure for diamond manufacturers to take responsibility for the relationship between their product and armed conflict throughout Africa. To avoid selling what are commonly known as "conflict diamonds," De Beers, in 2000, stopped purchasing diamonds that could not be traced to legitimate governments or companies. Oppenheimer's keynote speech at the World Diamond Council meeting in 2002 underscored his approach to CSR:

> We must continue our efforts to help bring the trade in conflict diamonds to an end. Not just because it has the potential to damage our industry and the integrity of diamonds, but because it is right to do so. We are the leaders of the industry and have a clear duty to the societies in which we operate to act, and act effectively.
>
> *(Bieri, 2016: 82)*

An essential feature of Oppenheimer's success with regard to De Beers's CSR strategy was his willingness – maybe even need – to cooperate with the government of Botswana, which shared a 50% stake in De Beers's operations. Notwithstanding, there is also much critique waged against the Oppenheimer family and the extent to which their CSR activities are indeed authentic (Watson, 2007). In this respect, corporate change agents are often scrutinised for using CSR as a reactive tool in light of criticism (Banerjee, 2009). This might largely be because this group of elites do not make grand claims for systems change. Corporate change agents base most of their initiatives on market-based economic growth, as Nicky Oppenheimer suggests: "the company will play its economic role in such a way that it will contribute to an ever more prosperous Africa" (van Wyk, Cronjé, and van Wyk, 2009: 31). As such, corporate change agents engage primarily in small-scale change projects and rarely propose any sort of systemic change.

Change leaders

In this category, change agents exhibit a grand theory of change, which they operationalise through an integrated strategy. As such, they do not express a distinction between their daily business operations and their intention to stimulate large-scale social change. Instead, change leaders, when speaking about how the business-society relationship *ought* to work, do so by realigning the virtues of capitalism as a mechanism for inclusive forms of economic development. They usually distance themselves from notions such as CSR, and often reject philanthropy as a form of ineffectual charity. Change leaders also refuse housing their change projects in organisations that are separated from their core business. Their business strategy and change strategy are completely intertwined. Arguably, there are few examples of change leaders within the African context.

Nonetheless, to provide an example of how change leaders operate, we opted for discussing the Conscious Capitalism movement, which engages in systemic change, and does so through an integrated strategy. Conscious Capitalism is attributed to its most avid proponents: John Mackey (CEO of Whole Foods Market) and Raj Sisodia (Co-founder & Co-chairman, Conscious Capitalism, Inc.). The term loosely refers to some form of "enlightened" business practice, or the idea that a company should transcend the traditional conception of business as solely for generating profits. Therefore, the focus is on businesses finding an intrinsic *purpose*, given that "intrinsic motivation is far more effective and powerful than extrinsic financial incentives" (Mackey and Sisodia, 2014: 55). Conscious Capitalism also stresses the interconnectedness between society and business; complexity is embraced instead of feared. Relatedly, Conscience Capitalism has been linked to promoting "vertical learning," which is beneficial for organisational change as argued by Brown (2013: 1): "[Conscious Capitalism] radically improves a leader's ability to navigate today's highly complex, ambiguous, and rapidly changing context, and cascade those new skills into the entire organization."

Since its conception, Conscious Capitalism has created significant buzz in popular press outlets including books and business press articles. Most notably, business news sources such as *Fast Company* (Shane, 2013) and *Fortune* (Schawbel, 2013) continue to extensively report on the progress of Conscious Capitalism as a concept and business practice. An impressive list of companies, including, for instance, Whole Foods, Trader Joe's, and Patagonia, have remarked that Conscious Capitalism (to varying degrees) fits with their sustainable business philosophy. At its core, Conscious Capitalism proposes that business transcend its obsession with short-term profits and do more. Conscious Capitalism describes several other tenets that make up the philosophy:

- *Higher Purpose:* Recognising that every business has a purpose that includes, but is more than, making money.
- *Stakeholder Orientation:* Recognising the interdependent nature of life and the human foundations of business, a business needs to create value with and for its various stakeholders.
- *Conscious Leadership:* Human social organisations are created and guided by leaders – people who see a path and inspire others to travel along the path.
- *Conscious Culture:* This is the ethos – the values, principles, and practices – underlying the social fabric of a business, which permeates the atmosphere of a business and connects the stakeholders to each other and to the purpose, people, and processes that comprise the company.

Business elites who ascribe to Conscious Capitalism are usually change leaders. This is because Conscious Capitalism does not separate business from non-business. For example, Conscious Capitalism stresses the need to consider the entire ecosystem within which it is embedded. In doing so, businesses begin to "recognize that, without employees, customers, suppliers, funders, supportive communities and a life-sustaining ecosystem, there is no business" (Conscious Capitalism, 2016). In addition, business elites that ascribe to this approach understand that there are systemic issues regarding modern-day capitalism, highlighting, for instance that "the drive for short-term gains has led to the destruction of many great companies like General Motors and Sears and the bankruptcies of Enron, WorldCom, Kmart, and Kodak" (Mackey and Sisodia 2014: xii).

Admittedly, although this category of business elite is largely absent within the African context as indicated earlier, there are noteworthy examples that come close. For instance, some organisations interweave their sustainability strategy with their core business despite using corporate foundations for their social change initiatives. This is evidenced with, for instance, financial service providers that target individuals traditionally excluded from banking given their lack of economic capital. Such companies include both microfinance banks that focus specifically on poverty alleviation (e.g., LAPO Microfinance Bank in Nigeria), and more traditional banks such as Kenya's Equity Bank, which targets lower-income households. Indeed, as stressed on Equity Bank's website, its business model is based on financial inclusion; the company strongly promotes a purpose-driven philosophy of stimulating socio-economic prosperity. These examples highlight that Change Leadership *can* be stimulated indigenously. But how can Change Leadership be stimulated in the future? A potential route here is embedding certain values within business and management education within African business schools. In this regard, values such as inclusiveness, systems thinking, and purpose-led business can be integrated within MBA programmes, amongst others, to ensure that students embrace more systemic ways of doing business that extends beyond an instrumental CSR approach (i.e., externalising social change initiatives to a corporate foundation).

Discussion and conclusion

We started this article by observing that the elite, and capitalism more generally, are facing a legitimacy crisis (du Gay and Morgan, 2013; Muller, 2013). Indeed, elites are often charged with furthering negative externalities produced by global capitalism including, for instance, inequality (Hojman, 1996; Piketty, 2014), environmental degradation (Hooks, 2005), and greed/self-love (Twenge and Campbell, 2009), which remain rampant and are in many instances arguably getting worse. However, in this article we presented an alternate understanding of elite power and elites' role in stimulating pro-social forms of economic development. We argued that much of the current literature on elites, whilst certainly insightful, generally considers elites as a homogenous group and often assumes a pejorative tone (Robinson, 2012). As discussed, this is mainly directed towards the inevitability that elite power almost always resembles undemocratic rule given the disproportionate allocation of power that rests the hands of a few. Yet, we find the obsession with this oversimplification unproductive, given the plethora of evidence regarding elites engaging in pro-social behaviour (Amsden et al., 2012; Clarke and Sison, 2003). For instance, whilst elites are known to engage in such behaviour to ultimately benefit themselves, according to social consciousness theory and notions of "enlightened self-interest" (Keim, 1978; De Swaan et al., 2000), there is also the possibility of a mutually recursive relationship between the elite and non-elite.

We admit that elites might be engaging in such behaviour for different reasons, some more authentic than others. In addition, elites may approach their engagement with social and environmental issues differently, have divergent strategies for implementing their ideas, and wish to make an impact on society in varying ways (Scott, 2008). As such, to account for this heterogeneity, we propose a framework that maps different types of business elites as change agents based on two dimensions. We distinguished between integrated vs. separated strategies, and contrasted this with the extent to which an elite engages in small-scale or systemic change. In doing so, we identified four change agent types: *Visionaries*, *Philanthropists*, *Corporates*, and *Change Leaders*. By providing examples of each type, we stressed how, rather worryingly, there is a clear dearth of the latter change agent – *Change Leaders* – within the African context. Whilst we certainly do not provide definitive answers as to why exactly this is the case, we do wish to suggest two propositions that may help promote elites' pro-social endeavours, including the managerial implications therein.

First, it is evident that whilst many business elites have grand ideas for change (Amaeshi and Idemudia, 2015), there remains a separation between their change endeavours and their core business. Indeed, as we highlighted, there is not always a clearly distinct separation between change endeavours and business operations. However, it is important to note that an elite's vision of change may trickle back into their actual business ventures. Similarly, whilst separation may occur, there are of course varying *degrees* to which elites decouple their business from their change endeavours. For instance, in their capacity as CEO, elites might be represented on the board of their external organisation – e.g., a corporate foundation – either as a mere formality or as an active, even key, member of the external organisation (Werbel and Carter, 2002; Cranenburgh and Arenas, 2013). Indeed, it is not uncommon for elites to become extensively involved with their philanthropic work, to the point of transitioning out of their business endeavours – as was the case with Bill Gates (Williams, 2014).

Nevertheless, separation does pose certain issues. All too often, separation fosters situations where an elite's pro-social change endeavours act as compensation for ills caused by either their own business (Pinkse and Kolk, 2010), or by weaker state institutions (Scherer and Palazzo, 2011). In this respect, decoupled entities, such as charities, foundations, and trusts, function as a remedy for the symptom, and not as a cure (Schandl et al., 2016). This can easily result in a situation where change *seems* to be happening but, in fact, positive change is offset in a negative way somewhere else. The danger here is that the allure of a good deed becomes hailed, despite knowing of its ineffectiveness. To escape this often-vicious cycle, business elites must re-couple their core business with their change initiatives. We provided an example earlier in this chapter of how the Conscious Capitalism movement has proceeded with promoting integrative strategies. In this vein, pro-social, sustainable thinking becomes part of a business elites' business DNA, which we stress may result in more prosperous societies, and potential enterprises too (Mackey and Sisodia, 2013).

This presents important managerial implications, as business elites may stimulate significant change within their own organisations. A clear spill-over effect is that employees would be affected by their organisations' purpose-driven approach. This, in turn, may cause further positive social change as employees mimic changes occurring at their workplaces within their local communities and at home. Furthermore, a closer association between a company's social change endeavours and their business practices is commonly theorised as inciting a culture of caring. In this vein, managers recognise the importance of corporate integrity; as Gao and Bansal (2013: 247) suggest, "managers in a caring organization will empathize with stakeholders and try to accommodate or support them, even in the face of necessary evils." Here, elites can inspire managers to engage with a higher purpose – i.e., socio-economic development – as opposed to fulfilling a narrow objective such as mere profit-making.

With respect to organisational change management, our proposal to integrate pro-social change endeavours and with core business activities resonates strongly with driving effective change leadership (Fiol, Harris, and House, 1999). In particular, such an approach must involve more democratic, as opposed to autocratic, leadership styles (Masi and Cooke, 2000). This should occur through wilful participation rather than forced cohesion; it is crucial for business elites, in their capacity as the head of a business, to ensure "buy-in" from their employees. If employees are not committed to the same degree, this may reproduce mere visions of change, as opposed to any sort of concrete action. Indeed, as indicated by Hamel (2009: 2) there is an increasing importance for managers to shed the traditional "big man" leadership style: "leaders will no longer be seen as grand visionaries, all-wise decision makers, and ironfisted disciplinarians. Instead, they will need to become social architects, constitution writers, and entrepreneurs of meaning." By foregoing the typical authoritarian mentality, it becomes more likely that there will be closer alignment between the values espoused by the change leader (in this case the business elite), and the value system of the organisation undergoing change (Burnes and Jackson, 2011).

Our second proposition regards how to direct the level of change from small-scale projects to addressing systemic issues. Systemic change is regarded as the most challenging sort of change to get right (de Lange, Armanios, Delgado-Ceballos, and Sandhu, 2016). This is because systems are inherently complex; they are also more ingrained into everyday practices and are often presented as being taken for granted. The irony here is that business elites attribute their success to these systems, especially economic systems such as capitalism or financial markets (Boltanski and Chiapello, 2008). Therefore, it takes a "special" type of business elite to address issues on a systems level. There is, in addition, a focus on finding long-term solutions since systemic issues frequently respond erratically – addressing poverty in one location may have adverse environmental effects elsewhere (Cilliers, 1998; Holling, 2001).

To foster systemic change initiatives, we suggest that elites invest in building relationships with strategic partners over time. This does not necessarily need to include other elites, although elites networks may prove beneficial too (Carney, 2014). In doing so, this allows for multiple voices and interests to be represented – thereby enveloping players within the wider system and resulting in change having more macro-level, as opposed to local, impacts (Calton and Payne, 2003). This might resolve the fact that, given the scale of many systemic issues, change can only happen when a large collection of players work together (Diani and McAdam, 2003; Ansari, Wijen, and Gray, 2013). Indeed, this does not mean that philanthropists need to necessarily change their project-based focus. The Tony Elumelu Foundation is a prime example of such a systemic change focus, as it aims to promote economic development in Africa by working with several international agencies and local governments. Systemic change, therefore, brings with it the highest reward both for society, and, over time, for business.

The managerial implications of a systems thinking approach are well evidenced (Maon, Lindgreen, and Swaen, 2008; Williams, Kennedy, Philipp, and Whiteman, 2017). Managers that embrace systems perspectives are commonly regarded as being able to address multiple conflicting tensions in a more effective manner. This is especially beneficial for organisations that are confronted with complex business environments, especially in developing-country contexts such as Africa. Here, complex decisions – including ethical decisions – become pronounced in particular within large, multinational firms that "are simultaneously challenged by a multitude of [. . .] issues and environmental demands are characterized by high dynamism, complexity, and heterogeneity" (Scherer, Palazzo, and Seidl, 2013: 275). Organisations should therefore stimulate thinking of social problems in a systemic way so that managers are able to adapt to the evolving nature of business environments. This would, in turn, likely improve the capacity for organisations to be innovative in turbulent times – both economically and in terms of political turbulence.

Placing emphasis on systems change also has implications specifically related to organisational change management. First, the notion that change happens only within organisations – i.e., among managers – is replaced by an emphasis on how change dynamics are embedded within broader social systems. This stresses the interconnectedness between internal organisational processes and external social dynamics. For example, change related to organisational culture – for instance, when promoting a purpose-driven business approach as suggested above – should not occur without explicit recognition of *why* this is necessary on a social level. By this we mean that organisational change activities should not occur only to fulfil immediate organisational objectives, but rather should be connected to a broader social goal. This is related to a wide variety of change endeavours: an efficiency programme could be connected to improved environmental sustainability; employee satisfaction schemes could be related to social wellbeing; worker participation initiatives could be associated with promoting democratic ideals; new human resource management systems could be linked to social inclusion, diversity, and so on. Of course, it is important to foster a culture that is apt in understanding how these examples form part of the same overarching network of interconnected relationships. Indeed, business elites are in a unique position to educate their workforce (and other elites too!) about the interconnectedness regarding social systems and core business.

Overall, it is evident that for African business elites to make a lasting contribution to the wellbeing of the continent, more emphasis must be placed on embedding "good" economic development within business, as opposed to externalising it. Moreover, there is much to be gained – for the elite as well as organisations – by focusing on big issues from a systems-based perspective. In other words, only through an integrated change strategy that addresses systemic change can African business elites foster sustainable and more equitable change that will benefit future generations to come. As discussed, this perspective has particular implications for organisational change management. These can be condensed into three key points. First, each category of business elite is different – both in their approach to social change and in terms of how this approach can be advantageous to organisational change. Second, for business elites to stimulate social change, business leadership must move away from its autocratic past to a more inclusive and democratic future. Third, managing organisational change is intertwined with addressing social change; this must be recognised in order to achieve both organisational success and improve social wellbeing.

References

Acemoglu, D., and Robinson, J. (2008) Persistence of power, elites, and institutions. *American Economic Review*, 98(1): 267–293.

Acemoglu, D., Johnson, S., Robinson, J. A., and Yared, P. (2008) Income and democracy. *American Economic Review*, 98(3), 808–842.

Ailon, G. (2013) From superstars to devils: The ethical discourse on managerial figures involved in a corporate scandal. *Organization*, 22(1): 78–99.

Amaeshi, K., and Idemudia, U. (2015) Africapitalism: A management idea for business in Africa? *Africa Journal of Management*, 1(2): 210–223.

Amsden, A. H., DiCaprio, A., and Robinson, J. A. (2012) *The Role of Elites in Economic Development*. Oxford: Univeristy Press Oxford.

Anderson, J. (2007) The Catholic contribution to democratization's 'third wave': Altruism, hegemony or self-interest? *Cambridge Review of International Affairs*, 20(3): 383–399.

Anheier, H. K., and Daly, S. (2006). Philanthropic foundations in modern society. In *The Politics of Foundations* (pp. 19–42). London, UK: Routledge.

Annan, K. (2002) *Both Business and Society Benefit From Working Together*. Retrieved from http://basd.free.fr/docs/speeches/20020901_annan.html

Ansari, S., Wijen, F., and Gray, B. (2013) Constructing a climage change logic: An institutional perspective on the 'Tragedy of the Commons'. *Organization Science*, 24(4): 1014–1040.

Banerjee, S. B. (2009) *Corporate Social Responsibility: The Good, the Bad and the Ugly*. Cheltenham, UK: Edward Elgar Publishing.

Berger, I. E., Cunningham, P. H., and Drumwright, M. E. (2007) Mainstreaming corporate social responsibility. *California Management Review*, 49(4): 132–158.
Bieri, F. (2016) *From Blood Diamonds to the Kimberley Process: How NGOs Cleaned Up the Global Diamond Industry*. London, UK: Routledge.
Bishop, M., and Green, M. (2010) *Philanthrocapitalism: How Giving Can Save the World*. New York, NY: Bloomsbury Publishing USA.
Boltanski, L., and Chiapello, E. (2008) *The New Spirit of Capitalism*. London: Verso.
Brown, B. (2013) *The Future of Leadership for Conscious Capitalism*. Sao Francisco, Brazil: META Integral Associates.
Burnes, B., and Jackson, P. (2011) Success and failure in organisational change: An exploration of the role of values. *Journal of Change Management*, 11(2), 133–162.
Calton, J. M., and Payne, S. L. (2003) Coping with paradox: Multistakeholder learning dialogue as a pluralist sensemaking process for addressing messy problems. *Business & Society*, , 42(1), 7–42. http://doi.org/10.1177/0007650302250505.
Carney, M. (2014) *Inclusive Capitalism: Creating a Sense of the Systemic*. Speech given by the Governor of the Bank of England at the Conference on Inclusive Capitalism, London, 27 May 2014.
Carroll, A. (1991) The pyramid of corporate social responsibility: Toward the moral management of organizational stakeholders. *Business Horizons*, 39–48.
Carroll, W., Carson, C., and Fennema, M. (2010) *The Making of a Transnational Capitalist Class: Corporate Power in the Twenty-first Century*. London, UK: Zed Books.
Carter, M. Z., Armenakis, A. A., Feild, H. S., and Mossholder, K. W. (2013) Transformational leadership, relationship quality, and employee performance during continuous incremental organizational change. *Journal of Organizational Behavior*, 34(7): 942–958.
Cilliers, P. (1998) *Complexity & Postmodernism: Understanding Complex Systems*. London: Routledge.
Claasen, C., and Roloff, J. (2012) The link between responsibility and legitimacy: The case of De Beers in Namibia. *Journal of Business Ethics*, 107(3): 379–398.
Clarke, G., and Sison, M. (2003) Voices from the top of the pile: Elite perceptions of poverty and the poor in the Philippines. *Development and Change*, 34(2000): 215–242.
Clegg, S. (2013) *Power, Rule and Domination*. London: Routledge.
Clemens, E. (2015) The democratic dilemma: Aligning fields of elite influence and political equality. In *Elites on Trial* (pp. 223–302). Bingly, UK: Emerald Group Publishing Limited.
Conscious Capitalism. (2016) *Stakeholder Orientation*. Retrieved from www.consciouscapitalism.org/stakeholder
Cranenburgh, K. C., and Arenas, D. (2013) Strategic and moral dilemmas of corporate philanthropy in developing countries: Heineken in sub-Saharan Africa. *Journal of Business Ethics*, 122(3): 523–536.
Daily Post. (2014) Africa's top donor Dangote raises new bar in philanthropy, donates N30billion in two years. *Daily Post*, 21 July.
De Beers Group. (2015) *Building Forever: Report to Society 2015*. Johannesburg. Retrieved from http://www.debeersgroup.com/content/dam/de-beers/corporate/documents/BuildingForever/Report to Society 2015.pdf
de Lange, D. E., Armanios, D., Delgado-Ceballos, J., and Sandhu, S. (2016) From foe to friend: Complex mutual adaptation of multinational corporations and nongovernmental organizations. *Business & Society*, 55(8): 1197–1228.
De Swaan, A. (1988) *In Care of the State: Health Care, Education and Welfare in Europe and the USA in the Modern Era*. New York: Oxford University Press.
De Swaan, A., Manor, J., Øyen, E., and Reis, E. P. (2000) Elite perceptions of the poor: Reflections for a comparative research project. *Current Sociology*, 48(1): 43–54.
DFID. (2010) *The Politics of Poverty: Elites, Citizens and States – Findings From Ten Years of DFID-Funded Research on Governance and Fragile States 2001–2010*. DFID Synthesis Paper, 104.
Diani, M., and McAdam, D. (2003) *Social Movements and Networks: Relational Approaches to Collective Action: Relational Approaches to Collective Action*. Oxford: Oxford University Press.
Domhoff, G. W. (1967) *Who Rules America*? Englewood Cliffs, NJ: Prentice Hall.
du Gay, P., and Morgan, G. (2013) Understanding capitalism: Crises, legitimacy, and change through the prism of the new spirit of capitalism. In P. du Gay and G. Morgan (Eds.), *New Spirits of Capitalism?: Crises, Justifications, and Dynamics*. Oxford: Oxford University Press, 45–66.
Edelman. (2016) *Edelman Trust Barometer*. Retrieved from https://www.edelman.com/trust2016/

Edwards, R. (2013) Can Africapitalism save the continent? *Guardian*, 12 July.
Elumelu, T. (2013) *Africapitalism – Path to Economic Prosperity and Social Wealth*. Lagos: The Tony Elumelu Foundation Africapitalism Institute.
Ferns, G., and Amaeshi, K. (2017) Struggles at the summits: Discourse coalitions, field boundaries, and the shifting role of business in sustainable development. *Business & Society*.
Fiol, C., Harris, D., and House, R. (1999) Charismatic leadership: Strategies for effecting social change. *Leadership Quarterly*, 10(3): 449–482.
Forbes. (2015) Africa's 50 richest. *Forbes*. Retrieved February 17, 2016 from www.forbes.com/africa-billionaires/list/#tab:overall
Forbes. (2018) *Aliko Dangote*. Retrieved May 10, 2018, from https://www.forbes.com/profile/aliko-dangote/
Gao, J., and Bansal, P. (2013) Instrumental and integrative logics in business sustainability. *Journal of Business Ethics*, 112(2): 241–255.
Good, K., and Taylor, I. (2008) Botswana: a minimalist democracy. *Democratization*, 15(4): 750–765.
Gurley, J., and Shaw, E. (1955) Financial aspects of economic development. *The American Economic Review*,45, 515–538.
Green, M., and Hulme, D. (2005) From correlates and characteristics to causes: Thinking about poverty from a chronic poverty perspective. *World Development*, 33(6): 867–879.
Hahn, T., Pinkse, J., Preuss, L., and Figge, F. (2014) Tensions in corporate sustainability: Towards an integrative framework. *Journal of Business Ethics*, 2(127): 297–316.
Hamel, G. (2009) Moon shots for management. *Harvard Business Review*, 87(2): 91–98.
Hojman, D. E. (1996) Poverty and inequality in chile: Are democratic politics and neoliberal economics good for you? *Journal of Interamerican Studies and World Affairs*, 12(2): 73–97.
Holling, C. S. (2001) Understanding the complexity of economic, ecological, and social systems. *Ecosystems*, 4(1): 390–405.
Hooks, G. (2005) Treadmills of production and destruction: Threats to the environment posed by Militarism. *Organization & Environment*, 18(1): 19–37.
Hossain, N., and Moore, M. (1999) Elite perceptions of poverty: Bangladesh. *IDS Bulletin*, 30(2): 125–160.
International Food Policy Research Institute. (2015) *Global Nutrition Report 2015: Actions and Accountability to Advance Nutrition and Sustainable Development*. Washington, DC: Intl Food Policy Res Inst.
Jennings, P. D., and Zandbergen, P. A. (1995). Ecologically sustainable organizations: An institutional approach. *Academy of Management Review*, 20(4): 1015–1052.
Keim, G. D. (1978) Corporate social responsibility: An assessment of the enlightened self-interest model. *Academy of Management Review*, 3(1): 32–39.
Kell, G. (2012) 12 years later: Reflections on the growth of the UN Global Compact. *Business & Society*, 52(1): 31–52.
Kolk, A., and Pinkse, J. (2010) The integration of corporate governance in corporate social responsibility disclosures. *Corporate Social Responsibility and Environmental Management*, 17: 15–26.
Mackey, J., and Sisodia, R. (2013) 'Conscious Capitalism' is not an oxymoron. *Harvard Business Review*, 14 January.
Mackey, J., and Sisodia, R. (2014) *Conscious Capitalism, With a New Preface by the Authors: Liberating the Heroic Spirit of Business*. Cambridge, MA: Harvard Business Review Press.
Maclean, M., Harvey, C., and Kling, G. (2014) Pathways to power: Class, hyper-agency and the French corporate elite. *Organization Studies*, 35(6): 825–855.
Maon, F., Lindgreen, A., and Swaen, V. (2008) Thinking of the organization as a system: The role of managerial perceptions in developing a corporate social responsibility strategic agenda. *Systems Research and Behavioral Science*, 25(3): 413–426.
Masi, R. J., and Cooke, R. A. (2000) Effects of transformational leadership on subordinate motivation, empowering norms, and organizational productivity. *The International Journal of Organizational Analysis*, 8(1), 16–47.
McWilliams, A., and Siegel, D. (2000) Corporate social responsibility and financial performance: Correlation or misspecification? *Strategic Management Journal*, 21: 603–609.
Meglino, B. M., and Korsgaard, A. (2004) Considering rational self-interest as a disposition: Organizational implications of other orientation. *The Journal of Applied Psychology*, 89(6): 946–959.
Michels, R. (1915) *Political Parties: A Sociological Study of the Oligarchical Tendencies of Modern Democracies*. Glencoe, IL: Free Press.
Mills, C. W. (1956) *The Power Elite*. New York, NY: Oxford University Press.

Mills, C. W. (2000) *The Sociological Imagination*. Oxford: Oxford University Press.
Morgan, G. (2015) Elites, Varieties of capitalism and the crisis of neo-liberalism. In *Elites on Trial* (pp. 55–80). Bingly, UK: Emerald Group Publishing Limited
Morgan, G., Hirsch, P., and Quack, S. (2015) Elites on trial: Introduction. In P. Hirsch, G. Morgan and S. Quack (Eds.), *Elites on Trial*. London: Emerald Group Publishing, 1–21.
Morgan, G., Quack, S., and Hirsch, P. M. (2015) *Elites on Trial: Research in the Sociology of Organizations*. Bingly, UK: Emerald Group Publishing Limited.
Mosca, G. (1896) Elementi di scienza politica. In G. Mosca (Ed.), *The Ruling Class*. New York, NY: McGraw Hill, 1–11.
Muller, J. (2013) Capitalism and inequality. *Foreign Affairs*. Retrieved from https://www.foreignaffairs.com/articles/2013-02-11/capitalism-and-inequality
Nsehe, M. (2013, January 31) *South African Billionaire Patrice Motsepe Joins Giving Pledge*. Johannesburg: Forbes. Retrieved from https://www.forbes.com/sites/mfonobongnsehe/2013/01/31/south-african-billionaire-patrice-motsepe-joins-giving-pledge/#386ced5449f5
Nurse, E., and Dougherty, J. (2013) Tony Elumelu: The 'Africapitalist' who wants to power Africa. *CNN*, 12 November.
Pareto, V. (1901) *The Rise and Fall of Elites*. New York, NY: Bedminster Press.
Piketty, T. (2014) *Capital in the Twenty-First Century*. Cambridge, MA: Harvard University Press.
Pinkse, J., and Kolk, A. (2010) Challenges and trade-offs in corporate innovation for climate change. *Business Strategy and the Environment*, 19(4): 261–272.
Porter, M. E. (2000) Location, competition, and economic develop- ment: Local clusters in a global economy. *Economic Development Quarterly*, 14(1), 15–34.
Porter, M. E., and Kramer, M. R. (2011) Creating shared value: How to reinvent capitalism and unleash a way of innovation and growth. *Harvard Business Review*, 1(2): 62.
Qobo, M. (2016) Why the rich should do more to save the world. *The Conversation*, 19 January.
Reed, M., and Wallace, M. (2015) Elite discourse and institutional innovation: Making the hybrid happen in English public services. In *Elites on Trial* (pp. 269–302). Bingly, UK: Emerald Group Publishing Limited.
Reis, E. P., and Moore, M. (2005) *Elite Perceptions of Poverty and Inequality*. London: Zed Books.
Rhodes, C. (2016) Democratic business ethics: Volkswagen's emissions scandal and the disruption of corporate sovereignty. *Organization Studies*, 1–18.
Riaz, S., Buchanan, S., and Ruebottom, T. (2016) Rhetoric of epistemic authority: Defending field positions during the financial crisis. *Human Relations*, 69(7): 1533–1561.
Robinson, W. I. (2012) Global capitalism theory and the emergence of transnational Elites. *Critical Sociology*, 38(3): 349–363.
Schandl, H., Hatfield-Dodds, S., Wiedmann, T., Geschke, A., Cai, Y., West, J., Newth, D., Baynes, T., Lenzen, M., and Owen, A. (2016) Decoupling global environmental pressure and economic growth: Scenarios for energy use, materials use and carbon emissions. *Journal of Cleaner Production*, 132: 45–56.
Schawbel, D. (2013) John Mackey: Why companies should embrace conscious capitalism. *Forbes*, 15 January.
Scherer, A. G., and Palazzo, G. (2011) The new political role of business in a globalized world: A review of a new perspective on CSR and its implications for the firm, governance, and democracy. *Journal of Management Studies*, 48(4): 899–931.
Scherer, A. G., Palazzo, G., and Seidl, D. (2013) Managing legitimacy in complex and heterogeneous environments: Sustainable development in a globalized world. *Journal of Management Studies*, 50(2): 259–284.
Scott, J. (2008) Modes of power and the re-conceptualization of elites. *Sociological Review*, 56(1): 25–43.
Seekings, J., and Nattrass, N. (2011) State-business relations and pro-poor growth in South Africa. *Journal of International Development*, 23(3): 338–357.
Shamir, B., and Howell, J. M. (1999) Organizational and contextual influences on the emergence and effectiveness of charismatic leadership. *The Leadership Quarterly*, 10(2): 257–283.
Shane, S. (2013) Beyond bogus corporate responsibility: It's time to get your hands dirty. *Fast Company*.
Sjöström, E. (2009) Shareholders as norm entrepreneurs for corporate social responsibility. *Journal of Business Ethics*, 94(2): 177–191.
Spence, C., Carter, C., Husillos, J., and Archel, P. (2016) Taste matters: Cultural capital and elites in proximate Strategic Action Fields. *Human Relations*. Article first published online: June 28, 2016. https://doi.org/10.1177/0018726716649247.
Taylor, I., and Nel, P. (2002) 'New Africa', globalisation and the confines of elite reformism: Getting the rhetoric right, getting the strategy wrong. *Third World Quarterly*, 23(1): 163–180.

Thomas, A. J. (2015) *Cholera: The Victorian Plague*. London: Pen and Sword.
Twenge, J. M., and Campbell, K. (2009) *The Narcissism Epidemic: Living in the Age of Entitlement*. New York, NY: Simon & Schuster.
Useem, M. (1980) Corporations and the corporate elite. *Annual Review of Sociology*, 6(1): 44–61.
van Wyk, D., Cronjé, F., and van Wyk, J. (2009) *Corporate Social Responsibility in the Diamond Mining Industry on the West Coast of South Africa*. Johannesburg: The Bench Marks Foundation.
Walder, A. G. (2003, December) Elite opportunity in transitional economies. *American Sociological Review*, 68(6): 899–916. Retrieved from www.jstor.org/stable/1
Watson, I. (2007, March) *De Beers, Diamonds and Angola: Developing an Understanding of the Role of Sustainable Development and Corporate Citizenship in De Beers' Exploration Strategy*. Master of Philosophy at the University of Stellenbosch, Supervisor: Professor Mark Swilling.
Weaver, G. R., Treviño, L. K., and Cochran, P. L. (1999) Integrated and decoupled corporate social performance: Management commitments, external pressure, and corporate ethics practices. *Academy of Management Journal*, 42(5): 539–552.
Werbel, J. D., and Carter, S. M. (2002) The CEO' s influence on corporate foundation giving. *Journal of Business Ethics*, 40(1): 47–60.
Williams, A., Kennedy, S., Philipp, F., and Whiteman, G. (2017) Systems thinking: A review of sustainability management research. *Journal of Cleaner Production*, 148: 866–881.
Williams, O. F. (2014) CSR: Will it change the world? *Journal of Corporate Citizenship*, 53: 9–26.
Zald, M. N., and Lounsbury, M. (2010) The Wizards of Oz: Towards an institutional approach to elites, expertise and command posts. *Organization Studies*, 31(7): 963–996.

11

Change leaders in the public sector

An interview with Governor Peter Obi

Franca Ovadje and Glory Enyinnaya

Introduction

In this chapter, we present an interview with a change leader in the public sector: Governor Peter Obi. He led the major transformation of Anambra State between 2006 and 2014. In the interview, he shares his experience on what it takes to lead change in the public sector. First, we present some background of Anambra State, the situation when he took charge in 2006 and some of his achievements. Finally, we present the interview.

Background

Anambra State was created in August 1991 as a state of the Federal Republic of Nigeria. It is located in the South-Eastern region of Nigeria. It has a population of 4 million and a population growth rate of 2.21% per annum. Over 60% of its people live in urban areas (mainly Onitsha, Nnewi and Awka), making it one of the most urbanized states in Nigeria (Anon, 2017).

Between the return to democracy in 1999 and 2007, Anambra State had five governors. Chinweoke Mbadinuju was governor from 1999–2003. He was succeeded by Dr. Chris Ngige, who held office from 2003 to 2006. Dr. Ngige was removed by a ruling of the Court of Appeal which declared that the election that brought him to office was rigged, and Peter Obi became the governor of the State in 2006. Peter Obi was impeached by a faction of the State House of Assembly but was reinstated three months later by a ruling of the Court of Appeal. In 2010, he became the first governor of Anambra State to serve a second term.

In 2006, when Peter Obi began his first term, Anambra had significant problems. It faced an enormous infrastructure gap, and the investment climate and regulatory environment were relatively poor. There were weaknesses in governance and institutional capacity. The political environment of the State was characterized by considerable unrest and gangsterism was widespread, as were kidnapping, militancy and corruption (Ajani, 2017).

The State's public services were deplorable. Education, for instance, was in shambles. Before 1999, secondary education was free in the State. Chinweoke Mbadinuju introduced school fees in all secondary schools during his tenure. This led to an unprecedented massive demonstration by secondary school students from all over the State. Teachers' salaries were not paid for several months. Aggrieved teachers in all the public secondary schools in the State embarked on a ten-month strike. Not surprisingly, many parents withdrew their children from public schools.

However, there were also some reasons for optimism. The State was blessed with mineral resources, such as bauxite and ceramic, as well as reserves of crude oil and natural gas. Its soil is almost 100% arable. It also had the lowest poverty rate in Nigeria, due in part to the ingenuity and industry of its people.

Peter Obi's achievements and legacy

Anambra State was transformed under Governor Peter Obi. From a State that was practically ungovernable, Anambra found peace and with it came development. Governor Obi left behind billions of Naira in government coffers for his successor to continue the transformation of the State.

According to two of his lieutenants, Stella Okunna and Patrick Obi: "Mr. Peter Obi emerged as the Best Governor in the implementation of the Millennium Development Goals (MDG). He was invited to speak on the MDGs at the 69th Session of the United Nations General Assembly in New York in 2014."

The Obi administration resuscitated education by partnering with the churches who originally owned the schools. From 2012, Anambra State had the best results in the West African School Certificate examination. Governor Obi won the Bill & Melinda Gates Award for outstanding performance in the health sector. He improved the road network in the State and built institutional capacity (secretariats for the State and local governments, schools, hospitals, etc.).

He instituted a social security system for citizens over 75 years of age. His administration paid arrears of outstanding salaries and pensions owed by the State since 1999. He improved the security system in the State such that Anambra State enjoyed peace and development.

According to Okunna and Obi (2015), Peter Obi is approachable, humane and humble to a fault; he demystified the cult of personality in leadership that has adversely affected the performance of several public office holders in all tiers of government. People now know that governance is about the people and not the incumbent.

Interview with Mr. Peter Obi, former governor of Anambra State, Nigeria (2006 to 2014)

Interviewer – We see clearly the need for change in the public sector in Africa but there are not many successful changes in this sector.

Governor Peter Obi – Which is where it is critical.

Interviewer – Yes, it affects the private sector and the lives of the citizens. I am interested in how you led change in the Anambra State and why it was successful. I would also like to explore your upbringing and values and how these may have contributed to your success in Anambra State. What did you meet in Anambra State when you became Governor in 2006?

Governor Peter Obi – Well, I don't know how to describe it. It was a situation where lunatics were in charge of the asylum. In 2001, we had a situation where schools in Anambra State were closed completely because the teachers were owed one year's salary. So there were no schools, and as you know, there were no rules.

I campaigned, won the election but I was not declared the winner. Since I believe in the rule of law, I went to court. People don't believe that the courts work, you don't have to do anything extra-ordinary. I followed the rule of law. The judges were transparent and eventually my mandate was given back to me.

When I took charge, I met a system that was not organised; I met a government machinery that had no direction. For example, I invited those in charge of various ministries to a meeting and asked them for their plans. There was no plan; there was no ministry of planning. I started this ministry.

My predecessor had done some good work in the area of road infrastructure in some parts of the State. But he did this without a plan. There was no vision. I asked members of staff in the Ministry of Education for their target and they had no idea. Of course, there was no planning and no vision, so there was nothing to measure. I asked people in Ministry of Agriculture the same question and I got the same answer. There was just nothing that could be used to do anything. It dawned on me then that we have a crisis. What do we do? How do we develop a vision for the State and plan properly?

Instead of formulating a new vision, we decided to adopt the United Nations development goals with its road-map for development which they christened Millennium Development Goals (MDGs). The MDGs had clearly defined goals so we had a direction; we adopted them as our vision. The MDGs cut across all the developmental strata. The first goals were:

- ✓ Fight poverty – hunger
- ✓ Education
- ✓ Health
- ✓ Environment

So having adopted the MDGs, we thought of the strategy for delivery. We developed what we called Anambra Integrated Development Strategy (ANIDS). It was simply a process that allowed us to plan for all sectors, budget properly to support our plan, execute the plan and ensure delivery. It was easy for us to measure. We moved both our planning, budgeting, execution and delivery from being supply driven to demand driven. We asked the people to tell us what is critical to them; what they need.

Interviewer – In every community?

Governor Peter Obi – We consulted with various communities. For example, we visited schools – I visited every secondary school and over 400 primary schools personally. I saw the buildings. This informed what we did.

With proper planning and budgeting, we could easily see the gaps in terms of the support we needed from development agencies, such as the World Bank. That is why you can see that no state in Nigeria had more support from the development agencies than Anambra State. Once we saw the gap we approached the development agencies. We were the first State to do poverty mapping in Nigeria.

Interviewer – What is that?

Governor Peter Obi – Because fighting hunger was our first goal, poverty mapping helped us identify the poorest areas in Anambra State. We were the first State to use statistical records to check our poverty indices. We saw that the poorest area of Anambra was Anambra West Local Government – Ogbaru and Orumba South.

Once we had located the poorest people we asked why they are poor. We discovered that their problem was lack of accessibility, road network. These communities were agricultural communities with no access to market where they could get more value for their products; they were selling far below market price. Our road construction projects began in these communities. When the roads were completed, we saw a reduction in poverty of the people: yam tubers which they used to sell for close to nothing now attracted five to ten times the price.

On education, in our first year in office, Anambra State was ranked 20-something in the WAEC and NECO examinations. It was the same thing in the second year and we wanted to know what was wrong. We concluded that the State should not be involved in the management of schools; nothing was being managed. All the resources we were pumping into education were transacted away. We needed to do something drastic. Schools were originally built by missionaries, owned by them and managed by them, so we had no business managing schools. I decided to return the schools to the missionaries and see if it works. Everybody protested; they said it will not work because the schools were taken over by the State about 40 years ago. They said there was no way we could reverse this. I said No; we have been on the wrong road for 40 years. We have to take the right road, we have to return the schools to the original owners and we will support them financially, we will give them subvention.

We returned the schools to the churches, what was said to be very difficult, almost impossible. We did not just return schools, we said those resources we used to invest in them when we managed them should go to them – we paid all the workers, teachers and tutorial and non-tutorial staff, etc. With this, we took off the load of financing activities of the school from the missionaries and they provided management. Those monies we used to spend on schools, instead of them spending through the ministry, we gave the schools directly. This happened in 2009. Two years later, Anambra State was ranked number one in the WAEC and NECO examinations. Everything changed: if you go to schools in Anambra State today you will see that the structures have been rebuilt.

I said everything changed, all we did is was to give back schools to the owners. Every year we budgeted a capital vote, we gave schools about 10 million Naira to spend the way they like – everything changed.

No School of Nursing or Midwifery was accredited when I took office; none was functional. During our tenure all the schools of Nursing and Midwifery, Health Technology, and Lab Technology were accredited. We found that the schools of Health Technology, Nursing and Midwifery were also owned by the missionaries, the churches. The hospital in Ogidi produced the first midwife in Nigeria. It had been shut down. So, we went back to the churches to ask them to resuscitate the School of Midwifery, School of Nursing and all the health hospitals. We worked with them. We did the same thing in St. Charles Borromeo hospital, St. Joseph hospital, Adazi, and Our Lady of Lourdes, Ihialla. They started resuscitating other facilities run by the church. We then built from scratch a Teaching Hospital attached to the University in Awka.

Because missionaries were able to utilize the monies given to them, we became innovative and decided to modernize the entire community. We decided that every community must have a Health Centre offering primary health care facilities; and every Local Government, a hospital.

We had a Good Governance Committee with a Chairman and committee members. Every quarter we met to evaluate how we were doing on the MDGs and decide what to do next. What did we do in Education, Health, etc.? Everything was systematically executed, infrastructure was developed and we measured everything.

Ministries were run as required by the law. We reduced the level of transaction and increased the level of transformation. I tell people that as a Governor, I was one of the freest people because nobody was looking for me. Because the Ministries were functioning, everybody was working, transactions were far less because people were not seeing money, the monies were being given to the Missions or to those who will execute. In our schools for example, we gave the money directly to the Principal and we supervised them.

Interviewer – The citizens of Anambra State did not demand good governance as such. If you had not initiated change it may have been OK. Why did you initiate change?

Governor Peter Obi – I don't know how to describe this but it hurts me, I don't know if it is the same with a lot of people in Nigeria. There is so much that this country can do with its resources in terms of human resources and God-given resources that is being wasted. For me I will say the quality of governance is too low. We should increase the quality and get people who are committed. What do you need? Simply, do something good and when you do the right thing the inner peace that you get is more fulfilling than everything you can get externally.

Interviewer – So you went into government with this in mind?

Governor Peter Obi – When I was campaigning, my Motto was – "Is Anambra State Cursed or are We the Cause?" And that is the question I ask myself today. Is Nigeria cursed or are we the cause? Both for Anambra State and Nigeria, we are the cause. It is not that we are cursed. It is just that the people are sick – the level of greed I found is unacceptable. You know, greed must have a limit or the person is ill. People acquire what they do not need and deprive other people. One can do a decent job and earn decent money.

Interviewer – What helped make the change happen? Pat Utomi and I wrote a case study on Dora Akunyili after she transformed NAFDAC. Some of the things that helped her make the change include – her integrity, her relationship with the President, the stakeholders she identified and partnered with . . . You were the Executive Governor of Anambra State. What are some of those things that helped you as Governor to make this change happen?

Governor Peter Obi – Well I will say my background; the way I was brought up. I am a Christian. I believe that we are children of God – we came here with nothing and we are going back with nothing. Whatever we are able to get here is a blessing from God. And if God has granted you a measure of success wherever you find yourself, it is for service to humanity. I was once a bank Chairman; the bank didn't buy me even a tyre! I live my life. I was a business man before.

I go to Mass every morning. When I became Governor, I did the same thing and I do the same thing today. I pray my rosary daily. My question is, if I do these prayers every day, how do I show that I truly believe? It is that fear of God and my belief in God that makes me know that I have to strive to do the right thing. I am not a saint but every day and every minute I strive to do what is right.

As Governor for example, when I finish work and I come back in the evening, I sit down and reflect on what I did because an unexamined life is not worth living. So I sit down and reflect on what I did that day that was wrong.

As a leader, I allow people to criticize and comment, because if you must lead, you must learn, you must listen to other peoples' ideas. I had a team and I let the team teach me. I didn't have stakeholders who were pushing me around but I had a team who were ready to disagree with me because I was learning. I always told my cabinet: if you agree with me in three meetings, I will dissolve the cabinet! I saw myself not as a Governor but as the head of a team so it was team work.

When we have our Good Governance meetings each quarter, the first person everybody criticizes is myself. The chairman of the Committee says – this is what you were supposed to do. You didn't do this and that. Everybody is measured on the same scale. Not that the governor is the governor, No! They tell me what I promised I will do which I did not do within that quarter and this is critical. You see, in Nigeria, we don't measure our leaders, so what they promised in the campaign is different from what they do in office. Nobody reminds them in March that they did not do what they promised in January.

As governor, everywhere I made a statement and I made a promise, the Chairman of my Good Governance Committee took note of it, and when we sat down for review, the first question was – you promised this school that you are going to re-roof their licking roof the last time you visited, has that been done? Commissioner, did we do it? When we went to that place, they showed you their problem with erosion, you said work will start on it in three months, did work start? So they were like a gadfly on everybody's back saying: "Hey! What did we say there? Are we doing it?" This is critical.

You can see that Americans are holding Trump to his promises: you said you will do this, what is happening? Even when I am sure he is doing something wrong but that was the promise – you know, it might not be acceptable to me but that was the promise. So if people are campaigning and they say they are going to do something, they should strive to do it. Let people see that you do it genuinely. You might not achieve it but let them see that you are trying.

Interviewer – Can you tell me a little bit about your upbringing – I hope this is not too intrusive, but I think it will be useful.

Governor Peter Obi – I was born into an ordinary Christian family, grew up going to church every day, went to Christian schools. My elder sister is a Reverend Sister and my immediate younger brother a Reverend Father.

My mother taught me many things. When I was going to Lagos the first time she gave me advice which has served me till today. She told me not to steal, not to envy others, to be grateful for all favours no matter how small . . .

I have never knowingly in my adult life stolen. I have never knowingly in my adult life envied anybody. I don't have a house in Lagos, I don't have a piece of land. I don't have a house in Abuja. I am not missing anything; I can afford it but it might disrupt other things that I am doing. People talk of others that own houses in Potomac, Washington, in London, in 5th Avenue, New York. I can't afford all these you know. I rented a place in Abuja and it was costing me almost ₦20 million. I go to Abuja three times at most in a month. One night in a hotel costs me ₦50,000. So why do I have to pay somebody ₦20million? They say it is for your prestige, but it doesn't make sense to me. They say it is for your status, I say what is status? It's a feeling.

The same thing drove me in government. When I went into government, I looked at the status of the State and I said we must live within our own means, within our income. We cannot as the government of Anambra State maintain a lodge in Abuja. Why will the Government of Anambra State own a lodge in Abuja? He doesn't live in Abuja, he has no reason to maintain a lodge in Abuja, we cannot afford it, we can't have a lodge in Lagos either. They say we have guest houses in Awka, where the Governor entertain guests – I said no, we can't maintain it. I go to work in the morning and come back in the evening, what do I need a lodge in Awka for?

The President doesn't live in Awka, so why should we build him a lodge for his three-day visit to the State? I moved out of the Governor's Lodge into a hotel and President Obasanjo stayed in the Governor's Lodge. The cost of governance is unacceptable, totally unacceptable. 30 people went with me on my first trip to Abuja as Governor. They said it was security! I changed that. Only one person flew with me on economy class after that: we paid for two tickets with the price of a business class ticket! What does a governor's office need 40 vehicles for? We are in a knowledge economy, not a baggage economy! If we had all listened to Ngozi Okonjo-Iweala when she begged us to save we would not be in this situation today.

Interviewer – What advice would you give someone who is going into the Public Sector and truly wants to make a change?

PETER OBI – Well my first advice is that he must be committed, because he is going to have enemies: those who don't want change because they live off the confusion. There are others at the margin: those who don't trust that you are going to succeed. The moment you are able to determine that this is the right thing, you have to pursue it with a level of insanity. Everybody will quarrel with you – nobody is happy with you. You have to go on and say listen: this is what we want and it will happen. Your friends, people you meet tell you that since you came here nobody is happy with you.

Secondly, select a team that is equally committed. Do not delegate too much. People don't do what is expected here, they do what is inspected. For example, to know the rut in the schools, I visited the schools. To know the quality of food children eat in schools, for over three months I was eating with them. I said listen, we are going to go to this school this afternoon to see what they are going to eat for lunch. So you must inspect directly, be part of it. Cut down the cost of governance, because there is a lot of waste in government. You can comfortably save up to 75% of what we are using today to run the office of governor or local government chairman.

So your eye must be on cost; read your memos carefully and look out for cost implications of whatever is written in the memos. If you are not a thief, if you are not corrupt, you will reduce corruption by 70%. You will not eliminate it – it will be there. What we need to fight is the greed, we are not going to eliminate corruption. Has that been eliminated anywhere in the world?

Where did we get money to do what we did? We reduced the greed. People knew that they were not doing anything for the governor, the governor was not interested. I can account for 75% of the Security Vote without looking at my books because I know where it went. We reduced the cost of governance, reduced the cost of transactions and we were able to achieve transformation.

Interviewer – Did you meet resistance? How did you handle it?

Governor Peter Obi – That is why I said you have to be insanely committed to the course. Whoever brings change has for enemy those who live off the old order and those who are not sure it will work. Whoever wants to bring about change faces obstacles and resistance. You must be committed – insanely committed to it, because everybody will be quarrelling with you.

I was the only Governor who did not have the office of the First Lady. I told them it is sheer madness – you have to reduce the confusion, the cost of governance. My wife stays at home and looks after me. We are very close but to create all these things is confusion. This was part of reducing the cost of governance. Convoys, dispatch riders, all these things cost money. We must save for tomorrow. Everybody knew I will read the memo and we will talk about cost! We made sure we were saving and left behind a surplus.

Interviewer – Where should one begin?

Governor Peter Obi – People say they are leading change. But in character and behavior, they have not changed. So how can they lead change? It is not only about what you do and what you can achieve. If you are in a leadership position, you must exhibit the character and behavior of a leader. My biggest achievement is bringing civility and order into the system. His Excellency, Distinguished, Honorable – people who have these titles should show it in their character and behavior in public. The way they move, things they do, that is where you start – because it is critical.

In my eight years as Governor, I do not recall inviting people for a party where I was dancing; nobody was dancing. I recall once I had a reason to attend somebody's party and I met university students, young girls there. I left. The person who invited me asked me why I was leaving and I said I just saw university students here. And he said to me: "Oh Peter, what is wrong with you?" I said to him: "Wait a minute, I am Visitor to the university, so during the day I am Visitor, at night I am dancing with them? What am I doing here? I am His Excellency; I have to live the life these people should emulate."

People want to go late to Church and sit in front. No! Front seats are not for late comers. You sit at the back quietly regretting why you came late. There is a Mass or Service schedule. I insisted throughout the time I was in office that if we arrive late we sit at the back and we tell the officiating priest that we are coming late and the reason why we will arrive late. It is not for you to come late and behave irresponsibly. Some people go into Church with armed guards! Where is their faith? There are so many things that are wrong. You don't use your title to jump a queue! The first place to start is conduct and public behavior.

Interviewer – You have been CEO, you have been Chairman of a bank and you have been Governor of Anambra State. Is there any difference in leading change in the private and public sectors?

Governor Peter Obi – I believe it is the same thing. Let me tell you the classical connection: those who have not created wealth should not manage wealth.

Interviewer – Why?

Governor Peter Obi – Because in the public space, you are managing the wealth of the people. I didn't say those who have worked for people – you know it is not exactly the same. Those who have genuinely walked through the difficult path are more in a position to manage the public wealth without losing their head over it, without seeing it as their personal wealth. Going through this path develops you in terms of conduct, behavior. In the public space, the individual who is in charge is critical, it is his character, conduct and behavior that drives the process. The CEO of an organization drives the organization.

Interviewer – So it is basically the same?

Governor Peter Obi – It is the same. There is not much difference. You always ask yourself, supposing this was my money? When I said I would not have a lodge in Abuja, they started wanting to put me into some of the big hotels. I told them, why don't I call Anambra people that own hotels in Abuja and ask them to give me a discount and they were able to give me 50% discount.

Throughout the time I was in office (maybe that is why the newspapers did not report what we were doing), people kept urging me – let's commission this, let's commission that. When we construct a road they tell me we must commission it. Unless somebody is paying, I find it very odd. Whenever I agree to commission something, they come up with a bill of 5 or 10 million Naira. But I can build two classrooms in a school with that money. The people who are using the road know we built it. Officials fear that somebody may come after us and claim that he constructed the road. My response is simple: forget about what people claim, let's get on with what we are doing. So you always look at every cost; because if this is your money you cannot use it anyhow.

Interviewer – A big challenge leaders face is that of making the change part of the DNA of the organization. Dora Akunyili transformed NAFDAC when she was the Director General of the Agency. People wonder today if that change was sustained. What can be done to institutionalize change so that it goes beyond the leader's tenure?

Governor Peter Obi – It is the people. Institutions are built by people, by peoples' persistence. President Trump introduced a new immigration policy. People challenged it, they went to court. CEOs came out and said Trump is wrong.

Dora and I were very close; she was my big aunty. She counselled me every now and then. Though we disagreed on a few things. She didn't believe I should save money because someone can come later and eat it. I told her that is not my business. My business is this: we are getting this money from a resource that will not be there forever – oil is a diminishing asset. We must save.

Channel less money through the ministry. We asked donors and the World Bank to give money directly to the schools and we monitored the schools. The senior prefects had my phone number. They sent me text messages to inform me of some issues in the school. For example, a text message could say: "our borehole is not working." I forwarded such messages to the Commissioner for Education and we solved the problem. We sometimes went to schools to celebrate the birthday of one of the senior prefects. The schools still invite me to their functions today.

While we should try hard to create institutions, it is the society and the people that sustain institutions. It is the people who can say this is not us.

We are not celebrating those who have tried to do what is right. We are still celebrating the criminality and rascality which we should do away with. Above all, when you find yourself in office, you will not achieve 100% of what is expected, but people want to see 100% effort, consistency and commitment. You will make mistakes. When you make mistakes, apologize, you are human. As a leader, you have to be committed, insanely committed. You also need character and you must do the right thing.

There was a need to inject a lot of money into education in the State, so we borrowed $40 million from the World Bank. We also borrowed $80 million to solve an erosion problem. We were able to negotiate a 40-year loan tenure, interest-free from the World Bank. We saved for the future, and to repay the loan. We put one-third of our savings in local equities, one-third in foreign bonds and one-third in local banks. My thinking was that if Anambra State did not invest anything new, at 6.81% yield, the value of our savings should be $1.4 billion in 2050. This is money I could have used to do the wrong things; I decided to use it for what is right.

References

Ajani, J. (2017) Oh Anambra! A state as metaphor for Nigeria's Fourth Republic. *Vanguard News*. Retrieved December 11, 2017 from www.vanguardngr.com/2014/06/oh-anambra-state-metaphor-nigerias-fourth-republic/

Anon. (2017) www.anambrastate.gov.ng Retrieved December 11, 2017.

Okunna, S., and Obi, P. (2015, July 19) *Salute to Peter Obi at 54: What Makes the Ex-Anambra Governor Special*. Retrieved from www.newsexpressngr.com

12

Fundamentals of organisational culture change

Who and what really matters in a Nigerian organisational context

Theresa A. Chika-James

Introduction

In light of the documented influence of culture on organisational performance (Kotter and Heskett, 1992; Denison and Mishra, 1995), several organisations have embarked on organisational culture change initiatives (see Krisher, 2012; Simons, 2012; Wankhade and Brinkman, 2014). Consequently, a steady stream of research has focused on the implications, feasibility and complexity of attempts to change culture in organisations (Ogbonna, 1993; Grugulis and Wilkinson, 2002; Harris, 2002; Smith, 2003) in order to produce actionable knowledge that can be used to enhance the effectiveness of organisational culture change efforts. Most of these studies, however, have concentrated on analysing Western organisational contexts. This chapter, therefore, attempts to provide an understanding of culture change and factors that influence change efforts in an African organisational context.

Drawing on Ogbonna and Harris's (2002) finding that like societal culture, organisational culture can and does change, and such change process is largely influenced by several factors, this chapter aims to uncover factors that influence culture change efforts within an African organisation. The chapter starts with a brief overview of the varied conceptualisations of organisational culture and organisational culture change. It then outlines the different frameworks of organisational culture change and presents the intricacies involved in the process based on extant research. Building on the preceding conceptual discussion, the chapter presents an analysis of culture change in an African organisational context using a Nigerian oil and gas company as a case study. The penultimate section provides an extended discussion of the findings, and the final section concludes with implications for change management in an African organisational context.

Conceptualisation of organisational culture

Organisational culture has been described as a cognitive phenomenon that resides in the minds of organisational members. Accordingly, some researchers describe culture as mental schemas, basic assumptions, patterns of meanings and knowledge systems amongst organisational members

(Goodenough, 1957; Rossi and O'Higgins, 1980; Schein, 1985; Hofstede, 2001). Other theorists, taking a symbolic view, describe organisational culture as a system of shared symbols including patterns of language, behaviours, myths and other artefacts (Geertz, 1973; Smircich, 1983). An understanding of the cognitive and symbolic perspectives indicate that culture in organisations includes both observable aspects, such as artefacts, behaviours, language, symbols and practices, as well as intangible qualities, including underlying assumptions, meanings, beliefs, values and expectations (House, Hanges, Javidan, Dorfman, and Gupta, 2004; Schein, 2010).

In conceptualising organisational culture, there is the notion that tangible and intangible elements are shared amongst organisational members, indicating a common experience of beliefs, values, interpretations, ideologies and behaviour (Dickson, Kwantes, and Magomaeva, 2014; Ehrhart, Schneider, and Macey, 2014). There is also the idea that organisational culture is unique, stable, founded in the history and tradition of the organisation and transmitted to new members as the correct way to respond to organisational issues (Schein, 2010; Ehrhart et al., 2014). The aspect of stability emphasises the enduring nature of its attributes leaving its imprints on the activities and operations of members (Schein, 2010; Ehrhart et al., 2014) such that new members learn instinctively or are deliberately taught the intricacies of culture in the organisation.

Other studies, on the basis of the 'uniqueness paradox', contend that cultural elements, rituals and stories are common across similar organisations, challenging the notion of the uniqueness of organisational culture (Martin, Feldman, Hatch, and Sitkin, 1983). In addition, the evolving nature of the environment and its potential influence on organisational culture indicates the likelihood that organisational culture is not entirely stable or able to sustain enduring characteristics. Furthermore, individuals and their varied personalities suggest that culture in organisations can be influenced by new intakes with differentiated beliefs and values, contradicting the idea of cultural socialisation and indoctrination of new members. The implication of these contradictory issues is that the construct, organisational culture, has varied attributes. These attributes has led to many and varied definitions of organisational culture (Alvesson, 2011; Ehrhart et al., 2014). A few examples are illustrated below:

- A shared and learned world of experiences, meanings, values and understandings which inform people and which are expressed, reproduced and communicated partly in the symbolic form.

  (Alvesson, 1993, pp. 2–3)

- A system of shared values (that define what is important) and norms that define appropriate attitudes and behaviours for organisational members (how we feel and behave).

  (O'Reilly and Chatman, 1996: 160)

- Culture is the collective programming of the mind which distinguishes the members of one organisation from another.

  (Hofstede, 1998: 478)

Recognising the varied conceptualisations of organisational culture, it is pertinent to clearly emphasise, as Ehrhart et al.'s (2014) study also demonstrates, that culture in organisations is somewhat shared, stable and unique. It is usually grounded in the history of the firm; provides procedures and policies towards functional operations; and creates, essentially, a source of collective identity and commitment amongst members. In order to provide clarity on the construct, this chapter adopts Edgar Schein's (2010) conceptualisation of organisational culture as:

> a pattern of shared basic assumptions learned by a group as it solved its problems of external adaptation and internal integration, which has worked well enough to be considered valid

and therefore, to be taught to new members as the correct way to perceive, think, and feel in relation to those problems.

(Schein, 2010: 18)

Schein's (2010) definition is largely based on the cognitive perspective that perceives culture as residing in the subconscious minds of people. However, Schein's (2010, 1991, 1990) studies also take into consideration other observable entities that partly express these assumptions or beliefs. This includes visible artefacts such as observed behaviour, and organisational structures and processes to include physical layout, dress codes and manner of communication. These observable entities are framed within Schein's (2010) three different levels of culture. The first level includes all occurrences that are visible to observers, such as the architecture of the physical environment, its technology and products, the language and emotional display of organisational members and other observable rituals and ceremonies. The second level denotes a greater level of awareness, and consists of espoused beliefs and values of the organisation, while the third level, which delineates a deeper level of the unconscious, consists of underlying assumptions. These underlying assumptions are often taken-for-granted norms or customary ways of thinking that subsequently guide behaviour and define entities and processes that are vital to the organisation. These three levels of culture, with emphasis on the first and second level of awareness, are incorporated into the conceptualisation of organisational culture in this chapter.

Organisational culture change: meaning, approaches, contingencies and implications

The conceptualisation of organisational culture change

There are two predominant meanings of organisational culture change in the literature. First, is the notion that as society evolves and organisations develop, cultural elements within organisations gradually transform, and in this evolving process, previous cultural forms are altered (Ehrhart et al., 2014; Flamholtz and Randle, 2014). Based on this premise, cultural transformation within organisations occurs naturally without any planned formal intervention (Schneider and Barbera, 2014). Second is the implied meaning that organisational culture change refers to deliberate attempts of organisational members to alter cultural content such as beliefs, underlying assumptions, values, behaviours and other artefacts for identified purposes (Armenakis, Brown, and Mehta, 2011). According to this notion, planned systematic procedures and practices are initiated to reconfigure existing cultural forms. The latter is the most widely implied meaning of culture change in the extant research (see Wankhade and Brinkman, 2014; Harris and Metallinos, 2002; Jorritsma and Wilderom, 2012). Thus, this chapter draws on this perspective in its analysis of organisational culture change.

Approaches to culture change in organisations

Several approaches have been proposed to guide organisational culture change efforts (see Silverzweig and Allen, 1976; Deal and Kennedy, 1982; Kotter, 1996; Cameron and Quinn, 2006). For example, Silverzweig and Allen's (1976) normative systems model of organisational change indicates a four-step framework towards culture change. First, the framework includes a sequential process of analysing the existing culture and establishing objectives towards the desired culture. Second, it proposes that members experience the desired culture by involving all work teams through several workshops. The third step involves a process of modifying the existing culture through eight critical cultural influences, which include leadership modelling; first line supervision; work teams; organisational structures and procedures; information and communication systems; performance and reward systems; trainings; and result orientation. Once the result of modifying the existing culture through systems installation is achieved, Silverzweig and Allen (1976) propose that the focus shift to the final step of sustaining the desired culture through ongoing evaluations. They argued that 'ongoing evaluation is necessary to ensure sustained results and to disclose the need for retooling and renewal of the change effort in one or more influence areas' (Silverzweig and Allen, 1976: 45).

In Deal and Kennedy's (1982) study, five managerial guidelines were highlighted to effect culture change in organisations. These were: providing skill building and training; significant opportunities for members to adapt to the culture change content; enough time for the change process; placing emphasis on communication and trust; and recognizing the influence of peer groups on the acceptance and negation of culture change efforts. In Kotter's (1996) analyses, the emphasis was more on leadership at all levels of the organisation, rather than senior management, taking the lead in effecting successful change efforts. Kotter's (1996) perspective is that leadership creates the change process, while management controls initiated concepts. On this basis, Kotter (1996, 2012) introduced an eight-step model that anchors changes in the organisational culture. This consists of the following steps:

1 Establish a sense of urgency: In the initial stage of the change process, Kotter (1996) proposes change agents eliminate any form of complacency through the creation of a rational opportunity that requires urgent attention. Kotter (2012) argued that an abiding sense of urgency on the need for the desired change from the top hierarchy of the organisation would influence other organisational members to be determined to move towards the opportunity for change, thus creating an awareness on the significance of the desired change.
2 Forming a guiding coalition: In the next step, Kotter (1996) proposed the formation of a guiding coalition to direct the change effort. The guiding coalition are members of the organisation who are selected from different departments and levels based on their expertise and outstanding management and leadership skills, as well as high level of trust (Kotter, 1996, 2012). It is expected that the social dynamics of this team, with in-depth knowledge about the organisational environment, managerial skills to control the organisation and leadership skills to drive change, would make good decisions on strategic initiatives and best practices to effect the change process.
3 Creating a strategic vision: Kotter (2012) argues that formulating a strategic vision as the next step in the change process will give the guiding coalition adequate direction to make consequential decisions. The strategic vision, he reasoned, should be feasible, easy to communicate, focussed and emotionally appealing.
4 Communicate the change vision: Upon completion of formulating the strategic vision, it is important to communicate the vision to all organisational members in a compelling way to create a buy-in. Kotter (2012) proposed that the vision should be communicated in ways that are clear, authentic, creative, and memorable. He argued that communication 'work best when it is so direct and so simple' (Kotter, 1996: 89).
5 Empowering others to act on the vision: In the next step, Kotter (1996) suggested actions be taken to remove as many barriers as possible to the implementation of the desired change vision in a timely way. Factors that may undermine the change process include middle management personnel, organisational structures, systems and skills that disempower and discourage workers, as well as slow the pace of the change effort. In order to empower workers for a broad-based action, change agents should confront problem managers in

honest dialogue on the change process rather than political strategies to manipulate them. Organisational structures and systems should be aligned to the vision, and adequate training on the right attitude and skills be provided to employees.

6 Planning for and creating short-term wins: In order to sustain the credibility and momentum of the change process, Kotter (1996, 2012) proposed that organisational members celebrate short-term wins. On the notion that 'success breeds success', Kotter (2012: 55) argues that successful feedback will buoy the guiding coalition members and volunteers, as well as motivate other employees to concede to the change process.
7 Consolidate improvements and produce still more change: In this step, Kotter (1996) advised that the credibility gained from celebrating short-term wins should be used to tackle additional and new change projects. Essentially, organisational members should not ease off the momentum because of the initial success; rather, additional employees should be incorporated, promoted and developed to facilitate the change process.
8 Institutionalise new approaches: In the final phase, Kotter (1996, 2012) advised that the developed and implemented change initiatives be incorporated into the day-to day activities of the organisation. In this process, change initiatives are embedded into the norms and shared values of the people, while inconsistent pieces that are incompatible with the change vision are eliminated. Kotter (1996) noted that the institutionalisation of new approaches would ensure the change efforts are firmly grounded in the culture of the organisation.

Kotter's (1996, 2012) model of leading and managing change focuses on establishing commitment towards the opportunity for change, reducing forms of resistance, and institutionalising initiated changes. Similar sequential approaches to culture change are proposed in Cameron and Quinn (2006) and Schein's (2010) work. Cameron and Quinn (2006), through their Organisational Culture Assessment Instrument (OCAI), proposed a six-step model for designing and implementing culture change efforts in organisations (see Cameron and Quinn, 2006: 90). In Schein's (2010) study, the focus is on three stages that follow the pattern of Lewin's (1947) change model of unfreezing, moving and freezing. In the first stage of unfreezing, Schein (2010) proposes leaders create motivation for change through crafting disconfirmation, survival anxieties and guilt, and also provide possible solutions towards anticipated or impending discomfort. The second stage introduces aspects of learning newly initiated concepts, meanings and standards of judgements; the final stage focusses on internalising learnt ideas and principles into individuals' identity and relationships.

Extant research indicates that there are several other models and prescribed approaches towards culture change in organisations (see Armenakis et al., 2011; Heracleous and Langham, 1996; Katzenbach, Steffen, and Kronley, 2012; DiDonato and Noelle, 2015). These propositions are quite similar to the early change models with emphasis on analysing the existing culture, identifying the desired culture and constructing plans towards achieving the desired culture (see Lewin, 1947; Silverzweig and Allen, 1976). Predominant themes of organisational culture change that emerged from these studies includes a focus on leadership; communication; training; recruitment and selection; performance and reward measures; incorporating changes in organisational structures, policies and procedures; and incorporating evaluation measures on initiated culture change efforts.

Contingencies and implications of culture change in organisations

In analysing the contingencies involved, theorists have identified certain opportune circumstances that may influence culture change. This includes leadership turnovers, mergers and acquisitions, organisational life cycles and the emergence of crisis situations (Lundberg, 1985; Schein, 2010; Spicer, 2011). Leadership turnover has been identified as one of the most potent contingencies for culture change in organisations (Siehl, 1985; Schein, 2010). The appointment of Chief Executive Officers (CEO), or change of existing managerial personnel to manage organisations, has been recognised as an avenue for these personnel to incorporate personal beliefs, values and behaviour among other organisational members. Analogous to this contingency are the occasions of a merger or/and acquisitions which tend to precipitate culture change in organisations (Kavanagh and Ashkanasy, 2006; Marks and Mirvis, 2011; Spicer, 2011). This operates on the basis that issues and challenges in the acculturation process of both organisations would influence the need to align cultural norms and behaviours to form a cohesive system towards desired organisational objectives.

In addition, transitional changes in the life cycle of an organisation, from its founding phase to growth stage, have been identified as a contingency to influence culture change in organisations. There is the notion that leaders with an understanding of these stages could facilitate the process of steering the existing phase towards a desired culture, particularly when the evolving change in the life cycle is 'slow or going the wrong direction' (Schein, 2010: 273). While there is relatively limited research on the opportunities this contingency may create to influence organisational culture change, there is a plethora of research on how the emergence of crisis situations provides opportunities to alter cultural norms and behaviours in organisations. For instance, the case of deliberate attempts towards culture change in Alexandria local government offices in the US was instigated by the financial crisis of 2008–2009 (Hartmann and Khademian, 2010). Reports of medical errors in the US and UK health sectors have also facilitated culture change efforts in these Western organisational contexts (see Institute of Medicine, 1999; Department of Health, 2015). These studies indicate that environmental uncertainties and managerial crises continue to precipitate culture change in organisations. It is presumed that organisational members would be receptive to culture change in such crisis contexts, as such change initiatives would potentially alleviate identified problems (Ehrhart et al., 2014).

Interestingly, while scholars have proffered these contingencies as potential opportunities to initiate culture change, others have noted implications of such planned culture change on organisations (Grugulis and Wilkinson, 2002; Harris, 2002; Hartmann and Khademian, 2010). The implications presented often connote unfavourable outcomes of effecting culture change in organisations. For instance, Grugulis and Wilkinson's (2002) study highlights a number of unintended consequences of culture change in British Airways with the appointment of a new CEO. The planned culture change initiated by the CEO resulted in several unintended issues such as strike actions by unionised employees, financial loss and resignation of the CEO. In instances of perceived and actual organisational crisis (increase in business competitors), the process of effecting culture change initiatives have resulted in employee withdrawal of support, expressions of fear and intimidation, and burnout and ill-health (Awasthy, Chandrasekaran, and Gupta, 2011). Other identified consequences considered unfavourable to organisations in the Netherlands, Australia and the UK include a wide perception of no significant cultural change towards an initial aim to improve existing culture, cynical and silo behaviours amongst workers (Jorritsma and Wilderom, 2012; Barratt-Pugh and Bahn, 2015) and short-term changes in values and behaviours (Wankhade and Brinkman, 2014). These unfavourable outcomes constitute a further rationale for the need to provide a better understanding of organisational culture change in order to mitigate the negative consequences of organisation culture change efforts.

The preceding review of the organisational culture change literature, and analysis of actual culture change efforts, highlights two key implications. The first implication is that the process of changing culture within organisations is complex. This is in spite of the myriad models, frameworks and contingencies posited as guides towards culture change. Secondly, while there have been reports of instances of successes, contemporary research indicates several unfavourable organisational outcomes. Yet this has not deterred organisations from initiating culture change. It is therefore necessary to further explore the practicalities of organisational culture change. In this process, a focal point would be to analyse the peculiarities of the context and process in which organisational culture change is initiated. This will be done by presenting a case study of culture change in a leading oil and gas company in Nigeria hereafter called Datvolgas (pseudonym).

The case of Datvolgas: a three-phase journey of culture change

Datvolgas was established in the late 1980s as a joint venture firm in the Nigerian energy industry. It is ranked amongst the top ten firms leading other blue-chip companies in Nigeria. Its core business is focussed on harnessing the natural gas resource within the country for both local and international markets. Datvolgas's overall vision in its business and social conduct is to remain a global firm with a drive towards contributing to the sustainable development of Nigeria. It is the company's ideology to set standards in business operations and relationships that would promote ethical conduct within Nigerian businesses. To this end, the early executive directors, composed of expatriates from its international partners, set up four core values: Integrity, Teamwork, Excellence and Caring (ITEC) to reflect the company's vision. These ITEC values were imprinted in the company's publications and websites, and passively communicated to all employees:

> Datvolgas workforce comprise direct hire staff, supported by secondees from shareholder companies, working together to achieve the company's corporate objectives, through a set of Shared Values . . . Integrity, Teamwork, Excellence, Caring.
>
> *(Company Annual Report, 2010: 10)*

> I remember when I joined, we just had these core values ITEC, and during the induction, it was just mentioned. There was no stress (emphasis) on it, as to the fact that, that's the way they want people to live out the values that they expect. It was just mentioned, it was not even, there was no culture. There was nothing said about how they expect us to behave.
>
> *(Public Affairs Officer)*

Over the years, each newly appointed management team continued in this act of displaying the core ITEC values in official publications and briefly communicated the same to new intakes. However, there was no collective manifestation of these values by management personnel or even amongst low-level employees. Operation, administration and implementation of tasks were accomplished without consideration of the ITEC values. What transpired in Datvolgas was a wide display of expressions and behaviours that reflected different beliefs, values, practices and work patterns. Behaviours and work practices were largely influenced by individual members' perception, previous work experiences and societal expectations. As informants explained, Datvolgas was known as a company with multiple cultures that were often contradictory:

> most people *(organisational members)* usually like to work in silos . . . they are not time conscious, people just don't care. They just do things anyhow. People don't listen. These lack of sense of urgency. Managers exhibiting this command and control kind of behaviour. They just want to be lord. They don't want to even collaborate and allow other people's ideas flow because 'I am a manager everything has to be like that'. All these things, complacency was found to be what characterised the company, also rumour mongering, a lot of these things.
>
> *(Public Affairs Officer)*

> As I mentioned to you earlier, there were a lot of different rules for different people in the company if you were in *Sueol Base Plant (SBP)*, and a different rule if you were in the head office. There was also 'man know man', if you are allegiant to a manager, you get rewards, and if you are not, you can just be punished. And managers could punish anyhow.
>
> *(Chief Executive Officer)*

> So, where you have divisions that the head is the general manager, and he is from NiG-Energy *(Nigerian Partner Company)*, you seem to have a traditional NiG-Energy way of things. For example, in HR, it is always more of NiG-Energy, so those were the things that affected that the culture being differently and perhaps grew up *(deepen)*. The typical finance staff who is under an NiG-Energy driven finance division seems to behave in that way and think in that way. They are very careful to approve things. They want things to be dotted, papers need to be signed. Somebody in HR which is NiG-Energy headed division. So that is how it was segmented, influenced differently.
>
> *(Assurance Officer)*

> as per the speed, I will attribute it to the international influence *(Foreign Partner Company)*. But NiG-Energy is like a sleep yawning local. It is a Nigerian thing. We do things here. Who knows who, is there *(favouritism)*. Influence is there . . . NiG-Energy, it is said to be free for all. The head man might be my clan man, and then we go on. He may be a Yoruba man to Yoruba man, or Hausa to Hausa man. Most of the time, perhaps throughout the day you may not relate *(communicate)* anything in English. It will be in local language . . . They have their own way of doing things. There is laxity, there is no speed of decision making.
>
> *(Supervisor, Logistics Services)*

There were instances where employees expressed values and behaviours that could be deemed ethical and constructive, such as open communication, trust and excellence. In other instances, some employees were predisposed to conceal information, suspicious of co-workers, and engaged in acts of nepotism, gossiping, bribery and corruption, amongst others. The composition of its workforce was a notable contribution to these differing values and behaviours.

Composition of the workforce

The workforce of Datvolgas is largely determined by senior management personnel of each shareholding firm that constitutes the joint venture. The shareholding firms include three multinational energy companies and a Nigerian oil and gas firm, hereafter referred to as MNC-1, MNC-2, MNC-3 and NiG-Energy respectively. Senior management staff of the distinct firms appoint members to serve as executive board of directors for Datvolgas. The board of directors, as representatives from each shareholding firm, appoint managerial personnel in Datvolgas to govern the affairs of the company. Based on set business policies, NiG-Energy appoints the Deputy Managing Director, Divisional Head of Human Resources and the Finance Executive; MNC-1 appoints the Managing Director and the Divisional Head of Production; and MNC-2 appoints the Divisional Head of the Commercial department. MNC-3 appoints no designated senior executive due to its limited number of shares in Datvolgas. These composed senior managerial personnel appointed by the shareholding firms then select personnel to serve as the Divisional Head for the Shipping department and the Public Affairs unit (see Table 12.1).

Table 12.1 Datvolgas's shareholders and their assigned executive positions for personnel

Shareholding companies	*Senior executive positons*	*Other executive positions*
NiG-Energy	**– Deputy Executive Director** **– Finance Executive** **– Human Resource Executive**	**– Public Affairs Executive**
MNC-1	**– Executive Managing Director/CEO** **– Production Executive**	**– Shipping Executive**
MNC-2	**– Commercial Executive**	
MNC-3	**No assigned executive positions**	

The shareholding firms, in addition to appointing managerial personnel, also assign employees from their company to work on a temporary basis in Datvolgas. Both appointed managerial personnel and low-level employees, termed 'secondees', usually work for a period of four years. The duration of their service can be extended by the shareholding firms based on individual task performance. There are other workers who are employed directly by Datvolgas on a permanent basis and others hired through third-party agents on a temporary basis. Workers employed on a permanent basis are termed direct staff, while those on a temporary basis are contract hires. The contract hires are Nigerian and foreign personnel assigned specific projects to execute on behalf of Datvolgas such as catering, medical, information technology, security and logistics services for all staff, as well as other corporate social responsibility services towards local communities across the nation. A significant difference between the direct staff and contract hires is the level of job security and remuneration package offered. While direct staff employment conditions are stable, with a significant remuneration package commensurate with global industry standard, the employment conditions of contract hires are unstable with low pay, little or no salary increments, delay in payments, poor employee benefit packages and impromptu dismissals.

At the onset of the company, the workforce was mainly expatriates from Europe, America and Asia. However, over the years, the workforce has transformed to mainly Nigerians in adherence to a specific legislation within the Nigerian oil and gas industry: the Nigerian Oil and Gas Industry Content Development Act 2010. This national Act mandates all business operators to give first consideration to the employment of Nigerians in executing services in the industry to increase the participation of Nigerians. However, in order to secure the interests of investors, the Act granted business operators in the industry a concession of maximum 5% of employment positions to be retained for expatriates. In adherence to this legislation, the Datvolgas workforce consists of over 90% of Nigerians, with some working in positions that were previously occupied by foreign nationals. While the workforce was mainly Nigerians, the shareholding firms still influenced its composition with transfer of Nigerian secondees to work in Datvolgas. In addition, demands from leaders within the local communities for Datvolgas to recruit members of the community also influenced the composition of the workforce. In order to satisfy the varied demands of shareholders and local community leaders, Datvolgas engaged in employing and retaining a diverse workforce of both skilled and unskilled workers. These workers initiated differing values and practices in Datvolgas from their parent companies, as well as local communities. The differing values and practices led to rising issues of unethical conduct such as nepotism, tribalism, rumour mongering, bribery and corruption, amongst others.

Contingencies for culture change in Datvolgas: new leadership and institutional demands

Initiatives towards culture change in Datvolgas commenced with the appointment of a new managing director from MNC-1. The new managing director, surprised and disappointed at the unethical practices within the firm, specifically practices of rumour mongering and bribery, initiated a culture change program toward conduct deemed ethical and aligned to the core ITEC values of Datvolgas. It was the opinion of the managing director that the 'reputation and success of the company is built upon a foundation of integrity – a commitment to act within the highest ethical standards and to conduct business honestly and legally' (Company Anti-Bribery and Anti-Corruption Policy, 2012).

In addition, institutional demands within the oil and gas industry, such as regulations towards compliance to anti-bribery and anti-corruption activities, instigated the need for culture change in Datvolgas. National regulations, such as the Independent Corrupt Practices and Other Related Offences Commission (ICPC) Act 2000 and the Economic and Financial Crimes Commission (EFCC) Act 2004, and other international regulations such as the United States Foreign Corrupt Practices Act (FCPA) 1977, the United Kingdom Bribery Act 2010 and the Organisation for Economic Co-operation and Development (OECD) convention on combating bribery and corruption in international business transactions, were key factors that influenced culture change within Datvolgas. The reputational risks of non-compliance with these regulations, such as poor quality of service, loss of revenue, customer attrition and damages to the reputation of the firm, were significant aspects considered by the managing director as rationale towards initiating a culture change program. Cases of unethical conduct which led to bankruptcy and closure of firms such as the Enron Corporation in the US, and Nigeria's Sunray Newspapers, Oceanic Bank and the National Fertilizer Company of Nigeria (NAFCON) were exemplary pointers used to indicate the implications of unethical conduct. For this core reason, the decision to change the existing culture of Datvolgas to also align with institutional demands was instigated.

Culture change efforts in Datvolgas

The managing director, in collaboration with senior management personnel and external management consulting firms, designed a culture change program to be effected within three phases over a three-year period (2012–2015) to include alignment, movement and embedding periods. Within the alignment phase, changes were focussed on aligning members' behaviours and practices with the core values of integrity, teamwork, excellence and caring (ITEC). Managerial personnel, in the initial period of the alignment, set up a culture change team (CCT) to identify desirable behaviours and practices to demonstrate the ITEC values. The expected values and behaviours are indicated in the following tables, with Table 12.2 illustrating the four core values and expected 10 behaviours, and Table 12.3 indicating the identified and proposed behaviours as against undesirable behaviours amongst organisational members.

Members of the CCT, on completion of the identification of desirable behaviours, commenced the introduction of massive culture change awareness programs, practices and display of symbolic objects in 2012. The culture change awareness programs include the establishment of a culture school to educate all members of the expected behaviours to express the ITEC values; an integrity club to promote a culture of transparency and honesty in all business relations; a senior management commitment retreat to ensure managers accept and remain loyal to the espoused culture; and an annual ITEC week to reinforce the espoused values and behaviours amongst all organisational members. Initiated practices include a real-time meeting feedback (RTMF)

Table 12.2 Espoused ITEC values and 10 behaviours of Datvolgas

Four values	*10 behaviours*
I-Integrity	Being fact-based
	Role modelling
T-Teamwork	Continuous improvement
	Effective/speed of decision making
	Creating a sense of urgency
E-Excellence	Listening
	Selflessness
C-Caring	Promoting collaboration
	Empowering to deliver
	Open communication

Source: Chika-James (2016)

Table 12.3 Datvolgas-identified undesirable behaviours vs proposed behaviours

Reality of identified issues	*Desired future state*
Silo mentality Lack of selflessness	Integration, collaboration and company first
Distrust and communication gap Rumours	Effective communication and trust Transparency
No sense of urgency Excessive bureaucracy Complacency	Robust performance management Motivated staff/role modelling
Command and control	Empowerment and accountability

assessment report on the behaviours of managers during official meetings; a culture moment for members to briefly discuss exemplary experiences in line with the espoused value and behaviour; and an anonymous ideas board and whistle-blowing hotline to comment, question or report any issue with regards to the culture change program, amongst others. The display of symbolic objects includes annual company magazines, a culture change website, digital signage, banners, company t-shirts and mouse pads indicating the ITEC values and expected behaviours. These activities and objects were intended to influence organisational members to align with the espoused culture.

In addition to the culture awareness activities, changes within the strategy of the organisation were incorporated concurrently in this alignment phase of the culture change program. Changes in the strategy were mainly related to policies and procedures to facilitate the acceptance and internalisation of ITEC values. Several policies were introduced, with reward and disciplinary procedures for members' compliance. However, three main policies and procedures were fundamental to the success of the culture change program. Foremost is the gift policy set up to aid organisational members who demonstrate the core integrity value and comply with industry regulations against bribery and corruption. The gift policy placed a cap of a hundred dollars (approximately 10,000 naira) on the financial worth of gifts organisational members are expected to give and receive. This includes both pecuniary and non-pecuniary gifts. As part of the policy and procedure, organisational members were expected to disclose and seek approval for gifts that exceeded the stipulated amount. It was also expected that members report occasions where there was a breach of the gift policy. Failure to comply with this policy, or intentions to conceal the violation of it, would lead to criminal proceedings and termination of employment. In line with this policy, several gift-giving and receiving initiatives were abolished, including gifts of hampers, alcoholic drinks and live animals to local community members and other government agencies.

The next strategic policy introduced by the CCT members was the public disclosure policy. The public disclosure policy, in line with the integrity value, was set to ensure information disclosed about Datvolgas was truthful and based on facts. Employees were expected to shun acts of rumour mongering or disclosing half-truths to organisational members and other external stakeholders. Failure to adhere to this policy was deemed an offence that resulted in the prosecution, suspension and payment of fines of defaulters. The third main policy introduced in attempt to sustain the value of excellence is the people and safety policy. The people and safety policy was established to provide fair treatment of all employees and support their wellbeing. It prohibits acts of discrimination based on ethnic origin and nationality, gender, religion, sexual orientations, marital status and disability. In adherence to this policy, it was expected that decisions about hiring, training, compensation, promotion and disciplining of organisational members be based on the qualifications, merit and performance of each worker. A breach of this policy would lead to termination of employment.

The next phase was the movement phase. This phase, which commenced in early 2014, aimed to assess members' conscious demonstration of espoused values, behaviours, initiated practices and policies. Several measures were used in attempt to achieve this purpose. This includes an evaluation of (a) reports on staff attendance at the culture school and participation during the annual ITEC week; (b) RTMF report on the daily behaviours of senior management personnel and line supervisors during official meetings; (c) focus groups and private reports from the consulting firm indicating organisational members' general assessment of the behaviours of managers; (d) 10-behaviour checklist of employees working in the logistics and information technology units; and (e) reports on success stories from members who demonstrated the espoused culture, and disciplinary measures on defaulters.

Towards the end of 2014, the senior management team, CCT members and officers from the consulting firms collated and evaluated the reports. Reports from the culture school and annual ITEC week indicated 90% and 35% of staff attendance, respectively. Based on the published RTMF report, 60–75% of managerial personnel complied with the expected 10 behaviours during official meetings. However, reports from the focus group sessions and private conversations with personnel from the consulting firm indicated that only 50% of managers demonstrated the expected behaviours outside official meetings. In assessing the behaviour of workers from the logistics and information technology unit, the reports indicated that 70% demonstrated the expected 10 behaviours; and upon analysing the success stories discussed, the report showed that 60% of the stories were published. Based on the statistical reports of the joint team members, it would appear that the culture change program in Datvolgas was taking a turn in the right direction. Even discussions amongst managerial personnel indicated that reasonable progress was achieved with the high turnout of staff in the culture school and workers' demonstration of the expected behaviours. On this basis, it was the decision of the managing director and senior management team to continue with the culture change initiative in the embedding phase as planned.

The embedding phase commenced in 2015 with a focus on reinforcing the need for culture change, as well as continuing with set policies, procedures and various routine activities. To this end, the managing director, amongst other official reports, sent daily emails to highlight the significance of the culture change program and its achievements. In addition, there were daily reports on RTMF; attendance in mop-up sessions in the culture school; continuation of the

ITEC week; the participation of senior management staff in management retreats where they pledged allegiance to the espoused culture; members' constructive comments sent to the ideas board; and continuation of the integrity club. Interestingly, further analysis indicated that there were also incidences and reports of embezzlement of funds by senior management staff; increases in acts of whistle-blowing; gift-giving over the expected limit; and dismissal of staff based on dishonest acts as well as the tolerance of defaulters based on business considerations. Attempts towards culture change in Datvolgas in the embedding phase were a combination of actual and surface demonstration of expected behaviours; outright resistance of initiated culture change policies and activities; and inconsistencies in the actions of managerial staff towards upholding the espoused culture.

Assessing effects of culture change initiatives

A detailed analysis of the strategic approach towards culture change in Datvolgas provides interesting insights into the knowledge of culture change in an African organisational context. These are discussed below.

I) Stimulated subjective awareness of self: There was evidence that the culture change program in Datvolgas activated the self-awareness of organisational members. A small number of employees agreed that the espoused values and initiated behaviours introduced during the two-year alignment phase triggered self-conceptions of their personality. They stated that the culture change program instigated the tendency to consciously exhibit the expected ITEC values and 10 behaviours that were already an innate aspect of their personality. As an informant noted: 'Culture alignment has made me understand that there are some desirable behaviours that I have and I've been displaying. But I have been doing it based on the fact that I am just behaving. I didn't know that these are actually virtues because we often call it common sense. But it is not common sense'. The reports from informants indicated that the culture change initiative triggered the decision to 'deepen and develop in the operation of these values'. In addition, they affirmed that it offered directions on how to express the espoused values and behaviours.

II) Fostered new communication terminology: The culture change program in Datvolgas also influenced an assertive style of communication amongst organisational members, fondly known as 'walk the talk slangs'. This style of communication was noted as an unintended consequence of the culture change effort, and within the first few years of the culture change program developed into an unconscious practice amongst workers. Organisational members would easily, clearly and tactically express their opinions and feelings on several issues by highlighting the expected behaviours in line with their needs. For instance, organisational members were apt to use the phrases 'Sir, this is not collaboration', 'Can you give me some more time? I want to ensure my report is fact-based' and 'Is your manager walking the talk? There should be a sense of urgency to this matter', amongst others, while communicating. For employees, this was an easy and approachable way to communicate without being perceived as disrespectful, especially to managerial personnel. Managers acceded to the demands of staff through this new terminology as it was used constructively to elicit favourable response. The use of this communication terminology, via face-to-face contacts, telephone calls and emails, reduced aspects of rumour mongering as organisational members had further clarification of facts in business operations and relations. In addition, it fostered open communication between senior and junior level staff by providing a platform to constructively question the actions and inactions of members.

III) Simulated demonstration of acceptance: Interestingly, while the culture change program instigated actual demonstration of espoused culture, increased communication and reduced rumour mongering, it also led to sham displays of accepting the culture. Discussions with senior management personnel and other low-level workers indicated instances where organisational members displayed superficial acceptance of the espoused culture. For example, informants indicated several occasions where managers had put up good listening skills, demonstrated acts of being approachable, lauded the significance of the culture change program and even signed up as executive members of the integrity club. However, it was noted, as informants explained, that the same managers were inconsistent in upholding the core values and behaviour, sluggish outside official meetings and involved in extra-marital affairs.

A public affairs officer explained inconsistency in demonstrating a sense of urgency:

> But my current manager, who is amongst the team preaching the culture journey, if you send him an email, this is without prejudice . . . you have to do him a reminder, one or two times, even three. So where is that sense of urgency? So, these are the things, personal idiosyncrasies play out everywhere . . . And in every forum, I have had wider or close circuit, I say leaders should lead us by example.

An engineering officer explains the issue of extra-marital affairs amongst executive personnel of the integrity club:

> But what a lot of people do not understand is that, for a lot of us integrity should be holistic point . . . When the integrity club was formed, the orientation people were given was that it is all about company integrity matter. Examples were given about company issues. But a lot of us were, personally, I felt that is not the way I want to think of it. Because I will see you just sneak out now, you are going for a training course and you are going with a girlfriend, meanwhile I know that you are married man. And then, you are telling me you are the head of integrity club. So, what is the sense? . . . There are so many things people do which you just know that they don't possess that integrity, so what is the point?

A lead engineering officer also commented on senior personnel, who were reputed to be committed to the organisation, involved in fraudulent acts:

> Our cooperative, messed up here and there by people in responsible positions. The same way, the same people who are messing up are also holding responsible positions in various divisions. So, if they can mess up our cooperative, embezzle money and make it useless, imagine what they are doing in the system which the system is not aware . . . These people have duped the cooperation and a lot of things are not working fine. People have abused it . . . But what I am trying to say is that, if you look at that, what we are seeing there, the same people, they are within the system, and they are seen as holy and moving high fliers.

For other low-level employees, there was wide evidence of feigned demonstration of being involved in the culture change program by attending the culture school and ITEC week; yet they remained inattentive to the details of the culture change programs. As a contract supervisor stated: 'Sometimes one is not even interested . . . I sit down there, pretend I am listening but I am not listening'. Other low-level contract hires merely attended the culture school to be seen and noted as imbibing the espoused culture. As a public affairs officer explained:

> A lot of people are doing some of these things just to tick the box. Even the activities that we do around the culture alignment journey, people just do it to tick the box and all that . . . just to say we've done this one.

It was reported that some employees breached the company policy on gift-giving by giving gifts that exceeded the stipulated amount and concealed these acts, and others tacitly supported members to do the same, while some were involved in several unethical acts like telling half-truths, embezzlement of company funds and sabotage. For instance, there were reports of contract drivers involved in stealing parts of company vehicles, including tyres, radiators and compressors. As a contract supervisor recounted: 'They drive the vehicle to the mechanic workshop, open and dismantle the engine, take out the compressor, radiator and bring back a mutilated engine. The next time you ask them, they will say, Sir the vehicle is faulty. I cannot work with it. I will need a replacement'.

It was noted that organisational members' simulating acts of accepting the espoused culture was basically to sustain job positions and enhance their career prospects via promotion. As a staff member explained: 'as long as we don't want to lose the job, until we are able to get another job, we keep what we have . . . getting out is difficult because opportunities are not much out there. There are so many graduates out there still looking for a job'. Their varied acts of resistance were also due to differing value orientations; misconstruction and disinterests in the culture change initiatives; perceived disunity amongst staff due to different conditions of employment; and pressures from external local community members to conform to cultural expectations of the society rather than the espoused culture of Datvolgas. For instance, on the disinterests in the culture change initiatives, contract hires attribute this to loyalty to their contracting firm:

> to be honest, if I tell you I know anything about culture alignment, I am joking because I really don't follow through because I am not a direct staff. So, most of those things they do, I usually don't get myself into it because if I do, that will be really mad for me. It will be madness; my head can't be there because I have a company I report to. So, it is actually my company's culture that I will be throwing myself to. Basically, the business we do here, is how to render services that will effectively cut cost for this people. The culture alignment is their own personal thing. Ours is really more business relationship. So, lot of this their activities bla, bla, bla . . . And basically, we have two managements we report to, and sometimes we have to strike a balance. So, for me, my own company would get like a 90%.
>
> *(Contract Supervisor, Logistics Service)*

A contract supervisor explains resistance issues related to different conditions of employment:

> When it comes to caring, apologies. They don't care how we feel . . . we have to pay our medical bills ourselves. That's a minus. You see what that means. Then we have to have the stress of thinking how to manage that salary that has changed from a very bad situation . . . like I said the caring is for their own staff. We are seen not to be their staff, so they don't care . . . What we go through is not their business . . . we are not part of the system, so why do anything? It doesn't help me. They are only shaking me up to give all the services and I get nothing in return. That's fraud. I am an intelligent human being, I can decide to just be there [culture training school] and I am not there. A lot of grudges.

In similar vein, an engineering lead contract officer, recounted challenges in imbibing the culture as result of different employment conditions:

> for the sake of argument, you are doing exactly the same job, but you are not getting the same compensation. So, it creates in you some resistance to something. So, it's there. You can't run away from that . . . I know that January to February is when these guys [direct hire] are smiling from here to there, when they receive all their allowances and then, in July as well . . . When you are a direct staff, because you feel that you are adequately compensated, and the company smiles on you every time, you work any hours. Now the bad reason for contract staff attitude towards the culture alignment is that the direct staff, as a whole, are not thinking of the contract staff . . . Exactly. I am saying, management is also doing the same, stating: 'after all, it is contract that they are doing'. And it ends there. So, it is that bad. And people have also seen the very negative effects of it . . . There was a contract staff that worked so many years . . . well over 10 years. He had an accident. And they tried to rush him to the hospital, because the best hospital in Sueol is the Datvolgas Residential Area hospital. They needed somebody, a direct staff to sign off his admission to the hospital. The contract staff's immediate supervisor was reluctant to sign, which is the supervisor's nature. And then what happened? The contract staff died. So, most of us are conscious of it, and just say, 'emmm, relax'. So, that does not align any culture to work together for every member of staff.

IV) Increased Fear, Tension and Frustrations: The culture change program in Datvolgas also instigated fear, tension and frustrations amongst some employees. Informants indicated that feelings of fear, worries and anxiety increased as a result of punitive measures towards defaulters, such as outright dismissal of some employees who were found dishonest, the withdrawal of projects from others who embezzled project funds and frequent reports of defaulters through acts of whistle-blowing. The culture change program had a negative effect on the psychological state of some workers. Interestingly the change effects on the mental-state of workers also resulted in a positive organisational outcome. On a positive note, the effects of disciplinary measures on the emotional state of members led to a reduction in receiving gifts from internal organisational members and external stakeholders. It even influenced members to discourage other external stakeholders from offering gifts. For instance, during festive season when it is customary to exchange gifts, a public affairs officer recounted how he discouraged a supplier from presenting gifts to his manager: 'They (suppliers) come and ask me, well this is Christmas oh! We are thinking of buying something for your boss. I just discourage them straight away and say don't even bother because my boss will not take the gifts; and I don't even give them the chance to even buy any'. It was noted that this effect subsequently reduced acts of bribery and corruption in Datvolgas, specifically the act of receiving gifts.

However, on the acts of gift-giving, members experienced a series of challenges from other external stakeholders, specifically officials from government agencies and members of the local communities. The act of giving expensive gifts was a prevailing norm used to facilitate the provision of services offered by government agencies, and also used as a means to sustain favourable relationships with the locals. With the introduction of the gift policy, organisational members were often frustrated by government officials, as these officers withheld offering the needed service to enhance Datvolgas operations. Informants recounted several occasions when customs officers delayed authorisation to clear imported goods resulting in high demurrage charges; government officers deferred the authorisation of car registration documents (stickers), leading to the confiscation of vehicles; and delays from officers at the Nigerian Communication Commission to issue licences to upgrade the internet bandwidth of Datvolgas, amongst others. As an information technology manager recounted on the internet licence:

> We have been on that license issue since this time last year . . . And the only reason we haven't gotten it approved is that . . . if I had personally met the guys as Mr Alejandro, taken them to lunch, offer them some money, I would have gotten the license in one week or at most a month. But we asked what is required for us to get it; make a long list and we provided everything. But we are still knocking on their door since. So, they are taking their time. It has its own disadvantage.

A supervisor of logistics services also indicated the challenges employees experienced when dealing with government officials in securing licence permits:

> I had the privilege of chatting or discussing with the guy who calls himself, the officer in charge. And he said we should pay 200,000-naira cash on this vehicle. And we said on whose account? He said, 'Datvolgas come and pay'. I said, 'Oga [Sir] sorry oh, Datvolgas cannot pay for the fact that it is not legal'. He said, 'Ok, if you cannot, go to Datvolgas and ask them, what can they release for you? Just collect something, just collect and we will give you receipts. Go to them'. So those are the influence that are coming. They don't want to know how you operate. All they know is that you must have those loopholes that enables them to siphon money . . . Things are not moving because you are not able to take, you are not able to give bribes.

This indicates that organisational members had to cope with problematic issues from some government officials. Their forbearance of this challenge was due to the nature of the risks to business operations, and managerial support in bearing the cost of delay in services, excess charges and confiscation of company property. However, in dealing with members from the local communities, the case was different. Members of the local community were also accustomed to the acts of receiving expensive gifts from organisational members. For community members, the act of gift-giving and receiving was a symbol of the communal and peaceful relationship between the community and Datvolgas. Gift-giving was a sign of respect and regard for traditional leaders, acts of care and understanding of community needs, and a significant inducement to facilitate business operations with the locals. Interestingly, most organisational members perceived it as means to avert corporate-community conflicts over the extraction of natural resources from the community. Hence, organisational members' adherence to the gift-giving policy towards the local community was a controversial issue. Members within the local communities were displeased with the new change and, through incessant demands, forced organisational members to concede to give gifts beyond the set limit. In return, some organisational members covertly gave expensive gifts to the locals, falsified and altered organisational funds to give beyond the set limit and tactily encouraged other members to do same. These differing reactions of organisational members were influenced by the risks involved with non-conformance to the expectations of the locals, and poor managerial support towards threats from these same community members. As an engineering lead officer explained:

> Every person (staff) in the pipeline unit know and are familiar with the way these community members behave. It is part of our bid to manage them. If they become aggressive, we talk to them and meet their needs . . . otherwise one day, they will beat us up and nothing happens to them. If they beat us up, nothing happens to them in the field. Datvolgas will not call the police or arrest them. The company will not do that. Are we going to remove our pipelines from there? We can't. We need to still go through them and look at their needs.

On this basis, some organisational members, particularly employees working in public affairs and production units, continued in covert acts of giving gifts beyond the set limit. Few others deliberated and negotiated with management on the gift policy towards local community members, indicating the challenges they encountered in attempts to uphold the espoused culture. In response to this issue, Datvolgas management later introduced the policy of donation towards local community members in 2015. The donation policy allows organisational members to present expensive gifts with no set parameters to local community members during special occasions such as chieftaincy coronations, wedding and burial ceremonies. As part of the procedure, management would have to approve the gifts presented. Then the local media will be invited to record and broadcast the event publicly so such acts of giving would not be misconstrued as offering bribes. The reformation of the gift policy suggests the ability of management to adapt to the constraints of its immediate environment as a result of the tension, risks and economic cost of non-conformance.

Implications of culture change in an African organisational context

The case of Datvolgas highlights empirical contributions towards studies on organisational culture management and managerial implications for business practitioners interested in culture management in an African organisational context. Empirical contributions are derived from findings in the case study analysis and managerial implications are recommendations for managers on planned culture change towards an ethical conduct in organisations.

Empirical contributions

Early studies on organisational culture change noted the feasibility of altering beliefs, values, behaviours and other artefacts in organisations towards specific identified purposes (Silverzweig and Allen, 1976; Deal and Kennedy, 1982; Peters and Waterman, 1982). Culture change efforts are predicated on the view that such deliberate attempts could enhance organisational performance. Subsequent studies have questioned the possibility of changing cultural patterns amongst organisational members on the basis that it is a complex process fraught with difficulties and unintended consequences (Harris and Ogbonna, 2002; Ogbonna and Wilkinson, 2003; Wankhade and Brinkman, 2014). The case of Datvolgas presents a moderate position to both extreme debates, as it illustrates the feasibility of planned culture change and also indicates the difficulties in attempts to change culture in organisations. The following key factors, based on analysis of the case study, have been identified to influence the feasibility of organisational culture change and also highlight the inherent complexities of the process. This includes the contingencies, processes, employment relations and content of the culture change program, as well as wider external stakeholders affected by culture change efforts.

I Contingencies for organisational culture management:

Siehl (1985) and Schein's (2010) studies indicate that change in leadership creates opportune moments for culture change in organisations. The feasibility of culture change becomes apparent with attempts of the new leader to incorporate personal assumptions, values, behaviours and practices amongst members. In addition, several studies (Frost, Moore, Louis, Lundberg, and Martin, 1985; Lundberg, 1985; Siehl, 1985; Ehrhart et al., 2014) indicate that organisational culture change becomes feasible in the event of a crisis situation, such as rising environmental demands. An analysis of the case study indicates that both changes in leadership and institutional demands facilitate organisational culture change. The consolidation and compatibility of both contingencies created an effective force in initiating and implementing a culture change program in Datvolgas. This indicates that leadership values and behaviours that are compatible with valid and acceptable standards of ethical conduct, when applied, constitute a potent force to facilitate culture change amongst organisational members.

II Process of organisational culture management

Interestingly, as the case study shows, both contingencies were effective when change initiatives aligned with the cultural expectations of senior executives and industry regulations were implemented. The process of effecting culture change in organisations is thus a significant aspect that influences the outcome of the culture change effort. A controversial discussion within process issues in organisational culture change is the length of time or duration of effecting the change. While some scholars argue that a longer duration of time that may extend into years could facilitate organisational culture change (Smith, 2003), others contend that the longer the change process, the more possibilities for things to go wrong (Kotter and Heskett, 1992), thus favouring short-term periods. This study indicates that significant aspects such as the series of initiatives and pace of implementation within a specified period of time can influence culture change in organisations. Thus, the study indicates that successful outcomes of culture change efforts are not necessarily tied to the duration of time, either short-term or long-term, but to the actions within the time given. For instance, in Datvolgas case, the alignment phase, with a two-year period of creating awareness through several policies and activities, largely influenced the subconscious minds of some employees to embrace the espoused culture. In essence, while a two-year awareness period in the alignment phase might be considered limited or adequate time, the initiatives introduced and the pace of implementation within the time period were vital aspects of successful outcomes amongst some organisational members.

III Employment relations and organisational culture management

The working conditions of employees has been identified as an influencing factor that could either facilitate or undermine culture change efforts in organisations (Grugulis and Wilkinson, 2002; Ogbonna and Wilkinson, 2003; Louw and Jackson, 2008). This study indicates that differences in working conditions amongst organisational members influenced managerial attempts towards organisational culture change. Differences in job security, remuneration and employee benefits offered to workers contributed a challenge to imbibing the espoused culture amongst contract hires. The resistance towards culture change from contract hires on the basis of unfair treatment illustrates that different working conditions constitute a militating factor to culture change efforts. This is more so when the desired culture aims to achieve a homogenous workforce built on common values and behaviours, yet with differing terms of employment.

IV Content of the organisational culture change program

The content of the espoused organisational culture is a significant aspect in attempts towards culture change in organisations. The content of organisational culture herein refers to both cognitive and symbolic structures (Goodenough, 1957; Smircich, 1983; Nebojsa, 2015). Cognitive structures include basic assumptions, values, beliefs and norms, while symbolic structures, often used to express these cognitive structures, include visible aspects of culture such as behaviours, practices and artefacts. A misalignment in the content of espoused culture could undermine managerial attempts to change organisational culture, as observed in the case of Datvolgas. It was expected that the integrity value as a cognitive structure could be expressed by members through symbolic practices of the gift policy. However, the symbolic practice of the gift policy connotes several meanings and values besides demonstrating the value of integrity. The gift policy represented acts of disrespect, disregard and poor understanding of the needs of local community members, and thus influenced the resistance of the espoused value of integrity amongst some organisational members. Based on this analysis, the complexity of culture change, in an African organisational context, lies in aligning cognitive and symbolic structures of management personnel, other organisational members and the local community members to reduce multiple meanings and interpretations. This might prove quite challenging to accomplish, but it presents a viable means to promote culture change programs.

V Effects of key external stakeholders

It is important to consider the influence from wider external stakeholders of the organisation. Previous studies have lauded the importance of understanding external adaptation in organisational culture studies (Ogbonna and Harris, 2014; Schein et al., 2015) but very few have analysed the implications of external stakeholders in culture change. This study indicates that key external stakeholders constitute a significant factor in culture change efforts. The influence of key external stakeholders becomes apparent when these stakeholders are affected by the culture change program. The gift policy in Datvolgas is a case in point that affected the corporate-community relationship with local community members. The gift policy, in demonstrating the value of integrity, abolished giving of expensive gifts to all stakeholders. This contradicted a cultural tradition amongst community members. It was therefore resisted by some organisational members. The decision to uphold cultural expectations of the society on the basis of its values superseded the rationale for demonstrating organisational practices. It therefore indicates that positive outcomes of organisational culture change within the larger society are linked to external stakeholders' acceptance or tolerance of the culture change effort. The implication of this factor is that an analysis of the cultural expectations of external stakeholders should be incorporated in the process of culture change in organisations.

Highlighting additional factors

The case of Datvolgas also indicates other factors that influence organisational culture change, including managerial support, financial commitments and reward and disciplinary measures. These factors have been discussed extensively in extant research (Deal and Kennedy, 1982; Kotter, 1996; Cameron and Quinn, 2006; Jorritsma and Wilderom, 2012; Gover, Halinski, and Duxbury, 2015). For instance, Jorritsma and Wilderom's (2012) study indicated that managerial support in terms of providing the needed training and communication was a significant factor in facilitating culture change in organisations. Deal and Kennedy's (1982) study also highlighted skill-building, training and communication as significant managerial guidelines in effecting culture change. This study indicates that managerial support through communication and training is essential for culture change within an African organisational context, as managerial personnel were engaged in communicating the need for change and offering the required training. In addition, management personnel also supported and accepted the expressions of new communication terminology amongst the workforce that resulted in some positive outcomes such as open communication and certainty of information shared.

The study also indicates that managerial support through the provision of financial resource to sustain the espoused culture across all stakeholders is necessary. For instance, managerial support of members to uphold the espoused culture while dealing with some Nigerian government agencies illustrates the significance of offering financial support in effecting organisational culture change. While this is a peculiar issue within this case study, it presents a significant aspect worth considering in effecting culture change within national contexts that are characterised by weak or embryonic government institutional structures that fail to support moral practices (see Chika-James, 2016; Kamoche, Chizema, Mellahi, and Newenham-Kahindi, 2012). The issue of financial commitment also extends to other aspects of a culture change program, such as financial commitment towards securing the services of management consulting firms and initiating massive awareness events and activities. Financial commitment is thus a significant factor that helps to initiate and sustain organisational culture change.

Reward and disciplinary measures have also been proposed as factors that could influence culture change in organisations (Silverzweig and Allen, 1976; Smith, 2003; Kerr and Slocum, 2005; Cameron and Quinn, 2006). In the case of Datvolgas, disciplinary measures proved more effective than rewards offered to members. Employees reacted more to disciplinary measures than short-term rewards because the penalties associated with disciplinary actions, such as withdrawal of contract projects or outright dismissals, outweighed the benefits of the rewards offered. However, the disciplinary measures triggered more overt displays of the expected behaviours than deep-rooted acceptance of core values, as some workers continued with sham displays of the espoused culture.

In analysing these culture change initiatives in Datvolgas with the analysis of culture change discussed in Smith (2003) and Kerr and Slocum's (2005) study, it is deduced that positive outcomes such as overt display of expected behaviours were more associated with disciplinary measures than rewards. Also, in view of the prerequisites for culture change in Kotter's (1996, 2012) eight-step model, it was observed that managerial personnel established a sense of urgency through the institutional demands for culture change. They also formed a guiding coalition, the culture change team (CCT); created expected values and behaviour towards the set vision; and communicated the change vision. In addition, they celebrated short-term wins and made attempts to institutionalise new approaches. However, the CCT members did not take into consideration the specific needs of all organisational members and the context of their local environment in the process of initiating changes to the culture. The implication is that an evaluation of these situational factors is significant in attempts towards culture change in an African organisational context, and while some factors may be similar and relevant within Western organisational contexts, few aspects may differ.

Managerial implications

The preceding findings suggest two key implications for managing culture change efforts in an African context:

1 Realities of culture change efforts: Attempts towards culture change in organisations begin with a recognition of a need for change, and designing change programs that will address such needs and initiate implementation of such plans (Silverzweig and Allen, 1976; Schein, 2010). While a deliberate design may guide actions towards the desired culture, it is pertinent to note that it does not always guarantee successful outcomes in each phase. Several factors influence the process of effecting culture change such that plans (policies) could be altered and adjusted to suit unforeseen circumstances. Thus, initial plans should be flexible enough to adapt to unexpected situations that may alter previous designs. The modification of plans is often time-consuming, and requires some expertise in the negotiation of meanings. It therefore requires culture change agents to be persistent, determined and flexible in attempts towards altering beliefs, values and behaviours of organisational members.

In addition, it should be noted that deliberate attempts to alter beliefs and values is often complicated. As the case of Datvolgas illustrates, while there was evidence of acceptance and demonstration of espoused values, it appears there were more overt behaviours without in-depth assimilation of expected values. It is unclear if actual expressions of beliefs or values were directly associated with the culture change efforts, or as a result of individuals' favourable dispositions towards the espoused values. The implication of this analysis is that planned culture change can alter observable artefacts such as behaviours of organisational members. Underlying assumptions, beliefs and values of organisational members could be easily influenced towards positive outcomes when individual personalities are compatible with espoused culture. Attempts to identify and select employees with compatible personalities would prove challenging, thus managers should, at best, focus on changing visible artefacts of organisational culture.

II Understanding organisational context: An understanding of the environment in which a firm is embedded is significant for its success in terms of production and distribution of services. It is equally significant to understand the unique environment of the organisation before commencing any culture change programme that would affect operations within that environment. In this case, it is vital to assess the needs of both internal and external stakeholders, while constructing desired culture to limit any form of resistance that may arise. For instance, equitable employment practices for internal stakeholders (employees) should be considered prior to commencing a culture change program aimed at attaining homogeneity of values and behaviours. Employees should be given fair treatment in regard to policies and practices associated with job security, compensation and employee benefits. Managerial executives should also engage key external stakeholders in ongoing negotiations over meanings, values, policies and

Table 12.4 Datvolgas culture change: Who and what matters?

Who matters	*What matters*
Managerial personnel: This includes senior executive members as well as other middle-level managers. Culture change initiatives require adequate support from managerial personnel in terms of demonstrating expected values in all aspects of business operations. This would require a consensus on every change initiative.	**Understanding organisational culture change:** An understanding of the concept of organisational culture and attempts towards altering existing culture in organisations would provide information on the aspects of culture that could be managed, observed and evaluated. Thus, enabling business practitioners to focus more on visible artefacts as changes in the underlying assumptions of individuals might be challenging to evaluate.
Organisational members: All organisational members who would be affected by the culture change initiatives, including permanent and temporary hires, as well as others who directly relate with external stakeholders such as public affairs officers.	**Communication and training:** Creating awareness of the significance of culture change and providing the needed training for organizational members will guide employees on expected behaviours to express. This includes new intakes from the society and other stakeholder groups.

(*Continued*)

Table 12.4 (Continued)

Who matters	*What matters*
Related government agencies and local community members: Emphasis should extend to both key stakeholders in government agencies and local communities to inform them of change efforts that would impact business relationship and also consider their expectations, ideas, and expressions of meanings relevant to the espoused culture.	**Financial commitment:** Any attempt to change culture in organisations requires financial investment. The extent of monetary commitment involved would depend on the size of the company and the content of culture change initiatives introduced.

practices in attempts to reduce rising issues and tensions from these stakeholders. Additional factors to consider in this process are the time and financial commitments needed to create reasonable and acceptable practice amongst all stakeholders. Table 12.4 illustrates a summary of significant factors in effecting culture change in an African organisational context.

Conclusion

Based on a case study of a leading oil and gas firm in Nigeria, this chapter has uncovered some prerequisites for culture change management in an African organisational context. This includes an understanding of the organisational context in which proposed culture change would be implemented, and taking into consideration the varied interests of workers and conditions of employment. In addition, it is important that the interests and expectations of key external stakeholders are considered, as a culture change initiative that deviates from the meanings, actions and expectations of key external stakeholders, especially when there are strong ties between the organisation and these groups, could negatively impact the culture change program. It is hoped that the implications of the findings of the case study reported in this chapter will provide an actionable knowledge base which the management of Africa-based organisations can leverage to effectively manage culture change initiatives as a way to adapt to the competitive pressures unleashed by globalisation.

References

Alvesson, M. (1993) *Cultural Perspectives on Organizations*. Cambridge: Cambridge University Press.

Alvesson, M. (2011) Organizaional culture: Meaning, discourse and identity. In N. M. Ashkanasy, C. P. Wilderom and M. F. Peterson (Eds.), *The Handbook of Organizational Culture and Climate*, 2nd ed. Thousand Oaks, CA: Sage Publications Inc., 11–28.

Armenakis, A., Brown, S., and Mehta, A. (2011) Organizational culture: Assessment and transformation. *Journal of Change Management*, 11(3): 305–328.

Awasthy, R., Chandrasekaran, V., and Gupta, R. K. (2011) Top-down change in a public sector bank: Lessons from employees' lived-in experiences. *Journal of Indian Business Research*, 3(1): 43–62.

Barratt-Pugh, L., and Bahn, S. (2015) HR strategy during culture change: Building change agency. *Journal of Management and Organization*, 21(6): 741–754.

Cameron, K. S., and Quinn, R. E. (2006) *Diagnosing and Changing Organizational Culture: Based on the Competing Values Framework*, revised ed. San Francisco, CA: Jossey Bass.

Chika-James, T. A. (2016) *Implications of Organisation-Host Community Relationship on Organisational Culture Management: The Case of a Nigerian Oil and Gas Company*. Unpublished PhD thesis. Cardiff Business School, Cardiff University

Company Anti-Bribery and Anti-Corruption Policy (2012). Anti-Bribery and Corruption (ABC) Policy. Lagos, Nigeria.
Company Annual Report (2010) Facts and Figures: Our People. Lagos, Nigeria.
Deal, T., and Kennedy, A. (1982) *Corporate Cultures: The Rites and Rituals of Corporate Life*. Reading, MA: Addison-Wesley.
Denison, D. R., and Mishra, A. K. (1995) Toward a theory of organizational culture and effectiveness. *Organization Science*, 6 (2): 204–223.
Department of Health. (2015) *Culture Change in the NHS: Applying the Lessons of the Francis Inquiries*. London: Willams Lea Group.
Dickson, M. W., Kwantes, C. T., and Magomaeva, A. B. (2014) Societal and organizational culture: connections and a future agenda. In B. Schneider and K. M. Barbera (Eds.), *The Oxford Handbook of Organizational Climate and Culture*. Oxford Handbooks Online 10.1093/oxfordhb/9780199860715.001.0001
DiDonato, T., and Noelle, G. (2015) *Changing an Organization's Culture, Without Resistance or Blame*. Retrieved March 8, 2017 from https://hbr.org/2015/07/changing-an-organizations-culture-without-resistance-or-blame#comment-section
Ehrhart, M. G., Schneider, B., and Macey, W. H. (2014) *Organizational Climate and Culture: An Introduction to Theory, Research, and Practice*. East Sussex: Routledge.
Flamholtz, E. G., and Randle, Y. (2014) Implications of organizational life cycles for corporate culture and climate. In B. Schneider and K. M. Barbera (Eds.), *The Oxford Handbook of Organizational Climate and Culture*. Thousand Oaks, CA: Sage, 235–256.
Frost, P. J., Moore, L. F., Louis, M. R., Lundberg, C. C., and Martin, J. (1985) *Organizational Culture*. Beverly Hills, CA: Sage Publications Inc.
Geertz, C. (1973) *The Interpretation of Cultures*. New York, NY: Basic Books.
Goodenough, W. H. (1957) Cultural anthropology and linguistics. In P. Garvin (Ed.), *Report of the Seventh Annual Round Table Meetings on Linguistics and Language Study*. Washington, DC: Kraus Reprint.
Gover, L., Halinski, M., and Duxbury, L. (2015) Is it just me? Exploring perceptions of organizational culture change. *British Journal of Management*, 1–16.
Grugulis, I., and Wilkinson, A. (2002) Managing culture at British airways: Hype, hope and reality. *Long Range Planning*, 35(2): 179–194.
Harris, L. C. (2002) Sabotaging market-oriented culture change: An exploration of resistance justifications and approaches. *Journal of Marketing, Theory and Practice*, 10(3): 58–74.
Harris, L. C., and Metallinos, G. (2002) The fact and fantasy of organizational culture management: A case study of Greek food retailing. *Journal of Retailing and Consumer Services*, 9(4): 201–213.
Harris, L. C., and Ogbonna, E. (2002) The unintended consequences of culture interventions: A study of unexpected outcomes. *British Journal of Management*, 13(1): 31–49.
Hartmann, J., and Khademian, A. M. (2010) Culture change refined and revitalized: The road show and guides for pragmatic action. *Public Administration Review*, 70(6): 845–856.
Heracleous, L., and Langham, B. (1996) Strategic change and organizational culture at hay management consultants. *Long Range Planning*, 29(4): 485–494.
Hofstede, G. (1998) Attitudes, values and organizational culture: Disentangling the concepts organization studies. *Organization Studies*, 19(3): 477–492.
Hofstede, G. (2001) *Culture's Consequences: Comparing Values, Behaviors, Institutions, and Organizations Across Nations*, 2nd ed. Thouisand Oaks, CA: Sage Publications.
House, R. J., Hanges, P. J., Javidan, M., Dorfman, P. W., and Gupta, V. (2004) *Culture, Leadership and Organizations: The GLOBE Study of 62 Societies*. Thouisand Oaks, CA: Sage Publications Inc.
Institute of Medicine. (1999) *To Err Is Human: Building a Safer Health System*. Washington, DC: National Academy Press.
Jorritsma, P. Y., and Wilderom, C. (2012) Failed culture change aimed at more service provision: A test of three agentic factors. *Journal of Organizational Change Management*, 25(3): 364–391.
Kamoche, K., Chizema, A., Mellahi, K., and Newenham-Kahindi, A. (2012) New directions in the management of human resources in Africa. *The International Journal of Human Resource Management*, 23(14): 2825–2834.
Katzenbach, J., Steffen, I., and Kronley, C. (2012) Cultural change that sticks: Starts with what's already working. *Harvard Business Review*, August: 110–117.
Kavanagh, M. H., and Ashkanasy, N. M. (2006) The impact of leadership and change management strategy on organizational culture and individual acceptance of change during a merger. *British Journal of Management*, 17(S1): S81–S103.

Kerr, J., and Slocum, J. W. (2005) Managing corporate culture through reward systems. *Academy of Management Executive*, 19(4): 130–138.
Kotter, J. P. (1996) *Leading Change*. Boston, MA: Harvard Business School Press.
Kotter, J. P. (2012) How the most innovative companies capitalize on today's rapid-fire strategic challenges- and still make their numbers. *Harvard Business Review*, 90(11): 43–58.
Kotter, J. P., and Heskett, J. L. (1992) *Corporate Culture and Performance*. New York, NY: Free Press.
Krisher, T. (2012) *GM CEO Says Old Culture Still Hinders Change*. Retrieved May 2015, 15 from http://phys.org/news/2012-08-gm-ceo-culture-hinders.htm
Lewin, K. (1947) Group decision and social change. In T. N. Newcomb and E. L. Hartley (Eds.), *Readings in Social Psychology*. New York, NY: Holt, Rinehart and Winston, 459–473.
Louw, L., and Jackson, T. (2008) Managing culture and change in South African organisations: The way forward for sub-Saharan Africa? Pre-refereed version. *Journal of Development Studies*, 38(1): 29–42.
Lundberg, C. C. (1985) On the feasibility of cultural intervention in organizations. In P. J. Frost, L. F. Moore, M. R. Louis, C. C. Lundberg and J. Martin (Eds.), *Organizational Culture* (pp. 169–185). London: Sage Publications, Inc.
Marks, M. L., and Mirvis, P. H. (2011) A framework for the human resources role in managing culture in mergers and acquisitions. *Human Resource Management Journal*, 50(6): 859–877.
Martin, J., Feldman, M. S., Hatch, M. J., and Sitkin, S. B. (1983) The uniqueness paradox in organizational stories. *Administrative Science Quarterly*, 28(3): 438–453.
Nebojša, J. (2015) *The hybrid approach in the research of organizational culture*. In ECRM2015-Proceedings of the 14th European Conference on Research Methods 2015: ECRM 2015 (p. 314). Academic Conferences Limited.
Ogbonna, E. (1993) Managing organisational culture: Fantasy or reality? *Human Resource Management Journal*, 3(2): 42–54.
Ogbonna, E., and Harris, L. C. (2002) Managing organisational culture : Insights from the hospitality industry. *Human Resource Management Journal*, 12(1): 33–53.
Ogbonna, E., and Harris, L. C. (2014) Organisational cultural perpetuation: A case study of an English premier league football club. *British Journal of Management*, 25: 667–686.
Ogbonna, E., and Wilkinson, B. (2003) The false promise of organizational culture change: A case study of middle managers in grocery retailing. *Journal of Management Studies*, 40(5): 1151–1178.
O'Reilly, C. A., and Chatman, J. A. (1996) Culture as social control: Corporations, cults, and commitment. In B. M. Staw and L. L. Cummings (Eds.), *Research in Organizational Behaviour*. Greenwich, CT: JAI Press, 157–200.
Peters, T. J., and Waterman, R. H. (1982) *In Search of Excellence: Lessons From America's Best-run Companies*. New York: Harper and Row.
Rossi, I., and O'Higgins, E. (1980) The development of theories of culture. In I. Rossi (Ed.), *People in Culture: A Survey of Cultural Anthropology*. New York, NY: Praeger, 31–78.
Schein, E. H. (1985) *Organizational Culture and Leadership*. San Francisco, CA: Jossey-Bass.
Schein, E. H. (1990) Organizational culture. *American Psychological Association*, 45(2): 109–119.
Schein, E. H. (1991) What is culture? In P. J. Frost, L. F. Moore, M. R. Louis, C. C. Lundberg and J. Martin (Eds.), *Reframing Organizational Culture* (pp. 243–253). Newbury Park, California: Sage Publications, 243–253.
Schein, E. H. (2010) *Organizational Culture and Leadership*, 4th ed. San Francisco, CA: Jossey Bass Ltd.
Schein, E. H., Costas, J., Kunda, G., Schultz, M., Connolly, H., Wright, S., Hofstede, G. J., and Wah, D. W. H. (2015) Opinions: All about culture. *Journal of Business Anthropology*, 4(1): 106–150.
Schneider, B., and Barbera, K. M. (2014) *The Oxford Handbook of Organizational Climate and Culture*. Thousand Oaks, CA: Sage.
Siehl, C. (1985) After the founder- an opportunity to manage culture. In P. J. Frost, L. F. Moore, M. R. Louis, C. C. Lundberg and J. Martin (Eds.), *Organizational Culture*. London: Sage Publications, 125–140.
Silverzweig, S., and Allen, R. F. (1976) Changing the corporate culture. *Sloan Management Review*, 17(3): 33–49.
Simons, R. (2012) *The Case Study: Henkel's Culture Shift*. Retrieved May 15, 2015 from www.ft.com/cms/s/0/6a85b182-1128-11e2-a637-00144feabdc0.html#ixzz3aDBgGQcV
Smircich, L. (1983) Concepts of culture and organizational analysis. *Administrative Science Quarterly*, 28(3): 339–358.
Smith, M. E. (2003) Changing an organisation's culture: Correlates of success and failure. *Leadership and Organization Development Journal*, 24(5/6): 249–261.
Spicer, D. P. (2011) Changing culture: A case study of a merger using cognitive mapping. *Journal of Change Management*, 11(2): 245–264.
Wankhade, P., and Brinkman, J. (2014) The negative consequences of culture change management: Evidence from a UK NHS ambulance service. *International Journal of Public Sector Management*, 27(1): 2–25.

13

Enhancing change implementation through virtuous leadership

A philosophical discourse

Santiago Martínez

Introduction

Africa is at a turning point. So is African society. Change shapes society because it changes its citizens. So does leadership. Change always needs leadership. The relationship between both terms is strong. Change as a concept belongs intrinsically to leadership literature, and that behind successful change there is always effective leadership (Kan and Parry, 2004; Voet, Kuipers, and Groeneveld, 2016; Caulfield and Senger, 2017). Indeed, it has even been argued that change is the main task of leaders. At the same time, though, approximately 70% of all change initiatives and actions fail (Burnes and By, 2012). This means that, for change to be successful, it needs proper leadership. Every change process needs the right leadership approach. Therefore, change also affects leadership. Change demands a new way of thinking and a new way of doing things. This occurs especially when there is not only a need for change, but a need for a new kind of change. And this is the case for Africa. This chapter aims at shedding light on why ethical leadership matters in times of change, and its importance in successful organizational and societal change through individual transformation.

The change Africa needs

In order to understand what kind of leadership Africa needs, it is necessary to understand what kind of change it needs. According to Burnes and By (2012), who refer in their research to the previous work of Kurt Lewin, Lippitt, and White (1939) and D. C. Wilson (1992), change can be planned or emergent. Planned change emphasizes the collaborative nature of the change effort, whereas emergent change defends the unpredictability of the process and the changing environments where organizations live. Similarly, Sue Pearlmutter distinguishes also between incremental and transformative change, the first aiming at fixing a problem or making an adjustment, and the second aiming at altering fundamental structures (Pearlmutter, 1998). Finally, Meyer, Brooks, and Goes (1990) distinguish between continuous, or first-order, change, and discontinuous, or second-order, change. First-order change "occurs within a stable system that itself remains unchanged" whereas second-order change "transforms fundamental properties or states of the system" (Meyer et al., 1990: 94). Whether planned, incremental or continuous order, common to all of them is the idea that "first-order change" aims at regular adjustment, whereas "second-order" change aims at a radical breakthrough. The continuum between them could be pictured with the path "adaptation, metamorphosis, evolution, revolution" (Meyer et al., 1990). Revolution, though, is an old-fashioned word that refers mainly to a rupture with the past in search of a better future. Africa does not need more revolutions, since it has had many and they have not brought the expected results. Africa does not need adaptation, nor metamorphosis either. Africa doesn't have to convert into something else. Africa has its own culture and traditions, on which it must live its present and build its future. Africa has its own model and does not have to follow any other pattern coming from outside. In short, Africa does not need change. What Africa needs is transformation. And this transformation must come from within, from its people, its history and its mores. Transformation must respect Africa's idiosyncrasy and values, which Wanasika and his colleagues (Wanasika et al., 2011), following their own research as well as the results from the Global Leadership and Organizational Behavior Effectiveness (GLOBE) project, identify as:

1 A deep recognition for the elderly and for gerontocratic and paternalistic relationships; together with a
2 Strong sense of hierarchy, where people in power keep distance and bestow favours and expect and receive obeisance or deference; supported with
3 The importance of clan or ethnic interests over individual needs, offering a unique perspective on in-group collectivism and reflecting a response to collective need rather than individual performance, mixed with
4 Respect for the dignity of others: the importance of interpersonal and more humane relationships over individual achievements, seen – for example – in tolerance and forgiveness and service for others in a spirit of harmony, resulting in
5 A strong group solidarity (an injury to one is an injury to all); teamwork (none of us is greater than all of us); and interdependence (each one of us needs all of us), what can be called *ubuntu*.

The above-mentioned values offer a good bedrock for the transformation process. But transformation would be empty if there is a lack of mission and vision, if there is a lack of purpose. Transformation requires a specific kind of leadership. Leadership is not value-free, as society is not value-free. And good leadership, as good citizenship, is not based on skills but on grounded moral values. It has been claimed that the deterioration of ethical values in leaders and role models is nowadays an important cause for a deficit in worldwide leadership (Wright and Campbell, 2011). This might be one explanation for the lack of sustainable leadership in Africa. A study carried out by the African Union at the beginning of the century, for example, estimated the cost of corruption in Africa to be roughly $150 billion USD per year. The World Bank estimates that Nigerian leaders have stolen around $300 billion USD in oil revenues during the last 50 years (Chukwudum Oforka, 2015). A more recent survey of 28 countries in sub-Saharan Africa, run by Transparency International during 2015 and 2016, showed that around 75 million people pay a bribe in Africa every year. In important African economies such as Kenya and Nigeria, the corresponding figures represented 37% and 43% of their respective populations. In Liberia it rose to 69% (Transparency International, 2017). Those figures show the level of structural and systemic corruption within African society. Its costs are expensive for Africa. For example, the Report on Illicit Financial Flows, produced by the UN Economic Commission on Africa, shown a yearly loss of $50 billion USD that leaves the continent through illicit financial outflows every year. The importance of that figure increases considering that developed countries donated $27 billion USD to Africa in 2016 (UN Economic Commission on Africa, 2014). The consequences of the above are seen in a survey done in 12 different African countries: when people were asked whether their country's political and senior administrative leaders were ethically credible, nearly 60% of the respondents gave a negative answer. The answer was even more unfavourable when people were asked whether political leaders of their country contributed to any major economic development accomplishment (65%), and it reached almost dramatic figures when the question was whether the president of their particular country promoted human rights, transparency and accountability towards the citizens (75%) (Dibie and Dibie, 2005).

The above-mentioned facts, together with renowned cases of country leaders, other politicians and business people, are just a few of many that illustrate the huge level of corruption that submits Africa to economic poverty and moral misery. Everything calls for a need to rethink African leadership and its purpose. Transformation without purpose would be just a mere transition from one stage into another. Transformation needs a reason, and so does leadership that transforms Africa from corruption into integrity.

Ethical leadership for change and excellence

There are numerous definitions of leadership, as well as many as leadership styles. Traditionally, leadership has been "often represented as the sole influence of an appointed leader, i.e. the manager who is positioned hierarchically above and external to a team with formal authority and outcome responsibility" (Binci, Cerruti, and Braganza, 2016). This vertical relationship between the leader and her followers is grounded in the power of the former over the latter; it easily becomes a mere transactional practice aiming at results, resembling authoritative management focused on tasks, where "followers are motivated by the leaders' promises, praise, and rewards, or they are corrected by negative feedback, reproof, threats, or disciplinary actions" (Ciulla, 2014: 177). Still, nowadays in Africa it is not uncommon to find, in the words of the late Sumantra Ghoshal, "the ruthlessly hard-driving, strictly top-down, command-and-control focused, shareholder-value-obsessed, win-at-any-cost business leader" whose "use of surveillance, monitoring, and authority leads to management's distrust of employees and perception of an increased need for more surveillance and control." Consequently, "for the employees, the use of hierarchical controls signals they are neither trusted nor trustworthy to behave appropriately without such controls. Surveillance that is perceived as controlling threatens people's personal sense of autonomy and decreases their intrinsic motivation" (Ghoshal, 2005: 84–85).

The above words by Ghoshal are an implicit censure of transactional leadership and management by tasks, whose only objective is efficiency. Still, efficiency as a target has been present in most of the leadership literature of the last decades. A good example is the distinguished work of the emeritus professor of Leadership John P. Kotter, who – through his prolific work on change leadership and consultancy work – has meritoriously helped companies in implementing organization change. His numerous books and articles about, among other topics, the errors most organizations fall into when trying to implement change or about the most appropriate leadership styles for particular situations and environments, have always had organizational efficiency as a target (Kotter, 2015). Like Kotter, most of the literature on change leadership has subordinated leadership to change and these two to efficiency. Franca Ovadje, in her reference to different leadership research in her book "Change Leadership in Developing Countries," implicitly reflects this subordination (Ovadje, 2014).

This traditional view of change leadership is becoming obsolete, though, and it has been argued that modern leadership theories need to "advocate fuller and more integrative focus" in order to cope with the challenges of the 21st century (Connell, 2014: 34). As a consequence, several theories have arisen during the last decades offering new leadership styles such as, for example, transformational leadership, authentic leadership, charismatic leadership, servant leadership and spiritual leadership, just to mention a few. Common to all these approaches is the acceptance that leadership is not based on commands, power and the authority of position, but instead, "leaders are now viewed as individuals who motivate their staff by establishing an emotional link with them through the power of their personality – their charisma" (Burnes and By, 2012: 241). At the same time, they all share the belief that leadership is not a technique. To a greater or lesser extent, they all share some positive moral perspective and values, positive modelling to followers, a certain degree of self-awareness and self-regulation and vision.

Recently there has appeared an approach to leadership that, while embracing all the new leadership proposals, crystallizes all the aspects that belong to leadership in one word: excellence. Excellence in organizations can be measured following four criteria, namely the "four Es of excellence": efficiency, effectiveness, ethics and enthusiasm.[1]

Efficiency and effectiveness comprise the technical factor of excellence, and aim at producing results. Though related, they refer to different aspects of excellent performance. Whereas efficiency refers to the capacity of producing results with few resources, effectiveness refers to the success in producing the desired results. The fewer means used, the more efficient an action – or an organization – is, and the closer an action – or an organization – is to its particular objectives, the more effective it is.

Ethics and enthusiasm, on the other hand, comprise the human factor of excellence and aim at respecting the individuals who produce the results. Ethics protect human dignity and foster a life which is worth living, and its aim is happiness. This is why ethics is related to enthusiasm or, for this purpose, the happiness individuals should find at work. Work is an important part of people's life, since they devote approximately 30–40% of their lives to work. Therefore, everyone should be able to find happiness at work and employers should foster enthusiasm at work, not only because a satisfied employee is more likely to be more efficient and effective – this kind of reasoning would instrumentalize people's happiness and subordinate it to effectiveness and efficiency, and that would be unethical – but because everyone deserves it.

Efficiency and effectiveness measure performance and focus on tasks. Ethics and enthusiasm measure relationships and focus on people. All together are the key for excellence. Task-oriented skills are related to organizational structure, goals and objectives. These functions are important not only for achieving organizational goals, but also for developing change initiatives. Person-oriented skills include behaviours that promote collaborative interaction among organization members, establish a supportive social climate, and promote management practices that ensure equitable treatment of organization members. These interpersonal skills are critical to planned organizational change implementation because they enable leaders to motivate and direct followers (Battilana et al., 2010).

Any organization that aims at sustainable and durable excellence, therefore, should aim at these four Es: efficiency, effectiveness, ethics and enthusiasm. Efficiency and effectiveness produce results, whereas ethics and enthusiasm produce stability. These four aspects being important, it seems that during the last decades African leaders have focused too often and too much on the first two elements and, in practice, have disregarded the other two. The result is a blatant moral deficit in social and organizational structures, as well as in many individuals. Thus, there is a need to identify an approach to leadership that, without neglecting efficiency and effectiveness, focuses on the ethical aspect of leadership and respects the humaneness of African values, enhancing the importance of relationships, the priority of the belongingness and the significance of reverence.

For leadership to be durable, it must offer not only technical excellence, but it also has to be ethical, which means that it must advocate for integrity, honesty, respect, and other core ethical values fundamental for the sustainable development of society. It must help citizens to develop those important human qualities and to understand why it is important to live by them. In other words, leadership must help to develop moral character amongst citizens. Moral character is the engine for moral change, and moral change is the ground for authentic transformation. Only then will this transformation – result of the combination of character and professional competence – become the cornerstone for an integrated culture that supports and challenges citizens to strive for excellence (Wright and Campbell, 2011). The former Nigerian Minister of Education, Oby Ezekwesili, summarized these ideas, saying:

> Character is the underlying factor that will define how our nation will make progress. If you want competency or capacity you can buy them, but character is not available to be bought. In this fourth industrial revolution of biotics, stimulations, signs and all kinds of science solution driven, all we need is a disruptive era of the character of the individual. The character of the individual matters most.
>
> *(Nigerian Tribune, 2017)*

This more integrative and holistic focus implies a combination of the latest trends together with a proper understanding of the anthropological roots of human beings, their aims and needs: it means leadership that is not based on transactions, but that creates relationships; that does not aim only at results, but at development; that does not aim at change, but at transformation. It means leadership that does not show only "how" but also "why" – in other words, leadership that has not only vision but also self-awareness and, above all, a deep sense of purpose and mission (Kempster, Jackson, and Conroy, 2011). Such an approach to leadership will be sustainable, and thus will create durable change and transformation.

Ethical leadership for the African context: an introduction to virtuous leadership

Ethical leadership is defined as "the demonstration of normatively appropriate conduct through personal actions and interpersonal relationships and the promotion of such conduct to followers through two-way communication, reinforcement, and decision making" (Brown, Treviño, and Harrison, 2005: 120). Within the array of approaches that can be included under the umbrella of ethical leadership, virtuous leadership offers a novel approach that fosters moral character in managers and people in top positions as well as in the so-called average citizen. It acknowledges the relevance of positive personal traits for the achievement of individual progress and fulfilment. At the same time, it also focuses on those qualities related to the development of society as well (Wright and Campbell, 2011). The final goal is to help citizens to become responsible, caring and contributing members of society. By improving their own and their followers' character, many leaders at various levels have transformed their organizations' culture, improved results, developed educated citizens and increased job satisfaction and retention.

Virtuous leadership seems especially appropriate for the African context, since its principles closely correlate with African values. Being both markedly humanistic and humane, virtuous leadership is based on an optimistic and respectful view of what a human being is. It believes that humans are endowed with intelligence and love and that individuals are communicable, sociable and self-transcending. The human being is open to the infinite as well as to all created beings, especially to all men and women of the world, because only insofar as she understands herself as related to a "you" can she say "I." The individual comes out of herself – from the self-centred preservation of her own life – to enter a relationship of dialogue and communion with others. Openness to transcendence, therefore, is intrinsic to the human person. Leadership is part of that transcendence, since leadership reinforces the sense of mission and purpose in life (Whetstone, 2002).

Virtuous leadership: anthropological background

Virtuous leadership acknowledges that humans are purposeful beings, whose acts have a *telos*, a goal. These purposes give a deep understanding of who the individual is and what she is trying to achieve. One's purposes represent all those things with which the individual has identified herself, all those things that tell the individual who she is. It is through what the individual intends that she becomes one kind of person instead of another. Her intentions not only shape her actions, they also shape herself (Wadell, 2009). Amongst all the different goals in life, some of them are very particular and some others are more general ones. There is one goal that is the most important one, the final *telos* of any individual: namely, the achievement of fullness in life, happiness in other words, whatever is best for her, that can bring a human being to the full and most perfect development of her self (Aquinas, 2007). Considered from this perspective, happiness is a matter of development; it is coming unto fullness through growing in excellence. For the individual to be happy, she has to transform herself by aiming at excellence in what she does, how she does it and why she does it – in other words, excellence in what she is. Happiness is excellence in being good; it is participating in goodness and growing in goodness. Happiness comes through a certain way of life, a virtuous way of life. But that is not easy, and it is not begun at all without the conscious cultivation of moral skills which enable the growth in the splendour of excellence. Such a transformation requires practice, commitment and time. Unless the individual adopts a way of life which nurtures and fashions this development, then not only will she fall short of it, she shall also become someone other than who she is meant to be (Wadell, 2009). She will stagnate in the desert of mediocrity. To end up someone other than who one is meant to be is neither difficult nor rare. This is why leadership seems to be only for a few. But no, leadership is for all. Where management is a task, leadership is a call (Havard, 2007).

This transformation requires the acquisition of habits. Habit is an acquired quality. It is not, however, an automatic reaction nor a response out of one's control. Neither is it an established personal routine, like, for example, the habit of brushing one's teeth before going to bed. Properly speaking, a virtuous habit is a good disposition that "ultimately emerges as a morally significant quality of the mind, a consistency in deliberate activity" (Zagar, 2010: 184). Habit as a "disposition is a vehicle of the will to act freely yet steadfastly. Animals can be 'habituated', only humans are disposed" (Zagar, 2010: 185).

Virtues and moral skill: tasks and relationships

Habits, or dispositions, are acquired by repetition. One act of temperance does not make a temperate person. She becomes temperate by habitually being temperate. As it has been noted earlier, "there is a very strong connection between what one does and who one becomes. Ultimately, the individual becomes what she most consistently does because the quality of her actions passes over into herself" (Wadell, 2009: 113). Good habitual dispositions are called virtues. "Virtues are qualities of the mind, the will, and the heart that instil strength of character and stability of personality" (Havard, 2007: 15). Virtues enlighten the intellect, strengthen the will, and purify the feelings because they help to see the right thing to do (mind), to want it (will) and to love it as good and enjoy the effort to attain it (heart). By doing so, virtues render any action steady, prompt and pleasurable. This process of self-transformation could be described as follows:

- Practice becomes a habit.
- Habit becomes a tendency.
- Tendency becomes an attitude.
- Attitude becomes a way of life.

The process is behind the continuum of personal development:

- Firstly, the individual is not aware of what she does wrongly, therefore she does not try to avoid it;
- Secondly, she becomes aware of what she does wrongly and has to struggle in order not to do it;
- Thirdly, she starts trying to do the right thing and struggles with it;
- Lastly, she does not have to struggle to do the right thing anymore because doing it becomes connatural to her.

It is possible to draw a parallelism between the process of personal development and the one described by Christoph Lueneburger and Daniel Goleman for a change initiative to become sustainable within an organization (Lueneburger and Goleman, 2010):

- Firstly, the organization is unconsciously reactive to change;
- Secondly, it becomes consciously reactive;
- Thirdly, it becomes consciously proactive;
- Eventually, it finally becomes unconsciously proactive.

Bringing the virtuous circle of the individual together with Lueneburger's and Goleman's institutional process for change initiative sustainability creates a set of outcomes that can help leaders to evaluate the transformation process in an organization from the perspective of human relationships. These four outcomes are:

- Engagement
- Involvement
- Commitment
- Loyalty

Virtues not only enhance transformation from the perspective of relationships, but also from the perspective of efficiency and effectiveness. As it has been said before, virtues are qualities

Table 13.1 The virtuous process of individual transformation and organizational change

Individual level	*Organizational level*	*Virtuous circle*	*Result*
The individual is not aware of what she does wrongly, therefore she does not try to avoid it.	The organization is unconsciously reactive to change.	Practice becomes a habit.	Engagement
The individual becomes aware of what she does wrongly and has to struggle in order not to do it.	The organization becomes consciously reactive.	Habit becomes a tendency.	Involvement
The individual starts trying to do the right thing and struggles with it.	The organization becomes consciously proactive.	Tendency becomes an attitude.	Commitment
The individual does not have to struggle to do the right thing because it is connatural to her.	The organization becomes unconsciously proactive.	Attitude becomes a way of life.	Loyalty

which enable an individual to move toward the achievement of the specifically human *telos*. Virtues perfect the human being by perfecting what she does, how she does it and why she does it. Virtues help the individual to aim at what she is really called for and, through the process described above, she will eventually expend less and less effort to do it since virtues become connatural to her, being therefore more efficient and effective.

Virtues and moral will: willingness to change

Humanity's moral decay has been accompanied throughout history by many moral tragedies. One of them occurs when people do not know what is the right thing to do, and this is called moral relativism. Another tragedy occurs when they know what is the right thing to do, but do not want to do it. This is called moral indifference. A third tragedy is when they know what is the right thing to do and, in theory, they abide by it but, in practice, they do not do it. This is moral inconsistency. There still exists a fourth moral tragedy, namely when people know what is the right thing to do and do it, but their heart is not in line with their mind: they feel unhappy doing what they think is right. This is lack of unity of life and the result of, among other things, the divorce between what is considered right and what is considered good.

The prevalence of this tragedy – in all its versions – explains the lack of ethical leadership and the prevalence of moral poverty in many African leaders. It also explains their reluctance to change, and why

> post-independence history has shown that political leaders and senior public administrators have not accepted the task confronting them in respect of transparency and accountability to the citizens. African political leaders seem to engulf with the principles of the vampire states that are characterised to have client status, personalised identity, centralised or overdeveloped morphology, a prebendal or rentier nature and an extractive impulse.
>
> *(Dibie and Dibie, 2005: 2)*

Against it rises virtuous leadership, one of its most attractive features being that doing the right thing – virtuousness – is a synonym of happiness. Virtuous leaders have the freedom of spirit proper to the people who have put their happiness, and not their obligation, into doing the right thing. Against one of the greatest misconceptions of virtue, virtuous leadership affirms that virtue and happiness are not stoic self-righteousness, one that suppresses feelings and emotions as if they were signs of human weakness and as if corporal pleasure would be evil. Corporality – the body, human flesh – is a constituent part of human identity and, therefore, it must be taken on board in the pursuit of happiness. Human excellence cannot be achieved at the expense of the body. Virtuous leadership understands that a comprehensive approach to the human person is the only way to acquire human excellence. Feelings, therefore, constitute an important element in virtuous leadership. Feelings and emotions allow us, for example, to communicate with others, to share with them and to establish communities of sentiment.

Feelings form an essential part of the person, since, as mentioned, human beings are social by nature and they are transcendental. Feelings open the door to transcendence and to communion with others. Virtuous leadership does not separate the individual from the rest of the world. Virtuous leaders are indeed happy, but not sublime. Leaders connect with people; they do not stay in their ivory tower. Leaders can be imitated, not only admired. Besides, since virtuousness becomes a lifestyle, it is connatural to the person. Virtuousness, in a virtuous leader, is authentic, and virtuous leaders, as exponents of ethical leadership, are authentic and genuine. This is why they "connect" with people. Virtuous leaders emphasize this relational phenomenon and develop a dynamic interaction between leader, follower, and context (Avolio and Gardner, 2005). Similarly, followers of virtuous leaders "are more likely to perceive themselves as being in social exchange relationships with their leaders because of the fair and caring treatment they receive and because of the trust they feel. As a result, they should be inclined to go above and beyond the call of duty for these leaders" (Brown and Treviño, 2006: 607). This is possible because leaders must be authentic to avoid the morality issues of pseudotransformational leadership, which is based on self-interest and deception (Bass and Steidlmeier, 1999; Barling, Christie, and Turner, 2008). It has been suggested that if followers consider their leaders authentic, they are more likely to show commitment and optimism towards change (Alavi and Gill, 2017). This is also caused by the fact that ethical leaders are more credible in the eyes of their followers (Sharif and Scandura, 2014).

Understanding virtues and passions – the role of feelings, will and reason – is crucial to understanding another key aspect of virtuous leadership: the difference between temperament and character. Temperament is the combination of mental, physical and emotional traits of a person; it is a natural, innate predisposition. Character, on the other hand, consists of "higher-order desires and values, beliefs, framing capacities, emotions, and enduring patterns of behaviour that have any bearing on moral matters" (Alzola, 2012: 387). Character is shaped by principles and motives that control one's life and behaviour. Temperament is a configuration of inclinations, while character is a configuration of habits. Character is disposition, temperament pre-disposition (Keirsey, 1984). Character is precisely the acknowledged struggle to overcome the challenges and to strengthen the good traits of one's own temperament. Good character is temperament forged by virtue. The individual develops character through the regular practice of sound moral habits. In so doing, "character leaves an indelible imprint on our temperament, which then ceases to dominate our personality" (Havard, 2007: 15).

Leadership can only be character. But if leadership is character, the fruits of good character cannot remain only in oneself and for one's benefit, as the fruits of leadership do not remain in the leader alone. Leadership is transcendental and, therefore, character must have also a transcendental dimension: excellent character must overflow for other people's benefit. From these perspective, character could also be defined as "those interpenetrable and habitual qualities within individuals, and applicable to organizations that both constrain and lead them to desire and pursue personal and societal good" (Wright and Campbell, 2011: 976).

Virtues, awareness and mission: humility and magnanimity

From the perspective of virtuous leadership, this extrinsic dimension of character is translated into two fundamental concepts: awareness and mission. There must be a reason to develop character, and this reason is twofold: one's own happiness (awareness) and the task at hand (mission). In other words, there needs to be consciousness of one's reality, one's origins and one's destiny, on one hand, and acceptance of one's calling in life, on the other. That is to say, the reason for developing character is understanding that one is happier the higher moral character she has, and that one's happiness is not for herself alone.

Behind the concepts of awareness and mission there are two virtues that, combined, account for the genuine originality of the virtuous leadership model: humility and magnanimity.[2] Both concepts are old in time, though new in fashion and rare in daily life. Unfortunately, it is even more uncommon to find both virtues in the same person. This is why virtuous leaders are scarce nowadays, since these two virtues make the bedrock of leadership.

Humility is key for awareness because humility is the truth, as Theresa of Avila wrote (Theresa of Avila, 2007). Truth is a necessary ingredient for genuine awareness. Humility makes it possible for the person to see one's reality as it is and accept it. This also explains why virtuous leaders are genuine and authentic. It is not only because virtues are neither artificial nor artificious to them, but because virtuous leaders accept what they are and how they are. Thomas Aquinas writes that humility means "that one keeps himself within his own limits; he does not stretch himself to what is above him" (Aquinas, 2015). This acceptance of one's reality implies also the recognition of one's gifts and abilities. Otherwise, excellence in character – leadership – couldn't be achieved. This is an important revision of humility and one of the keys to understanding the relationship of humility with leadership: humility is needed to see the truth about one's origin, one's potential and one's destiny and, therefore, to see one's mission in life. The recognition of one's origin helps one to understand that many gifts are given and, therefore, there is a reason to be grateful and to feel an everlasting sense of debt. This sense of gratefulness and of "having been granted a credit" is one of the reasons to be willing to further develop those gifts, to develop one's potential. Understanding one's destiny enlightens one to see one's mission.

If virtuous leadership reinvents humility, it also rediscovers another virtue that – opposite to what many may think at first sight – supports humility at the same time as it needs it: magnanimity. Magnanimity is the "the pursuit of great things according to right reason" (Aquinas, 2007, Summa Theologica – Pars II-II – Q. 161). If humility makes it possible to be aware of one's origins, potential and destiny, magnanimity makes it possible to see the greatness of those origins, that potential and that destiny, and to behave in a way consistent with that belief. The base for a magnanimous mission is the awareness of one's dignity and confidence in one's potential. At the same time, where magnanimity is grounded in one's greatness, humility enables the same person to see the greatness of others and in others. This is why humility is also a passion to serve, because a humble person sees both her own dignity as well as the dignity of others. And, again, it is precisely the virtue of magnanimity that moves her to serve others with excellence. A leader is a person who has embraced the mission of serving others in an excellent way and is happy accomplishing that mission.

Humility and magnanimity don't oppose or hinder each other. On the contrary, like other virtues, they dignify each other: without magnanimity, humility could deteriorate into pusillanimity, and without humility, magnanimity could easily become ambition. Often it is said that leaders are ambitious. No, they are not. Ambition is recurrently confounded with determination and with magnanimity. But this is wrong. Magnanimous and ambitious persons aim at great things, but whereas a magnanimous person does it unselfishly and liberally for the sake of the mission at hand, an ambitious person does it for the benefit and glory that those great objectives bring to her. A magnanimous person enjoys the effort to attain the goal, whereas an ambitious person is focused only on the outcome. The liberality of a magnanimous person attracts other people around her. People may follow ambitious leaders freely, but people only follow magnanimous leaders for free. For them, the reward is the accomplishment of the mission that inspires them, as it is for the leader they follow. On the other hand, people who follow an ambitious leader expect a reward for their effort, as the leader is looking for benefit and glory. Magnanimity and ambition aim at doing great things, but only magnanimity aims at doing things great. Humility and pusillanimity remind one of one's nothingness, but only humility reminds of one's uniqueness.

Virtue and transformation before change

The excellence of genuine humility and authentic magnanimity can be seen in the preference for transformation over change. It is easier to find advocates for change than for transformation, because change does not compromise as much as transformation. Change refers to the future and looks at the final result, whereas transformation refers to the present and looks at the process. As C.S. Lewis wrote, "humans live in time, and experience reality successively. To experience much of it, therefore, they must experience many different things; in other words, they must experience change"

(Lewis, 2011: 50). A disordered quest for change, though, may lead to the belief that "unchanged" is synonymous with "stagnant." There is no room for organic development since people think of "the Future as a promised land which favoured heroes attain – not as something which everyone reaches at the rate of sixty minutes an hour, whatever he does, whoever he is" (Lewis, 2011: 51).

Transformation, on the other hand, brings commitment to the present and to the process. It is the answer to what Romano Guardini very discerningly wrote in 1965, and to what can be considered as the ultimate test for leadership: "the only measure for properly evaluating an age is to ask to what extent it fosters the development and attainment of a full and authentically meaningful human existence, in accordance with the peculiar character and the capacities of that age" (Guardini, 1957: 61). It is characteristic to virtuous leaders – humble and magnanimous leaders – to be able to interpret the signs of their times while being faithful to the perennial reality of human nature. In order to succeed in this task, virtuous leaders can follow four ideas that Pope Francis – one of the most genuine virtuous leaders of current times – has pointed out in his exhortation *Evangelii Gaudium*. Leaders, Pope Francis writes, should acknowledge the following principles:

1 **Time is greater than space**. A humble and magnanimous person accepts the constant tension

> between fullness and limitation. Fullness evokes the desire for complete possession, while limitation is a wall set before us. Broadly speaking, "time" has to do with fullness as an expression of the horizon which constantly opens before us, while each individual moment has to do with limitation as an expression of enclosure. (. . .) This principle enables us to work slowly but surely, without being obsessed with immediate results. (. . .) One of the faults which we occasionally observe in socio-political activity is that spaces and power are preferred to time and processes. (. . .) Sometimes I wonder if there are people in today's world who are really concerned about generating processes of people-building, as opposed to obtaining immediate results which yield easy, quick short-term political gains, but do not enhance human fullness.
>
> *(Francis, 2013: 224)*

2 Leaders should also remember that **unity prevails over conflict**. Change may bring conflict, whereas transformation does not. There is a difference between Hitler and Gandhi, Robespierre and Mother Theresa. A leader who aims at transformation keeps unity strong. A humble and magnanimous leader builds communion amid disagreement. This "can only be achieved by those great persons who are willing to go beyond the surface of the conflict and to see others in their deepest dignity". This requires humility. The passion to serve brings a desire for "solidarity, in its deepest and most challenging sense". A virtuous leader acknowledges a principle indispensable to the building of society: "unity is greater than conflict" (Francis, 2013: 228).

3 Leaders should also serve people not ideologies, for **realities are more important than ideas**. This principle

> calls for rejecting the various means of masking reality: angelic forms of purity, dictatorships of relativism, empty rhetoric, objectives more ideal than real, brands of ahistorical fundamentalism, ethical systems bereft of kindness, intellectual discourse bereft of wisdom. . . . Ideas disconnected from realities give rise to ineffectual forms of idealism and nominalism, capable at most of classifying and defining, but certainly not calling to action.
>
> *(Francis, 2013: 232)*

4 Finally, virtuous leaders have to avoid being "overly obsessed with limited and particular questions," because **the whole is greater than the part**. Still, virtuous leaders do not fail to ignore the part of the whole.

> An innate tension also exists between globalization and localization. We need to pay attention to the global so as to avoid narrowness and banality. Yet we also need to look to the local, which keeps our feet on the ground. Together, the two prevent us from falling into one of two extremes. In the first, people get caught up in an abstract, globalized universe, falling into step behind everyone else, admiring the glitter of other people's world, gaping and applauding at all the right times. At the other extreme, they turn into a museum of local folklore, a world apart, doomed to doing the same things over and over, and incapable of being challenged by novelty. (. . .) We constantly have to broaden our horizons and see the greater good which will benefit us all. But this has to be done without evasion or uprooting. We need to sink our roots deeper into the fertile soil and history of our native place.
>
> *(Francis, 2013: 235).*

The interconnection of virtues

Humility, magnanimity, excellence, mission, awareness, service. This is the core of virtuous leadership and what inspires the individual towards transformation. There are also many other positive character traits that could be labelled as virtues. Virtuous leadership underlines four of them, namely: courage or fortitude, temperance or self-control, prudence or practical wisdom and justice. These four virtues are, like humility and magnanimity, interconnected. Where humility and magnanimity form the bedrock of leadership, courage, self-control, prudence and justice form the four pillars for leadership, and bring character to the level of excellence. Self-control, for example, is – contrary to what many may believe – not a limitation but, like magnanimity, greatness of soul. This virtue introduces order and measure into desire, firm and moderate mastery of reason over passions. Its exercise is not reduced to a pure negation, which would be a caricature of this virtue. Self-control makes possible for the individual not to love only what is pleasurable but also what is reasonable – in other words, what is worth being loved. Courage, on its behalf, empowers the individual to overcome what is arduous and achieve what is excellent; it boosts the will so that it can rule over the prevalent tendency towards easiness. When the heart is free from corruption and the will steady to act, prudence can enlighten reason to see objectively, make the correct decisions and put them into action. Justice will show the guidelines to reason so that, reminding the individual of her origins and of other people's dignity, her decisions give everyone her due. Justice will also ignite her heart, faced with the unfairness she sees around her, into magnanimous desires for a better world. Courage, self-control, prudence and justice enhance magnanimity and humility to the level of excellence:

- Without courage, leadership becomes cowardice, finding its recourse in the power of coercive manipulation rather than in the strength of moral authority.
- Without self-control, leadership becomes self-destruction, loving only what is beneficiary and pleasurable and hating what is appropriate and reasonable.
- Without justice, leadership becomes corruption, remembering only its own benefit and forgetting everyone's due.
- Without prudence, leadership becomes arbitrariness, disguising subjective self-interest under the cloak of objective decisions.

- Without humility, leadership becomes an ambitious desire for success instead of becoming a genuine ambition to serve.
- Without magnanimity, leadership becomes a pusillanimous attempt at control instead of becoming an ideal to develop everyone's potential.

Conclusion

Corruption hinders Africa's development for two reasons: firstly, it steals resources that could otherwise be used for the betterment of society and, secondly, it keeps leaders unwilling to change. This latter is an obstacle for sustainable change: corruption causes a lack of positive attitude in leaders towards changing existing structures. Therefore, those who should be change agents become a unfortunate burden upon social and institutional transformation.

This chapter has offered a model of ethical leadership for change based on virtues and character development. Virtuous leadership fosters personal excellence and aims at a stable change in attitude, which is the key for sustainable institutional transformation. Grounded in strong anthropological origins, it advocates for the practice of virtues, or qualities of the mind, will and heart that foster strength of character and stability of personality in leaders. Two of the pioneers of organizational development identified the belief that the needs and aspirations of human beings provide the prime reasons for the existence of institutions as one of the core values of organizational development (French and Bell, 1973). Following the same line of thought, virtuous leadership connects organizational change with personal transformation. Aiming at excellence through efficiency, effectiveness, ethics and enthusiasm, virtuous leadership's novelty lies in its comprehensive approach, taking into account task-oriented skills and person-oriented skills producing excellent outcomes and excellent relationships, with stronger follower commitment and loyalty. Through humility, a virtuous leader is aware of the value of her own dignity and potential, as well as the dignity and potential of others; through magnanimity, a virtuous leader wants her potential to reach the highest level of excellence, which one achieves through the practice of other virtues like courage, prudence, justice and self-control. These and other virtues forge one's temperament into good character, allowing one to identify the realities that must be changed, to decide to change them and to embrace that decision with enthusiasm.

Notes

1 I am indebted to Professor Manuel Guillén, from University of Valencia, who originally developed the theory of three Es of excellence in his book *Ética de las organizaciones. Construyendo confianza.* With his approval, I have expanded it with the fourth "e," enthusiasm.

2 I have had the privilege of lecturing on virtuous leadership on five continents and have witnessed how the model's approach to humility and, especially, magnanimity are, by far, the most enriching discoveries people experience when they first hear about virtuous leadership.

References

Academic articles

Alavi, S. B., and Gill, C. (2017) Leading change authentically. *Journal of Leadership & Organizational Studies*, 24(2): 157–171.

Alzola, M. (2012) The possibility of virtue. *Business Ethics Quarterly*, 22(2): 377–404.

Aquinas, S. T. (2007) *Summa Theologica*. Father of the English Dominican Province (Eds.). New York, NY: Cosimo Classics.

Aquinas, S. T. (2015) *Summa Contra Gentiles*. London: Aeterna Press.

Avolio, B. J., and Gardner, W. L. (2005) Authentic leadership development: Getting to the root of positive forms of leadership. *Leadership Quarterly*, 16(3): 315–338.

Barling, J., Christie, A., and Turner, N. (2008) Pseudo-transformational leadership: Towards the development and test of a model. *Journal of Business Ethics*, 81(4): 851–861.

Bass, B. M., and Steidlmeier, P. (1999) Ethics, character, and authentic transformational leadership behavior. *The Leadership Quarterly*, 10(2): 181–217.

Battilana, J. et al. (2010) Leadership competencies for implementing planned organizational change. *Leadership Quarterly*, 21(3): 422–438.

Binci, D., Cerruti, C., and Braganza, A. (2016) Do vertical and shared leadership need each other in change management? *Leadership & Organization Development Journal*, 37(5): 558–578.

Brown, M. E., and Treviño, L. K. (2006) Ethical leadership: A review and future directions. *Leadership Quarterly*, 17(6): 595–616.

Brown, M. E., Treviño, L. K., and Harrison, D. A. (2005) Ethical leadership: A social learning perspective for construct development and testing. *Organizational Behavior and Human Decision Processes*, 97(2): 117–134.

Burnes, B., and By, R. T. (2012) Leadership and change: The case for greater ethical clarity. *Journal of Business Ethics*, 108(2): 239–252.

Caulfield, J. L., and Senger, A. (2017) Perception is reality: Change leadership and work engagement. *Leadership & Organization Development Journal*, 38(7): 927–945.

Chukwudum Oforka, V. (2015) *The Bleeding Continent: How Africa Became Impoverished and Why It Remains Poor.* Xlibris.

Ciulla, J. B. (2014) *Ethics, the Heart of Leadership*. Santa Barbara: ABC-CLIO.

Connell, P. K. O. (2014) A simplified framework for 21st century leader development. *The Leadership Quarterly*, 25(2): 183–203.

Dibie, R., and Dibie, J. (2005) Analysis of the paralysis of government leadership in sub-Saharan Africa. *Africa's Public Service Delivery and Performance Review*, 5(1): 1–13.

Francis. (2013) *Apostolic Exhortation Evangelii Gaudium.* Rome: Editrice Vaticana.

French, W. L., and Bell, C. H. (1973) *Organization Development.* Englewood Cliffs, NJ: Prentice Hall.

Ghoshal, S. (2005) Bad management theories are destroying good management practices. *Academy of Management Learning & Education*, 4(1): 75–91.

Guardini, R. (1957) *The End of the Modern World: A Search for Orientation.* London: Sheed & Ward.

Guillén Parra, M. (2006) *Ética de las organizaciones. Construyendo confianza.* Madrid: Pearson – Prentice Hall.

Havard, A. (2007) *Virtuous Leadership: An Agenda for Personal Excellence.* New York, NY: Scepter.

Kan, M. M., and Parry, K. W. (2004) Identifying paradox: A grounded theory of leadership in overcoming resistance to change. *The Leadership Quarterly*, 15: 467–491.

Keirsey, D. (1984) *Please Understand Me: Character and Temperament Types.* Del Mar, CA: Prometheus Nemesis Book Company.

Kempster, S., Jackson, B., and Conroy, M. (2011) Leadership as purpose: Exploring the role of purpose in leadership practice. *Leadership*, 7(3): 313–334.

Kotter, J. P. (2015) What leaders really do. *Harvard Business Review*, November: 1–13.

Lewin, K., Lippitt, R., and White, R. (1939) Patterns of aggressive behavior in experimentally created 'social climates'. *Journal of Social Psychology*, 10: 271–299.

Lewis, C. S. (2001) *The Screwtape Letters: Letters From a Senior to a Junior Devil.* NewYork, NY: Harper Collins.

Lueneburger, C., and Goleman, D. (2010) The change leadership sustainability demands. *MIT Sloan Management Review*, 51(4): 49–56.

Meyer, A. D., Brooks, G. R., and Goes, J. B. (1990) Environmental jolts and industry revolutions: Organizational responses to discontinuous change. *Strategic Management Journal*, 11: 93–110.

Nigerian Tribune (2017, November 11) *Character Is Basis of Good Governance.* Retrieved from http://www.tribuneonlineng.com/character-basis-good-governance-ezekwesili-awolowo-dosumu-ibru-others/

Ovadje, F. (2014) *Change Leadership in Developing Countries.* New York, NY: Routledge.

Pearlmutter, S. (1998) Self-efficacy and organizational change leadership. *Administration in Social Work*, 22(3): 23–38.

Sharif, M. M., and Scandura, T. A. (2014) Do perceptions of ethical conduct matter during organizational change? Ethical leadership and employee involvement. *Journal of Business Ethics*, 124(2): 185–196.

Theresa of Avila. (2007) *The Interior Castle.* Mineola, NY: Dover Publications.

Transparency International. (2017) *Transparency International Corruption Perception Index 2016.* Retrieved from https://www.transparency.org/news/feature/corruption_perceptions_index_2016

UN Economic Commision on Africa. (2014) *Report of the High Level Panel on Illicit Financial Flows From Africa.* Retrieved from https://www.uneca.org/sites/default/files/PublicationFiles/iff_main_report_26feb_en.pdf
Voet, J. Van Der, Kuipers, B. S., and Groeneveld, S. (2016) Implementing change in public organizations: The relationship between leadership and affective commitment to change in a public sector context. *Public Management Review*, 18(6): 842–865.
Wadell, J. (2009) *The Primacy of Love Paulist.* Mahwah, NJ: Press New York.
Wanasika, I. et al. (2011) Managerial leadership and culture in sub-Saharan Africa. *Journal of World Business*, 46(2): 234–241.
Whetstone, J. T. (2002) Personalism and moral leadership: The servant leader with a transforming vision. *Ethics: A European Review*, 11(4): 385–393.
Wilson, D. C. (1992) *A Strategy of Change.* London: Routledge.
Wright, T. A., and Campbell, J. (2011) The role of character in ethical leadership research. *The Leadership Quarterly*, 22(5): 975–978.
Zagar, Y. (2010) *Acting on Principles: A Thomistic Perspective in Making Moral Decisions.* Eugene, OR: Wipf & Stock.

14

Transformational change in Africa

A case study of sustainable economic growth in Kenya

Michael J.R. Butler, Suncan Pavlovic, Anastasia Pavlovic and Bahar Ali Kazmi

Introduction

Sustainable economic growth is a current and vitally important issue for all transitional economies, yet such growth is hard to achieve in practice. This case study makes a contribution by providing evidence for a new framework of actionable knowledge for Kenyan policy makers and managers to consider when making their decisions about how to drive growth.

The framework emerges in a governance context similar to the UK circa 2000, in which there is a lack of 'adequate theory and strategy of how to mobilize and sustain organizational and cultural change in a complex, volatile and multi-level pattern of governance' (Hartley, Butler, and Benington, 2002: 401). The solution is also similar, recognising the need for organisational theory to consider factors in the external environment together with demands from central government. In other words, theory needs to be based on a dynamic and multi-layered view of change. However, the Kenyan context differs in its focus on micro, small and medium enterprises (MSMEs) as a positive driver of economic growth, and in highlighting the importance of capacity building with MSME owners, both in the formal and informal economy.

The chapter will critically discuss each factor within the framework in turn. First, radical participative management is defined in the context of external forces for change affecting Kenya. The external environment is a downward pressure of change, influencing Kenya to comply with United Nations (UN) sustainable development goals. Second, the internal forces for change will be explored, noting the emphasis on MSME business start-ups in sustainable economic growth. Central government, in responding to the external environment, is creating favourable business conditions to encourage entrepreneurs to implement their ideas. Third, contemporary and international approaches to facilitating MSME growth will be reviewed, and their application to Kenya highlighted. In particular, a dominant model is provided by the Global Entrepreneurship Monitor (GEM), but complementary emerging approaches are appearing, such as research in the practice and process of growth by The TRANSFORMATION Project. Fourth, the chapter will evaluate three business support case studies by the Institute for Small Business Initiatives (ISBI), indicating the variety of business innovation and individual circumstances within the formal MSME sector. Fifth, the chapter will extend the discussion to a new variant of business innovation, the informal MSME economy, which not only helps in peace-building processes in northern Kenya and Somalia, but is also an important part of Kenya's economy. Sixth, the threads are brought together in the new change framework, revealing future policy, practice and research directions.

External forces for change

Sustainable economic growth is high on the international policy agenda which is acting as an external force for change within Kenya. The United Nations (UN) (2015) has set seventeen sustainable development goals, which came into effect on 1 January 2016, and which will guide the decisions it takes over the next fifteen years until 2030. Two goals are of particular interest to this chapter:

> Goal 8. Promote sustained, inclusive and sustainable economic growth, full and productive employment and decent work for all
>
> Goal 9. Build resilient infrastructure, promote inclusive and sustainable industrialization and foster innovation
>
> *(UN, 2015)*

Goal 8 links economic development to decent work, and Goal 9 suggests that growth is associated with infrastructure, industrialisation and innovation. Implementation of the goals is supported worldwide, including the UK government's Department for International Development (DfID) which clearly states:'Britain has officially backed the UN framework' (see www.gov.uk/government/news/greening-britain-backs-the-global-goals-for-sustainable-development).

Although these aspirations are laudable, academics have critically discussed such policy measures in terms of the emergence of a New Development Management (NDM) (Cooke and Dar, 2008). NDM is viewed as 'a political tactic' (Cooke and Dar, 2008: 10) to facilitate a neoliberal agenda in which market ideas are applied to international development. Within this managerialist framing of transforming sustainable development, Thomas (1996) identified three types of material that should be taught in development management programmes. The first includes 'conventional management theory in a development context' (Thomas, 1996: 108). The second highlights that the co-option of organisations other than the state to implement NDM, such as non-government organisations, might be the source of conflict, because there may be competing goals and values (Thomas, 1996; Dar and Cooke, 2008). Thomas' (1996) third type of material, according to Cooke and Dar (2008: 10), has been 'utterly ignored or silenced.' The third type is described as 'radical participative management methods aimed at enabling and empowering, arising from cases where development management may be viewed as the management of interventions on behalf of the relatively powerless' (Thomas, 1996: 108).

The central contribution of this chapter relates to the third of Thomas' (1996) three types of material for development management programmes. The contribution suggests that there is now the emergence of participative management methods aimed at management for development which enables and empowers entrepreneurs. The focus in the chapter is on transformational change and its application to growing MSMEs in Kenya. In particular, three approaches to MSME capacity building will be critically discussed. First, the role of knowledge exchange processes through more traditional MSME events and site visits in Nairobi and Southern Kenya will be discussed. Second, the establishment of ISBI within a higher education setting, Strathmore Business School, Nairobi, and ISBI's deep engagement with the formal economy through entrepreneurship education with about 200 MSMEs will be outlined. Third, an emergent trend in peace-building processes is acknowledged by recognising the importance of informal MSMEs in Kenya and other East African countries. Specifically, the discussion will highlight the interconnections between development practice and management tools, especially the tools from, and the subsequent impact of, The TRANSFORMATION Project's MSME Growth Programme in Kenyan MSME growth. The focus is on MSMEs because of the authors' recent engagement with this type of organisation and civil society organisations in Kenya, in partial response to Bremmer's (2015) assessment of Kenya in Fortune magazine, as one of only seven new global places to invest.

Internal forces for change

Allied to the external forces are internal forces for change: namely, opportunities for growth, but with recognition that Kenya does have instabilities that need to be managed, opportunities for business start-up supported by central government legislative change, and international models which underscore the feasibility of institutional and culture change in Kenya.

Growth and instability

Currently, Kenya is a success story with a robustly growing economy, though there are instabilities such as periodical election-related violence (which resurfaced during the 2017 elections), terrorist attacks, and the armed conflicts in the Greater Horn of Africa that could hinder growth. It is therefore important to review the immediate past economic history of Kenya in order to reveal how change is indeterminate, in continuous flux, and therefore difficult to manage. There are four phases: poor performance, accelerated growth, decline, and the current resurgent phase.

In phase one, before 2003, Kenya performed 'considerably lower than the average of least developed countries (LDCs). Part of the relatively poor performance lies in the comparably slow transformation to an industrial-based economy' (ILO, 2013: 1). During this period, economic growth had been 2% or less at least one-third of the time over the previous 30 years, during the 1970s, 1980s, and 1990s (ILO, 2013). In the second phase, in 2003, there was real GDP growth from 0.3% in 2002 to almost 7% in 2007 (ILO, 2013). Despite sustained drought which affected agriculture, there was the revival of tourism (ILO, 2013). In phase three, in 2008, decline set in with the outbreak of violence following a general election (ILO, 2013). This low level of economic performance slowed job creation, hampered improvements in living standards, and especially impacted younger workers (12–24-year-olds) (ILO, 2013). This was exacerbated by the global financial and economic crisis, when commodity process increased (ILO, 2013). In the fourth phase, an indicator of recent success of the Kenyan economy is that, in 2014, GDP growth was 5.3%, with projections for 2015, 2016, and 2017 being 5.5%, 6.0%, and 6.4% respectively (Odero, Reeves, and Chokerah, 2016). Growth came from construction, manufacturing, finance and insurance, information, communications and technology, and wholesale and retail (Odero, Reeves, and Chokerah, 2016). The key drivers for growth are 'increased rainfall and enhanced agricultural production, a stable macroeconomic environment, continued low international oil process, the stability of the Kenya shilling (KES), improved security boosting tourism and reforms in governance and justice' (Odero, Reeves, and Chokerah, 2016: 2).

Within these drivers is a re-balancing of the economy from a reliance on agriculture and manufacturing to information and communications technology (ICT) by encouraging ICT industrial parks (Odero, Reeves, and Chokerah, 2016). The reliance on agriculture is evidenced by its still contributing 30.3% to GDP in 2014, followed by finance, real estate, and business services, which collectively contributed 11.1% to GDP in 2014 (ILO, 2013; Odero, Reeves, and Chokerah, 2016).

Growth is in part supported by economic co-operation, regional integration, and trade. There has been the establishment of the East African Community (EAC), which facilitates the free movement of goods, labour, services, and capital. In short, there is the removal of economic barriers. M-Pesa is a financial service operated through mobile telephones. In addition, Kenya plays an important role in promoting peace and security across the EAC. (Odero, Reeves, and Chokerah, 2016). As international symbols of the emergence of success, in 2015, Kenya hosted three high-profile visits: the President of the US, the Pope, and the WTO.

This context, however, is dynamic and contains instabilities which may dampen growth. EAC could be considered more of an aspiration than a practice because there are implementation issues; for example, a Single Customs Territory is not yet in place despite having the protocol (Makame, 2012). The African economic outlook report for Kenya (Odero, Reeves, and Chokerah, 2016) notes that the economy slowed in 2014, partly due to fewer tourists arriving following terrorist attacks in the country. One attack, for example, left 150 students dead at Garissa University. The report also mentions the operations of criminal gangs in 2015 leading to deaths in various counties, including Nairobi.

In terms of developing human resources, there are contradictory indicators. More negatively, at the primary level, illiteracy rates increased for those who have been in school six years. More positively, at the university level, numbers increased by 22.8% during 2013–2014. (Odero, Reeves, and Chokerah, 2016).

Long-term challenges threaten structural transformation and sustainable cities. In other words, there is the rapid growth of urban areas, leading to daily struggles for food and water (OXFAM, 2009; Hope, 2013). Nairobi in particular, over the decade leading up to 2015, grew about 75%, from two million to 3.5 million inhabitants. This phenomenon is taking place across urban areas. This trend is leading to increased investment in agriculture to attract people back to rural areas (Odero, Reeves, and Chokerah, 2016).

Business start-up

One feature of the re-balancing of the economy is a series of Acts in 2015 to facilitate a positive business climate (the Companies Act, the Insolvency Act, the Special Economic Zones Act, the Business Registration Service, the Companies and Insolvency Legislation (Consequential Amendments) Act, and the Finance Act Amendments). Legislation was innovative, for example, the Special Economic Zones Act was the first in Africa. Collectively, legislation made it much easier to start up a new business. (Odero, Reeves, and Chokerah, 2016).

The application of the legislation is as important as the passing of the commercial Acts. Odero, Reeves, and Chokerah (2016) suggest that this is likely and predictable because of the 2010 constitution which restructured the judiciary. They specifically highlight the comprehensive appeals process which includes all parts of the judiciary system, from Magistrates' Courts to the Supreme Court.

Independent assessments by the World Bank (2016) and the World Economic Forum (WEF) (2015) reflect the development towards a positive business environment and a stable legislative system. WEF's (2015) Global Competitiveness Index (2015–2016) ranks Kenya 61 (out of 140 countries) for judicial independence. The World Bank's (2016) index for the ease of doing business revealed that Kenya was now 108 (out of 189 countries) in the ranking, a move up of 21 places. These rankings indicate Kenya's path to improvement, but there is more progress to be made to secure higher rankings.

As a report published by the International Labour Organization (ILO) (2015: 16) points out, 'Micro, Small and Medium Enterprises (MSMEs) operate in all sectors . . . The sector plays important roles.' Five key roles are highlighted:

- Delivering Kenya Vision2030 by contributing to the socio-economic transformation of the production of goods and provision of services
- Increasing income opportunities for all the population within farming/non-farming businesses and the formal/informal sectors employing 1–99 workers
- Contributing between 18–20% of annual GDP
- Promoting job creation, especially by 'being a main contributor to the creation of decent jobs.'

(ILO, 2015: 17)

The ILO's list of five key roles for MSMEs raises three critical issues: informal employment, labour laws, and job creation amongst the young. The ILO (2015) revealed that there were 2,149,000 workers in the formal sector, but 10,511,200 in informal employment. The informal sector is likely to operate outside a formal system which enacts effective labour laws. In response, the ILO (2015) is stressing the benefits of complying with labour laws and running training courses to strengthen the capacity of the MSME sector. The ILO (2015) emphasises the importance of labour laws in improving worker morale, their performance and public relations, avoiding workplace unrest, high staff turnover, and legal disputes. The ILO (2015) proposes a practical programme of eight modules introducing the benefits of labour law compliance. The ILO (2013) is particularly concerned about youth employment, because this signals a more inclusive approach – the young are part of the solution, not a problem. It is suggested that the ILO's training courses could target this age group to increase job opportunities and employability skills.

International trends

The ILO (2013) sets Kenya's current growth trajectory within an international context to pragmatically indicate that institutional and cultural change is possible. They focus on other emerging nations, especially in South America and Asia. For example, in terms of formalising the informal sector, the ILO (2013) highlights that in Brazil, credit was extended to MSMEs to fund growth, that the number of steps to formalisation was reduced from 41 to 7, and that tax burdens were reduced for sole traders and for businesses with one employee . Peru adopted a different approach related to their conditions and who has property rights. The Praedial System granted property titles to 1.2 million families, helping 380,000 firms enter the formal sector (ILO, 2013).

China took another approach, again related to their context. The ILO (2013) reports that China promoted non-farming activities in rural areas to establish links between the agricultural sector and the rest of the economy. This has been a success in helping to increase rural household income.

Globally, there has been an effort to increase youth employment through developing a range of skills. These initiatives may provide examples of good practice which Kenya can adopt in order to achieve job creation amongst the young. Korea and Singapore have addressed the quality of secondary and tertiary education, and vocational skills. Chile and the Dominican Republic have included soft skills for the youth labour market. Within Africa, there has been a more comprehensive approach, for example, in Egypt, a UNESCO-funded programme promoted re-integration into both the labour market and society. The Programme introduced literacy training, computer skills, and learning a foreign language. The *Northern Uganda's Youth Opportunities Programme* focused on 16- to 35-year-olds in order to encourage business start-ups. Cash grants enabled tools, materials, and training to be purchased (ILO, 2013).

Entrepreneurial models of change

In addition to external and internal forces for change, in order to enact change within MSMEs, specific models of change related to the entrepreneurial context are required to guide management decisions. These models need to be suitable for understanding and managing sustainable economic growth in Kenya. This section will review contemporary and international approaches to facilitating MSME growth, and their application to Kenya. Having discussed a dominant model provided by the Global Entrepreneurship Monitor (GEM), the section will turn to complementary emerging approaches such as research in the practice and process of growth by The TRANSFORMATION Project.

GEM Conceptual Framework

The GEM Conceptual Framework (GEM2017: 14) is presented in Figure 14.1.

The figure divides the entrepreneurial process into its main elements and the relationship between the elements. Starting from left and moving right, the wider social, cultural, political, and economic context contains two categories: national framework conditions and entrepreneurial framework conditions. The national framework conditions take into account the stage of economic development and draw on the World Economic Forum's (2015) classification: factor-driven, efficiency-driven, and innovation-driven. The factor-driven stage consists of

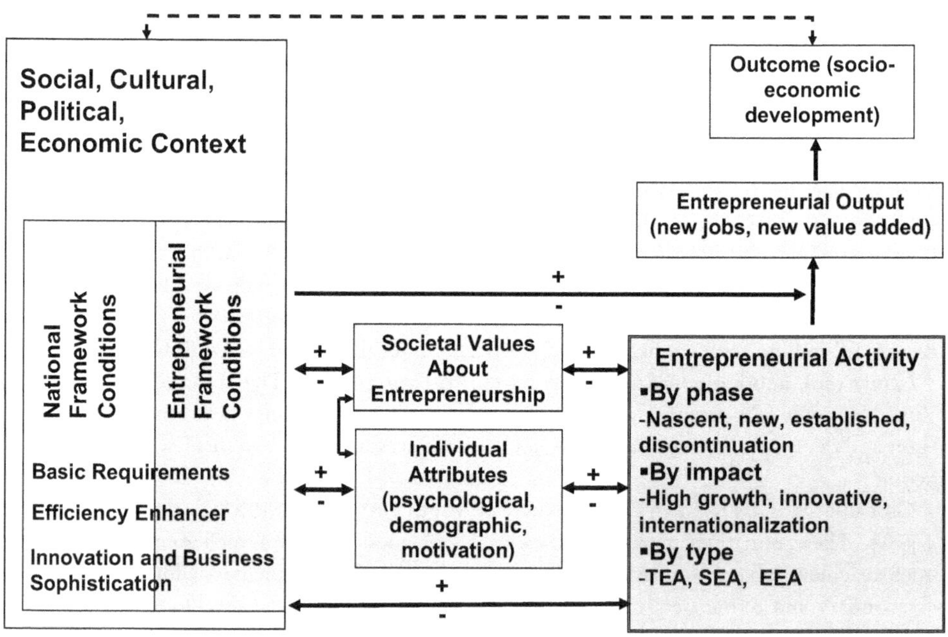

Figure 14.1 The GEM Conceptual Framework

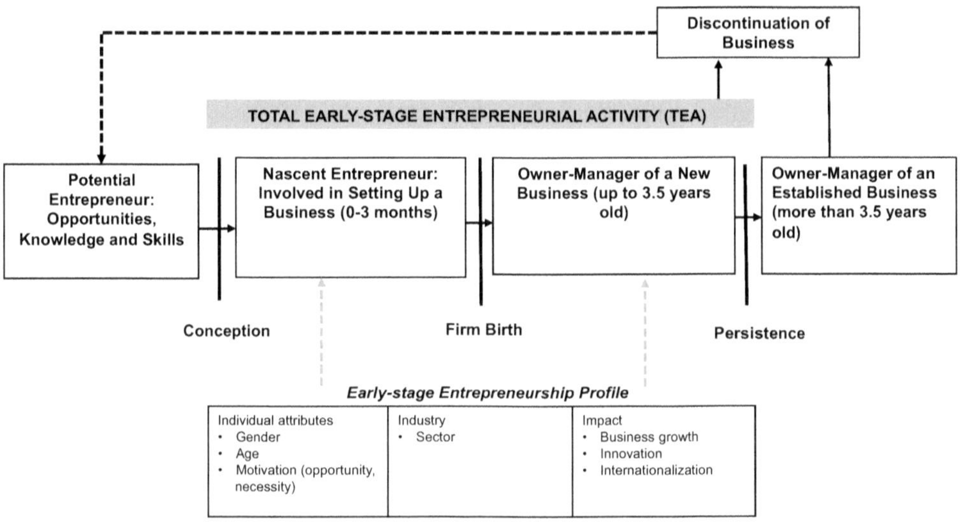

Figure 14.2 GEM model of business phases and entrepreneurship characteristics

subsistence agriculture and extraction businesses, with a heavy reliance on unskilled labour and natural resources. In the efficiency-driven stage, the economy is more competitive with more efficient production and product quality. The innovation-driven stage includes the emergence of knowledge-intensive businesses and service-sector expansion (see WEF, 2015).

The entrepreneurial framework conditions focus more on the quality of the entrepreneurship environment, for example, relevant finance, policy, government programmes, education, research and development, commercial and legal infrastructure, regulations for internal market entry and dynamics, infrastructure, and cultural and social norms (GEM, 2017).

Together the national framework and entrepreneurial framework conditions set the basic requirements and efficiency enhancers for economic growth through entrepreneurial behaviour in innovation and business sophistication. Moving to the right of the figure, these conditions set the social values for creation, in which the individual entrepreneur is located. Moving to the right again, the conditions are now in place for entrepreneurial activity and entrepreneurial output – new jobs, new added value. In turn, all this establishes a positive feedback loop to further develop the socio-economic conditions for more entrepreneurial activity (GEM, 2017).

The GEM model of business phases and entrepreneurship characteristics (GEM2017: 15) is presented in Figure 14.2. It expands on the entrepreneurial activity section of the previous figure; in particular, it highlights the activity by phases (nascent, new, established and discontinued).

In an ideal growth scenario, a potential entrepreneur develops their idea by setting up a business, which survives more than 3.5 years, allowing it to become an established business. The bottom section of the figure also overlaps with the previous figure. A potential entrepreneur will have key attributes, for example, high motivation aligned with key knowledge and skills, in order to take advantage of emerging opportunities. The entrepreneur will operate in a sector which facilitates business growth, innovation and, potentially, internationalisation (GEM, 2017).

Application to Kenya

An e-mail exchange at the time of writing this chapter with GEM indicates that there are no specific reports focusing on Kenya. More widely, GEM's (2017) Global Report reveals that the African countries they surveyed in 2016 were either factor- or efficiency-driven, either driven by subsistence agriculture or more efficient production. Those that are factor-driven include Burkina Faso, Cameroon, and Senegal. The efficiency-driven countries are Egypt, Morocco, and South Africa. Although WEF (2015) rates Kenya a factor-driven economy in its stage of development, Kenya is probably moving towards being between factor- and efficiency-driven. This is because there is still a reliance on agriculture (Odero, Reeves, and Chokerah, 2016), which indicates a factor-driven economy (GEM, 2017). There is also a drive towards ICT industrial parks, which will support finance, real estate, and business services (Odero, Reeves, and Chokerah, 2016), which indicates a more efficiency-driven economy, if not a kernel of innovation-driven activities (GEM, 2017).

The emergence of a more advanced economy is also supported by recent legislative changes, the Acts in 2015, and the 2010 constitution which restructured the judiciary. Together, they facilitate a positive business climate (Odero, Reeves, and Chokerah, 2016), in particular, the ILO's (2015) emphasis on the emergence of MSMEs to the socio-economic transformation of production and services.

As noted earlier in the chapter, in contrast to the emergence of a more advanced Kenyan economy, there are more negative headwinds which cannot be ignored. For example, in the long term, though university numbers have increased, illiteracy at the primary level has increased, suggesting that the pipeline of entrepreneurs could be compromised (Odero, Reeves, and Chokerah, 2016). In the short term, many more workers are in informal employment rather than in the formal sector (ILO, 2015: 16), which makes it much more difficult to influence the re-balancing of the economy.

Alternative ideas: the TRANSFORMATION Project

Contemporary research is identifying alternative ideas which complement GEM's work. The TRANSFORMATION Project, through its Transformation for Growth Programme (www.thetransformationproject.co.uk), supplements GEM's model of business phases and entrepreneurship characteristics (GEM, 2017). Founded on prior research in the practice and process of change (Butler, 2003; Butler and Allen, 2008; Butler and Gheorghiu, 2010; Butler, 2012), the Transformation for Growth Programme is more specific about how to move through the business phases by enhancing individual and organisational capabilities. The Growth Pathway and the 4-Stage Process systematically structure a set of MSME organisation development activities in a sequence. It is this specificity and the subsequent impact that the MSMEs in Nairobi wanted to learn about. As part of an international knowledge exchange process, the first author was an invited keynote speaker at a workshop to review the work of The TRANSFORMATION Project with a range of entrepreneurs (ILO, 2015); for example, one worked with the UN, whilst others had founded businesses in emerging service areas such as digital marketing. The first author facilitated a discussion on the theme of 'MSME Capacity Building – The Impact of The TRANSFORMATION Project and What We Learnt.'

Between 2013 and 2015, Transformation for Growth, a partnership with Birmingham City Council and part-financed by the West Midlands European Regional Development Fund Programme (ERDF) (£479,276), achieved the following impact:

- Worked intensively and directly with 38 SMEs
- Added £2,356,942 gross value to the economy in the West Midlands

- Created 62 jobs in the West Midlands
- Hosted four conferences with internationally renowned speakers and 400 attendees
- In support of the Equality and Diversity theme, worked with SMEs which identified themselves as Asian or Asian British, Black or Black British, and White British
- 37 of our SMEs had not previously worked with the Work and Organisational Psychology Group at Aston Business School, Aston University
- Enhanced the TRANSFORMATION Project website to capture all the learning with written and video case studies (www.thetransformationproject.co.uk)

Two interlocking processes were used to achieve MSME growth. First, Figure 14.3 captures the three steps involved in The Growth Pathway. In order to reveal measurable growth and a change in organisational culture to one which supports performance improvement, the Receptivity for Change Toolset was used before and after an intervention by the Business Engagement Team. In this way it was possible to identify a need for change and check that the need had been met. The intervention was a modified and light-touch version of the CHAMPS2 project process.

Second, in the second step of The Growth Pathway, the intervention involved a 4-Stage Process (see Figure 14.4). In order to successfully pass from one stage to the next, a stage gate needs to be completed. This is an audit of the MSMEs achievements in the previous stage, and an action plan for the next. The benefits to MSMEs from using the 4-Stage Process is that it can enable organisations of any size to undergo change, whilst developing expertise within the MSME. It supports change across a wide range of MSME needs. The key strengths of the 4-Stage Process are that it focuses on defining and then realising outcomes, by being a tool to redesign an approach to service delivery, whilst continuing to focus on customer requirements. The 4-Stage Process is designed to review all aspects of service delivery in a structured approach to delivering change.

The capacity-building session in Nairobi was part of a number of meetings across Kenya, including site visits with MSMEs in the Maasai Mara and Mombasa. The first author spent much time with the second and third authors to learn about their ISBI Entrepreneurship Education Programmes and their role at Strathmore University, both located in Nairobi (see www.isbi-kenya.org/about/). In turn, ISBI learned about the work of The TRANSFORMATION Project and how the management tools linked to the Growth Programme, outlined above, can help to recalibrate ISBI's MSME interventions – this is a form of technology transfer. Before outlining the mutual knowledge transfer and its impact between The TRANSFORMATION Project and ISBI, ISBI's deep engagement with the formal economy through entrepreneurship education will now be explored in much more detail.

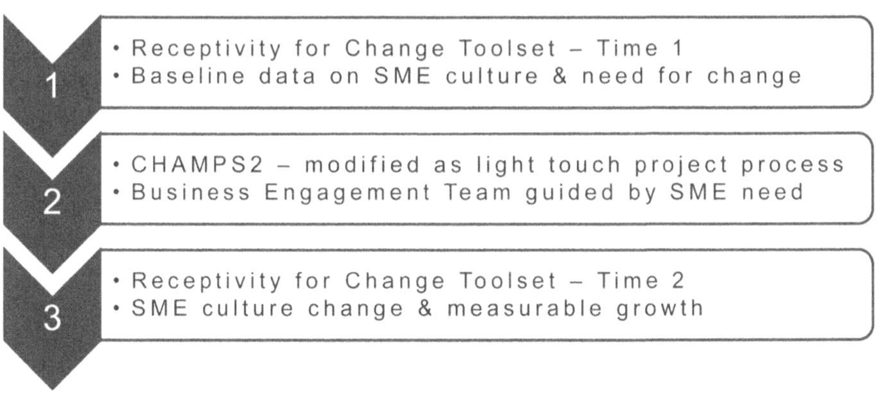

Figure 14.3 The growth pathway

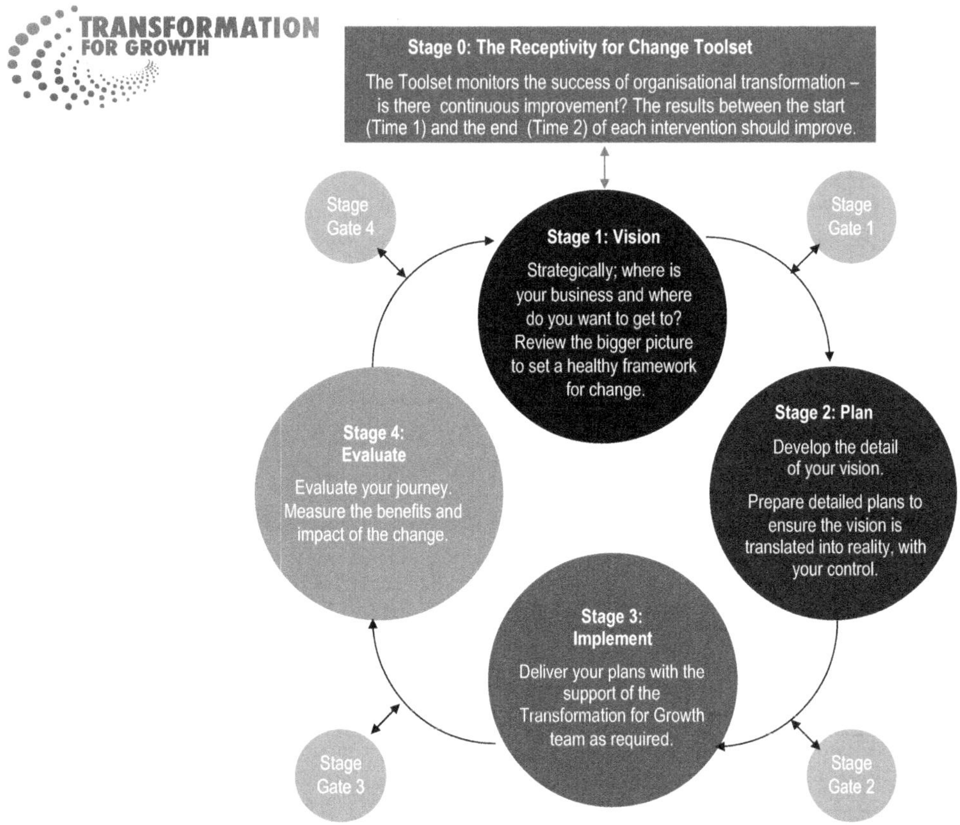

Figure 14.4 4-Stage Process

MSME capacity building in the formal economy: three business support case studies

A final layer of change management is that the transformation for growth of Kenyan MSMEs required three approaches to capacity-building. The first, the role of more traditional MSME events and site visits in Nairobi and Southern Kenya, was discussed in the last section. Here, the second approach is discussed – ISBI's capacity-building with the formal economy. The third approach, an emergent trend in peace-building processes which recognises the importance of the MSME informal economy, is discussed in the next section. In this section, the context for ISBI's work is highlighted, followed by three case studies of their work with three different types of MSME, and then the learning from the cases is reflected on.

Background

The Institute for Small Business Initiatives (ISBI) (www.isbi-kenya.org/) was founded by an Austrian NGO, ICEP (https://icep.at/organisation/?lang=en), and Strathmore Educational Trust (SET), with the goal of promoting business and financial skills amongst MSMEs in Nairobi. ISBI operates from Strathmore Business School (http://sbs.strathmore.edu/about-sbs/welcome/) because of its trusted position amongst MSMEs. Suncan Pavlovic is Managing Director of ISBI, which was founded in May 2014. From August 2015, he also became a Lecturer in Financial Analysis, Valuation and Case Studies at Strathmore University's School of Finance and Applied Economics, Nairobi (www.strathmore.edu/en/). Anastasia Pavlovic is the lead researcher.

ISBI was established to support the economic growth of MSMEs in all sectors, helping to deliver Kenya Vision2030 (ILO, 2015). In particular, ISBI addresses a perceived gap in the market for individual mentoring and tailor-made consulting to overcome barriers to further MSME growth, and to offset high failure rates with starting one's own business. The mentoring and consulting is practice- rather than theoretically-led, providing entrepreneurs with key financial and professional and skills. ISBI title this a Teaching-Training-Mentoring-Consulting (TTMC) Programme. Unlike other providers, entrepreneurs pay for this assistance with a view to recovering the course costs within three to six months through business growth and job creation. However, ISBI's development costs were financed by ICEP and the Austrian Development Agency. Since May 2014, almost 200 entrepreneurs have participated in ISBI programmes. ISBI's potential to work with more MSMEs is tempered by a challenging market in which sponsored MSME programmes provide free training, tending to emphasise numbers of participants trained over tracking change on the business activity.

There are three programmes (Basic, Intermediary, and Advanced), which depend on the entrepreneur's stage of development. GEM (2017) identify three stages: nascent entrepreneur, new business (less than 3.5 years old), and established business (more than 3.5 years). ISBI defines the three stages in economic terms:

- Basic or nascent entrepreneur: No pre-requisite to join the course
- Intermediary or new business: A pre-requisite is records for at least three months, and a loan capacity of KES 200,000 (USD 2,000). Loan capacity was chosen because it is a proxy for the stage of business development – this amount indicates that there has been more than one loan, further suggesting the original loan was repaid and the business has been in operation for some time
- Advanced or established business: A pre-requisite is the fulfilment of any of three criteria: annual turnover of KES 10 million or more, credit capacity of KES 5 million or more, minimum of five full-time employees, fully formalised operations, or undergraduate diploma

The Basic programme teaches business finance and cost management based on the record-keeping application RecApp© developed in-house together with Safaricom. The end product leads to better record-keeping. The Intermediary programme teaches strategy, marketing, business planning, and presentation. Entrepreneurs will receive feedback about their business plan. The Advanced programme teaches the same as the Intermediary programme, but with more depth and adds investment and banking, employee management, decision-making, and negotiations. Participants in this programme can opt for feedback about their business plan or receive a consulting report.

Given Kenya's dynamic market and MSME growth (ILO, 2015), the programmes are under review. The absence of record-keeping during the Intermediary programme, and the reliance on assumptions, means that this programme is being suspended whilst the Basic programme is being used to establish foundation knowledge. The Basic programme becomes a prerequisite for the new Intermediary programme. Another programme, higher than the Advanced programme (Mastering), is being approved by Strathmore University.

Teaching is done in groups of sixteen to 24 entrepreneurs, whilst the training is in smaller groups of four all sharing a common industry so that learning is industry specific. The class framework helps the entrepreneurs to network and exchange ideas with like-minded participants.

The entrepreneurs are their own business case studies. This is important because when ISBI interviewed entrepreneurs about their businesses, they tend to overestimate their revenues by two times. Without financial management skills, entrepreneurs are not able to calculate their profits properly, confusing profit with cash flow and mixing business and personal expenditures. Three cases are now explored in detail, demonstrating the wide variety of MSME needs (inefficient use of capital, strategy and employee management, and operational improvements), which require individual and sustained attention. The MSMEs come from construction, automotive spare parts, and butchery.

Case 1: Construction

ISBI's experience of training and consulting MSMEs in Kenya has exposed several critical challenges, including inefficient use of existing capital. The fastest way to achieve significant improvement of MSME profitability is to eliminate operations that employ the capital unproductively.

M & Co was established over 40 years ago by the entrepreneur's father. The company, quite prosperous in the past with a turnover between KES 400 and 500 million, had been gradually falling into decay. It was losing tenders, turnover decreased, and the number of employees fell from 500 to 200. The entrepreneur, John, approached ISBI after taking the Advanced programme with a mandate to help him restructure the loan of KES 100 million. The total turnover amounted to KES 200 million with the resulting operating profit of KES 22 million; after deducting KES 19 million in the interest costs and paying KES 1 million in taxes, the company remained with the net profit of KES 2 million, i.e., a 1% profit margin.

The analysis was aggravated by the absence of data. Financial statements were prepared exclusively for tax purposes and data aggregated into totals, which made it impossible to judge the profitability of each project separately. Financing was the cheapest on this market. M & Co had an overdraft of KES 100 million and was paying 19% on the proportion used. The overdraft, however, was constantly exhausted to the full, hence the interest costs of KES 19 million yearly. As a result of lengthy and arduous information collection, the following was revealed. The company performed two types of jobs: exterior construction or 'wet works' and interior design. Exterior construction corresponded to roughly 20% of sales, but employed over 60% of capital. Moreover, based on the information out of the interviews with the field managers, it was evidently a lot less profitable (if not loss-making; as mentioned previously, no per-project-analysis was possible) than interior design works that generated 80% of sales, but required only 40% of capital.

As a result, ISBI detected an optimisation potential of KES 14 million by introducing the following measures:

- Stop undertaking exterior construction works. It would gradually free up the capital, eventually reaching the utilisation level of KES 40 to 50 million, which would allow them to cut KES 10 million on interest costs in the following year
- Transform KES 30 million of the remaining overdraft into long-term debt
- Focus exclusively on interior designs, which might result in a further (at that stage hard-to-quantify) benefit: sales might potentially increase due to concentrating the freed resources on their competence area
- Introduce thorough tracking systems to be able to assess the profitability of each project, which will surely help to detect further improvement potential
- Introduce other smaller operational improvements, like tighter control of hourly wage workers, which would bring about another KES 4 million in savings

Case 2: Automotive spare parts

ISBI's experience also revealed the critical challenge of effective strategy and employee management. Maria had a spare parts shop ideally located around a garage area and close to a central 'matatu' stage, where many drivers stop to repair their vehicles. A sales employee led the shop acquiring customers, doing purchasing and selling, including negotiating the price, since Maria had no price list and preferred to set the price on the spot judging by what a customer could afford – or rather, she expected her sales person Jacinta to do so in the best interests of the company. Maria herself was rarely at the shop and little concerned about it, because she focused on her main activity: tenders to supply car spare parts in large quantities to the state institutions, like ministries and military. Maria also did not live from the shop; it served only as a shell business to satisfy the tender requirements. The shop was highly unprofitable: it generated a turnover of KES 10,000 to 15,000 monthly, whereas the shop rent and the salary alone cost her KES 11,000 and KES 20,000 respectively. Moreover, the stock was kept at a constant level of KES 300,000. But she still kept the shop despite its unprofitability, because it was a formal condition for the tendering business. Maria also had an overdraft of KES 3 million at 20% interest with a usual utilisation of KES 1 to 3 million, rarely falling below 0.5 million.

After the Advanced programme Maria chose consulting and defined her main challenge in the shop as not being able to find the right sales person. Her employee at that time, Jacinta, was neither particularly knowledgeable nor overly interested in cars. A previous employee was really passionate about it, but he left after a year and opened his own spare parts shop in close vicinity. Jacinta might well not have been the right person for this job, because she was neither trained nor interested in cars. However, her motivation might have been due to her salary, which was fixed at a survival level and not tied to her performance. With the absence of fixed prices, she was actually encouraged to steal the biggest chunk of the negotiated mark-up. Nor could Maria check at what prices the goods were sold, as she herself abolished any price list. Jacinta was also entrusted with some of the most crucial elements of tendering, like preparing the documents and sourcing the parts. So she saw the profit on paper, but didn't see the 'facilitation fees' and all the effort that went into it. She probably felt unfairly treated, severely underpaid, and taken advantage of.

The mission focused on helping Maria crystallise her strengths and her needs. Her strength and profit stemmed from tendering. She needed the possibility to retain the shell shop (and the small office room in the back) without having to incur losses on it. On the other hand, the shop as such could have been a good business opportunity if managed properly. The location was ideal. The KES 20,000 she was paying for it was over 30% to 40% below the market price for this location, since Maria had the advantage of an old contract. She had rented it 20 years ago. Anyone willing to rent a shop at this location would be required to pay a monthly rent of KES 30,000 and over KES 100,000 as a one-time upfront goodwill. She had all the prerequisites and only needed to find the way to offer it to someone on conditions better than the market. Recommendations were the following:

- Abandon the shop business operationally and concentrate solely on tendering
- Keep the shop formally registered under her name in order to continue fulfilling the tendering requirements, but find a partner who will operate under her company name on his own account
- She will continue being responsible for the accounting services
- Sub-let the shop at the market price of KES 30,000 to a suitable person, retaining only the small office behind
- Sell her stock at cost price for KES 300,000 to the new operator instead of demanding goodwill

In this way Maria would be able to continue doing the tendering, but instead of bearing costs of over KES 30,000 a month (20,000 for the office and 11,000 in salary), she will get a surplus of KES 10,000, getting to use the office for free. The new operator would enjoy the conditions far better than the market, being able to pay the goodwill in the form of acquiring the stock and paying for all company-related expenses, since Maria would retain the company and hence reporting obligations in the face of the authorities. Next to incremental cash flow of about KES 500,000 p.a. (12 * (31,000 + 10,000)), Maria would free KES 300,000 of capital previously tied up in inventory, which would save her another KES 60,000 a year on interest.

Case 3: Butchery

In addition, ISBI's experience revealed the critical challenge of effective operational improvements. This case stems from a micro MSME segment. A butchery owner came to the Intermediary programme with an initial idea to open a second butchery and needed a business plan to apply for a loan for the expansion, which included the extra working capital and acquisition of an electric bone saw. Jack estimated that his running butchery generates a profit at around 20% of turnover. In the course of the programme, his mentor encouraged him to start keeping records. By the end of the course he realised that he was sacrificing approximately half of the profit to stealing (getting only 20% instead of 40%). Whereas he had silently come to terms with a certain 'default' share, he didn't expect it to be this much. It further transpired that his employees colluded with their colleagues in other butcheries and were combining waste to present to their bosses.

The recommendation to him was to temporarily stop the expansion plans and concentrate on optimising (in other words, introducing controls in) the existing butchery. If successful, the operational margin would double, without the extra cost of financing. Jack engaged his mother-in-law, whose dedication and perseverance helped him eventually halve the loss and double the profit as predicted.

Cross-case learning for managing change

Three issues for managing change can be learned from the case studies. First, there are a wide variety of MSME needs requiring specialist business and financial advice and, as a consequence, organisational interventions have to be tailored to individual situations. This is a complex process requiring a mix of training and either coaching or mentoring over a sustained period of time. The Transformation for Growth Project worked in a similar context, in which MSMEs require individual advice over a period of time. Whereas The Transformation for Growth Project was able to collect some impact data about how their case studies had improved, because of the dynamism of the business culture within Kenya, in which business activities change rapidly and are less likely to be recorded, impact data is harder to find. Impact data is likely to emerge from case 1, but in case 2, infrastructure redevelopment led to a relocation of the matatu stop and the rationale for this type of shop changed, and in case 3 the butchery has become a fruit and vegetable store – the owner copying another successful operation.

Second, there is a lack of crucial strategic and financial management skills from informal micro-businesses to the formal and established MSMEs with hundreds of millions of shillings in turnover. This results in poor capital management which costs the MSMEs and the economy as a whole. High financing costs may well be partially explained by the high failure rate amongst the MSMEs and their consequent default on the loans. The fact that it does not translate into the default for the financing institutions is owed to the fact that loans up to a certain level are bundled into groups in which each member pledges for the rest. Efforts directed towards lowering refinancing costs for financial institutions would be better utilised if redirected towards overcoming skill gaps and promoting record-keeping.

Third, an implication of the case studies is that despite working with the formal economy, ISBI has identified a blurring of the boundary between the formal and informal economy, which slows MSME growth. More than that, as was noted in case 2, having an employee's salary at a survival level contradicts the UN's (2015) eighth sustainable development goal of providing decent work. The recommendations above highlight one approach to tackling this situation through formalising MSME work processes (ILO, 2015). Another approach is highlighted the following section, which argues that working with the informal economy is often the first stage to more formal MSME economic growth, and the informal economy can also be used for important social purposes.

MSME capacity building in the informal economy: the case of peace-building processes

As noted in the last section, the third approach to MSME capacity building is now discussed. This approach recognises and manages the informal economy as a new variant of change. Business profoundly affects the conditions that shape peace and conflict. The dominant view tells revealing tales of how private companies contribute to generating, maintaining, and escalating conflict by financing groups in civil wars, trading and distributing conflict-relevant goods, and taking advantage of regulatory gaps. Essential though this analysis is for achieving sustainable peace, it nonetheless is partial, as it disregards the business practices that prevent political violence and sustain peace. Increasingly scholars and practitioners of corporate social responsibilities (CSR) are arguing that it is essential to identify these business practices and include them in national and international policy frameworks that aim at accomplishing sustainable peace (Oetzel, Westermann-Behaylo, Koerber, Fort, and Rivera, 2009; Slim, 2012).

This plea has led to the formation of an international network of organisations, developing new ways of understanding the connections between business practices and peace. In March 2001, for example, a UN initiative, the Global Compact, organized the first learning forum on the role of 'Business in Zones of Conflict.' Since then, it has made significant progress and led to the formulation of a 'Business Guide for Conflict Impact Assessment and Risk Management' aiming to show the relationship between conflict and investment decisions. In 2004, the UN Security Council has established a working group on the role of 'Business in Conflict Prevention, Peacekeeping, and Post-Conflict Peace-Building.' Furthermore, the OECD Guidelines for Multinational Enterprises (MNEs), the 'Business Leaders Initiative on Human Rights' and, more recently, the Ruggie's (2011) 'Protect, Respect and Remedy' Framework, have played an important role in shaping the interaction between business organisations and human rights. In the context of civil wars, armed conflicts, and localised political violence, this interaction requires stronger accountability and transparency.

Many of these initiatives have given more attention to the roles and responsibilities of MNEs because of their power and influence to affect the lives of the civilian population. Recently these international learning forums have begun to give serious consideration to the effect of violent conflicts on MSMEs and the role they can play in preventing violence and building sustainable peace. Slim (2012) argues that the debate on the war economies overlooks the large informal business sectors, run by family businesses desperately trying to survive in unstable political environments. Protecting these MSMEs, Slim (2012) argues, can safeguard the vital supplies and employment opportunities that are essential for the survival of the civilian population.

Recent research, which one of the authors has conducted for the UN initiative on peace and reconciliation in Somalia (Kazmi and Loyaan, 2017), suggests that in Somalia it is the 'informal' international network of large, medium, and small Somali businesses operating in livestock, telecommunications, and remittances (Hawala) that run the Somali economy and contribute proactively to humanitarian and development assistance. The Hawala (money transferring) system, which is a de facto banking system, is a lifeline for 40% of the Somali population that count on the financial support (estimated to be $1 billion annually) provided by the diaspora for their production, consumption, and humanitarian/development activities in Somalia. Many of these businesses, run by the Somali refugee community, are a part of the informal sector of Nairobi and their estimated trade volume is Ksh 2.9 billion per year (Farah, Opanga, and Abdishakur, 2016).

The refugee-driven informal sector, in this sense, has not only been reducing the risk of deprivation which can potentially aggravate conflict, displacement, and violence, but it has been significantly contributing to the economy of Kenya. It has also been a source of innovative business models which facilitate businesses to perform state-like roles, providing humanitarian assistance and establishing cross-clan interaction in Somalia. There is no doubt that MSMEs are the backbone of countries with weak statist institutions and therefore Brück, Naudé, and Verwimp (2012), by using Baumol's (1990) analysis, argue that entrepreneurship can have a dark side – that is to say, it can be used for destructive activities. For example, many international banks are reluctant to work with Somali communities and companies because of the fear of unwittingly getting involved in financing armed groups. MSMEs without national or international regulatory frameworks may hinder peace processes.

Discussion and conclusion: sustaining MSME economic growth in Kenya

This last section returns to the key issue identified at the start of the chapter, the difficulty of sustaining economic growth in transitional economies. One potential answer to this conundrum is presented now, a new framework for managing transformational change in Africa so that Kenyan policy makers and managers can make better decisions about how to drive growth. Specifically, these stakeholders can reflect on whether the conditions for change will be motors of or barriers to change and, if they are not conducive to change, how they may be positively influenced. The framework identifies the key inter-related factors driving effective change related to sustaining MSME economic growth in Kenya (Figure 14.5).

Underpinning the framework is Thomas' (1996) radical participative management as a tool in fostering effective change management, because it enables and empowers entrepreneurs within development management. Participative management emphasises working with local communities for a series of small wins which collectively lead to transformational change.

Within the Kenyan context there is the alignment of forces for change, models of change, and MSME capacity-building. Forces for change can be subdivided into external and internal forces. In terms of external forces, this chapter began by indicating that sustainable economic growth is high on the international policy agenda, notably because the eighth of the UN's (2015) seventeen sustainable development goals targets inclusive growth. In addition, there are international models which indicate that institutional and culture change is possible – examples were given from elsewhere in Africa, South America, and Asia. In terms of internal forces, Kenya is re-balancing its economy to facilitate a positive business climate, making it easier to start up a new business, especially MSMEs (ILO, 2015). It is anticipated that MSMEs will contribute between 18–20% of annual GDP (ILO, 2015).

Aligned with forces for change is the availability of entrepreneurial models of change which guide management decisions. The GEM Conceptual Framework (2017) has proved useful

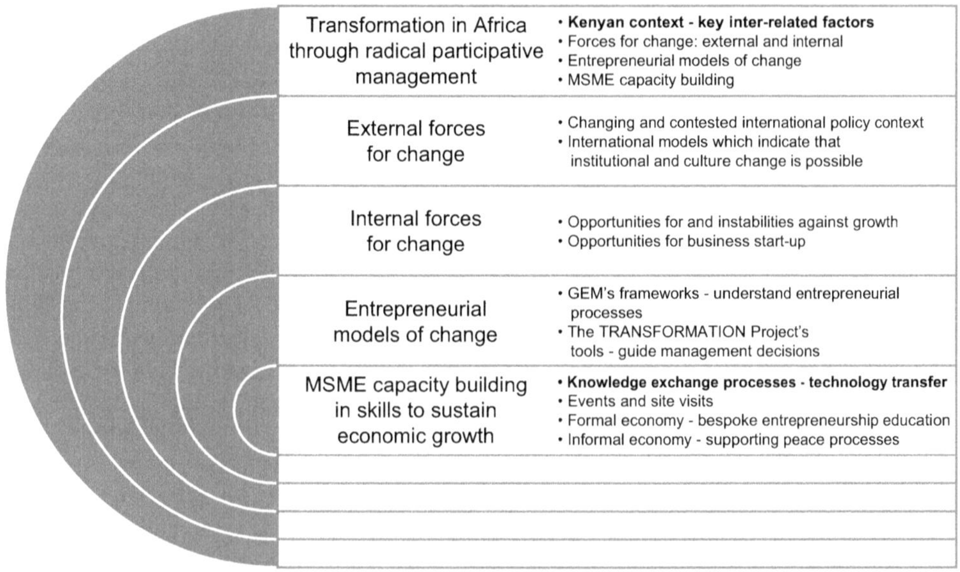

Figure 14.5 Framework for transformational change in Africa: Radical participative management for sustainable economic growth in Kenya

in revealing the national and entrepreneurial framework conditions for economic growth in Kenya. There is momentum for MSME growth created through legislative changes supported by enforcement measures (Odero, Reeves, and Chokerah, 2016). GEM's (2017) second model helpfully links MSME business phases to entrepreneurship activities. However, the Transformation for Growth's Pathway and 4-Stage Process complement GEM's (2017) work by being more specific about how to move through the business phases by enhancing individual and organisational entrepreneurship capabilities. They provide a structure for organisation development, flexible enough to be able to adapt to multiple situations.

ISBI's case studies map onto the 4-Stage Process by reaching stage three, implementation, having passed through setting a vision and planning implementation. This demonstrates that the management tools developed in the UK context can be transferred to an international context, in this case, Kenya. This is probably because the 4-Stage Process has been applied in both countries in a specific sector: MSME growth. The key difference is that it is harder to reach stage four in Kenya, evaluating success. This difference allowed the Transformation for Growth Programme to collect impact data. It is acknowledged, as the case studies reveal, that the informal work practices in Kenya make it very hard to establish and implement credible recommendations for growth, never mind having the resources to measure impact. Indeed, the blurring of the boundary between the formal and informal economies in Kenya potentially slows MSME growth. Nevertheless, stage four provides persuasive evidence about how to facilitate long-term sustainable change – the key ambition of most economic growth programmes, such as the UN's (2015) sustainable development goals.

The entrepreneurial models of change are not enough, and three approaches to MSME capacity-building to sustain economic growth have been highlighted. This is the central contribution of the chapter because the approaches directly address Thomas' (1996) radical participative management. The approaches are related to knowledge exchange processes to facilitate technology transfer, and include events and site visits, bespoke entrepreneurial education for the formal economy, and recognising the informal economy which supports peace processes.

Knowledge exchange events, such as the seminar with MSMEs from Nairobi, are important because they share the latest research findings about how to transform MSMEs for growth. The high turnout (the room reached its capacity of about 40 people) supports the notion that more knowledge exchange events should take place. Knowledge exchange site visits like the one between the first author and the ISBI team allow for capacity-building between higher education organisations, in our case, the UK's Aston Business School and Kenya's Strathmore Business School. If the UN sustainable development goals are to be achieved, then more institutional capacity-building will be required. This will need to be grant funded by relevant public or private institutions, and Kenya needs to be included as a location for such activity, which has been a difficulty faced by the authors of this chapter. This spreads capacity-building beyond the initial locale.

The establishment of ISBI within a higher education (HE) setting, Strathmore Business School, Nairobi, is consistent with UK practices. Universities are pivotal for entrepreneurship education because, as Christina Slade, Vice-Chancellor of Bath Spa University, UK, states: 'the key challenge [of HE] will be to get people ready for portfolio careers, to encourage them to become entrepreneurial. It's a combination of helping people to become resilient through these changes and equipping them with hard skills' (quoted in Faragher, 2017: 20). However, entrepreneurial education needs to be independently assessed to ensure that Slade's key challenges are being met. The Small Business Charter (SBC) award recognises only 36 UK business schools that effectively support small businesses, local economies, and student entrepreneurship. To achieve the award there is rigorous assessment of the depth and effectiveness of business engagement and business support. The SBC facilitates knowledge sharing networks to promote entrepreneurship education. (See https://charteredabs.org/small-business-charter/.) Kenya could adopt a similar policy, having a Kenyan SBC, so that the work of ISBI and Strathmore Business School is recognised.

ISBI is providing structured entrepreneurship education through the three programmes. Their work could be expanded within the portfolio of programmes offered by Strathmore Business School, subject to more support. This is because ISBI, like the Transformation for Growth Programme, have found a business model which assists the wide variety of MSME needs. In particular, ISBI has identified a fundamental need for more strategic and financial skills. ISBI argues that growth based on projects or activities that generate a return on investment below the average cost of capital adjusted for risk destroys rather than creates value for the MSME, as well for society. In this context, recommendations for policy makers could focus on raising business and financial literacy among all Kenyan MSMEs, which has the potential to improve MSME profitability dramatically and to boost economic growth. The focus could be on:

- Enhancing current operations: Abandon unprofitable activities and optimise cost structures
- Optimising capital use: This leads to either a reduced need for a loan or the redirection of these resources into a more profitable activity
- Delaying growth and expansion: These may only come later, once sound operations and a healthy capital structure have been established

In summary, knowledge transfer between The TRANSFORMATION Project, based in the UK, and ISBI, located in Kenya, has been possible because the two projects have focused on the same issue, facilitating MSME growth, and they both operate with an HE setting. The knowledge transferred to ISBI is the technology of the two management tools outlined earlier in the chapter which drive MSME growth by directly working with MSMEs in a systematic method. The current impact on ISBI by The TRANSFORMATION Project is the recalibration of their entrepreneurship programmes in three ways. First, there is the systematisation of their interventions into a 4-Stage Process. Second, as a result of the process, it has led to an emphasis on the last stage, measuring ISBI's impact. Measuring impact reveals the effectiveness of their advice to MSMEs by identifying growth. Third, knowledge exchange events upskill a larger population of MSMEs, extending the impact beyond ISBI directly to MSMEs in Nairobi. The follow-on impact on ISBI by The TRANSFORMATION Project will be to help embed performance measurement, which will increase MSME participation in ISBI's programmes once it is clear that entrepreneurship education leads to economic growth. The systematised collection of impact data will achieve this goal – we are working on this future collaboration. Following Kenny (2008), who argues that there are opportunities for reverse learning from Kenya to the UK, ISBI's three entrepreneurship programmes could be applied to support growth in the UK. The current impact on The TRANSFORMATION Project is to reflect on how it can share its performance measurement systems with ISBI. In doing so, the follow-on impact will be demonstrating how the management tools can work internationally in Kenya, and perhaps in the surrounding region in the MSME informal economy.

Finally, the growth and performance of enterprises operating in the informal economy in the East African region, to an extent, makes Kenya a coordinating hub, integrating local, national and international markets, and linking the activities of a large number of MSMEs with the formal sector (for example, trading, telecommunication, construction, consumer goods, and banking). More research on the integration and intersection of the informal MSME sector with the formal sector is needed to fully grasp the co-dependency of these sectors and the contribution of the former to the success or failure of the later. Nonetheless, and in conclusion, this chapter evidences Kenya being a positive case of sustainable economic growth.

References

Baumol, W. J. (1990) Entrepreneurship: Productive, unproductive, and destructive. *Journal of Political Economy*, 98(5): 893–921.

Bremmer, I. (2015) The new world of business. *Fortune*, 22 January. Retrieved June 26, 2017 from http://fortune.com/2015/01/22/the-new-world-of-business/

Brück, T., Naudé, W., and Verwimp, P. (2012) Business under fire: Entrepreneurship and violent conflict in developing countries. *Journal of Conflict Resolution*, 57(1): 3–19.

Butler, M. J. R. (2003) Managing from the inside out: Drawing on 'Receptivity' to explain variation in strategy implementation. *British Journal of Management*, 14 Special Issue December: S47–S60.

Butler, M. J. R. (2012) Five readiness factors for organisational change. In C.-L. Rathbone (Ed.), *Ready for Change?* London: Palgrave MacMillan, 29–51.

Butler, M. J. R., and Allen, P. (2008) Understanding policy implementation processes as self organizing systems. *Public Management Review*, 10(3): 421–440.

Butler, M. J. R., and Gheorghiu, L. (2010) Exploring the failure to protect the rights of the Roma child in Romania. *Public Administration and Development*, 30(4): 235–246.

Chartered Association of Business Schools (CABS). (2017) *Small Business Charter*. Retrieved June 26, 2017 from https://charteredabs.org/small-business-charter/

Cooke, B., and Dar, S. (2008) Introduction: The new development management. In S. Dar and B. Cooke (Eds.), *The New Development Management*. London: Zed Books, 1–17.

Dar, S., and Cooke, B. (Eds.). The New Development Management. London: Zed Books.

Department for International Development (DfID). (2015) *Britain Backs the Global Goals for Sustainable Development*. Retrieved June 26, 2017 from www.gov.uk/government/news/greening-britain-backs-the-global-goals-for-sustainable-development

Faragher, J. (2017) Analysis: How can universities weather the storm? HE leaders debate challenges of changing job market and political instability. *Times Higher Education*, 13–19 July, No. 2314: 20.

Farah, I., Opanga, V., and Abdishakur, S. (2016) Eastleigh 'Little Mogadishu' and its traditional integration into the East African economy: The secret, challenges and opportunities. *Horn of Africa Bulletin*.

Retrieved August 7, 2017 http://life-peace.org/hab/eastleigh-little-mogadishu-and-its-traditional-integration-into-the-east-african-economy-the-secret-challenges-and-opportunities/

Global Entrepreneurship Monitor (GEM). (2017) *Global Report 2016/17.* Retrieved June 26, 2017 from http://gemconsortium.org/report/49812

Hartley, J., Butler, M. J. R., and Benington, J. (2002) Local government modernisation: UK and comparative analysis from an organizational perspective. *Public Management Review*, 4(3): 387–404.

Hope, Sr. K. R. (2013) The growth of urban communities in Kenya. *African Identities*, 113: 274–289.

ICEP. (2018) *ICEP: weltweit mehr unternehmen – Partner for Development.* Retrieved 14 May 2018 from https://icep.at/organisation/?lang=en

Institute for Small Business Initiatives (ISBI). (2018) ISBI at Strathmore Business School: It's about Impact! Retrieved May 14, 2018 from www.isbi-kenya.org/

International Labour Organization (ILO). (2013) *Kenya: Making Quality Employment the Driver of Development.* Retrieved June 26, 2017 from www.ilo.org/wcmsp5/groups/public/–africa/documents/publication/wcms_231155.pdf

International Labour Organization (ILO). (2015) *Labour and Non Labour-related Laws for the Micro, Small and Medium Size Enterprises in Kenya: Participant's Handbook.* Retrieved June 26, 2017 from www.ilo.org/wcmsp5/groups/public/–africa/–ro-addis_ababa/–ilo-dar_es_salaam/documents/publication/wcms_493747.pdf

Kazmi, B. A., and Loyaan, F. A. (2017) *A United Nation's Briefing Paper: Business-led Peacebuilding in Somalia – Opportunities and Challenges.* Unpublished.

Kenny, K. (2008) 'Arrive bearing gifts. . .': Postcolonial insights for development management. In S. Dar and B. Cooke (Eds.), *The New Development Management.* London: Zed Books, 56–73.

Makame, A. (2012, August 16) *The East African Integration: Achievement and Challenges.* GREAT Insights (Maastricht, ECDPM). Retrieved August 7, 2017 from http://ecdpm.org/great-insights/trade-and-development-making-the-link/east-african-integration-achievements-challenges/Odero, W., Reeves, W., and Chokerah, J. (2016) *Kenya 2016.* Retrieved June 26, 2017 from www.africaneconomicoutlook.org

Oetzel, J., Westermann-Behaylo, M., Koerber, C., Fort, T. L., and Rivera, J. (2009) Business and peace: Sketching the terrain. *Journal of Business Ethics*, 89(4): 351–373.

OXFAM. (2009) *Kenya Threatened by New Urban Disaster.* Oxford: OXFAM.

Ruggie, J. (2011) *Guiding Principles on Business and Human Rights: Implementing the United Nations "Protect, Respect and Remedy" Framework.* Retrieved August 7, 2017 from https://business-humanrights.org/sites/default/files/media/documents/ruggie/ruggie-guiding-principles-21-mar-2011.pdf

Slim, H. (2012) Business actors in armed conflict: Towards a new humanitarian agenda. *International Review of the Red Cross (IRRC)*, Autumn, 94(887): 903–918.

Strathmore Business School (SBS). (2018) *About SBS: Our Overarching Mission at SBS; Service to Society Through the Development of International Executive Business Management and Leadership Programs.* Retrieved May 14, 2018 from http://sbs.strathmore.edu/about-sbs/welcome/

Strathmore University (SU). (2017) *Your Strathmore Journey Starts Here.* Retrieved May 14, 2018 from www.strathmore.edu/en/

Thomas, A. (1996) What is development management? *Journal of International Development*, 8(1): 95–110.

The TRANSFORMATION Project. (2017) *World-Leading Ideas and Innovation, Founded on Engaged Scholarship, From Research to Application.* Retrieved June 26, 2017 from www.thetransformationproject.co.uk

United Nations (UN). (2015) *Transforming Our World: The 2030 Agenda for Sustainable Development.* A/RES/70/1. Retrieved June 26, 2017 from https://sustainabledevelopment.un.org/content/documents/21252030%20Agenda%20for%20Sustainable%20Development%20web.pdf

The World Bank. (2016) *Doing Business 2016: Measuring Regulatory Quality and Efficiency* Retrieved June 26, 2017 from www.doingbusiness.org/~/media/WBG/DoingBusiness/Documents/Annual-Reports/English/DB16-Full-Report.pdf

World Economic Forum (WEF). (2015) *The Global Competitiveness Report 2015–2016.* Retrieved June 26, 2017 from www3.weforum.org/docs/gcr/2015-2016/Global_Competitiveness_Report_2015-2016.pdf

15

The challenge of institutionalizing organizational renewal

A case study of Equity Bank

Franca Ovadje

Introduction

Strategy and change management researchers have tried to understand why some firms are able to renew themselves and respond to environmental changes that threaten their viability. Organizational renewal is particularly important in uncertain environments characterized by frequent and discontinuous changes. However, in spite of the challenges in the African environment, little is known about how organizations anticipate and/or respond to environmental shifts on the African continent. Given the high level of uncertainty and complexity of these countries, a study on organizational renewal in the African context should provide many insights for researchers and managers.

Africa's GDP growth averaged 3.3% between 2010 and 2015 (McKinsey Global Institute, 2016). According to George, Corbishley, Khayesi, Haas, and Tihanyi (2016: 377) much of this growth is driven by emerging consumer markets, investments in infrastructure, technological leap-frogging, and the opening up of new markets. Information and computing technology has created huge opportunities for growth. It is projected that by 2025 half of the population will have internet access. Research by The Economist shows that mobile phones are revolutionizing Africa. The number of active mobile phones is about 1 billion. Mobile telephony has enabled financial inclusion and created whole new industries on the continent.

In spite of the economic growth, the environment remains volatile and uncertain. It is not surprising that in this environment the rate of small business failure is high (Marlow, 2005 cited in Adisa, Abdulraheem, and Mordi, 2014: 2). South Africa is said to have the highest failure rate of small businesses in the world (George et al., 2016). The environment is particularly harsh on small businesses who are less likely to have the resources to neutralize the effects of environmental disincentives (Ibeh, 2003). Yet small businesses play a pivotal role in the economic development of any country. They employ a large majority of the population and can be a source of innovative products and services.

George et al. (2016: 377) opine that the greatest challenge of African countries is the persistence of what Palepu and Khanna (2010: 16) called institutional voids. The latter identified three such voids in emerging markets: absent or unreliable sources of market information, an uncertain regulatory environment, and inefficient judicial systems. These voids negatively affect the ease of doing business in Africa. For example, uncertain regulatory environment creates huge challenges for organizations in Africa and demand frequent and adequate responses if these organizations are to survive (Ovadje, 2014: 1). They must reconfigure existing resources and create new ones that enable them win in a constantly changing environment (Jurksiene and Pundziene, 2016: 433). Not many organizations have been able to do this successfully, if we go by the failure rate of small businesses in Africa. Few family businesses have been able to move successfully to the second generation.

One organization that has renewed itself and survived in this rapidly changing environment is Equity Bank. In 1993, Equity was moribund: it had total losses of 33 million Ksh and a non-performing loan portfolio of 54%. It was to be shut down by the Central Bank of Kenya. Instead, the latter asked Equity to hire a change agent (he later became the CEO) and implement change. By 2015, Equity Bank was the most profitable bank in Kenya. It had subsidiaries in five African countries, total assets of 341,329 million Ksh (ranked second in Kenya), and a profit after tax of 22,288 million Ksh. How did Equity achieve this feat in an uncertain and volatile environment?

In this chapter we discuss organizational renewal in Africa. First, we review the literature on dynamic capabilities and ambidexterity. This review provides the theoretical framework for understanding the case study we present in the next section of the chapter. The case is of an African organization that is constantly renewing itself, and is thriving. We describe how Equity Bank has transformed itself since its foundation in 1984.

Equity Bank built organizational renewal into its culture; it expects to disrupt itself every ten years. It has developed dynamic capabilities for sensing the environment and seizing the opportunities (Teece, 2007). Equity combines exploratory and exploitative innovation to meet its environmental challenges (Jurksiene and Pundziene, 2016: 437). We describe how Equity Bank achieves ambidexterity and the enablers of ambidexterity. The chapter closes with a discussion of the findings and the implications for managers in Africa, who must constantly renew their organizations to survive and thrive in their uncertain and often volatile environments.

Theoretical framework

The Resource Based View is a theoretical framework for understanding competitive advantage among firms (Eisenhardt and Martin, 2000). Organizations are viewed (conceived of) as bundles of resources which are unevenly distributed among firms. Those organizations that possess resources which are valuable, rare, inimitable, and non-substitutable (VRIN) can achieve sustainable advantage over other firms. Research suggests that having this stock of resources is a source of advantage in relatively stable environments (Barney, 1986).

An organization may have developed capabilities which enable it to thrive in a stable environment: it has a strategy which is well aligned to the culture, structure, and processes (O'Reilly and Tushman, 2016). This fit or alignment makes it possible to outperform competitors. However, in dynamic contexts where change is often radical, fit may lead to rigidities, the inability to adapt to change which could lead to the demise of the organization (Hatum, Pettigrew, and Michelini, 2010: 258). In developing countries, it may be particularly necessary that organizations develop capabilities that enable them thrive in uncertain macro-economic, political, and social environments. In such unpredictable, changing environments, having a stock of VRIN resources may not be enough to achieve competitive advantage. In markets where the competitive landscape is shifting, dynamic capabilities become the source of sustained competitive advantage (Eisenhardt and Martin, 2000: 1106).

Teece, Pisano, and Shuen (1997: 516) define dynamic capabilities as "the firm's ability to integrate, build and reconfigure internal and external competencies to address rapidly changing environments". Capabilities which are VRIN must be refreshed in changing environments (Ambrosin and Bowman, 2009) if the organization is to sustain competitive advantage. It must create new resources, or alter the resource mix in order to realign with the shifting environment (Teece et al., 1997). In environments characterized by shocks, where there are unknown unknowns, dynamic capabilities are most relevant (Teece and Leih, 2016).

Hatum et al. (2010), in their study on building organizational capabilities, identified five capabilities required to adapt under turmoil: diversity of top management, decentralization and de-formalization of decision making process, low macroculture embeddedness, environmental scanning, and strong organizational identity. Teece (2007: 1336) argued that to sustain dynamic capabilities, decentralization is important as it brings top management closer to new technologies, the customer, and the market.

Chang, Chang, Chi, Chen, and Deng (2012: 442) argue that some capabilities are essential for radical innovation: a firm's ability to explore, adapt, tolerate, and experiment with new products, processes, and services for non-mainstream businesses. They identified four radical innovation capabilities: *Openness capability* (willingness to explore); *strategic integration capability* (alignment, adaptation, or ambidexterity); *autonomy capability* (tolerance of creativity and differences); and *experimentation capability* (ability to learn and probe).

Teece (2007: 1319) identified three elements of dynamic capabilities: sensing and shaping opportunities and threats, seizing opportunities, and maintaining competitiveness through enhancing or re-configuring the organization's intangible and tangible assets. Sensing involves environmental scanning, exploration, and learning. Entrepreneurs and managers try to figure out how to interpret new events and developments (Teece (2007: 1322). Senior managers must be able to accurately *sense* changes in their competitive environment, including potential shifts in technology, competition, customers, and regulation (Harreld, O'Reilly, and Tushman, 2007: 24).

Seizing opportunities involves the development of new products and processes, design of new business models, the establishment of new decision rules, and resource allocation processes. To seize opportunities, managers must be detached from current decision rules and be open to new ones.

The third category of dynamic capabilities is reconfiguration. According to Teece (2007: 1335), this is key to sustained profitable growth. It is the ability to recombine and reconfigure assets and organizational structures as the organization grows and as markets and technologies change. As the environment changes, organizations must learn new skills and reallocate resources. Sustained competitive advantage comes from the firm's ability to leverage and reconfigure its existing competencies and assets in ways that are valuable to the consumer but difficult for competitors to imitate (Harreld et al., 2007: 24). Thus, dynamic capabilities provide insights to managers about how they become more effective in adapting to discontinuous change (Birkinshaw, Zimmermann, and Raisch, 2016: 36).

The African environment is dynamic, and arguably one with deep uncertainties. Unstable macro-economic environment, frequent changes in regulations and government policies, recent changes in demographics, and the rapid increase in access to mobile phones have created a highly uncertain, even volatile business environment. To survive, African firms must adapt to the shifting environment; they must develop dynamic capabilities to sense the changing environment and seize the opportunities in it.

For example, Equity Bank in Kenya sensed the impact of telecommunications on the banking industry early in the day. M-Pesa, a financial product introduced by Safaricom (a telecommunications giant in Kenya) had become very popular. The senior management of Equity Bank sensed that the boundaries between financial services and telecommunications were getting blurred. Many banks were focusing on the retail segment, which had a huge percentage of the unbanked. Moving away from branches to "Your Phone, Your Bank" made sense in this environment. Equity Bank sensed this environment, interpreted it correctly, and seized the opportunity by setting up a Fintech (reconfiguring its structure).

As the environment shifts, firms in dynamic environments must be able to adapt; they may require new strategies, structures, etc. Hatum et al. (2010) argued that very long-standing or persistent capabilities that are not flexible enough to incorporate new competences and skills may evolve into core rigidities and eventually impede organizational adaptation. Efficiency in current markets and technologies, as well as flexibility and experimentation for future markets and technologies, is essential for the long-run survival of an organization, especially in an uncertain environment (O'Reilly and Tushman, 2013: 1).

Organizational ambidexterity

In the view of Birkinshaw, Zimmermann, and Raisch (2016: 37), ambidexterity is a useful complement to the dynamic capabilities framework: it clarifies the strengths and weaknesses of different organizational arrangements chosen by executives to sense and seize opportunities and reconfigure their internal activities. Ambidexterity has been positively associated with increased firm innovation, better financial performance, and higher survival rates (O'Reilly and Tushman, 2013).

Organizational ambidexterity is the ability of an organization to explore new opportunities while at the same time working diligently to exploit existing capabilities (O'Reilly and Tushman, 2004: 74). An ambidextrous organization is able to manage the present and at the same time harness opportunities that will ensure the long-run survival of the organization. Birkinshaw and Gibson (2004: 47) call these two abilities *alignment* (a clear sense of how value is being created in the short term and how activities should be coordinated and streamlined to deliver that value) and *adaptability* (the ability to move quickly towards new opportunities, to adjust to volatile markets and to avoid complacency). They emphasize that an organization must find the right balance between adaptability and alignment. Ambidexterity is one of the capabilities for cultivating and supporting radical innovation; it ensures the survival of an organization not only in the short-term, but also in the long-term. (Chang et al., 2012: 444).

If organizations in Africa are to thrive in their turbulent environments, they must do two things well: exploit current opportunities and explore future opportunities (O'Reilly and Tushman, 2013). They conceptualize exploitation as the ability to compete in mature technologies and markets where efficiency, control, and incremental improvement are needed; and exploration as the ability to compete in new technologies and markets where flexibility, autonomy, and experimentation are required. These organizations simultaneously pursue incremental innovations in their existing businesses while seeking radical innovations (radical changes) in new businesses, products, etc.

Past research has examined the question of how ambidexterity is achieved in practice. Ambidexterity can be achieved sequentially, by shifting structure; simultaneously, by establishing separate units for exploration and exploitation of opportunities, each internally aligned (O'Reilly and Tushman, 2013); and behaviourally, by creating a context that allows employees to decide how to spend their time between exploitation and exploration (Gibson and Birkinshaw, 2004). With sequential ambidexterity, the organization focuses on exploitation or exploration at different times, usually over a long period of time. No new structures are created under behavioural or contextual ambidexterity; employees are encouraged to make judgments on which activity to pursue and which to let go. Ambidexterity can also be achieved through the creation of new structures which focus on exploration while the rest of the organization concentrates on exploitation activities. However, O'Reilly and Tushman (2016: 10, 14) show that if an organization is to exploit existing assets and capabilities by getting more efficient, and provide for sufficient exploration that they take advantage of changes in markets and technologies, what is needed is not physical separation of exploitation and exploration, but a more sophisticated separation that also includes targeted integration, strong senior management support for the new business, and an overarching organizational identity. These enable the new business to leverage the assets and capabilities of the existing business and executives can give the exploratory unit the protection and oversight it needs to succeed.

O'Reilly and Tushman (2013) highlighted two factors which may affect the choice of the type of ambidexterity: the nature of the competitive landscape and time. In stable markets, sequential ambidexterity may be appropriate to take advantage of the occasional environmental jolts. In dynamic markets, a simultaneous focus on exploitation and exploration (structural ambidexterity) may be more appropriate as firms try to resolve the conflict between the present and the future. They argue further that in dynamic markets, once the exploratory unit gains traction, it may be integrated into the exploitation structures (O'Reilly and Tushman, 2013: 330).

The antecedents of ambidexterity

Wang and Rafiq (2014: 61) argued that an organizational culture characterized by shared vision and diversity promotes contextual ambidexterity. Organizational diversity was defined as the set of organizational values and norms that encourage and tolerate differences, and recognize and reward individuals' different viewpoints, skills, and knowledge. Shared vision is the set of organizational values and norms that promote the overall active involvement of organizational members in the development, communication, dissemination, and implementation of organizational goals.

Birkinshaw and Gibson (2004: 51) found in their study of 41 business units in 10 multinational companies that supportive *organizational contexts* are associated with high levels of ambidexterity. Organizational context is characterized as performance management and social support. Performance management includes stimulating people to deliver high-quality results and making them accountable for their actions, and social support involves providing people with the security and latitude they need to perform.

Structure (the ability of an organization to develop appropriate structural mechanisms to enable it cope with the competing demands of exploitation and exploration) has also been identified as an antecedent of organizational ambidexterity (Raisch and Birkinshaw, 2008). They make the case that organizational units pursuing exploration should be small and decentralized with loose processes, while those pursuing exploitation should be larger, more decentralized, and with tight processes. According to them, it is important to make this distinction because the demands of exploration and exploitation differ. For instance, exploration may require very loose, decentralized structure where employees are free to come up with creative ideas and try them out, whereas successful exploitation of existing capabilities would require clear structure and systems and working within boundaries to achieve specific results. According to Gibson and Birkinshaw (2004), developing structural mechanisms for coping with the competing demands of alignment and adaptability aids the achievement of ambidexterity.

Several scholars have identified leadership as an important antecedent of organizational ambidexterity (O'Reilly and Tushman, 2016; Raisch and Birkinshaw, 2008; Lubatkin, Simsek, Ling, and Veiga, 2006; Gibson and Birkinshaw, 2004). Raisch and Birkinshaw, 2008 found that firms whose founding teams had diverse characteristics and experiences showed a higher degree of ambidexterity. In other words, team composition and behavioural integration (defined by Lubatkin et al., 2006: 647 as the degree of senior management team's wholeness and unity of effort) are important precursors of organizational ambidexterity. Leadership is essential in the implementation of different kinds of ambidexterity and necessary to promote a supportive organizational context (Raisch and Birkinshaw, 2008: 391; Gibson and Birkinshaw, 2004: 210). According to O'Reilly and Tushman (2016: 39), leaders must be able to help their organizations compete in mature businesses that are typically the source of today's profits by exploiting existing assets and capabilities while they prepare for the future markets by using these assets and capabilities to explore new ventures.

Summary

African markets are dynamic, even uncertain markets characterized by frequent changes in regulation, technology, demographics, etc. To remain competitive, African firms must renew themselves. This renewal may consist of incremental changes to the existing business or more transformational changes which could ensure the long run viability of the firm.

Research suggests that to succeed in today's market, organizations need to align their strategies with their structure, culture, and processes. It is this alignment that enables firms to enjoy superior profits. However, the alignment may be so tight that the organization becomes rigid and out of sync with its environment. In a dynamic, uncertain environment, organizations must build capabilities that enable them thrive in this environment. *Organizational capabilities* are those unique internal management processes and intangible resources that enable an organization to constantly renew itself. Competences and skills may degenerate into core rigidities, which can be detrimental to the long-term survival of the firm. Firms that are careful about the capabilities they develop relative to the environment in which they operate can transform and adapt quickly in dynamic markets (Hatum et al., 2010: 258).

Dynamic capabilities are most relevant in rapidly changing, uncertain environments (Teece and Leih, 2016). They are comprised of sensing and shaping opportunities, seizing opportunities, and reconfiguring the organization's assets (Teece, 2007). According to Birkinshaw et al. (2016: 37), ambidexterity is a useful complement to the dynamic capabilities framework. Ambidextrous organizations are able to manage present conditions and create value in the short term (exploitation) while also moving quickly towards new opportunities (exploration). They explore new opportunities while at the same time working diligently to exploit existing capabilities (O'Reilly and Tushman, 2004).

Three types of ambidexterity were identified in the literature: sequential, structural, and contextual or behavioural ambidexterity. We also highlighted some antecedents of organizational ambidexterity from the literature: organizational culture, supportive organizational context, structure, and leadership (See Wang and Rafiq, 2014; Birkinshaw and Gibson, 2004; Raisch and Birkinshaw, 2008). In the next section, we discuss the case of Equity Bank, an organization that has regularly renewed itself in a dynamic environment.

Equity Bank Ltd.: a case study

Introduction

Equity Bank (hereafter called Equity) is a financial services provider with its headquarters in Kenya. It offers retail banking, microfinance, investment banking, insurance services, consulting, and other related services to its customers. It has subsidiaries in Uganda, South Sudan, Rwanda, and Tanzania. Equity began operations as a building society in 1984 and transformed to a commercial bank in 2004. As at December 31, 2015, Equity had 11 wholly owned subsidiaries and 79% of the shares of ProCredit Bank Limited in the Democratic Republic of Congo (DRC).

Equity changed the face of financial services provision in Kenya through financial inclusion giving dignity to the *mwananchi*, or ordinary Kenyan. By the end of 2015, Equity had over 10 million customers, and its customer deposits grew by 23% (Kshs 303.2 billion) in 2015. In 2015 as well, its profit before tax and exceptional items increased by 12% to Kshs 24.0 billion from Kshs 21.3 billion in 2014. Its total assets and net customer loans increased by 24% and 26%, respectively.

In 2015, Think Business Kenya awarded the Best Bank of the Year to Equity. In fact, Equity won ten of the 24 awards. The Bank also received other awards, including: *Most Innovative Bank and Best in Mobile Payments* (Banker Africa Awards); *Best Financial Services Firm, Social Corporate Category* (Social Media Awards); *CEO of the Year* and *Best Performing Company* (in the Ai40 Awards). A distinguishing feature of Equity is its commitment to the social and economic empowerment of the *mwananchi*. The evolution of the Bank can be divided into four periods each of which is characterized by a major change or transformation.

1984–1994: Equity 0.0 Equity Building Society

Equity started operations in 1984 as Equity Building Society. Its mission – the social and economic transformation of the *mwananchi*, the ordinary Kenyan – was clear from inception. As a Building Society, it aimed at empowering the lowest stratum of the society by providing them mortgage loans. This group (low-income population) was marginalized at the time; they had little or no access to financial resources. Equity removed barriers (such as minimum credit balance, limits on withdrawals) and enabled the *mwananchi* to access financial services. The company's logo, a modest house with a brown roof, signified the desire of the founders to create a better life for the people of Kenya.

With only a few branches in rural Kenya, Equity Building Society provided access to mortgage facilities. In 1993 however, Equity was declared "technically" insolvent by the Central Bank of Kenya (CBK), citing poor management and ineffective governance. But the CBK was reluctant about recommending the winding down of Equity because of the fact that the company had affected the lives of many ordinary Kenyans positively. The CBK therefore allowed the company to continue in existence after a change agent, James Mwangi, was hired as the company's Finance Director.

1994–2004: Equity 1.0 Change in business model and strategy

In 1994, Equity changed its business model and obtained a license to operate as a Micro Finance Institution. This change in business model met with a lot of success, as it addressed the real needs of Equity's customers: people wanted small loans to grow their businesses, not to buy homes. With this change, Equity was able to obtain deposits and provide short term loans to its growing clientele. The Management team articulated the mission and vision of the Bank.

Equity attracted professionals to its Board and increased its capital base. Training programmes were organized for staff and the culture of the Bank was articulated and communicated; efforts were made to ensure that all employees imbibed the new culture.

2004–2014: Equity 2.0 Legal and structural transformation and repositioning for the future

In 2004, Equity went through another major transformation: it became a commercial bank. This change involved a change in legal framework, structure, processes, etc. The Bank identified critical success factors (CSFs) for its mission and business model: an organizational culture that values people, enhances performance, and supports people; customer focus;

high-quality asset portfolio; operational efficiency and scalable operations; robust systems; maximizing value for all stakeholders; and regional expansion. Goals, targets, and measures, as well as activities, were agreed upon for each of the critical success factors, and each CSF was assigned to a director and his/her performance and contribution were measured along those lines. The CSFs enabled the alignment and execution of the company's new strategy.

Mary Wangari Wamae, the Director of Strategy, remarked:

> The biggest change was in 2004. First of all, we changed the legal form of the Company from a Building Society to a Limited Company, and then a Bank, a fully-fledged Commercial Bank. We made drastic changes to the Board of Directors. We made changes in the management. We made changes in even products and services – you know the way you deliver the service to the customer, all that changed.

Other incremental changes were made during the 2004–2014 period. The board of directors was restructured. The initial board of directors was constituted by a group of friends who shared the same vision, people who believed in the transformation of the ordinary Kenyan. Directors from reputable organizations with diverse experiences were recruited. The Board now had a truly Kenyan identity with each region in Kenya having a representative on the Board. Equity built the capacity for change in the staff by training them on the new strategy and focus.

Between 2004 and 2014, the Bank scaled up its distribution network to 170 branches in Kenya and embarked on a massive expansion into East Africa: Equity Bank Uganda was established in 2008, Equity Bank South Sudan in 2009, Equity Bank Rwanda in 2011, and Equity Bank Tanzania in 2012. It was also during this period that Equity built a network of ATMs, launched its Internet Banking platform, and began Agency Banking. It was listed in the Nairobi Stock Exchange in 2006.

In addition to the changes highlighted above, Equity changed its core banking application to Finacle – an IT solution for providing universal banking. Following the drop in mobile phone prices and an anticipated increase in mobile phone ownership, Equity began some innovations in mobile and online banking. After M-Pesa was introduced by Safaricom in 2007, Equity partnered with Safaricom to introduce M-Keso. It also began a financial supermarket strategy in 2006/7 with product offerings in insurance, investments, and custodial services.

2014 to 2024: Equity 3.0 Technology focused on emerging trends and future disruptions

In 2014, the Bank decided to converge banking and telecommunications and redefine banking. A bank became something you do, not somewhere you go. Equity launched Equitel, a revolutionary platform for performing financial transactions using a smartphone. With an Equitel SIM card, customers could send money securely to another phone, send money to a bank account, pay bills, pay for goods and services, buy airtime for Equitel and other networks, use the account to save money, get an *Eazzy* loan, and also save for a goal. The possibilities with the *My Money* feature of Equitel were many, and basically the customers' phone became his/her bank.

According to James Mwangi, the MD/CEO:

> There were two things that overtook the traditional model of banking. The first one was technology. The second was telecommunication . . . So what we decided was: what if we make the bank a Fintech? If it is technology that is moving faster than the bank, then make the bank a Fintech . . . Why don't we converge banking and telecommunication? And this is a story of making Equity a Fintech: a convergence of telecommunication and banking so that you can fully digitize and you can use telecommunication as a channel, the mobile phone as a channel delivery and you can see how well it has performed.

Mary described the new Bank:

> Equity Bank needs to become part of your lifestyle. It doesn't matter what you do. You buy insurance, shop, pay a bill, you do anything, Equity is there for you.

Equity introduced two additional critical success factors (brand protection and customer experience) in 2015 to ensure alignment of the new strategy, and is currently exploring partnerships and strategic alliances, especially in the area of big data. Equity became a group holding company in 2015 and continued its expansion by acquiring Pro Credit Bank in the Democratic Republic of Congo.

Summary

Following the development of Equity, one observes that every ten years, there is a major change (a radical innovation) followed by several incremental changes within the ten-year period (see Figure 15.1). 1984 saw the establishment of Equity Building Society. In 1994, Equity changed its business model from a Building Society to a Microfinance Institution. Between 1994 and 2004, the capital base was increased, and efforts were made to develop human capacity, build an organizational culture, and communicate the vision.

2004 was the year of legal and structural transformation and repositioning for the future, the year Equity was registered as a Commercial Bank with the capacity to carry out universal banking functions. To ensure alignment with the new strategy, the Bank identified the critical success factors for the strategy. This major change was accompanied by several legal, operational, and structural changes, as well as the introduction of mobile and online banking, and scaling up of distribution networks, ATMs, and agency banking.

In 2014, Equity Group launched Equitel and redefined banking. It identified two additional critical success factors in 2015: *brand protection* and *customer experience*.

It is pertinent to note that since its foundation, Equity's mission and vision have remained the same, even as the business was transformed. There have been changes in the organizational structure, strategy, people, and technology but its culture (which was built between 1994 to 2014) has remained the same. In the next section, we discuss strategic alignment and self-disruption as a way of life at Equity.

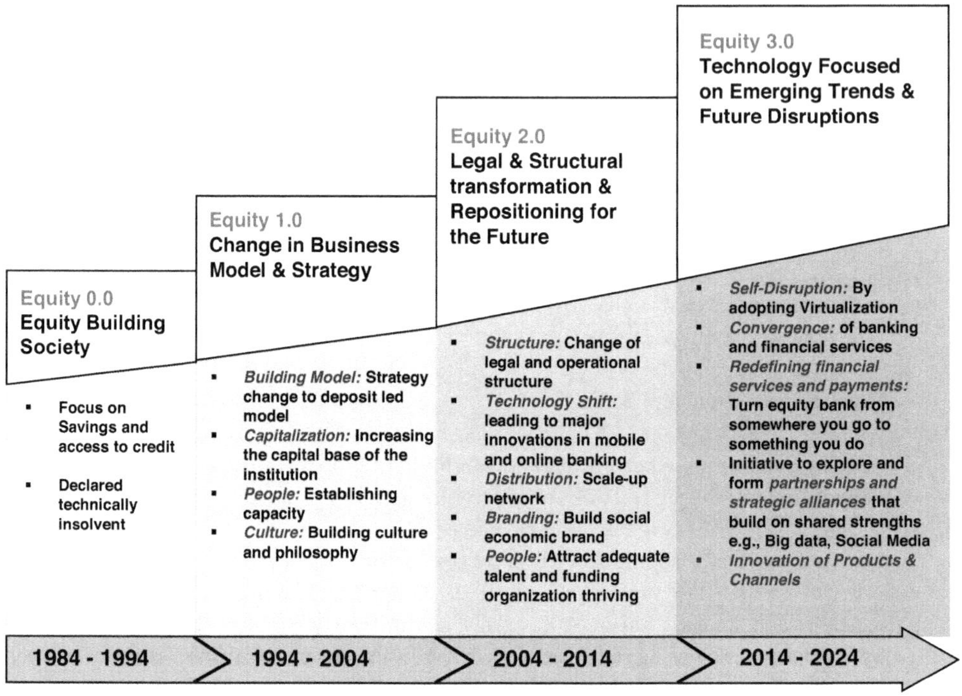

Figure 15.1 Evolution of Equity Bank

Source: Equity Bank Document

Self-disruption as a strategy

From the foregoing, it is clear that Equity has transformed in four decades from a Building Society to a Micro Finance Institution to a Commercial Bank with universal license, and to a holding company that manages several subsidiaries, including Fintech, which brings together banking and telecommunications. These radical changes happened during ten-year periods. Within each decade, Equity implemented several incremental changes or innovations. For example, during Equity 2.0 (from 2004 to 2014), many incremental changes were implemented, including online banking, M-Kesho, ATMs, and Agency Banking. The Bank also identified critical success factors for implementing the new strategy.

James Mwangi, the MD/CEO, explained why it took ten years to disrupt at Equity:

> Disruption is a massive transformation... It's not something you can do overnight. It requires that you change everything – board members, leadership team, systems and processes – because you are disrupting, you are looking afresh. So, if you do it frequently you will not execute the transformation fully and you'll not have thought the next disruption through.

Disruption at Equity is a deliberate, carefully planned action. The planning took about 2–5 years, and the implementation another 2–5 years. The organization tried its best to obtain sufficient data to justify the radical change and ensure that the change was not reversible or destructive.

According to the CEO, disruption can be destructive, especially for a large organization. He explained:

> You can't simply make a quick turn. You have to go to the next roundabout, and a lot of planning has to be done. To change an organization, there has to be a lot of planning and execution. It takes 3–5 years before you complete execution of disruption and then sweat for 5 years so that you get the impact. Meanwhile as you sweat, you are collecting data for the next wave of change.

According to a senior manager in the Strategy department of Equity, the Bank has a culture of renewal – deliberately shaking things up and sustaining change. He said:

> Equity Bank has a culture of renewal, a culture of change . . . We deliberately disrupt ourselves every ten years but in between, we implement a lot of changes. It is deliberate; it is critical. Everybody knows that change is going to happen irrespective of leadership; it has to happen.

Equity sees disruption as a complete cycle with different phases: planning, execution, reaping the benefits of the investment, carrying out research, validating and confirming it, consulting the stakeholders, and finally execution, and the cycle goes on. If the appropriate time frame is not given for disruption to yield its desired results before another one is implemented, the objectives may not be achieved. After all, disruption is not done for its own sake, but to create value, and creation of value takes time.

The CEO of Equity identified three major disruptive forces in the environment. Knowledge is one of the major disruptors. Another important cause of disruption is *technology*. Changes in technology could reduce the cost of operations substantially and render obsolete some products and/or services. In Equity, technology is seen as an enabler, a hygiene factor. But changes in technology cause major challenges which business must respond to if they are to survive. A new technology platform can enable a competitor do more and better things at a lower cost. In other to leverage its investments in technology, Equity sought technology that is scalable.

The environment is another source of disruption. Demographic changes, changes in regulation, consumer needs, and competitive dynamics are driving innovation, especially in developing countries. Equity does not wait for the market or the environment to change; rather, it anticipates environmental changes and thus avoids a situation where the environment changes faster than the organization. According to the General Manager of Communications:

> It's never about finding a comfort zone. We believe in self-disruption. We do not wait for the market to disrupt us; we disrupt ourselves. And that word is commonly used around here: let's disrupt ourselves. Let's not build comfort zones because the world is dynamic, the marketplace is dynamic, the consumer is dynamic. Let's not wait for the consumer to run ahead, let's run with the consumer. Let us even discern the needs of the customer and that is why the customer asks: "what is coming next?"

Strategic intent and alignment

The focus on exploration of future opportunities is what drives self-disruption at Equity. This is important for long-term survival. However, survival in the short term requires alignment of current strategy with the environment and the structure, people, culture, and operations. Alignment makes execution possible and enables value creation.

At inception, Equity Building Society's business model was not aligned: customers needed micro finance services and the firm offered mortgages. The business model was not aligned with current market realities nor with the internal systems, processes, etc. It is not surprising, therefore, that the company faltered. From 1994, special efforts at alignment were made. While the mission and vision remained essentially the same, with each transformation, efforts were made to align the new strategy with the structure, culture, and people. Critical success factors for the strategy were identified in 2004 and have not changed much in the last 20 years. Together with the mission, vision, and culture, the critical success factors (CSFs) have been the bedrock of the transformations and incremental changes at Equity.

In 2004, Equity became a commercial bank. This led to changes in the board, the organizational structure, technology, and people (with respect to experience and skills). To properly align the change, eight critical success factors were identified: an organizational culture that values people and supports the business; customer focus; operational efficiency; high-quality assets portfolio; a robust system that is scalable; maximizing value for all stakeholders; regional expansion; and customer experience.

In 2014, the organization carried out a technological revolution which required that customers do banking transactions using their mobile phones. The "Your Phone, Your Bank" strategy meant that some customers will never go to an Equity branch. This change in delivery channel required new skills. For example, customer relationship managers in the branches had to transform to SME advisors. To align the strategy, two additional critical success factors were identified: brand protection and customer experience. To build brand loyalty among these customers and to preserve its identity as an organization that cares for the social and economic wellbeing of the people, Equity aligned its Corporate Social Responsibility with its new strategy. While the branches continued to support social projects such as provision of water to communities, sports events, etc., the Equity Group Foundation carried out two high-impact programmes: the "Wings to Fly Scholarship" Programme and "Equity Leaders Programme."

Wings to Fly was launched in partnership with The MasterCard Foundation, and provides scholarships, mentorship, and leadership training to gifted students from economically disadvantaged backgrounds. USAID, KFW, and UKAID have in recent years supported the initiative. *The Annual Education and Leadership Congress* enables scholars to learn from and interact with local and international leaders. Ten thousand people are expected to benefit from the programme in the next ten years. The Equity Leaders Programme is a post-secondary programme that equips young people from across Kenya with the professional and leadership skills they need to succeed in the global marketplace. Both initiatives increased the brand awareness of Equity at the national level and brought a lot of goodwill to Equity.

According to the Director of Operations:

> Wings to Fly is across the whole country. Everywhere you go you hear people talk about Equity Bank because we are creating a new path for the society and a huge impact on the community.

A keen awareness of the environment is necessary for self-disruption and for incremental innovations. In the next section, we examine how Equity sees the future.

Environmental scanning

Self-disruption has become part of Equity's DNA. But how does the Bank know what is coming? How does it identify disruptive forces in the environment? One of the strategies for organizational renewal at Equity is environmental scanning. Town hall meetings are held at the branch level twice every week to sample opinions and enhance communication within the organization. The Bank receives feedback regularly from customers, it also conducts research.

The tagline of Equity is the listening caring partner. The Bank is a customer-focused organization. Customers feel they have rights, that the bank exists to serve them, and this deepens their commitment to the bank. It is this sense of ownership that makes the customer walk into a branch or the head office to point out something they want to see differently, an innovation they desire to see introduced. The Director of Operations expatiated:

> We have given the bank to the customers. They feel they own the bank and this is why they say they are members, not customers. A customer can come in and say, "I don't like the way your accountants are looking" or "I don't like the way this product is designed" . . . They have that ownership because we have projected the bank as theirs so they tell us what type of bank they want to serve them.

Equity customers get involved and believe the bank is there to serve them. They make invaluable recommendations on how the bank can serve them better. Some of them even call the MD to make complaints or give suggestions.

There is also a strong feedback culture at Equity, described by the CEO as an "*open feedback loop*." Feedback matters a lot at Equity because they believe that an open feedback loop builds trust. In other words, when feedback is analyzed and properly acted on, it builds trust and confidence and opens up the path for more feedback. It is treated as very important: it is analyzed and used when, how and where appropriate. The CEO explained:

> It's important you constantly demonstrate that feedback is of value to you for people to continue to give you feedback. We always ask ourselves: How much are we adapting? How much are we synthesizing the information? The level of feedback that we get is determined by how we act on feedback. The more you act, the more you receive and the more you perfect.

The Bank also tries to anticipate customer needs. When it introduced ATMs, for instance, many customers did not want to use them even though the queues in the branches were very long. Customers preferred the personal interaction with the tellers; they were also awed by the new technology. Equity hired hawkers who joined the long queues and explained to customers the benefits of the ATM and taught them how to use the machines.

Equity recognizes that the customer is always changing. According to the Director of Strategy, the average age of Equity customers ten years ago was between 40 and 45, but today the average age is 34. These younger customers demand to be served differently. They prefer online banking to visiting physical branches, while the older generations are accustomed to personal interactions.

Increasingly, customer feedback comes from Equity's Contact Centre via voice, email, and social media platforms. The Centre is run by two very senior managers. Feedback is analyzed and reports are sent to the CEO and relevant units twice a day. Equity's social media presence is widely acknowledged in Kenya. The Bank won the national award as the *Most Committed Bank on Social Media in Kenya* in 2015.

Decisions at Equity are usually based on extensive research and information-gathering. Changes are made in response to anticipated changes in the environment (demographics, life style, the macro-economy, etc.). A research team at Equity conducts extensive research on the evolving trends in consumer behaviour and provides managers with information for decision making. Initiatives and interventions typically originate from analysis and understanding of the environment.

Equity uses scenario analysis and role-play in making choices about the future. During company retreats, employees are encouraged to imagine the future, envision possible scenarios, and act them out. This enables them immerse themselves into the future and make choices after considering the implications of the different scenarios. This is, perhaps, one of the most distinctive innovative strategies at Equity.

According to James Mwangi, the CEO,

> When we create scenarios and act them, it's fully understood, and fully internalized, and that's the essence of role-play . . . Role-play is stimulating. It helps you to simulate and see the situations and gaps, and simulation is very important before execution.

In a bid to better measure and manage feedback from the environment, Equity is moving into Big Data analysis. Analytics has helped Equity automate the credit decision process. This has made it possible for customers to obtain credit facilities through their mobile phones. The CEO expatiated:

> It is important to synthesize information given that we have 11.6 million customers. Once we do that, we have information on payment gateways, on mobile channels, etc. We are privileged to have very big data and one of the biggest data processors in the world. The question is: how do we internalize and interpret this data?

The role of the C-suite in seeing the future must be emphasized. The MD/CEO serves on several boards of directors. These boards offer him a wide range of opportunities for learning and exposure to current trends in the market and the world at large. James explained:

> I think I'm very privileged: what I initially thought were responsibilities turned out to be my most useful learning forums. I sit on the IFC high-level panel on SMEs, on the G8 Advisory Board on Inclusive Finance, G8 on SMEs, on the Advisory Board of the MasterCard, McKinsey, the Clinton Global Initiative and the Bill and Melinda Gates Foundation. I'm also on the World Economic Forum, etc. These forums have become my biggest learning forums.

James is also Chairman of Kenya's Vision2030. He speaks at business schools and interacts with professors and students. These experiences and opportunities for learning present the leadership of Equity Bank with reliable knowledge on the environment and current market realities.

Organizational purpose and culture

Equity Bank has gone through a number of transformations since it was founded in 1984. Its mission and vision however, have remained the same: to transform the lives and livelihoods of the ordinary Kenyan – the *mwananchi*:

> We exist to transform the lives and livelihoods of our people socially and economically by availing them modern, inclusive financial services that maximize their opportunities.

It is this overarching purpose that guides and informs all of Equity's activities and innovations. According to James Mwangi (who led the transformation in 1994 and has been CEO since 2004):

> We go for volume business rather than margin and are usually market ready . . . We exist to transform the lives of our people socially and economically, availing them modern financial

> services that maximize their opportunities. We are mere facilitators; facilitating how people want to live their lives. We are a catalyst of lifestyles, of maximizing opportunities and we are very inclusive: we do not discriminate.

This core identity accounts for its customer focus and is a source of motivation for the staff. The core values are captured in the acronym PICTURE, which stands for Professionalism, Integrity, Creativity and Innovation, Teamwork, Unity of Purpose, Respect and dignity for customers, and Effective Corporate Governance.

Employees learn these values very quickly. They are trained and reminded at all times to be mindful of the way they treat the customers because the customers, even the poorest of them, are the reason why Equity is in business. To an outsider, it could seem like an obsession with the customer.

In addition to the respect and dignity accorded customers, Equity has a culture of creativity and innovation, "a very daring culture of possibilities" as James Mwangi put it. The culture of creativity and innovation as well as the customer focus are arguably the major driving forces for disruption in Equity. Staff members are encouraged to be creative in the performance of their daily duties and responsibilities and to share whatever insights they may have with the management. Staff feedback is possible because the leadership is open to new ideas and suggestions. Mary Wamae, the Director of Strategy, commenting on the culture of innovation and creativity at Equity said:

> People are always asking us, "What's next? What's the next big change?" People expect something new from us. Some say, "Okay, you guys, what are you cooking now?" For us change is natural; we have made creativity and innovation part of our core values; we encourage our staff to think creatively and do things differently, serve the customer differently, think about small things that work in their area that will make a difference. In one of the branches, they decided to give roses to all our customers who walked in just to surprise them and the customers were impressed. Others decided: "Okay, today is a cold July morning, so we are going to serve a cup of tea and Mandazi to all the customers that come in and the customers were so excited."

The corporate DNA and the leadership were said to be very open to change. According to the GM Mobile Innovations:

> The CEO is a person who likes to disrupt himself creatively and positively and this has been cascaded down. From the leadership all the way down, no body resists change in this organization. If you resist, you will find yourself out without being forced out. The entire organization is open and free to change. When we say, "let's move," we move. I think the successes we have obtained from these changes have reassured our team that change is good. We have survived many disruptions: we see ahead, prepare and we change.

With respect to the last major change (Equity 3.0), he commented:

> We think like a technology company. Of course we use technology to drive the business. We don't have those barriers, you know the conventional banking, risk oriented kind of stuff that keeps you in one place. We think, we innovate and then we call in the risk people to ensure everything is okay. If there is a strong conviction that we can do it, we go for it. We bring in other supporting teams to ensure that speed is controlled, the governance is there, risk is managed.

Innovation spaces

Innovation is an essential component of organizational renewal, and Equity takes this very seriously. Effort is made to create the right spaces for innovation to thrive. This ranges from adopting the right structure for innovation, to people selection and using feedback, and building risk management into innovation.

A lot of importance is attached to building cross functional teams, which are needed to manage the innovative ideas and convert them into profitable solutions. Equity builds strong, cohesive teams comprising of people with expertise in specialized areas to lead innovations. A team is created for a specific project. Employees with a diversity of skills are identified and pulled together to drive and manage innovation. For example, once the idea of converging banking and telecommunications was accepted, a cross-functional team was set up. The team "produced" Equitel and related innovations.

The best people are put together in the team, and the team leader is not necessarily the most senior person, but the person who has the capacity to lead. People bring their knowledge and not their authority to the team.

Initiatives are broken into small task forces and people are assigned to the small teams based on their competencies. Teams define what is to be done and create and manage their own governing structure and decision making, independent of the bank. The CEO expatiated:

> We break the initiatives into small task forces based on their competence. They don't have to be taught; they just need to be explained what is expected. How they do it is theirs to define. And then you give them authority so they create their governing structure and decision making; they don't need the rest of the bank. We remove it from the normal governance structure because the normal governance structure is an operational structure; it's not a strategic structure. If you try to use the normal operational structure, you will never make strategic decisions because they are not experts in strategic initiatives. You give autonomy to the strategic initiatives to put its own governance structures and decision making and you hold them accountable.

Not only do project teams have their governance structures, they are physically separated from the rest of the Bank. For example, 50 leaders on Project Everest were moved to a hotel for several months while they worked on the project. Procedures are deliberately flexible for the innovation spaces. For example, they do not go through the normal procurement procedures; once the budget is approved, nothing is allowed to slow them down.

Equity also has a portal where staff can log in their innovative ideas and say what they want to see improved in the organization. Employees no longer have to suggest their ideas to line managers who may not take the ideas to the management meeting or execute those ideas.

People and leadership

According to James Mwangi, an organization can change as much as its people. Finding the right people, developing them, and retaining them is therefore critical to organizational renewal. Day-to-day operations as well as the innovation spaces are run by employees who graduated from the Pre-University Programme. They were the best and brightest in their divisions in the Pre-University National examination. They received a scholarship from Equity to go to university, and worked for the Bank during their gap year and during vacations while they were at university. Before they are employed by the Bank, many of them have imbibed its values and culture.

The general manager of mobile innovations, for example, started his career as a teller at Equity. He was spotted as a creative person and moved to an innovation space.

While many managers have remained in the Bank for over a decade, Equity has refreshed its senior management a number of times. Effort is made during recruitment to ensure entrants have the required skill, experience, fit with the culture and values, and belief in the organization's mission and vision. The management team is very diverse in terms of experience, background, and nationality. James Mwangi has been CEO for over a decade. He sits on several boards and brings a wealth of knowledge and experience to the Bank.

Leadership is the most critical factor that drives organizational change and renewal at Equity. James Mwangi joined Equity as the Company's Finance Director and eventually became MD/CEO in 2004. James led all the major transformations at Equity. He is said to be open to ideas and is committed to the mission and values of Equity. He said:

> I never do anything even subconsciously that goes against the values and mission of Equity.

Equity has grown from a commercial bank to a holding company with banking and non-banking subsidiaries. Each of these subsidiaries has its own management team, board, and board committees. They are all held together by a corporate office, headed by a London School of Economics-trained banker, who worked with HSBC, City Bank, and then Standard Chartered Singapore before joining Equity. He brings his wealth of experience in the financial industry to bear in the management of all the Directors of the group.

There is a diversity of experience in the senior management. Equity boasts of a diverse team: the Director of Payments is Zimbabwean; the Director of Treasury is Kenyan; the Director of Special Projects is Kenyan; the Director of Analytics was a Professor of Analytics in South Africa; the Director of Finance is Nigerian; and the Directors of Risk and Compliance and Corporate Banking are both Indians. About this diversity, James said:

> It is very important to ensure this is a globalized leadership team to test whether this culture can permit unity across races.

This culture of diversity not only serves to bring the right people with different expertise together but also harnesses the diversity of cultures and national backgrounds. The CEO described how he works with senior management:

> You have to be able to coordinate that type of talent, that type of diversity both in culture, socialization, experience, almost everything. This requires a great deal of humility. I try to create a harmonious environment for this type of people. Maybe my greatest strength is humility. In spite of my humble education, I am willing to have everybody better educated than I and yet report to me. I try to be emotionally intelligent to allow them thrive, to allow them shower me with their skills and knowledge without my feeling humiliated or inadequate . . . knowing that I also have a contribution to make.

James attributes the success of the bank partly to the quality of its management. According to him, poor quality of management is one of the major reasons why banks fail:

> Some banks burn up because you subject an MD to a Board that does not have technical experience. You need to subject him to people who are better than him technically so they can say to him "where you are going is wrong."

Discussion

The ability to implement exploratory and exploitative innovation simultaneously allows firms to meet their environment and market challenges (Jurksiene and Pundziene, 2016: 437). This may account for Equity's success over the years. Equity Bank is ambidextrous; not only does it seek an alignment of current strategies to structure, processes, culture, etc., it also explores future opportunities: it has a specific time frame for radical change, and it self-disrupts every ten years. In the first decade of its existence, Equity's strategy was not aligned externally with the needs of the customers. It offered mortgage loans while customers needed small loans to finance their businesses. This lack of alignment contributed to its near demise in 1993. The Management learned the lessons, including that of alignment. Future radical changes were followed by alignment: the Bank identified the critical success factors for the strategy and ensured that the responsibility for these factors were assigned and performance indicators agreed. This alignment to both the external and internal environment is at the core of Equity's success in the marketplace.

Equity is also flexible. It avoids what the strategy literature has termed core rigidities: the danger of being so aligned that adaptability becomes very difficult, if not impossible. Renewal, change, and flexibility seem to be in the Bank's DNA. The Equity culture is one that is comfortable with change. Members of staff have seen the benefits of change and are thus more open to it.

Equity achieves simultaneous or structural ambidexterity (O'Reilly and Tushman, 2013). The Bank simultaneously explores future opportunities and exploits current opportunities. Exploration activities are carried out in a separate structure (innovation spaces) with its own procedures, processes, and decision-making mechanisms. Exploration activities are carried out in separate units and decision making is decentralized. The top team ensures that exploration and exploitation are speaking to each other, but the procedures and structures of the Bank do not apply to the exploration unit. Thus, exploration can be carried out independently. As the General Manager of Mobile Innovations put it: employees in the innovation spaces are not constrained in their thinking. When new ideas have been conceived and developed, risk management is brought in to ensure it is doable and that risks are mitigated.

In order to ensure that innovation spaces are attractive to top talent, a career management system is in place. Employees who join an innovation space are sure of a fulfilling and attractive career after a project. Time spent in the innovation spaces is considered valuable and the Bank benefits when the incumbents return to the exploitation structures.

Equity combines structural and behavioural (or contextual) ambidexterity. Employees are encouraged to think creatively about their jobs and share their insights. Mechanisms have been created to capture these new ideas. For example, employees can log in new ideas on a portal created for this purpose. Since creativity and innovation are values of the Equity culture, there is no distinction in time between when employees carry out exploitation and exploration activities.

Behavioural or contextual ambidexterity lies in the culture of the Bank. It is not that employees decide how to spend their time between exploitation and exploration activities (Gibson and Birkinshaw, 2004); rather, they explore in the context of their exploitation activities.

Accounting for ambidexterity at Equity Bank

Sensing opportunities

Equity has many antennae for sensing the environment and seeing the future. In addition to a well-staffed research unit, it has developed ways to listen to the customer and use the insights obtained to innovate. Customers regularly give feedback to the organization. There are instances of customers who went to the head office to see James Mwangi to give him feedback directly. Employees know that suggestions are not only encouraged, but feedback is given on how the Bank is using these suggestions. Environmental scanning has been identified as one of the capabilities required to adapt under turmoil (Hatum et al., 2010). In an environment where obtaining data is difficult and people are overly optimistic, Equity obtains reliable data for decision making. They often ask themselves: what could go wrong? In the African culture with its high external locus of control, this question is not often asked, and is not easy to face the harsh reality. Yet, confronting reality is important for successful innovation.

Seizing opportunities and reconfiguring

In order to seize opportunities in the market, Equity uses innovation spaces to explore new ideas and develop new products. Task forces or project teams are moved out of the head office to outside locations; sometimes they spent months in a hotel. By separating them physically, innovators are able to focus on the task at hand. They are also shielded from the normal organizational procedures and hierarchy. Innovators are sure of their career paths; they often go back to the Bank with more skill and experience and into higher responsibilities. Therefore, while on the project, they have no cause to worry about their future.

Equity draws from its wealth of financial resources to implement innovations. With a consistent growth in profit over the years (profit grew by 12% in 2015 and Return on Equity and a Return on Assets of 25.5% and 4.5% respectively), Equity Bank is able finance its growth: it is able to invest in several initiatives and continue is expansion. It has developed a history of taking innovations to market. This encourages even more creativity and innovation.

According to Uhlaner, van Stel, Duplat, and Zhou (2013), knowledge is at the heart of change; without new knowledge, it is impossible to innovate. Equity Bank hires the best graduating students through its pre-university programme. Employees are socialized into the Equity Culture. Exposure through training, mentoring, and learning journeys to other countries are encouraged. James Mwangi is considered a trainer and coach, especially to the branch managers. Senior management is a very diverse team of talent, experience, nationality, etc. New knowledge is acquired, created, and utilized in the organization. According to the MD, an organization changes as fast as its people; if the people do not have new knowledge, new insights, it is impossible to change.

While Equity Bank has seven corporate values, two in particular make renewal and self-disruption possible: strong customer focus, and creativity and innovation. These values have been embedded in the Bank. O'Reilly and Tushman (2013) noted that ambidexterity can be achieved through a supportive organizational context that encourages creativity and innovation among employees. Self-disruption and renewal are built into the DNA of the Bank. Both staff and customers want to see the next big thing. The fact that change has brought a lot of benefits for the Bank has reinforced the belief that change is necessary and is good. There is consequently some pressure for innovation and change.

Perhaps the most important reason for organizational renewal at Equity Bank is the leadership. Innovation spaces or physical separation of innovation units may not be enough to encourage flexibility (O'Reilly and Tushman, 2016). In fact, while some new businesses have been created, such as the Investment, Custodial, and Insurance businesses, the major innovations or disruptions at Equity Bank have been changes to the Bank itself. Senior management support for the new business and an overarching organizational identity were indispensable for successful renewal.

Equity bank is ambidextrous because the leadership supports it. The leadership makes it possible for both exploitation and exploration to exist side by side. In other words, the company is not just focused on efficiently exploiting existing capabilities, but also on exploring new opportunities through self-disruption. James has been at the centre of the organization's conscious self-disruption every ten years, and he has encouraged the staff to imbibe it such that everyone knows and expects a major disruption every ten years. This is in addition to the incremental changes that occur during the course of the ten-year period.

While the Equity culture facilitates change, senior management makes serious efforts to win commitment to the changes. For example, during the implementation of Equity 3.0 (the convergence of banking and telecommunication), the CEO and the senior managers went to all the branches to sensitize the members of staff on the change and what is expected of them. Employees had the opportunity to ask questions and make suggestions, some of which were incorporated into the change plan. Needless to say, they felt engaged, involved, and there was buy-in. According to the Director of Operations:

> You can't move with speed, if you are not moving with everyone. So, when we decide to change, we rally our teams. We do a lot of training of our managers on leadership skills so they can inspire their staff to do what is required. James spends a lot of time training them on leadership, culture, and the corporate philosophy of the organization. So, there is a lot of involvement and a lot of training so that whatever we want to do, we do it as a team, we do as an organization.

James' ability to connect emotionally with the staff is another reason for the success of change initiatives. Sometimes, he draws on the emotional bank account, telling the employees "you can't let me down." He commented on the leader-follower relationship:

> One of the things I've understood about leadership is that it is a privileged position, but privileges go with expectations. You are entitled to those privileges if you are delivering on the expectations of the position. Anytime there is a disconnect, leadership is destroyed in the eyes of the followers. We are willing to follow you, but we have expectations of you to deliver to us. And one of the things that I have really understood about leadership is that if you do not win the trust of your followers, you're not going to be followed.
>
> The second thing is that they must see your capability to take them to the destination. If you don't have capability, they will not follow you. And it is demonstrated capability. They will only follow if they know you care about them and have their interest deep in your heart. If they know this, they'll follow without first of all sitting down to deliberate on what is there for me. They know they'll be taken care of. And lastly, values help a leader out. Values make you predictable; ability can be ascribed to you based on the values, trust can be bestowed on you based on values.

Implications

An interesting research question in the organizational change literature is: why do some organizations renew themselves and others do not? This question is particularly relevant in Africa, where few organizations make the transition from small to medium and then large organizations, and where many firms fail or remain marginal. Organizational renewal is particularly important in Africa if organizations are to survive beyond the first generation, and change is of huge importance for survival in an uncertain environment.

Organizations in Africa must build dynamic capabilities (including the capability for resolving tensions between the present and the future) to thrive in this environment. Equity Bank has developed ambidextrous capabilities which no doubt account for its success in the marketplace.

The case study shows that African organizations must think alignment and flexibility at the same time; they must think today and the future; they must be ambidextrous.

To survive this dynamic environment, organizations in Africa need to do two things well: ensure alignment of strategy with the internal and external environment, and develop capabilities for sensing and seizing the future (Teece, 2007). First, the business model should be aligned with the organizational structure, culture, and processes. As the strategy changes, it is important to re-align: for example, new structures may have to be introduced and they have to be aligned. The values of the culture should be examined for alignment with strategy.

While alignment is important for survival, in a dynamic environment, alignment alone may become dangerous: flexibility and adaptability are critical. African organizations must develop capabilities for sensing and seizing the future. Environmental scanning is a discipline that enables an organization anticipate the future: how will consumer tastes change in the future? What demographic changes are taking place and what are the implications for the business? Which regulations are likely to change or be enforced in the future and what is the likely impact of this on the business? What are competitors or would-be competitors doing that could significantly change the industry dynamics? An organization that can anticipate the future is better positioned to seize it. As they sense opportunities, they test hypotheses and place bets (Harreld et al., 2007: 23).

However, the ability to see the future is often constrained by attachment to the status quo (Ovadje, 2014). There is a need to look at decision-making and resource allocation processes which may be biased towards the status quo; the new and the untried may threaten some constituencies in the organization and slow down investment in innovation.

In the Equity case study, ambidexterity was achieved through the setting up of autonomous, structurally separate units for exploration (Tushman and O'Reilly, 1996) while the rest of the organization continued exploiting current opportunities and introducing incremental changes. The innovation teams had independent decision-making processes, were very decentralized, and old authority structures were replaced with knowledge structures. The MD showed strong commitment to the exploration units. The case also showed that ambidexterity can be achieved in more than one way. Equity used both: structural and behavioural ambidexterity.

Organizations in Africa should consider both structural and behavioural ambidexterity. The latter helps shield the exploratory unit from the rest of the organization and, with the right leadership, can ensure the units have the independence they need to pursue innovative ideas. Employees could be encouraged to think of new ideas and their suggestions can be captured by the innovation teams.

An organization that seeks to develop dynamic capabilities should consider whether or not it has the enabling environment for their development. The Equity case shows some characteristics of this environment: people, culture, and leadership. This begins with finding the right people – talent. This is challenging in the African environment, given the paucity of talent due mainly to the educational system. Organizations like Equity choose the best candidate and over a number of years induct them before even offering them a job. In this environment, finding the right talent and getting them ready to perform are a necessary condition for success. After all, the organization can be innovative if its employees are knowledgeable, exposed, and constantly updating their knowledge base.

Organizational culture is a strong enabler of ambidexterity. Respect and dignity for the customer and creativity and innovation are some of the values of the Equity culture. If customers feel ownership rights over the organization and have fierce loyalty to it, they are likely to give feedback to the organization which it can use to renew itself. A culture of openness, of candour, of customer obsession is likely to create the environment for ambidexterity. The Equity case suggests that innovation must be part of the organizational culture and not an add-on. While a time frame for self-disruption puts some pressure on the organization to innovate, the length of time required for innovation will vary. It is, however, necessary to have tentacles constantly open to sense the environment. A culture of innovation, of continuous renewal keeps organizations supple and responsive (Teece and Leih, 2016: 9).

What holds the ambidextrous firm together? From the Equity case study, it is the organizational mission and the leadership that holds the firm together. Equity has transformed itself several times, but has remained true to its mission of social and economic transformation of the poor since its inception. Organizations need missions that are worth committing to. These missions serve as a rallying cry or force for employees. The customer is at the heart of Equity's mission. It is not surprising that innovation to better serve the customer is one of the values of Equity's culture. Organizations that recognize the centrality of the customer and align strategies, structures, and processes around serving the customer are likely to be more successful in building dynamic capabilities.

Finally, the role of leadership in providing an enabling environment for the achievement of ambidexterity cannot be overemphasized. How comfortable leaders are with managing the current business while exploring future opportunities may determine an organization's ability to survive in dynamic environments. Leadership must recognize the need to manage the present and the future; they must themselves be ambidextrous. They must support the exploration structures while ensuring that there is alignment of the current strategy to the structure, culture, and processes.

A strong focus on the mission and vision of the organization is necessary. The leader galvanizes the efforts of all employees towards the achievement of the mission. He helps the organization see the benefits of ambidexterity to the customer, the employees and the shareholders. To do this, the leader must be trusted by his or her followers and must have demonstrated capacity to lead them into the future.

References

Adisa, T. A., Abdulraheem, I., and Mordi, C. (2014) The characteristics and challenges of small businesses in Africa: An exploratory study of Nigerian small business owners. *Economic Insights – Trends and Challenges*, 111(4): 1–14.

Ambrosini, V., and Bowman, C. (2009) What are dynamic capabilities and are they a useful construct in strategic management? *International Journal of Management Reviews*, 11(1): 29–49.

Barney, J. B. (1986) Strategic factor markets: Expectations, luck, and business strategy. *Management Science*, 32(10): 1231–1241.

Birkinshaw, J., and Gibson, C. (2004) Building ambidexterity into an organization. *MIT Sloan Management Review*, 45(4): 47.

Birkinshaw, J., Zimmermann, A., and Raisch, S. (2016) How do firms adapt to discontinuous change? *California Management Review*, 58(4): 36–58. doi:10.1525/cmr.2016.58.4.36.

Chang, Y. C., Chang, H. T., Chi, H. R., Chen, M. H., and Deng, L. L. (2012) How do established firms improve radical innovation performance? The organizational capabilities view. *Technovation*, 32(7): 441–451.

Eisenhardt, K. M., and Martin, J. A. (2000) Dynamic capabilities: What are they? *Strategic Management Journal*, 21(10–11): 1105–1121.

George, G., Corbishley, C., Khayesi, J. N., Haas, M. R., and Tihanyi, L. (2016) Bringing Africa in: Promising directions for management research. *Academy of Management Journal*, 59(2): 377–393.

Gibson, C. B., and Birkinshaw, J. (2004) The antecedents, consequences, and mediating role of organizational ambidexterity. *Academy of Management Journal*, 47(2): 209–226.

Harreld, J. B., O'Reilly III, C. A., and Tushman, M. L. (2007) Dynamic capabilities at IBM: Driving strategy into action. *California Management Review*, 49(4): 21–43.

Hatum, A., Pettigrew, A., and Michelini, J. (2010) Building organizational capabilities to adapt under turmoil. *Journal of Change Management*, 10(3): 257–274.

Ibeh, K. I. N. (2003) Toward a contingency framework of export entrepreneurship: Conceptualizations and empirical evidence. *Small Business Economics*, 15: 49–68.

Jurksiene, L., and Pundziene, A. (2016) The relationship between dynamic capabilities and firm competitive advantage. *European Business Review*, 28(4): 431–448. doi:10.1108/EBR-09-2015-0088.

Lubatkin, M. H., Simsek, Z., Ling, Y., and Veiga, J. F. (2006) Ambidexterity and performance in small-to medium-sized firms: The pivotal role of top management team behavioural integration. *Journal of Management*, 32(5): 646–672.

McKinsey Global Institute. (2016) *Lions on the Move II: Realizing the Potential of Africa's Economies*. Retrieved from www.mckinsey.com/insights

O'Reilly III, C. A., and Tushman, M. L. (2004) The ambidextrous organization. *Harvard Business Review*, 82(4): 74–83.

O'Reilly III, C. A., and Tushman, M. L. (2013) Organizational ambidexterity: Past, present, and future. *Academy of Management Perspectives*, 27(4): 324–338. doi:10.5465/amp.2013.0025.

O'Reilly III, C. A., and Tushman, M. L. (2016) *Lead and Disrupt: How to Solve the Innovator's Dilemma*. Redwood City, CA: Stanford University Press.

Ovadje, F. (2014) *Change Leadership in Developing Countries*. London, UK: Routledge.

Palepu, K. G., and Khanna, T. (2010) *Winning in Emerging Markets: A Road Map for Strategy and Execution*. Brighton, Massachusetts: Harvard Business School Press Books.

Raisch, S., and Birkinshaw, J. (2008) Organizational ambidexterity: Antecedents, outcomes, and moderators. *Journal of Management*, 34: 375–409.

Teece, D. J. (2007) Explicating dynamic capabilities: The nature and microfoundations of (sustainable) enterprise performance. *Strategic Management Journal*, 28(13): 1319–1350.

Teece, D. J., and Leih, S. (2016) Uncertainty, innovation, and dynamic capabilities: An introduction. *California Management Review*, 58(4): 5–12. doi:10.1525/cmr.2016.58.4.5.

Teece, D. J., Pisano, G., and Shuen, A. (1997) Dynamic capabilities and strategic management. *Strategic Management Journal*, 18(7): 509–533.

Tushman, M. L., and O'Reilly, C. A. (1996) The ambidextrous organizations: Managing evolutionary and revolutionary change. *California Management Review*, 38(4): 8–30.

Uhlaner, L. M., van Stel, A., Duplat, V., and Zhou, H. (2013) Disentangling the effects of organizational capabilities, innovation and firm size on SME sales growth. *Small Business Economics*, 41(3): 581–607.

Wang, C. L., and Rafiq, M. (2014) Ambidextrous organizational culture, contextual ambidexterity and new product innovation: A comparative study of UK and Chinese high-tech firms. *British Journal of Management*, 25(1): 58–76.

16

Riding the waves of change

An interview with Mitchell Elegbe, CEO Interswitch group

Franca Ovadje

Introduction

Interswitch was founded in 2002 and has grown into a multi-million-dollar company. It began as a switching company and has contributed to the growth of the electronic payment space in Nigeria. Whether one is paying taxes or import duties, Interswitch facilitates transactions behind the scenes.

The company is a wholly Nigeria-owned and proudly African company. It has four divisions run by four deputy CEOs: Switching & Processing; Verve & consumer-facing business; Financial inclusion services; and Industry vertical markets business. It had about 500 employees in Nigeria, Kenya, Gambia, and Uganda. In spite of the recession in 2016, Interswitch remained highly profitable and continued on its growth trajectory.

Change has been part of Interswitch from inception. It started business with ₦200 million. The business plan required ₦450 million but the owners (a number of Nigerian banks) could not invest ₦450 million, and there were no venture capitalists in the market at the time. At the second Board Meeting, three or four months after inception, Mitchell Elegbe, the project manager who became the founding managing director, told the Board that there was a need to change the direction of the company. One of the Board members asked the Chairman what kind of company they had invested in. How could they change the strategy in just three months? Mitchell responded that since the firm could not get the ₦450 million it needed, it was unwise to behave as though it had ₦450 million. Many of the things they thought they could do were no longer feasible. The focus changed, but they kept their eyes on where they were going.

In 2017, a private equity firm bought $100 million USD worth of shares in Interswitch when the unofficial exchange rate was $1 USD to ₦500 NGN. According to Mitchell, no one will put that kind of money into Nigeria if the company is not doing well. The investors probably saw that Interswitch had weathered the storms over the years.

The interview with Mitchell Elegbe

Interviewer: What is driving change in the industry and how has Interswitch evolved?

Elegbe: We started the company in 2002. At that time, customers went to the bank, got a tally number and spent hours on the queue. Employees left the office and did not come back to work; their excuse was: there was a long queue in the bank. There was a lot of inefficiency in the banking system. A number of companies (including Accenture) researched the problem. They concluded that there was too much cash in the system; Nigeria was an overwhelmingly cash-based economy with all the inefficiencies of cash. The solution was to eliminate cash. NIBSS tried to do this through cheques. ValueCard, now Unified Payments, tried to eliminate cash through the use of electronic purse. We felt that the solution was not to eliminate cash but to change the way we use cash. Why is Nigeria trying to eliminate cash? Why go against the waves? Why not ride the waves of change?

We decided to ride the waves and make cash available. Instead of using Point-of-Sale, we decided to focus on ATMs. The latter gives you cash just in time. Because it is always available, you take the portion you need. Before the ATMs you withdrew enough cash for the weekend. Armed robbers knew you had cash at home so they came to attack you during the weekend. The first wave of change was to introduce our people to cards, but not to eliminate cash, but to get cash just in time. We created the infrastructure to enable banks to run ATMs. We did not go against the tide; we rode the waves. It is not easy to stand when the waves are coming, you have to look for a way. This phase lasted from 2002 to about 2006. Cash was a big wave. We tamed cash.

After taming cash, we saw a lot of efficiency, so what else could we do? The next wave was the collections wave. Everybody, including government, wanted to know who paid money into their account, through what channel, who received the money and where the money was kept? Ifueko Omoigui, the Executive Chairman of the Federal Inland Revenue Service, was the key driver of this change. She came to us and said: "this is the challenge I face. How can you help me?" We created a system that allowed you pay your tax into any bank; but we kept a record of it and she could see a simple report showing what is paid, into which bank branch, etc. Today we do collections for about 33 state governments, a lot of corporates (Airtel, Lafarge, Dangote . . .). This was the second wave; create convenience for your customers so they can pay you.

While this wave was going on, another wave kicked in; what I call the wave of disbursement. If you can collect money electronically, why can't you pay electronically? So why do we write cheques to pay our contractors? Why carry files to the bank to pay staff salaries when we can electronically swipe the money? This phase started at the end of 2005 till 2010 though it is still on.

But between 2009 and 2010, something happened in the environment: there was massive fraud in the banking system. Consumers' confidence began to drop. We had to stop all we were doing and think about the consumer and create a more secure platform for them to interact, one that gives them more confidence. This led us to Chip-and-Pin cards. MasterCard, Visa and Verve came into the market to create better security. We spent the next few years consolidating. When Charles Soludo, the Central Bank of Nigeria (CBN) Governor at the time, came up with the FSS Vision 2020, he introduced another phase of change where any and everybody wanted to do business electronically. This phase continued for about five years. The next phase was cashless Nigeria. Government wanted a larger proportion of Nigerians to be able to make payments electronically. People were penalized for withdrawing cash over the counter.

Interswitch led these changes by creating a product that was required at each stage. First it was ATM switching; then Paydirect for collections; disbursements with Quickteller and Autopay; and we went into secure cards with Verve. When we see an opportunity, we create the right product.

If you look at our growth and success, you see that as the market was changing, we had something ready or created it and grew with the changes with minimal effort. Being able to read the environment is critical to predict what will happen next. Positioning, to be ready just before it happens, is critical. You need to begin to bring your three sights to play at the same time; hindsight (your knowledge of what has happened in the past); insight (your knowledge of what is happening right now) and foresight (your vision of the future). Sometimes, you can create the future you want by anticipating change.

Interviewer: What has been the impact of regulation, competition and technological change on Interswitch?

Regulation has been good, bad and ugly. It was good because it forced the banks to take action particularly when there were challenges around fraud. Regulation was bad when they attempted to fix prices thereby creating a disincentive for the private sector to get involved. Regulation was bad when policies that were not well thought through were thrown out there. The result was that nobody wanted to innovate because of the uncertainly of the reaction from the Central Bank of Nigeria (CBN). Some regulations were ugly; they were well intended but the outcomes were bad. For example, CBN directed that banks should stop deploying ATMs to offsite premises and focus on ATMs at the branches. It was hoped that private companies would deploy ATMs. They did not. Before this policy was made, Nigeria was one of the fastest growing ATM markets in the world. After the policy was introduced, the growth rate declined and never picked up. It was supposed to be a good policy, but the unintended consequences were negative.

Innovation is tied to regulation. This market innovated when there was freedom to do stuff. Now, before you can do anything, you have to inform the regulator. Sometimes they put policies in place which make products unviable. Sometimes what the market wants and what the regulator is saying you must do, do not tally. The net result is that people slow down. Sometimes we are forced to make investments in areas that if given a free hand we would not invest in. But overall, the industry has innovated. Consumers continue to be very demanding. To remain in business, you have to meet their expectations.

Competition has always been there. But over the years, we all found our niche. Payments in Nigeria is at a nascent stage. Even up to now we do not have up to 10% penetration. You have to be extremely lazy in the payments space not to carve out a niche for yourself. E-transzact, Unified Payments, NIBSS, everyone is doing well. The opportunity is huge. Having said that, there are a lot of new entrants in the industry all threatening to disrupt the traditional business but they need scale. Payment is a scale business. You can wish to disrupt but you need scale, so you need to come up with that killer application but nobody has been able to do that. All the new entrants are doing is trying to improve on what is there. There are many players now eating into your market share in different areas. This is expected.

Interviewer: How do you see the need for change?

Our industry is very dynamic. Our regulator is extremely active, in my view, sometimes too active. Our competitors are even more active than the regulator. Our business is one business new entrants can get into; anybody can create what you creating and there's always one bank who will listen to them because banks are looking for ways to create brands for their customers. So if you look at Porter's five forces as far as this business is concerned, the barrier to entry is low.

I will say that I'm very privileged in the sense that my number two was my classmate at university. I told him: "Akeem, I'll like to start up a business in the future and I'll like to work with you. But if you start up first, let me know, I'll come join you." Our number three, Charles, was somebody who worked with us when we developed the business plan. So, you can see that in a way, the top leadership is close-knit.

I must say that 13 years down the line, change is one of the most difficult things. For the first time, all three of us have different perspectives as to where the business is going. And I've used a very democratic management style where concessions must be made before we move forward. That has become a challenge because today there are about 15 of us in senior management. Getting agreement from 15 people with different views is difficult.

Business has been changing rapidly; every second of the day means loss of market of share. So, suddenly I discovered that I have to change my approach to doing things. That change of approach itself creates a challenge with some of my colleagues who have been used to the traditional way of doing things.

The Greiner growth model states that companies go through six stages in their life time and at every stage there is a disruption. I had that kind of disruption many years ago when I was trying to make some little change and I couldn't understand why everybody was up in arms, holding unto their positions. This used to be a very simple business where we all knew who the enemy was. For the first time we were asking what exactly is going on? And while in that confusion, trying to understand what was going on, I went online and I googled, "how do you lead change?" and I found the Greiner Growth Model. I read it and I saw what the problem was.

In order to solve that problem. I sent a copy of that article to my colleagues. They read it and change took place immediately. The point I'm trying to make is that people need to understand what is happening to them. It is like somebody who is not feeling too well; if you know what your ailment is, you are not confused. That means you know what the problem is. You will have more problems if you are not feeling too well and doctors don't know what is wrong with you and everybody is saying a different thing. But the moment you understand what the problem is, the solution is a lot easier. Our problem was that at that stage, we were a very peculiar organization. We had reached a stage where processes and standards were required and people were resisting. "What is this regulation?" "What is this process?" "What is this ISO they are talking about?" "What happened to the good old days when we could sit down, take a decision and move on?" "Why is Mitchell forcing us to follow these processes? They are just annoying."

The moment they realized that these are traits of an organization at this stage, if we don't make the transition, the company will decline, change was a lot easier. Not the easiest, but a lot easier. I often refer them to that article and I start the management meeting with, "Let's look at this article one more time and identify where we are in our life cycle." And we spend time debating where exactly we are. Once we all agree where we are, it is easy to see what the changes should be. The most popular quote I use in my office is: "when the facts change, what do you do?"

Interviewer: When the facts change what do you do?

This quote allows me get through a lot of things. "Gentlemen, the facts have changed. So, we need to change." I usually use this to justify the frequent changes I make. A few months after we started business, I went to the Board and told them that I want to change the direction of the company. If I can do that to the Board, imagine what I can do to staff. We change almost every day and there is a reason.

Flexibility is required in the kind of business we do. This quote is from John Maynard Keynes, who proposed Keynesian theory. After making the entire country believe this is the way to go, a few days later he said: "Sorry, I made a mistake, we need to go in the opposite direction." And a journalist asked him, "Are you confused? Don't you know what you are doing? Why would you tell us something one day and the next day you are telling us the opposite?" Keynes replied: "When the facts change, I change my mind. What do you do, sir?"

So, one day, I went to the Board and said to them, "We are not going to do Agency Banking even though the Central Bank has just approved it; it doesn't make sense. It is Interswitch working for the banks and the banks making all the money. We do all the work and there is no value added. So, we are not going to do it." A few days later, I had a discussion with a company that had come to connect to us. We do Quickpayment and Quickteller for example and the biggest customer there is Multichoice. Of course, we have the likes of GoTV and Startimes. The latter has more subscribers than DSTV but you hardly see Startimes customers pay online. So, these guys came to us and said, "Mitchell, we want to connect to Interswitch so we can use Quickteller and your Startimes platform."

I told them "this doesn't make sense. You want to address people that don't have money." But I allowed them to continue and guess what? Overnight, we saw the volume of business of Startimes began to grow. What these guys did was digitize cash. You want to pay your Startimes bills in Ajegunle, so you go to an agent. The agent collects cash from you and uses his card to make the payment online for you. The gentleman had no bank account so he did not have a card and therefore could not make payments online.

Then it dawned on me that there are a 150+ million Nigerians and we are struggling for 40 million with MasterCard and Visa. No one was going after the 100-and-something million. The only way to go after this business was to get into the agency business. So I went back to the Board and I said, "Gentlemen, the facts have changed. There is a market of 100 million people that we ignored. We have to focus on it now." That led to the creation of a subsidiary, Interswitch Financial Inclusion Services.

What is fact? This question comes up anytime I try to initiate the change process in Interswitch. We have very smart guys in the room who use their phones to google up things and are ready for you. They are waiting for you to make a fool of yourself so they can tell you, "We shouldn't be going in that direction. We should be going in this direction." I said to them a fact is a proven truth. When you want to take a decision as management, you are looking for facts.

Why did this gentleman resist change for so long and why has he suddenly changed his position? What was the lightbulb that went off in his head? Most of the times, it is when you are able to differentiate between truth and facts. So, if you go into a meeting, and you say $1 + 1 = 2$, and you have somebody in the room who reasons in the opposite way, who starts from 2 equal something, the first thing you must do is to shift his thinking from 2 equals something to $1 + 1 = 2$.

Apart from trust, the one thing I think is important is that leaders must not be lazy. It is lazy leaders, leaders who have lost focus, whose companies die. Any smart leader will know that there is a problem coming. Most of us assume it will just go away. The problem has been shown to you, it doesn't go away. You have to solve it.

There is a common saying that when one door closes, another opens. I usually ask the question: who opened up the other door? All the doors were always there; you saw only one. You begin to see the other door when you begin to apply yourself. Don't apply yourself when the problem comes, apply yourself before the problem comes. See everything and choose one but don't be blind to the other doors. This is a way of dealing with change. There are no surprises. If there is fraud and banks are losing money, do you think the regulator will fold its hands and leave you? They are going to take drastic measures so you should be asking yourself what kind of solutions are they likely to come up with? You can pick up the phone and call someone. Sometimes leaders become complacent. I know everything that can affect this company. You cannot say you did not know; your intuition will tell you that something is going to happen.

Interviewers: Do you use consultants to see the need for change?

We called Oliver Wyman to analyze our business and tell us the issues they think we should deal with. They looked at our strategy, operations, our subsidiaries in Kenya and Uganda, and our marketing team, and they raised 23 issues.

We grouped them into five areas. When we unpacked all of those issues, we had 23 core objectives, 41 strategic initiatives, 64 one-off projects, and 41 operational objectives. Each of these things required change! Even if we focused all our efforts doing one project per week, in a year we will not be done and in the market that is very dynamic, there must be something very wrong with this process. So the strategy team sat down and went through all of these issues one by one. It came down to four core objectives and 16 strategic initiatives.

So, the question here is, this industry is changing and everybody understands that this industry is changing. Today, we support several channels – ATM, POS, Internet, Mobile, Kiosk, Bank branches, Agents . . . Is there one channel that is growing very fast, that if we lose out on that growth, it will potentially become a problem for us in the future? Everybody said yes, there is one: Mobile. So we acquired BANSO – the industry leader. You can see that strategy drives the initiatives. The moment we acquired BANSO, the organizational structure had to change. BANSO was in the payment business. Everybody understood why BANSO had to come in because they were part of the strategy session. So, if you understand why BANSO has to come in you have to accept some of these changes that are going to come. Isn't that logical?

Interviewer: Let's talk about internationalization. Why did Interswitch internationalize and what has been the experience?

Three reasons. First: Nigeria was becoming a challenge to our growth so we felt we should diversify. Regulation was becoming too frequent and too serious. We felt sticking to one country could be a risk. Secondly, there is a lot you learn from other countries that you can bring to your country. We needed international experience. What works in Kenya may not work in Nigeria but what works here could be applied there. Thirdly, to be honest, I was getting bored; I needed to go conquer somewhere else. So boredom was one reason for expansion.

Apart from experience we gained, it was a lot of waste of time. If you want to do international expansion, you need a very long-term strategy. It is not a quick fix. If you buy a company that is not doing well, there must be a reason why it is not making money. The model might be wrong. It took us five years to get our business in Uganda profitable. Looking back, we have realized that the reason why it took us so long is that we missed something simple: the total number of bank accounts in the whole of Uganda is less than five million. That is less than the number of accounts of First Bank in Nigeria! If you look at the population you are deceived. Our business model was switching bank transactions so we had to look for ways to do more business outside of banks and the moment we figured that out we became profitable.

In Nigeria, because the market is big, you can stick to banking alone. In Kenya, financial inclusion is very big. We are trying to buy two companies in Tanzania: we are going there with the knowledge we have acquired. I look at the last five years as learning the ropes in internationalization. Unfortunately, even though we learnt the basic things in business schools, the real lesson is when you hit the ground. With the knowledge of the theory and the reality on ground, we think we are now ready.

We continue learning. We keep our eyes open for the lessons. Anticipate the lessons. Before now the lessons hit us. Now we actually seek for the lessons. We learn the lessons and we quickly apply what we have learnt. So, I think international expansion is becoming interesting and I think we are better prepared.

Interviewer: It seems change has been a companion on your journey these 15 years. How do you win the commitment of your staff members to change?

You have to show your managers what you are seeing. Not many CEOs are willing to spend the time to get everybody on the same page, and so, what they try to do is what I did many years ago as a young engineer. I thought being aggressive was the best way to get results. I had the reputation of someone who doesn't take nonsense. I broke all the rules and I got results. My CEO backed me because I got results. But HR disliked me because I did not follow due process. Finance did not understand what I was talking about because I had not retired the cash for the last trip and I wanted to travel again. And guess what, when they said they won't give me money for the trip, I said no problem, I'll use my money.

I soon realized that I was having victories but no success. It's like going to war with a thousand people and you win the battle, and when you raise up your hands to jubilate, you turn round to see your team, but there is nobody. Everybody is dead. So, you turn round and look for the next victims.

To make change happen, you need to spend time to get everybody on the same page. Everybody never comes to the same page, by the way. But you need to be clear that while you are bringing everybody to the same page, you are not standing on one spot.

"Guys, we need to move towards . . . Get your things, let's go." As long as you keep moving, they know this man has come again; he has a direction he is going. So, let's begin to align quickly. That aligning is important to be honest because when you get to the door and nobody is there, you come back. So, while you are moving towards the door, you are actually gauging to make sure that people are falling in line so that by the time you get to the door, everybody is in line. If they are not with you, it makes sense to stop and ask "Why are you guys not following me?"

Our business is growing very fast. We started with ₦200 million. Eight years later we were valued at ₦26 billion. Today, we are in the region of ₦120 billion. There's no payment business in Nigeria that is even close. Because I am seeing some possibility in the future, I am trying to focus around it. But something that is less than 2% of our revenue stream now will never get focus, not from the CEO. So, the only way to get that is to break it out and get a new CEO to lead that business. This is a major change. Every time, you take from someone's portfolio in a company that is controlled by private equity, where results quarter-by-quarter is what they look at, you begin to hear statements like the ones I hear from time to time: "Mitchell, are you setting me up for failure?"

Now, when people who have worked with you for 15 years begin to talk like this, you should watch it. This statement was made three times by the same individual so I sent him an email telling him to be very careful lest he believe the statement. If somebody seriously thinks that you are setting him up for failure, every idea you come up with will be looked at from that perspective.

So, it is important to take time to address these kinds of issues when they come. So, I told this guy: "When I moved Jonah to Calabar to run Smartgolf, a very small business (he left his family in Lagos) was I setting him up for failure? When I told Muyiwa to go to Uganda to run the business was I setting him up for failure? Vincent is leaving Gambia now and he is going to become Group CEO in East Africa where we are combining four countries together. Jonah is back in Lagos and is now chief strategy officer. The company needs to make these changes for growth, and certain people will have to go for smaller portfolios to make this growth happen. But they should not forget that they went there for a reason." I had to give him examples of people we have moved and all of them have become better persons.

The first issue here is that when you get into the room and you want to talk about facts that have changed, they wonder which facts have changed? It is safe to assume that these guys don't all see the same thing. So, which facts are you talking about?

I'll give you an example. One of my senior managers said to me that operations was becoming a big issue: one error could kill the company. We need a very good and experienced person to run operations and the person should report to me directly. The moment I told him I liked his idea and I think the best person to run operations is his number two, everything changed; he became resistant. I was taking away his best guy. We sat down to discuss the issue. He said I gave him a very difficult task to do and the best guy who is just settling into the role is the person I want to take away. Valid concern. So, what do I do? He saw the logic of what I was talking about and he knew that person was the right person. It just happened that that person was the right person for his department too.

One day, I said to one of my colleagues: "let's have a trust conversation." I asked her if she trusts me. If she thinks I trust her. If her colleagues in management trust her and if she trusts them.

Finally, I asked her if her subordinates trust her. She was to answer these questions on a scale of one to five and send me the report. The result was very interesting. I discovered there were colleagues who did not trust each other. There were colleagues who said they trusted me 100%. I didn't believe it. And there were those who were bold to enough to say, not 100% anymore; I used to, but not like before. Nobody will say they don't trust you but those who you have known long enough are saying it used to be 100% but now I'm not too sure. And then, some said that they don't think their subordinates trust them.

If you have a team where people don't trust each other, change cannot take place. Every idea is looked at with suspicion; there must be an agenda. Even when it is 1 + 1 = 2, they will say, 1 is not 1. Something that should take a few hours to resolve could drag for weeks. Managers are trying to find out if there is a hidden agenda. They do not see what you see. Where I sit, I see a lot of things, I do a lot of things. Where they sit, they do not necessarily see what other people are seeing. So, if you want to effect a change that is good for the group but will potentially affect one person negatively, you need to spend time, to sit down with that individual to help him/her understand why that change is important, what it means for the organization and why it is not a hidden agenda.

So, one day, I sent an email to this colleague of mine who said: "Are you setting me up for failure?" I said to him: "We have been working together for 13 years. Can you point out one action that I have taken that suggests that your interest was not taken into consideration and you are not catered for?" Two weeks later, there was no response so I told him that I am still waiting to hear one thing I have done in 13 years that suggests that I acted against your interest. Two weeks later, I asked him the same thing. The truth is that there is none.

Interviewer: What else have you found important in making change stick?

When people are angry with you about change, at the back of their heads they have two arguments: equity and equality. They don't prefer one to the other; they simply use the one that is more convenient at a point in time to argue their case. Sometimes I hear, "Mitchell, you need to be fair; why won't you treat us equally?" Another manager says: "Mitchell, I am the baby in the room. I need all the support I can get. I'm not saying you should treat us equally; all I'm asking is that you be equitable."

One guy in the room is talking about equality. The other guy is talking about equity. So I explain to them the dilemma I face when we have issues of change. Without trust, you cannot accept any change, even change that is good for you. You won't accept it if you don't trust the system. You must recognize that there are times where equality works and there are times when equity is the right thing to do.

Some of the managers tell me they "built this company for 13 years. When our salary was very poor, these other guys were not here. They were in Zenith Bank, First Bank, MTN, earning fantastic salaries while we laboured. Now the meal is prepared, we want to start enjoying and these new guys come and they want to be treated equally? How can that be?"

And they twist equity. "Mitchell, in fact, those of us who have been in this company for a long time are the little ones who should be getting more." These are life conversations in management meetings and everybody has a point. It boils down to one thing: will they trust your final position? Luckily for me, the trust level is still very high, so I use it all the time and I end such conversations like this: Gentlemen and ladies, I've heard all your points and all your points are valid. Let me go and reflect on what you have all said and I'll come back to give my final position.

And before I come back with the final position, I call each one of them and I say "This is going to be my final position and this is how I think it is going to affect you and this is how I think you are going to react. I'm asking you not to react this way because I know what you are going to do. I know you very well, you are a bad boy. At the end of the day, it will be better for us all." I call the next person and tell them same thing. Sometimes, somebody benefits and I say, "today you appear to be the beneficiary of this decision. Just bear in mind that tomorrow it will be somebody else's turn to be a beneficiary. So when that time comes, I want you to behave in a very honourable manner." Some of these conversations are not easy. But we are still a very close-knit team and I've been at Interswitch since inception. So, maybe I have that leverage. I'm not sure what my successor will do when it comes to effecting change.

But there are some basic principles that I think have worked for me which I will like to share. I was attending a programme once, and I asked the professor the role of a CEO. Everybody in the room was a CEO. The professor asked everyone in the room and summarized the comments: All of you have the role of ensuring that your business is integrated with the market and ensuring that there is internal cohesion within the organization to serve that external market. Then, he went into a discussion of what external integration means – you want to sell things to the market, you want the market to pay a good price and you want the market to feel they got a fair deal. It came down to one thing – TRUST. The market must trust the organization, that you said you can do this and you really can do it. They are buying your trust; they are not buying your product. He then looked at internal cohesion and same thing, at the end of it all it came to one single thing – TRUST. And I told myself, if that is all I can take out of that class, it's been worth it. Let the market trust your organization and let the people within trust each other. If you can achieve those two, every other thing around change becomes a lot easier.

So, back to problem I mentioned earlier. One day while having a trust conversation with the manager who suggested we create an operations role in the company, I said to him: "You changed. You suggested we create an operations department and I've been chasing this thing and all of a sudden, it's as if you don't believe in it." He said, "Mitchell, I still believe in it. What I have an issue with is the way you went about it." I said, "What did I do wrong?" He said, "When you told me you are going to take my number two to run this thing, you told me to go and think about it and come up with ideas. I did not know that while you were telling me to go and think about it, it was already decided." I said, "how did you come up with that?" He said, "HR told me that she agreed with you and suggested I should get myself aligned." I said, "I never said so." So, I called HR and said, "HR, this is the issue I have, kindly confirm our conversation," and HR confirmed our conversation exactly the way I said it. "So why did you go and tell him what you did?" HR said, "Ah-ah, I was joking with him? I said he should stop resisting change."

The guy said, "Mitchell I'm sorry. Don't mind these HR people." And that was it. There was nothing else I did other than: Do you trust me? If you trust me, why are you acting this way? After all, you brought this idea to me. I bought it and you abandoned me in the race.

I think trust is extremely important and if you have a system where there is no trust, I think you have to spend some time to create that trust, otherwise you will kill ideas for no reason. In fact, some people enjoy killing ideas for the fun of it. It's like this is their cartel. They forget that we are all here for the same thing.

Interviewer: Are incentives important in driving change? How do you get your direct reports to work for the group and not only for their businesses?

The kind of incentives you create determines how quickly people react to change. If you look at all the decisions we have taken, you will understand why they were taken. It may not have been good for one department 100% of the time, but over time it was better for the group. Our incentives are at the group not the business levels.

The way you structure the reward system is also very important. In Interswitch, we have a calendar of payments we make to staff. Our salary is benchmarked to the 75th percentile of banking and telecommunications group. We also benchmark the top four consulting firms.

We have a performance based bonus scheme that is tied to your individual performance; your own scorecard. I have a scorecard that my chairman signs after a very elaborate process. I spent three hours discussing my Balance Scorecard with my Chairman. It is not a trivial process. I share it with my direct reports and they build from mine.

Performance is a very critical issue for us. First, there is the individual bonus. It doesn't matter how the company performed, you agreed to do ABCDE. You did them. 40% of your annual salary comes to you as bonus. There is a group performance bonus which is what we call profit share: 10% of the total profit of the company is shared at the end of the year once profits are declared.

We have a long-term incentive plan. Every staff of Interswitch has shares in the business including the drivers. After about five years, something happens: people sell part of their shares. Right now, we are about to sell 25% of our shares. This will give members of staff who are thinking of buying houses enough money to do so. What that does is because the shares are tied to the centre, value creation is at the centre. So it is very easy for us to be say in the management meeting: "Tara, I know you want to go after this opportunity. If your unit goes for it, the group benefits and you benefit too." The only way to manage the tension between the businesses is to reward at the group level. If the reward were at the business unit level, brotherly love could varnish.

Tie the incentive to the centre and let everybody be aligned to that centre, then change may not be so difficult. But if people have their different cabals, sitting in their different businesses, one business will cannibalize another business and nobody would care. Change is a lot easier if people are aligned at the centre and therefore decisions are taken based on that alignment.

Interviewer: Can you give us an example?

We are launching a credit product that we think is revolutionary. It's called Verve Self-made Credit. We are saying, you don't need collateral, because you don't have. So, let's not disturb you. You have been using Quickteller for 13 years and we have your history but you just never knew. What it means is that I know everybody you transfer money to monthly on Quickteller. I know the amount of airtime you buy. I know how much you pay for your toll. Okay, I know you have 5 DSTVs in your house; I don't know what you are doing with them; I don't know if it is a hotel you are running!

That is enough information to paint a picture and say: "This person is a reliable guy. He's been banking with two banks since banking came into Nigeria. And just on our platform alone, this is the volume he does, I don't think giving him up to ₦500,000 credit is a bad idea. He's not going to run away." In fact, I'm trying to do it in such a way that we will be paying your DSTV on your behalf, but your history shows that you pay ₦10,000 every month. Just give it to us. Out of your credit, we will just pay for you. So, we call it Verve Self-made Credit. In other words, go online, answer a few questions, as you are answering, we are checking your answers with what we know about you to see if you are telling the truth, and based on that we apply a score. And a bank will offer you credit on our monies. No collateral.

The manager who is running this platform wanted to partner with one of the foreign cards for it and the manager in charge of Verve said: "I am here and you want to give the business to somebody else?" So, we agreed that Verve must be the only partners, for one year.

Interviewer: Why one year?

Lead time, before any other person can come in. But he could have said, "No no, Mitchell, it's not your responsibility. Any card can come and use my service. It's just a platform I'm running. It's only a platform. Anybody can use it. Why am I limiting anybody? If Verve wants to use it,

Verve should move fast and run with it." That is a very logical answer. But we would have told him: "No, if those guys win, we may get the money, but only a portion of it comes to us, but with Verve a 100% of it comes to us. So, this makes more sense."

Interviewer: Talk to us about the next five to ten years of Interswitch.

Let me share with you an exercise we have just gone through. We are preparing a company retreat later this week to plan for the next five years. Already, I am thinking of how to carry the people along. I called the Chief Strategy Officer and said to him, let's get the whole company involved in the strategy session. Let's talk about what strategy is. We circulated reading materials to all staff with some questions. Every unit was to meet to discuss these documents and send in their answers to the questions. Everybody read the cases. They sat down to discuss it in groups. There are serious debates going on, this is the best way to learn. Now, when we talk about operational efficiency, people know what you are talking about. The outcome of this exercise is that if you are in a customer facing business, your primary goal should be customer intimacy. If you are in a support function or core operational function, your primary goal should be operational efficiency. If you are in product or R&D your primary goal should be product leadership. Everybody understands why and they know that these three areas reinforce each other. People understood where the company should be going.

We told the staff that as companies grow they face a myriad of challenges. We then asked them to identify the next challenge we are going to face and plan for it. They all read about the Greiner Growth Model. The question was: is Interswitch a fast-growth, moderate, or slow-growth company? They said Interswitch is a fast-growth company in a fast-growth space. What does this mean? It means we have to learn to accept change and to adapt much faster. For us, if we don't adapt in six months we are dead!

Where is Interswitch in the growth phase and which challenges are we facing now? Everybody is saying we are at the collaboration stage. Which challenges do you expect in this phase? They said, red tape. Many of them are feeling that things are slowing down, there is a lot of rules and regulations; there is red tape. To deal with red tape, what do you do? You need to work in teams. You need to put teams together, solve the problem, and disband the teams. Everybody can understand where we are. I told them there is no problem we are going to face that companies have not faced before. There is no problem that Google, Apple have not faced. So how did they deal with it? They have millennials, they are a fast-growing company in a fast-growing space, how did they deal with their issues?

What kind of structure do we need in this phase? They said a matrix structure; one group said the organization has reached a level of maturity where it can handle a matrix structure. I have been trying to implement a matrix structure for almost a year. What they are studying now is a matrix structure. Everybody knows where we are, they know the matrix structure is what we need. What kind of changes do leaders need? Some leaders want to be the only one to rate the performance of their subordinate. The younger employees love it. But the senior managers are struggling; they are used to having total control. Now they cannot have it; they have to negotiate.

You use a matrix structure when the rate of change of a business is high and you are dealing with more than one thing at the same time. You are dealing with competition, changing customer expectations . . . one person alone cannot handle it. You need deep knowledge, both vertical and horizontal knowledge. You need to know for example, the HR issues with millennials, you need to tap into the expertise of different groups of people.

When the company becomes complex, you need to create teams of experts to lead. The single big thing we need to do is that senior leaders have to accept that decision making is no longer one person's prerogative; it is collective. And you need to be able to negotiate. Secondly, resources are scarce, you need to fight for resources. Thirdly, to have this kind of collaboration, meetings have to be effective. The days of calling meetings where six experts spend 30 minutes waiting for one more member to arrive are gone. You have to start on time. It even influences you way you structure your office. You need a lot of meeting rooms. Therefore, the culture has to change. You cannot come to a meeting with your phone.

I talked to all the staff about the three types of people and their attitude to change. Type I gets involved, likes to know when the change is happening and to contribute. They drive the change. Type II persons think that somebody else will do it. They don't really care. Type III are those that things happen to. I asked them what type of person they are. Nobody wants to be called Type III. We have not started the change and people are already asking what they should be doing.

Change should be inclusive; let people anticipate it. Everybody wanted to be Type I but guess what? Some of them are actually Type II but they began to display Type I behaviours. Everyone is exposed now. The behaviours of each Type are known. I told them if you know of any Type II or III in your department, go to them and tell them you are a Type II or III. Repent, Mitchell said you should repent. If somebody tells you to repent, do not attack the person, the person is just my messenger. I am going to be walking around (by the way, google up "Management by Walking Around"). They think: "you mean when he is walking around he is managing? What kind of stupid management is that?"

It is a learning organization. People are accepting change even though they do not know in detail what the change will involve. We wanted to be Lean Six Sigma certified. HR got a company online and in less than one month, all 500 of us were certified; we all passed the examinations. People are now driving change at their level. We are offering a prize of ₦150,000 for the winning initiative.

I am looking forward to this financial year because to be honest with you, the energy I am seeing, the way people are moving it is going to be amazing.

Interviewer: Even the way you lead change is changing . . .

The way you deal with children is not the same way you deal with adults. If they have knowledge they will use it. Don't leave the knowledge in a few hands. What do you do with the money you make? We have profit share. And the business is growing. We are going to increase salary because the business did well.

Our financial year ends in March. Usually, this is when everybody is trying to make the last Naira. But no one is thinking about that because we met our target. So people are focusing on the next year. Helios is selling part of their shares. The new buyers are giving us tough conditions. For example, they asked us to disclose everything we know if we don't we will forfeit all the money we make from selling our shares. This is tough but I agreed to sign; nobody is hiding anything. There is some money that needs to be paid to us in dollars. I went to the bank and asked for a domiciliary account for the staff. I want the staff to collect the dollars and go change it in the black market if they want to. It is a lot of effort, some of them will never have opened a domiciliary account. The people trust their leaders, that they have their back. Anything we say here, they accept. I tell them I have never given a bribe before and I have never collected one. It takes you thrice the effort to commit a crime than to do good. You plan the bad action as you would the good one. Then you plan how not to get caught. You must consider the possibility of being caught and plan for that too! Why spend so much energy when you can simply do the right thing?

Leaders must realize that they have a responsibility for the people they lead. You are responsible for their future. Will they have good retirement benefits? Once they know that this is your objective, it is easy. We wanted to fire a couple of people. I realized that if we fire them immediately, they would lose their shares. So I called their boss and said let's wait a few months for their shares to be vested so even after we have fired them they can enjoy the shares. We don't want to ruin your life. Yes, you can't work with us anymore, you have to go but the fact that we are not working together anymore does not mean that your years here should be wasted.

Leaders must not be lazy. It is lazy leaders; leaders who have lost focus whose companies die. Any smart leader knows when a problem is coming. Most of us assume it will go away. You have seen the problem, it won't go away. You have to plan for it.

There is a common saying that when a door closes, another opens. I usually ask the question: who opened up the other door? All the doors were always there; you saw only one. You began to see the other door when you began to apply yourself. Don't apply yourself when the problem comes, apply yourself before the problem is manifested. Make a choice but don't be blind to the other doors. This is a way of dealing with change. There are no surprises. If there is fraud and banks are losing money, do you think the regulator will fold its hands and leave you? They are going to take drastic measures so you should be asking yourself what kind of solutions are they likely to come up with? You can pick up the phone and call someone. Sometimes leaders become complacent. I know everything that can affect this company. You cannot say you did not know; your intuition will tell you that something is going to happen.

Leaders must also be fair. Your followers read all the messages, they see things. They see your vibes; they know what you guys think about yourselves. They may conclude: they don't care about us. Some of the decisions we take at management meetings somehow get to them. People say followers deserve the kind of leaders they get. But leaders also deserve the kind of followers they have. Leaders can create the kind of followers they want.

We are going for the Retreat in a few days. I am looking for a presentation I made in 2010 when Helios was about to invest in Interswitch. Most of the things we said we will do have happened. We are going to this exercise with that seriousness. We are creating this company for future people. The company is doing very well; our owners are happy despite the devaluation of the Naira. New owners are buying shares of about USD $100 million. Nobody will put that kind of money into Nigeria if the company was not doing well. They are pushing on: they know the company; they know the country.

So, we are going to this exercise with that degree of seriousness knowing that what we decide could make or break this company in the next ten years. Chances are that most of us will not be here in ten years' time so we are creating this company for other people. We have weathered many storms. So, there is a discipline to see what is coming, prepare, and ride the waves. This is our story. One of our millennials told me: "five years from now when we review this strategy, I will know that I contributed to the strategy which made the company great."

17

Conclusions

Toward effective change management in African organizations

Samuel Aryee and Franca Ovadje

Despite the change implications inherent in the external and internal forces shaping the African continent, there is a dearth of research on change management in African organizations. Although the continent evidences thriving organizations amid the turbulence, they are clearly in the minority, and the African continent has had its fair share of failed organizations. As the survival and growth of these organizations is critical to ensuring employment opportunities, and therefore the realization of the Africa growth pole narrative, it is imperative that research generates actionable knowledge that management of these organizations can leverage to effectively initiate and manage change interventions. The scarcity of research on turnarounds in Africa makes this undertaking particularly important, if only to minimize organizational decline and the consequent financial and human costs. This Handbook aims to fill this void by presenting, for the first time, a contextualized account of change management in Africa and, in the process, contributes to the wider scholarly literature on change management. It brings together what we know about change management in Africa today, identifies trends such as the role of business elites and responsible management education in bringing about change on the continent, and maps out some directions for future.

We adopted a multidisciplinary perspective and viewed change management from strategic, organizational behaviour, human resource management, economic policy, and philosophical viewpoints. Collectively, these chapters not only underscore the complexity of change management efforts, but also provide insights into how African organizations and their top management can develop a change management capability to effectively respond to the increasingly turbulent environment in which they operate. In the rest of this chapter, we bring together the various themes running through the handbook and map out some directions for change management research and practice in the African context.

The environment and change

One theme that emerges from the chapters is the nature of the African environment. Although it has been variously described, it is safe to assert that African organizations operate in a highly volatile and complex environment. While this environment provides a number of opportunities, as seen in the recent mushrooming of IT-related firms, it poses considerable threats for the continent's large and predominantly small- and medium-sized enterprises. The complexity is heightened by the need to navigate institutional voids which George, Corbishley, Khayesi, Haas, and Tihanyi (2016: 379) describe as 'the business support infrastructure or "ecosystems" that determine resource availability and enable fair market access for inclusive growth.' According to Utomi and Akor, this institutional void, and the predatory activities of government officials, is the biggest challenge organizations face in Africa. The two CEOs we interviewed corroborated this; their companies were thriving because they had found ways to anticipate change, to be steps ahead of a constantly changing environment. One of them observed that regulation hampers innovation in the industry. He has learnt to stay ahead of even regulation. The two companies, Interswitch and Equity Bank, are ambidextrous; they combine a focus on present challenges with seizing opportunities in the future.

Two emergent change drivers identified in this Handbook are the role of business elites and the role of internationalization. Although there is a dearth of research on the internalization of African organizations relative to those from the developed and transitional economies, recent years have seen a small but growing interest in the subject (Adams, Nyuur, Ellis, and Debrah, 2017; Davis and Luiz, 2015). To enhance our understanding, and therefore effective management, of internationalization or the intra-African expansion of African organizations and the change implications, it is imperative that research begins to shine a light on a number of related issues. How and why do African firms internationalize? What are the challenges and what accounts for successful internationalization? For example, while some firms may follow their clients into international markets, they may also internationalize to gain the reputation of an international firm which will enable them compete more favourably in their home countries.

The boom-bust-boom-bust cycles in Zoogah's murmuration model of change capture both the complex African environment and the difficulty of sustaining change. He points out that reversals happen, and that change is often not sustained. This is particularly true of culture change. As Chika-James pointed out in her chapter, a culture change may not guarantee changes in the values and beliefs of organizational members. The case study of Equity Bank shows how the bank embeds change; it has a timeline for implementing and embedding major changes. It has built change capacity in the organization such that every ten years it embarks on a major organizational renewal. More research on embedding change while maintaining flexibility to adapt to an uncertain environment is necessary.

Winning commitment to change

This seems to be of paramount importance to leading change in Africa. Three contributors focused on the role of Ubuntu and authentic and virtuous leaders in leading change in Africa. Ovadje (2014), in her decision-making model of change, also emphasized the importance of winning commitment to change. She argued that at every decision point about the change, how commitment to the change will be won must be considered.

Without commitment, fundamental or strategic change may not take place. Misati and Walumbwa argue that authentic leaders are change leaders. They have the attributes required to lead successful change in the African environment. These leaders may be the CEO or the human resource manager or other change agents. In his discourse on virtuous leaders, Santiago Martínez emphasizes their role in winning commitment to change. These leaders fit the African cultural environment and are thus well suited to be change leaders in this context. Authentic and virtuous leadership may have great promise for Africa. These leaders are attuned to the African culture represented by Ubuntu. In the Sokoto dialect, the saying 'Mutum mutane as shi,' meaning 'the people around a person make that person,' is reminiscent of Ubuntu in southern Africa. More empirical research in Africa is necessary.

As change and strategy implementation in general is much dependent on employees, the strategic partner role of the HR function brings into sharp focus the need to professionalize the function in order to effectively execute its change agent role. To that end, Samuel Aryee's chapter and the proposed model highlights the content and processes through which an HPWS for agility, as a change intervention, can develop the change management capability to promote the marketplace agility of African organizations. Although there is a steady stream of research on HR in Africa (Horwitz, 2015; Kamoche, Chizema, Mellahi, and Newenham-Kahindi, 2012), much of this research is not grounded in the strategic HR management literature, and has therefore not addressed the implications of a strategic partner role for the function. Research is urgently needed to understand the role of HR as capabilities builder (George et al., 2016), as well as the competencies required of HR professionals and the contribution of the HR function to the marketplace agility of African organizations.

Change in the public sector

Although the continent has witnessed a series of public sector change interventions, most of them have been failures. Indeed, Peterson (2011: 205) noted that successful public sector reform is rare in Africa. Perhaps one reason why reform has not been successful in Africa is the number of tensions in public sector reform and transformation relative to the private sector. For example, few in the public sector may understand the need for change, the competing interests of the varied stakeholders, or the perception of public sector employees of what it means to work in this sector.

The interview with Peter Obi provided a snapshot of what it takes to lead change in the public sector. He was a businessman who went to the public sector with the purpose of effecting change. Is this the recipe for change in the public sector in Africa? Should change leaders be people grounded in the private sector? What does it take to lead change in the public sector of Africa?

In the few cases where change was successful, was it sustained? Peterson (2011: 211) asserts that sustainability is the weak link in public sector change in Africa. There are huge opportunities for research on institutionalizing change in the public sector in Africa. Such research will provide empirical evidence that can guide policy makers, NGOs, and private-public sector interactions.

Conclusion

Boisot and Child (1998: 238) observed that 'the complexity that organizations are required to enact or adapt to reflects human cultural activity and level of development. These shape both the forces that an organization must respond to as well as the representations and behavioural dispositions through which the response is channeled.' Despite the complexity of the environment in which African organizations operate and its inherent change triggers, there is a lack of research on understanding this context and how organizations can effectively adapt to it through effective change interventions. This is particularly unfortunate as change is the 'new normal' and 'organizations are now being asked to: (i) drive performance today while changing their business models for tomorrow; (ii) leverage their current advantaged capabilities and build new capability sets; (iii) optimize their current product/service portfolios and offer customized solutions; and (iv) minimize their current carbon footprint and adopt sustainable practices by introducing disruptive innovations and fundamentally different ways of operating' (Worley and Mohrman, 2014: 216). As organizational adaptation reflects a human cultural activity and level of development, this handbook provides conceptual lenses for a contextualized understanding of the drivers of change in an African context and actionable knowledge that organizations and their management can leverage to enhance their survival and growth. Additionally, it maps out some directions for multidisciplinary research on change management in the African context.

We have highlighted the prospects and challenges of change management in Africa rather than in each African country. Future studies may want to look at individual countries or regions within Africa.

References

Adams, K., Nyuur, R. B., Ellis, F. Y. A., and Debrah, Y. A. (2017) South African MNCs' HRM systems and practices at the subsidiary level: Insights from subsidiaries in Ghana. *Journal of International Management*, 23: 180–193.

Boisot, M., and Child, J. (1998) Organizations as adaptive systems in complex environments: The case of China. *Organization Science*, 10: 237–252.

Davis, D. N., and Luiz, J. M. (2015) The devolution of the human resources function in South African multinational companies. *International Journal of Human Resources Management*, 26: 2763–2785.

George, G., Corbishley, C., Khayesi, J. N. O., Haas, M. R., and Tihanyi, L. (2016) Bringing Africa in: Promising directions for management research. *Academy of Management Journal*, 59(2): 377–393.

Horwitz, F. (2015) Human resources management in multinational companies in Africa: A systematic literature review. *International Journal of Human Resource Management*, 26: 2786–2809.

Kamoche, K., Chizema, A., Mellahi, K., and Newenham-Kahindi, A. (2012) New directions in the management of human resources in Africa. *International Journal of Human Resource Management*, 23: 2825–2834.

Ovadje, F. (2014) *Change Leadership in Developing Countries*. New York, NY: Routledge.

Peterson, S. B. (2011) Plateaus not summits: Reforming public financial management in Africa. *Public Administration & Development*, 31(3): 205–213.

Worley, C. G., and Mohrman, S. A. (2014) Is change management obsolete? *Organizational Dynamics*, 43: 214–224.

Index

Page numbers in italic indicate a figure and page numbers in bold indicate a table on the corresponding page.

For Product Safety Concerns and Information please contact our EU representative GPSR@taylorandfrancis.com Taylor & Francis Verlag GmbH, Kaufingerstraße 24, 80331 München, Germany

Batch number: 10726294

Printed by Printforce, the Netherlands